Leaving the Ivory Tower

The Causes and Consequences of Departure from Doctoral Study

Barbara E. Lovitts

ROWMAN & LITTLEFIELD PUBLISHERS, INC.
Lanham • Boulder • New York • Oxford

ROWMAN & LITTLEFIELD PUBLISHERS, INC.

Published in the United States of America
by Rowman & Littlefield Publishers, Inc.
4720 Boston Way, Lanham, Maryland 20706
www.rowmanlittlefield.com

3 Henrietta Street
London WC2E 8LU, England

British Cataloging-in-Publication Information Available

Library of Congress Cataloging-in-Publication Data

Lovitts, Barbara E., 1960-
  Leaving the ivory tower: the causes and consequences of departure from doctoral study
/ Barbara E. Lovitts.
    p. cm.
  Includes bibliographical references and index.
  ISBN 0-7425-0941-9 (alk. paper)—ISBN 0-7425-0942-7 (pbk.: alk. paper)
  1. Universities and colleges—United States—Graduate work. 2. Doctor of philosophy
  degree—United States. I. Title.

  LB2386 .L68 2001
  378.1'55—dc21

                                                                                00-066465

Printed in the United States of America

⊗™ The paper used in this publication meets the minimum requirements of American
National Standard for Information Sciences—Permanence of Paper for Printed Library
Materials, ANSI/NISO Z.39.48-1992.

To Ted Greenwood for believing in me
and to all the departers who made this study possible
but should not have had to.

Two roads diverged in a yellow wood,
And sorry I could not travel both
And be one traveler, long I stood
And look down one as far as I could
To where it bent in the undergrowth;

Then took the other, as just as fair,
And having perhaps the better claim,
Because it was grassy, and wanted wear;
Though as for that the passing there
Had worn them really about the same,

And both that morning equally lay
In leaves no step had trodden black.
Oh, I kept the first for another day!
Yet knowing how way leads on to way,
I doubted if I should ever come back.

I shall be telling this with a sigh
Somewhere ages and ages hence:
Two roads diverged in a wood, and I—
I took the one less traveled by,
And that has made all the difference.

—Robert Frost, *The Road Not Taken*

Contents

Figures and Tables

FIGURES

TABLES

Preface

Perhaps in the social sciences more than any other domain of knowledge, research projects emerge from the author's personal experiences. This study is no exception. It results from my own unhappy experiences as a graduate student and departure from not one but two doctoral programs.

On the morning of 9 November 1985, during my last semester as a graduate student, I woke with tears streaming down my cheeks, wondering where to find the book that would tell me that my life was going to be okay. I knew such a book didn't exist and resolved to write it. I knew that my experience was not unique, that about 50 percent of those who start Ph.D. programs leave without the degree, yet we were isolated from one another. There were no support groups, no networks. No one cared about us. We were outcasts.

I jumped out of bed with the title *Leaving the Ivory Tower* in mind, grabbed a pad of paper, and spent the morning sketching out the questions for a survey on the causes and consequences of departure from doctoral study. I hoped that by conducting the research, I could turn a negative into a positive, answer my own questions, and help others going through the same experience.

I would briefly like to tell the rest of the history of this project because it reflects some of the obstacles (and opportunities) that noncompleters confront as they try to negotiate the world without those "three magic letters" (James, 1911) after their names and, in the process, relate how some of those obstacles and opportunities have shaped this study.

After leaving graduate school, I initially worked as an office temp and freelance writer while working on the original survey and trying to do some (very unstructured) background research. A little over a year after my departure from grad school, I was called to interview at an organization where I had dropped off a résumé more than a year before. The position was advertised for a postdoc. During the interview it became clear that because I had not finished my degree I would not get the position. I did, however, get the position, *but* the salary was cut $4,000. Hence, the concern with credentialism and human capital–related issues in the chapter on labor market consequences of departure.

About a year later, in May 1988, I attended a luncheon where Clifford Adelman of the U.S. Department of Education (ED) was speaking. He mentioned that ED was about to begin a study on the master's degree. I returned to my office, wrote him a letter about the study I wanted to do. Cliff called me immediately and said, "Let's do it!"

During the summer and fall of 1988, I periodically slipped out of my office and met with Cliff. We hammered out a methodology for the study and selected a sample of universities. That October, I wrote to the deans of twenty-four universities to see whether they would be interested in participating in the study. Before I had a chance to follow up, Michael Dingerson, vice chancellor and dean of the Graduate School at the University of Mississippi, called me and said, "This is important. How can I help?" Mike, who came to Washington, D.C., regularly, quickly became an important ally and key supporter.

In January 1989, with the advice and assistance of Cliff and Mike, I wrote a grant proposal and started searching for an institutional home. No organization was interested in taking me on as an unaffiliated nobody without a Ph.D., yet I persisted. In the interim, I was pushed back into graduate school. Numerous people had told me that the research I was proposing would make a good dissertation and that I would be taken much more seriously in my professional career if I had the terminal degree. I chose to return to graduate school in sociology at the University of Maryland (my previous attempts were in psychology and history of science at the University of Wisconsin and Johns Hopkins University, respectively) because I realized that what I was proposing to do was effectively a study in the sociology of higher education, and the project has benefited from this turn of events in many ways.

While Mike and I were preparing to submit a preliminary proposal to the National Science Foundation (NSF) in the fall of 1991, my current position was terminated, and I was hired as a program officer at the NSF—a major achievement for someone as young as I was and without a Ph.D. This hire, however, created an immediate conflict of interest, thus eliminating NSF as a possible funding source.

By fall 1992, I was still unfunded. I was also starting my last year of coursework, and I began to wonder whether I might not yet again become an attrition statistic if I could not do the research I had gone back to graduate school expressly to do. I decided it was time to pull out all stops. If I were going to go down, I would at least go down having given it my best shot. Consequently, I littered the foundation world with copies of my grant proposal.

At this point in the narrative, let me say that I was extremely lucky to be living and working in Washington, D.C., where I had easy access to education foundations and federal offices. Things would have worked out very differently had I been living in a different labor market (hence, the inclusion of a rural and an urban university in the study).

My grant proposal ultimately ended up in the hands of Ted Greenwood at the Alfred P. Sloan Foundation. Ted took a serious interest in the project, although he had doubts and suspicions about me. I did not have a Ph.D., after all, and I had a less than stellar track record with graduate education. Ted called several of my references and requested letters of recommendation from several people who had worked with me on the project. And I had to convince him that I was not a graduate student who happened to have a job but a working person who happened to be going to graduate school (there is a *big* difference). In June 1993, more than seven and a half years from the project's inception, the Sloan Foundation awarded me $85,000.

The award, which I was more than delighted to receive, was not large enough to allow me to quit my job and work on the project full-time. As a federal employee it was illegal for me to draw salary from the grant, so I could not change my employment status to part-time. Thus, I found myself in exactly the one situation I did not want: working full-time and working on a major research project during evenings and weekends. Fortunately, NSF has a professional development program that allowed me to take one day a week out of the office to work on my project. In addition, the federal government has a mechanism for detailing employees to other organizations, which I used to get myself detailed to the Council of Graduate Schools for six months, where I completed my dissertation.

In fall 1996, I received notice from the Sloan Foundation that they would fund me full-time to revise my dissertation into a book and add chapters on personal and professional consequences of attrition, which had been omitted from the dissertation. I took a major career risk and promptly resigned my position at NSF. I spent 1997 in the Graduate School at the University of Maryland writing this book. My risk paid off. I am currently doing part of what I initially set out to do—research. By choice, I work for a government contractor. And I am at last happy in my career.

Although this study does have a policy cast, my own interests and concerns in conducting it have always been with the individual and the effect of the experience on the individual's life. For what is the purpose of policy if not to make individuals' lives better? Unfortunately, this motivation often gets lost when issues are raised to the policy level. This study was conceived and conducted in a very unstable policy climate. In 1985 when I first conceived it, there was not much national interest in graduate education, much less in graduate student attrition. Then forecasts of an undersupply of Ph.D.'s were announced, raising a great deal of concern in the policy community. A few short years later, the labor market turned sour and we were confronted with a Ph.D. glut, which almost undermined my ability to get this study funded. Interest in graduate education is again on the upswing, as noted by the increasing number of publications and conferences on this topic. I hope this book will add a human face to the dialogue.

The process of conducting this research has been enormously personally rewarding. I am gratified by the degree of interest that so many people have taken in the project. The thirty noncompleters I interviewed and with whose words and experiences I worked closely for almost three years, have in my mind become close friends. I never judged their experiences. Rather, I accepted them as genuine because, in the words of W. I. Thomas, "If men [*sic*] define situations as real, they are real in their consequences" (Thomas and Thomas, 1928, p. 572).

The pseudonyms used in this study have their own histories as well. I had to come up with ninety. For my own amusement, I decided to take names out of *Gone with the Wind* (Mitchell, 1936)—a book with a lot of characters. Shortly after making the decision, I realized how apropos the decision was, because many students who leave graduate programs confront a cultural divide and social dislocation, which is what *Gone with the Wind* is about. To paraphrase the book slightly, "They are swept away from their sheltered lives and dropped down in the midst of haunted desolation" (p. 397).

The two universities in this study have pseudonyms as well to protect their identities. Even if I had not been required to do this, I would have done it anyway so that readers could not say, "Not my department, not my university."

The term *dropout* is never used in this study because it connotes individual failure—a failure of the individual to measure up to the demands of graduate life and study regardless of the character and content of the graduate experience (Tinto, 1987). Rather, the terms *departer* and *noncompleter* are used interchangeably for people who started but did not complete the Ph.D. *Departer* was chosen because of its positive connotations, as in departing on a trip or new beginnings. *Noncompleter* is used in contrast with *completer*. The term *persistence* is frequently used in preference to attrition and retention. Attrition and retention are dichotomous acts, whereas persistence is continuous, and it captures the behavior of both completers and noncompleters: You can continue to persist, or you can stop persisting.

Acknowledgments

Over the years that it has taken to conduct this research, many people have helped me in a large variety of ways. I would like to thank them in roughly chronological order of their contributions. The support, advice, and encouragement of Clifford Adelman and Michael Dingerson have already been mentioned. Without their help, this project would never have gotten off the ground. Next comes Ted Greenwood, my program officer at the Alfred P. Sloan Foundation, to whom this book is dedicated. As a former program officer myself, I know all too well just how much of a risk he took for me, and I am deeply grateful. Had he not shepherded my grant through the funding process, this research would never have been conducted.

My dissertation adviser, Jerald Hage was always ready with a big idea and a new concept to explore, and he helped me navigate the shoals of a large and complex project. My committee—William Falk, V. Lee Hamilton, Robert Berdahl, and Frank Schmidtlein—also provided good advice and criticism.

Special thanks go to my contacts in the graduate schools at Rural and Urban Universities. Unfortunately, I cannot mention their names without revealing the identities of the universities, but they know who they are. I would like to thank all the former graduate students who returned completed surveys, especially the departers who participated in telephone interviews. Additional thanks go to the faculty and directors of graduate study who also participated in interviews.

Johnny Blair, associate director of the University of Maryland's Survey Research Center (SRC), ably oversaw the execution of the survey phase of the project. Many thanks go to Beata Kozak, David Rohall, Gregory Slater and Dana Wagner, my project coordinators at the SRC, and to all the personnel at the SRC whose names and faces I do not know, but without whose efforts this project would not have come off as well as it has. Alan Lehman served as statistical consultant to the project. His enthusiasm for my research topic and allied data kept me going during some long lonely months. Anna Nemesh and her staff at Terp Service—Marlene Barner, Sally Ely, Emily Porter, and Renee Worly—did a fine job transcribing eighty-one interviews. Mildred Yen managed my grant. Steven J. Byun, a work-study student, pulled together the data on faculty retention and productivity.

I am indebted to Daryl Chubin, my boss at the National Science Foundation, for not only allowing but also encouraging me to take extended periods of professional development time and go on a six-month detail. I am grateful to Joseph Lengerman for letting me use his office during the summer of 1995.

Extra special thanks go to Jules LaPidus and Thomas Linney at the Council of Graduate Schools (CGS), where I spent my six-month detail, for giving me the time and the space to think and write. They, and the rest of the staff at the CGS, provided me with the best homestretch experience a dissertator could have.

Clifton Conrad, Diane Jacobs, and Elaine Seymour served on the advisory board to the book project. They provided superb advice on how to revise a dry, technical dissertation into an accessible book for a more general audience. I am grateful to Dr. Ilene Nagel, dean of the Graduate School, University of Maryland, and her staff for giving me an office as well as support and encouragement during the book-writing process. Anne Preston served as the economic consultant. Without her efforts to make sense of some very unclean data, we would know considerably less about the labor market consequences of attrition than we now do.

The Sloan Foundation's desire to have my research reach a wider audience led to me to Cary Nelson, who provided advice and guidance on the book and has collaborated with me on articles. Amy Rovelstad not only did a lot of listening but also read and critiqued the manuscript from an engineer's perspective. Robert Ibarra, one of my reviewers, provided direct assistance on revisions and helped me clarify issues related to organizational culture and minority students, as did my colleague Carlos Rodriguez. Like my previous employers, Diane Pelavin, my current employer, gave me the gift of time to revise the manuscript for publication. DeWan Lee and Michael Simone formatted the figures.

Finally, thanks and love go to my parents, Hannah and Albert Lovitts, for supporting—and putting up with—my academic peregrinations. I am fortunate that my father knew I had successfully defended my dissertation, and I regret that he did not live to see me graduate or this book reach publication. And last but not least, thanks and love go to my recently departed canine companion, Katie, for all the walks we didn't take and all the sticks I didn't throw.

Chapter 1

The Invisible Problem

To say that doctoral student attrition is one of academe's best kept secrets would be to speak a fallacy. The statement would only be true if the attrition rate were a guarded secret. It's not. The situation is worse than that. For large segments of the country's faculty and administrators, the problem does not exist because the problem—and the student who leaves—is largely invisible.

Witness the reaction of two faculty interviewed for this study to some recently released institutional self-study data on their departments' attrition rates. Professor Jackson* remarked, "I was amazed at the attrition rate. [We] only recently found out that something close to half of the students who come do not finish. They leave for one reason or another, and that seems very high to me. . . . I don't know if it's different for other departments in this country or if it's something special to our department. So it's something to be concerned about. I don't know what the reasons for it are at this point." Similarly, Professor Bedford commented, "[W]e've compiled some statistics. . . . [W]hen we all heard the numbers . . . we were surprised that the attrition rate was as high as it was. And it was also higher for women students than for men. . . . We had a lot of meetings about this. We still don't understand the causes, really."

Not only were these professors—professors who each had more than thirty years of tenure in their departments—surprised and amazed when they learned the magnitude of their departments' attrition, each was also perplexed about what could have contributed to such a high rate. Professor Jackson was also uncertain as to how his department's attrition rate compared with other departments around the country. In fact, it compares favorably. Although no hard core national data exist (National Research Council, 1996), the overall

---

*Pseudonyms are used throughout this book to protect the identities of those who participated in this study.

rate of doctoral student attrition in the United States has consistently been estimated to be around 50 percent; this figure dates back to at least the early 1960s.[1]

Professor Bedford's department's gender-skewed attrition is also not unique. The attrition rate of women—as well as that of racial and ethnic minorities—is considerably higher than 50 percent, but the exact figure is unknown (see Benkin, 1984; Magner, 1989; National Science Foundation, 1990; Nerad & Cerny, 1991; Office of Scientific and Engineering Personnel, 1987a, 1987b; Vetter & Babco, 1989; Widnall, 1988).

The high and persistent rate of attrition and the causes of departure from doctoral education are the focus of this study. The first issue is examined in chapter 2; the second (along with the consequences of departure) is the subject of the remainder of the book. Indeed, three ideas will be explored and argued throughout:

- It is not the background characteristics students bring with them to the university that affect their persistence outcomes; it is what happens to them after they arrive.
- Graduate student attrition is a function of the distribution of structures and opportunities for integration and cognitive map development.[2]
- The causes of attrition are deeply embedded in the organizational culture of graduate school and the structure and process of graduate education.

However, before exploring these issues, it is important to address the question, Why should we be concerned? After all, if 50 percent of doctoral students have been dropping out of graduate programs for the last several decades, the attrition rate must be functional. Universities have been producing, perhaps even overproducing, an increasing numbers of first-rate new Ph.D.'s. And the students who leave are not complaining; their decisions must be appropriate. Is there really a problem?

REASONS TO BE CONCERNED

Costs to Faculty and Departments

During periods of economic austerity, low Ph.D. production rates—and by implication high student attrition rates—put the very existence of doctoral programs (and the faculty who teach in them) at risk. During the 1970s and again in the 1990s, fiscal constraints, downsizing, and political pressures for accountability, efficiency, and effectiveness inspired governments and boards of higher education in several states[3] to review their systems with the goal of eliminating programs judged to be unnecessary or ineffective (see Cage, 1989; *Chronicle of Higher Education*, 1989; Mooney, 1991; Schmidt, 1996, 1997).

As a result of these recent reviews (Schmidt, 1997), university systems were given legislative mandates to weed out all unproductive, outdated, or duplicative academic programs. This led some universities to eliminate dozens of doctoral programs and, in some instances, whole departments, while others were subjected to restructuring, enrollment caps, and limits on state funding.

Doctoral programs in private universities were not immune to these pressures (see *Chronicle of Higher Education*, 1992, 1993, 1995, 1996; Heller, 1990b; Jaffe, Lipman, & Lowengrub, 1996; McMillen, 1989; Wilson, 1996). Such well-known private universities as Chicago, Columbia, Cornell, Johns Hopkins, MIT, Princeton, Rochester, Stanford, and Washington University addressed their current and projected fiscal deficits by cutting jobs, programs, and departments.

Doctoral programs in areas of "national need" such as chemistry, mathematics, and engineering were as likely to be cut or consolidated as programs in anthropology, comparative literature, education, history, linguistics, and sociology. When departments are cut or consolidated, or even when they are threatened with cuts or consolidation, the graduate students in them face tough options (Wilson, 1996). They can transfer to another institution and lose a year or more of study, or they can stick around and watch as their program shrinks in stature and the number of faculty and students dwindle. This upheaval not only demoralizes many students but also causes some to give up and abandon their fields and their career aspirations.

Costs to the University

Compared with large corporations, higher education as a business has few standards by which efficiency and productivity are measured (Blumenstyk, 1993). Consequently, the true financial costs of graduate student attrition to the university are not known. However, such attrition cannot but waste scarce administrative and academic resources.

Administrators know that it is cheaper to retain an undergraduate than to recruit a new one (Bean, 1990). Even though no research exists on the costs of recruitment versus retention at the graduate level, Hossler (personal communication, fall 1994) contends that it must hold true for graduate education as well. Indeed, the costs of recruiting graduate students may be even greater than that of recruiting undergraduates. These costs include producing, publishing, and sending off catalogs; processing applications; entering academic and financial information into data systems in several administrative units;

and sometimes underwriting the cost of a campus visit. The costs of retention include the costs of student services as well as the costs of processing loans for students who take them; payroll, health, and retirement expenses for teaching and research assistants; and the zero return on investment when fellowship support does not result in a Ph.D.

Less tangible are the costs of attrition with respect to the time and effort faculty devote to educating and training graduate students who do not complete. These costs are greater when students depart in the later, as opposed to earlier, stages of their programs (Bowen & Rudenstine, 1992). For each student lost to the system, the cycle—and the costs—start over again when a new student is recruited and admitted.

Costs to Society

Attrition is costly to society. Society needs highly educated people from all disciplines to fill a wide variety of positions both inside and outside of academe. A large percentage of Ph.D.'s do not seek or end up in academic positions, and they never have.

A 1995 report from the National Academy of Sciences and Engineering and the Institute of Medicine (Cage, 1995) found that the proportion of new doctoral recipients who started in university positions declined from 57 percent in 1973 to 45 percent in 1991, while the proportion employed by business and industry rose from 24 percent to 36 percent. These statistics not only reflect the realities of the limited academic job market for new Ph.D.'s in the 1980s and 1990s—a cyclic market that booms and busts—but suggest an expanding job market for Ph.D.'s outside the academy. They also indicate that for at least the last twenty years a high percentage of new Ph.D.'s sought and found nonacademic employment.

In addition, some unknown but not insignificant percentage of Ph.D.'s who hold university positions (faculty and administrative) leave the academy to fill vacancies in society that require their knowledge and expertise. Indeed, Ph.D.'s (both old and new) can be found throughout society as CEOs and division directors of corporations and research institutes; heads and staff of philanthropic and nonprofit organizations; program directors and analysts throughout all levels of government; legislative assistants to congressional representatives; editors and journalists of specialized publications and broadcast media; administrators and teachers in the K–12 system; artistic directors and managers of symphonies and operas; curators of museums and archives; directors of galleries, auction houses, and historic preservation associations; and consultants in almost every conceivable field. Moreover, they have been filling these positions (see Fitzpatrick, 1996; Heller, 1990b; Jones, 1990; LaPidus, 1997) long before the recent calls (see Cage, 1995, 1996; Magner, 1994, 1996; National Academy of Sciences, 1995; Nelson, 1995; Nelson & Berube, 1994; Tobias & Chubin, 1996; Tobias, Chubin, & Aylesworth, 1995) to train graduate students for "alternative" careers began.

This reality stands in stark contrast with the deep and widespread belief among graduate faculty that they are training doctoral students for academic (and occasionally for industrial) research positions, period. But not all students enter doctoral programs with the intention of pursuing an academic or a research career. Also, many students who planned an academic career when they enrolled become disillusioned with academe and the academic lifestyle during the course of their graduate careers and give up the desire to pursue one. Many of these students would like to complete their degrees, but because they are no longer interested in an academic or research career, they are not encouraged to and receive little or no counseling about where and how they could use the Ph.D. outside academe. Consequently, many bright and able graduate students leave without the terminal degree and self-select out of or are de facto excluded from consideration for high-level positions they could have otherwise filled. Society thus loses not only their knowledge and skills as disciplinary experts but also their ability to channel that knowledge in a socially productive manner as an administrator, manager, or consultant.

Society also loses the perspectives that noncompleters could bring to bear on social and scientific issues. Emmie, a very insightful former graduate student in sociology who was interviewed for this study, raises important questions not only about the process of graduate education, the differences between completers and noncompleters, but also the effect of those differences on social policy and the types of research questions that do and do not get asked:

> *Emmie*: In those schools where you don't have that kind of human interaction, you really have to be extremely focused and very self-reliant and just move straight through and not be cognizant of anything else. You think, boy, it takes a certain kind of person and you wonder, Well, then, who does make it? and What kind of research then are they bringing to the forefront? and What are they saying about social policy? To me, it raises a lot of questions about personality type. Certainly students who went through the same experiences as I did, finished. But what was it about their personalities that they finished the program? And what does that say now about the kind of research that they're doing?

Just how much knowledge and talent is lost to society as a result of attrition is unknown. Indeed, many of the questions raised and perspectives taken in this study were unlikely to have come from someone who never experienced noncompletion. The fact that it took a noncompleter to focus on the problem of attrition from the perspective of the student who leaves is very telling.

Costs to the Student Who Leaves

The most important reason to be concerned about graduate student attrition is that it can ruin individuals' lives. The financial, personal, and professional costs of attrition to the student are immense. In response to rising concern about the level of indebtedness of new Ph.D.'s, the National Research Council (NRC) added questions about debt to the Survey of Earned Doctorates in 1987. In 1990 when the data were first released (Watkins, 1990), the NRC was pleased to announce that of those who *received doctorates* in the 1987–88 academic year, 53 percent did not owe any money for their education; among those in debt, 37 percent owed less than $5,000, with only 4 percent owing $30,000 or more. However, these data completely overlook the indebtedness of the student who does not complete the Ph.D. As we shall see in chapter 5, noncompleters are less likely than completers to receive research and teaching assistantships and are more likely to not to have received any support at all. Consequently, they are more likely than students who complete the Ph.D. to have taken out loans to support their education. Thus, the high levels of debt the NRC was expecting but did not find among Ph.D. recipients is actually concentrated among those who leave without the Ph.D.—and the magnitude of their debt is unknown.

Lack of academic ability and academic failure account for only a small percentage of all attrition.[4] Tucker (1964) found that students admitted to doctoral programs with low undergraduate GPAs (less than a 3.0) completed the Ph.D. at a rate almost identical to that of his total sample. In addition, less than 2 percent of the students in his sample who did not complete the Ph.D. reported that they did not maintain a satisfactory GPA or failed required courses. Twenty years later, Benkin (1984) found that students with less than a 3.0 GPA were just as likely to complete the doctorate as any group, except those with the highest GPAs.

By all accounts, then, completers and noncompleters are equally academically able. They are people who have been successful their entire lives and view themselves as superior students, as people who can surmount any academic obstacle, and as people who finish things they start. Yet, when they find themselves unable to get through their programs, they confront failure for the first time in their lives. This "failure" can be devastating. Indeed, noncompleters describe the experience of deciding to leave as "gut-wrenching," and they feel "really shaken up," "horrible," "shell-shocked," "disappointed," and "depressed" by it. Some leave feeling suicidal, some attempt it, and some appear to succeed.[5]

Attrition also affects noncompleters' early labor market experiences. Those noncompleters who, during a telephone interview, mentioned that they had left with diminished self-esteem and self-confidence initially took jobs in the blue-collar sector of the labor market. In other words, people with up to three and four years of graduate education took jobs as farmhands, salesclerks, and waitresses—and felt lucky to have those jobs.

Regardless of their emotional state at the time of departure, most graduate students who leave without the Ph.D. have to reconstruct their lives. They have to give up an often deeply held image of themselves as a person with a Ph.D., although some never do. They have to construct a new professional self-image and pursue a career and a lifestyle that is often far different from the one they had been envisioning. And they have to do this at a time when they are demoralized, broke and often deeply in debt, living far from the supportive reach of family and close friends, and in a place they may not want to be and that may not have employment opportunities for someone with their educational background. In short, the costs of attrition on the financial, personal, emotional, and professional lives of students who leave are not small, and they can be devastating and long lasting.

WHY IS THE PROBLEM INVISIBLE?

How is it that the exodus of such a large number of doctoral students has been so invisible to so many faculty and administrators for so long? Part of the answer lies in how "doctoral student" or "doctoral study" is defined, part of the answer lies in the way graduate education is structured, and part of the answer lies in the way doctoral students leave.

Ph.D. programs vary greatly in their definition of who is a doctoral student or, more precisely, when doctoral study begins (National Research Council, 1996). Within the same university, different departments structure doctoral education around one of three basic models. The MA-First Model requires students to have or to complete a master's degree before they are admitted to the department's Ph.D. program. The German Model does not consider a student to be a doctoral student until the student is admitted to candidacy—that is, until the student has completed all the requirements for the Ph.D. except the dissertation. Thus, any student who leaves an MA-First program before entering the Ph.D. program or who leaves a German Model program before attaining candidacy is, by definition, not a doctoral student. Consequently, even though most students who intend to obtain the Ph.D. consider themselves to be doctoral students at the time of admission, their department does not. Hence, they are not viewed as having "dropped out" of the doctoral program if they leave before they are technically defined as being in it. Only the American Model treats all newly admitted graduate students as members of the Ph.D. program. Therefore, only programs structured around this model are likely to capture early-stage doctoral attrition as such—and a high percentage of attrition takes place in the early years.

In their study of six disciplines at six universities, Bowen and Rudenstine (Bowen & Rudenstine, 1992) found that 13 percent of graduate students had left before the start of the second year (stage 1). Of the 696 students in this study for whom duration data are available,[6] 14 percent had left before the start of the second year. Among the 256 noncompleters, 7 percent had left by the end of the first term, and another 28 percent had left by the end of the first year, bringing total first-year attrition for noncompleters to 35 percent.

During the development-of-competence stage (stage 2), which spans from the start of the second year through completion of all requirements for the Ph.D. other than the dissertation, Bowen and Rudenstine found that 17 percent of students who made it past the first year left graduate school during this stage, bringing total pre-ABD (all but dissertation) attrition to 30 percent. Although this study did not capture duration by stage, 36 percent of the entire sample was gone by the end of the fourth year, the amount of time by which most graduate students should have achieved candidacy. Among the noncompleters, the attrition rate was 77 percent.

Finally, several studies (Benkin, 1984; Bowen & Rudenstine, 1992; Moore, 1985; Nerad & Cerny, 1991) estimate that between 15 and 25 percent of graduate students who advance to candidacy for the Ph.D. (stage 3) never complete. This study's attrition rate data are consistent with those estimates. Thus, the trickling out, as opposed to mass desertion, of doctoral students makes their attrition less perceptible.

Doctoral student attrition goes unnoticed for a variety of structural reasons as well. One reason has to do with the reward system of graduate education. Most departments are rewarded for maintaining high enrollments, and these enrollments are frequently maintained by admitting rather than retaining students. Although departments often have to provide administrators with annual data on enrollment and graduation rates, they are rarely asked for data on attrition, and unless they are asked to provide these data, few departments have an incentive to collect it. This lack of accountability not only conceals departments' attrition rates but also allows departments to waste graduate students intentionally, as the comments from several professors interviewed for this study demonstrate:

> *Lincoln*: The way we are set up at the moment, we rely on [the] teaching assistants to do all the teaching. And the way the university is financially set up, our budget is such that we need teach[ing assistants] to do the teaching. So one way to decrease the attrition rate would be to admit fewer students. . . . [W]e [could] admit . . . the same students, only maybe the top half of them. Then this way we'd probably get more students who would be more interested in [the discipline] and we would have a smaller attrition rate. We could do this, but we haven't because we need the teaching assistants.

> *McDonough*: [A] high rate of retention follows from the admissions policy. . . . I've thought in some sense we've had our incoming class too big. In part, they were

big because . . . we have a lot of service courses, and TAs [teaching assistants] were a primary source of establishing those courses. . . . There is a danger of trying to get enough graduate students to fill the [slots], rather than trying to set your target well. . . . [W]e should not lower our standards beyond this. And as it [the class] gets bigger, I think you make more mistakes.

The assumption contained in these remarks is that the majority of their departments' attrition takes place among the bottom half of the students they admit—which, as we have seen, is a false assumption. Furthermore, because these students are not "The Best," they are of no import or concern to the department beyond teaching the service courses the faculty do not want to teach. In fact, these "poorer-quality" students are expected to leave after they have fulfilled the department's need for their teaching services, irrespective of the hopes, dreams, and aspirations these students brought with them to graduate school. Yet, the faculty know that they cannot predict who the best or most successful students will be based only on their undergraduate records[7] or even their performance in their first year of graduate school:

Bedford: We screen students for academic aptitudes, so that's a given. But if you were trying to predict who's going to finish our program, we often wring our hands at faculty meetings that we just don't have the information to make that prediction commonly when students present their dossiers as a graduating senior. . . . [S]o the phenomenon of the paper tiger is very real.

Meade: [I]t's making that transition from an exam taker to a research doer. Some people just love it and the transition is easy, but for a lot of people it seems to be hard as hell, and that's the critical thing. . . . If you ask the faculty at the end of the first year which people in this class are going to be going to independent research, we wouldn't be very good predictors. You get surprised. . . . I don't think we understand that process well enough.

Another reason doctoral student attrition goes unnoticed has to do with the structure, or lack thereof, of the first-year class. Unlike law school or medical school where an entering cohort proceeds through the program in lockstep, the first-year class in most graduate programs is rarely together as a class, outside of a few required courses, and does not move through the program as an intact cohort. It is difficult to look at a class and notice who is missing, because few, if any, faculty have seen the class as a whole. This lack of lockstep progress through the program provides a camouflage for attrition. In addition, lengthy times to degree are taken for granted, further concealing who is or is not in the program.

The structure of the advising process also helps hide the quantity of attrition. When asked how many graduate students they had advised at any point in their graduate career, the vast majority of the faculty interviewed for this study responded as if they had been asked about the number of

Ph.D. *candidates* they advised—that is, students whose dissertations they directed, even though most have predissertation advising responsibilities. Given the fact that faculty generally do not view predissertation students as students for whom they have much, if any, responsibility, it is not surprising that the faculty were unaware of the magnitude of the attrition in their departments. Indeed, when asked what percentage of their advisees left before completing the Ph.D., compared with data they supplied on their Ph.D. productivity rates and data on their department's attrition rates, the faculty, in general, systematically underestimated their own attrition rate as well as their department's. This underestimation helps explain why faculty, departments, and universities have not been concerned about attrition: Low numbers by individual faculty are acceptable, and students who do not make it to the dissertation stage are invisible. However, a large percentage of attrition takes place in the predissertation stage, and when the low numbers proffered by individual faculty are aggregated over a whole department, the numbers are not so small.

Finally, the way in which students leave further conceals their attrition. Not only do departing students trickle out over an extended period of time, but they tend to trickle out silently. Many never discuss their thoughts about leaving or actual attrition decisions with faculty or administrators. They simply leave and make their attrition "known" by failing to register for courses. Universities do not require students to give formal notice of their departure or engage in exit interviews. Thus, unless the student is at the dissertation stage or has an adviser, or unless the student tells a professor he or she is leaving, or unless someone in the department is keeping track of who is registered, graduate students can—and do—slip out unnoticed.

In sum, graduate student attrition is neither a small nor inconsequential problem. It has costs and consequences for universities, departments, faculty, and society, and, most important, it has serious and sometimes dire costs and consequences for the student who leaves.

Not only does the current structure of graduate education make the problem of attrition largely invisible, but it also prevents graduate students from voicing their dissatisfactions and discontents. Consequently, students exit in silence, thereby denying faculty and administrators the feedback they need to invalidate their assumptions and redress the underlying causes of attrition.

Even though at the time of this writing the job market for new Ph.D.'s in many disciplines is poor and there is much public discussion about a Ph.D. glut, that problem is a market problem, one of cyclic booms and busts. By contrast, the graduate student attrition rate has been relatively constant for at least as long as there has been data on the issue—over forty years—indicating that the problem is deeply entrenched in the structure and process of graduate education. These two countervailing problems create a tension between the belief that even with a 50 percent attrition rate we are overproducing first-rate Ph.D.'s and the belief that the market will be further flooded with lesser-quality Ph.D.'s if the attrition rate were reduced. However, this conjoint problem is really a nonproblem, one worsened and confused by deep and widespread beliefs among academics that students who leave doctoral programs are not as good as the ones who complete and that everyone who goes to graduate school plans an academic career or still desires one by the time they have finished. The data—nationally and objectively collected— simply do not support these views. Finally, regardless of whether or not they intend an academic career, graduate students who sincerely desire the Ph.D. are far better off completing the degree, deriving the pride and satisfaction that comes with its achievement even if they do not find the type of job they were hoping for, than going through life blaming themselves for their attrition, struggling with feelings of failure, and grappling with a case of the "could have beens."

INVESTIGATING
THE INVISIBLE PROBLEM

This study uses six sources of data to explore the persistently high rate of attrition and its causes: (1) survey responses from a cohort of completers and noncompleters, (2) interviews with a sample of noncompleters, (3) interviews with the directors of graduate study (DGSs) from each participating department, (4) interviews with a sample of high- and low-Ph.D.-productive faculty from each department, (5) faculty retention rates, and (6) observations made during site visits to each university and department. The remainder of this chapter provides an overview of these sources. Technical details on the survey, procedures for the study, and statistical and qualitative analyses can be found in Lovitts (1997).

The Sample of Graduate Students

The 816 students in the sample (511 completers, 305 noncompleters) were members of the fall 1982 to fall 1984 entering cohort at two universities in nine departments.[8] All of the students were enrolled full-time in Ph.D.-granting programs, and all attended United States colleges and universities as undergraduates.

The universities, which I call Rural University and Urban University, are among the top forty Ph.D.-granting universities in the United States. Rural University is a public research university located in a small town. It had an attrition rate of 33 percent for the departments included in the study.[9] Urban University is a private research university located in a major city. It had an attrition rate of 68 percent for the departments included in the study.

The nine departments are traditional liberal arts disciplines and come from each of the three major domains of knowledge (sciences: mathematics, biology, chemistry; social sciences: sociology, economics, psychology; humanities: English, history, music). These disciplines were selected based on the degree to which Ph.D. recipients in those fields seek academic versus nonacademic employment.

Table 1.1 presents the departments' attrition rates by university. Note the large differences in the attrition rates between Rural's and Urban's economics and sociology departments. The dissimilarity indicates that the cause is not inherent in the discipline and that Urban's attrition rates can be other than what they are.

The sample was 61 percent male, and 38 percent female, with 1 percent of unknown gender. Relative to their proportions in the sample, women, regardless of university, were more likely to depart than men.

Regardless of completion status, the sample was predominantly white (88 percent). Asians constitute the next largest ethnic group at 8 percent; blacks, 2 percent; Hispanics/Latinos, 1 percent; and other combined with race/ethnicity unknown, 2 percent.[10] Although their enrollment rates were low, the attrition rates for the minority students (Asian, 38 percent; black, 57 percent; Hispanic/Latino, 45 percent) were higher than that for whites (25 percent).

The low numbers of minorities in the sample are roughly consonant with more recent (1996) data on minority graduate enrollment rates (Asian, 5 percent; black, 8 percent; Hispanic/Latino, 5 percent) (Council of Graduate Schools, n.d., table 1.5). Differences between the sample and current rates may stem from a number of causes. First, enrollments for underrep-

Table 1.1. Graduate Student Attrition Rates by Department and University (in percent)

	Rural University	Urban University
Mathematics	32	47
Chemistry	19	42
Biology	39	65
Economics	22	82
Sociology	28	72
Psychology	41	23
History	30	61
English	34	76
Music	44	65
Total	33	68

resented minority groups have been increasing over time. Second, the 1996 figures include minority enrollment in all graduate programs, whereas the sample was restricted to students who enrolled in doctoral programs in nine liberal arts disciplines, and some minority groups are more likely to enroll in the professions (e.g., education, social work, law, medicine) than in many of the disciplines in the sample (Council of Graduate Schools, n.d.; Ibarra, 2000). Third, minority students frequently commence their postsecondary educations in community colleges and transfer to or start in smaller, regional nonresearch-oriented institutions. They are subsequently judged by the level of educational quality associated with those institutions and thus are less likely to receive admittance to graduate programs in prestigious Research I institutions such as Rural and Urban Universities (Ibarra, 2000). Fourth, some minority students may have enrolled at Rural and Urban Universities as part-time students, a category that was not included in the sample. Fifth, some minority students in the sample may have chosen not to respond to the survey.

The very small numbers of minority students in the sample made it exceedingly difficult to conduct meaningful analyses by race/ethnicity, though two analyses are presented tentatively and cautiously in chapter 5 because they further and support central arguments. Moreover, combining Hispanic/Latino ethnic groups (e.g., Puerto Rican, Mexican American, Cuban American, and other Central and South American populations) into one category may mask real differences among them; the same holds true for domestic and foreign-born Asian ethnic groups (e.g., Chinese, Japanese, Korean, Indian, Pakistani) and Native American tribes. Thus, the conclusions about graduate students and their experiences in graduate school contained in this book may be incomplete. Consequently, the theory and supporting evidence put forward in this work represent the general case for graduate students writ large and can serve as a platform for further inquiry into the experiences of special populations.

In an effort to parallel the "Decision to Leave" section of the noncompleter survey, the completer survey asked students whether they had ever seriously considered leaving graduate school without completing their degree and, if so, to respond to a series of questions about why they considered leaving. Overall, 42 percent of the completers (44 percent from Rural University, 35 percent from Urban University; 40 percent of the males, 47 percent of the females) indicated that they had seriously considered leaving without finishing. Because differences between *at-risk completers* (completers who seriously considered leaving) and *on-track completers* (completers who never considered leaving) are often quite similar to those between completers and noncompleters, differences between the two types of completers will be discussed throughout the book, where appropriate.

The completers and noncompleters are virtually indistinguishable on self-reported undergraduate GPA (3.53 vs. 3.55), as are on-track completers and at-risk completers (3.55 vs. 3.52). Similarly, students who attended Rural and Urban Universities were equally qualified (3.53 vs. 3.56). These data support those of earlier studies (Benkin, 1984; Tucker, 1964) that, using objective data, found that completers and noncompleters enter graduate school on equal academic footing.

The female students, however, reported significantly higher undergraduate GPAs than the male students (3.59 vs. 3.51); the probability of seeing a difference this large is less than one in one hundred. Although the gender-by-status interaction effect was not statistically significant, it is worth noting that female noncompleters reported the highest undergraduate GPA (3.62).[11]

The Noncompleter Telephone Interviews

Thirty noncompleters, approximately two from each department from each university, participated in an hour-long, focused (Merton, Fiske, & Kendall, 1990) telephone interview to explore issues that could not be addressed adequately by the survey instrument. The data set contains twenty-nine useable interviews (one female, Rural student's interview did not record). This sample is composed of fifteen males and fourteen females; fourteen attended Rural University, and fifteen attended Urban University. Despite efforts to purposively select nonwhite students for this part of the study, the interview sample contains twenty-four whites, two Hispanics (both Puerto Rican), two Asians (both Japanese American), and one black.[12]

As already mentioned, to protect the identity of the students, faculty, and universities, all interviewees (students and faculty) were given pseudonyms. All potentially identifying information such as names, locations, dates, specialty areas, and the like was altered, taken to a higher level of generality, or deleted entirely when the transcripts were edited. On a few occasions, the gender of the speaker or the person spoken about was changed.

The Director of Graduate Study Interviews

Half-hour, semistructured telephone interviews were conducted with the directors of graduate study (DGSs) in each department to gain background information on the departments' formal and informal structures and processes for educating graduate students. The interviews explored the departments' policies for admitting, funding, training, and retaining graduate students; the information provided to graduate students to help them develop an understanding of their programs; the nature of the departments' academic and social activities; actions the department had taken in the previous ten years to improve retention or reduce attrition; and the DGSs' beliefs about factors related to retention and attrition.

The Faculty Interviews

Thirty-three faculty members, roughly two from each of the participating departments—one who had produced many Ph.D.'s and one who had produced few—participated in half-hour, face-to-face interviews to discern systematic differences in the attitudes, beliefs, and behaviors of those most responsible for educating and training graduate students. The interview covered the nature of the faculty's academic and social interactions with the students they advise, how they help their students' develop an understanding of the program and the profession, and their beliefs about why students do or do not complete their degrees. Eighteen of the professors were designated as high producers by their chairs, and fifteen were designated as low producers; three departments at Urban University were unable to provide a low-productive faculty member. None were identified as minority; two were female.

As a backup on faculty productivity, a work-study student went through all *Dissertation Abstracts International* from 1987 (the earliest any member of this study's cohort was likely to have completed a Ph.D.) to June 1994 (the latest available edition) (University Microfilms International 1987a–1994a, 1987b–1994b) and tallied the number of dissertations supervised by each faculty member in the participating departments. The faculty selected as high producers were among the most productive in their departments, and the faculty selected as low producers were among the least productive. However, it should be noted that entries in *Dissertation Abstracts International* for Urban University rarely included the name of the dissertation adviser, so there was little independent corroboration of faculty productivity for Urban University.[13]

Faculty Retention Rates

Faculty retention rates are an indicator of the quality of a department's environment. The greater the retention, the more cohesive, collegial, and supportive a department is likely to be.[14] Faculty retention rates were computed as follows: Urban University's 1980 and 1993–94 *Guide to Graduate Programs* and Rural University's 1981–82 and 1993–95 *Guide to Graduate Programs* were used to compile a list of faculty members in each department and their status (assistant professor, associate professor, full professor, professor emeritus) for each time period. The number of faculty who were present in both time periods was divided by the total number of nonemeritus faculty present during the earlier time period. Emeritus faculty were included in the later time period to control for turnover resulting from retirement.

To assess how actual faculty retention rates compared with what might reasonably be expected, an expected retention rate was calculated as follows. First, it was assumed that the average attrition rate for faculty is 5 percent a year;[15] that is, it was assumed that departments, on average, replace about one out of every twenty faculty members annually. Thus, the expected retention rate[16] for faculty at Rural University over the thirteen-year period used in the analysis is 35 percent. Similarly, the expected retention rate for faculty at Urban University over the twelve-year period used in the analysis is 40 percent. To standardize retention rates across universities, deviation from expected retention was calculated for each department. Table 1.2 shows the faculty retention rates for each department at each university, with their deviation scores in parentheses. Four departments (italicized) had higher than expected faculty attrition rates.

The deviation scores were compared with completers' and noncompleters' survey response rates to determine whether a relationship existed between faculty retention and student response rate. No relationship between completers' response rate and faculty retention rate was found. However, there was a significant curvilinear (quadratic) relationship between noncompleters' response rate and faculty retention rate. If it is accepted that faculty retention rate is related to the collegial nature of a department, then the results indicate that completers' response rate was independent of the nature of the department they were in but that noncompleters' response rate was dependent on it. Noncompleters in departments with the highest and lowest faculty retention rates (most and least collegial) were more disposed to respond than students in departments with more "typical" faculty retention rates. However, the curve has a strong, independently significant linear component, which indicates that the

Table 1.2. Faculty Retention Rates by Department and University over 12 to 13 Years in Percentages

	Rural University (1980–83)	Urban University (1981–93)
Expected faculty retention	35.0	40.0
Actual faculty retention	54.7 (19.7)*	43.7 (3.7)
Mathematics	73.5 (38.5)	48.5 (8.5)
Chemistry	52.4 (17.4)	48.4 (8.4)
Biology	51.8 (16.8)	*31.4 (–8.6)*
Economics	42.9 (7.9)	50.0 (10.0)
Psychology	*34.2 (-0.8)*	64.2 (24.2)
Sociology	57.6 (12.6)	42.9 (2.9)
History	51.4 (16.4)	55.6 (15.6)
English	72.0 (27.0)	*31.5 (-7.5)*
Music	55.5 (20.5)	*30.0 (-10.0)*

*Numbers in parentheses indicate deviation from expected retention.

higher the faculty retention rate (the more collegial the department), the more likely noncompleters were to respond. Thus, the study's noncompleter results may be biased. Noncompleters who returned surveys may have had more positive experiences than those who did not respond.

Observational Data and Artifacts

During week-long site visits to each university, I made unobtrusive observations (Webb, Campbell, Schwartz, & Sechrist, 1966) of the physical space and the nature of the social and academic interactions that took place in each department. I took field notes on the existence, structure, and upkeep of faculty and student portrait and bulletin boards, and miscellaneous postings in hallways including the decoration, or lack thereof, on faculty and student office doors. I made special efforts to observe graduate student offices and to note student–student and faculty–student interactions in the hallways, lounges, conference rooms, department administrative offices, and graduate student offices. In addition, I collected current department handbooks/catalogs, guides for graduate students, department newsletters, student newspapers, and so on, as available.

The observations and artifacts were used to glean information about the collegial nature of the universities in general, and of the departments in particular, as well as the type of information available to students to help them construct a coherent understanding of their program and the rules, policies, and procedures they have for getting students through their programs. Although much of this information has changed since the study's cohort was enrolled, it is reasonable to assume that most changes are improvements because revisions are usually made to correct deficiencies.

NOTES

1. The 50 percent figure can be found in Benkin (1984), Berelson (1960), Bowen and Rudenstine (1992), Katz and Hartnett (1976), National Research Council (1996), Nerad and Cerny (1991), Office of Technology Assessment (1988), and Tucker (1964).

2. Integration is a sense of community membership and cognitive maps are mental models. These concepts will be explained more fully and developed in chapters 3, 4, and 5.

3. At the time of this writing, Louisiana, Illinois, Massachusetts, North Carolina, Ohio, and Oregon had conducted reviews of their systems; Alabama, Colorado, Idaho, and Tennessee were preparing to do them.

4. Data on this issue can be found in Belt (1976), Benkin (1984), Berelson (1960), Tinto (1987, 1993), and Tucker (1964).

5. One of the thirty noncompleters in the interview sample reported being suicidal for many years following her attrition. At least 2 of the 305 noncompleters in the survey sample

attempted suicide; both were female, making the known attempted suicide rate among female noncompleters 2 in 151. In addition, in her study of graduate student attrition in four departments at one university, Golde (1996) heard about 1 suicide among 147 noncompleters. To put these findings in context, data from the National Institutes of Mental Health (NIMH) (1996) show a suicide rate of 15.2 per 100,000 in the twenty-five- to twenty-nine-year-old population (4.9 per 100,000 for women; 25.4 per 100,000 for men). Although no data on attempted suicide are available, there are an estimated eight to twenty-five attempted suicides to one completion. More men commit suicide (4:1 ratio); more women attempt it (2:1 ratio). According to the NIMH fact sheet, the majority of suicide attempts are expressions of extreme distress; depression is among the strongest risk factors. Data in chapter 9 show that noncompleters, women in particular, experience a high degree of emotional distress as well as a high degree of depression at the time of departure.

6. Duration data were captured from a life history calendar rather than by a direct question. Consequently, there were 120 missing cases, which were distributed proportionately between completers and noncompleters.

7. Sternberg, who analyzed GRE scores of 167 Yale psychology students over twelve years, found that GRE scores predicted only first-year grades but did not predict success or failure in graduate school. Furthermore, he found that only the analytic section was a good predictor of first-year grades in graduate school, but only for men (Basinger, 1997).

8. The University of Maryland's Survey Research Center (SRC) traced the sample using information provided by Rural and Urban Universities that was disclosable under the Family Educational Rights and Privacy Act (1988). The find rate for the entire sample was 85 percent. The SRC located 86 percent of the Urban sample (82 percent of the completers, 88 percent of the noncompleters), and 84 percent of the Rural sample (86 percent of the completers, 81 percent of the noncompleters). The formal mail survey was conducted between October 1994 and June 1995 using the Total Design Method (Dillman, 1978). The overall response rate for the entire sample for students with good addresses was 62 percent (69 percent for completers, 54 percent for noncompleters). Two questionnaires were returned shredded and mutilated.

9. The universities' and departments' attrition rates were calculated by dividing the total number of noncompleters eligible to be in the sample (i.e., respondents and nonrespondents) by the total number of students (completers and noncompleters) eligible to be in the sample.

10. *Black, Hispanic,* and *Asian* were the terms used in the survey. I cannot guarantee that members of those groups are Americans and so avoid using the terms *African American* and *Asian American,* for example.

11. Completer and noncompleter undergraduate GPA by gender are as follows: female: completer, 3.57, noncompleter, 3.62; versus male: completer, 3.52; noncompleter, 3.49.

12. Inclusion in the interview sample was premised on responding affirmatively to a survey item that asked noncompleters whether we could contact them by phone for a follow-up interview. Few minorities responded affirmatively.

13. During the site visit to Urban University, I had dinner with a friend on the faculty who made a number of good (uncorroborated) guesses about who the high and low producers were in his own and other departments.

14. Faculty retention was originally included to assess the degree to which social forces operating during the time the study's cohort was enrolled are still operating today. The analysis is based on the assumption that barring major changes in policies and procedures

concerning graduate student education and training, the manner in which faculty interact with (treat and train) graduate students changes little over time. Thus, the higher the faculty retention rate, the more likely the forces operating in a department today resemble the forces operating in the department in the early to mid-1980s. Although not related to faculty retention, the DGSs were queried about changes their departments made in the last ten years to increase retention or reduce attrition. Few DGSs indicated that any major changes were made, further supporting the relative constancy of the social forces.

15. Although no hard data exist, the Council of Graduate Schools (n.d.) estimates that the annual faculty turnover rate is 5 percent.

16. Expected retention rate = 1 – expected attrition rate

= 1 – (0.05 per year × number of years)

Chapter 2

Explaining the High and Persistent Rate of Attrition

Most graduate programs have responded to the problem of graduate student attrition by placing greater emphasis on selection, assuming that if they could only make better admission decisions, attrition rates would decline.[1] Yet, the problem persists and may be getting worse (Bowen & Rudenstine, 1992).

The emphasis on selection suggests that universities believe the problem lies not with graduate school but with the students themselves. To the university, the student who leaves is just another statistic, a dropout. As Tinto (1987, 1993) points out, the term *dropout* connotes individual failure—a failure to measure up. The label "dropout" leads universities to believe that student departures—voluntary and involuntary—are primarily due to students' inability to meet the social and academic demands of the graduate experience and, therefore, reflect individual rather than institutional failure. Consequently, universities and graduate faculty believe that they have little to do with these departures. If the student is at fault, then nothing needs to change except the admissions process. Therein lies the problem.

To explain the persistently high rate of attrition, this chapter explores the selective admissions myth and then brings together attribution theory from social psychology (Jones & Nisbett, 1971; Ross, 1977); exit, voice, loyalty and neglect theory from political economy (Hirschman, 1970); and the theory of greedy institutions from sociology (Coser, 1974). It locates the cause of attrition in the organizational culture of graduate school and in the social structure and cultures of the larger process of graduate education, and it shows that the way the university community interacts leads it to misjudge the reasons for attrition, thereby preventing the true causes of attrition from surfacing and being redressed.

THE SELECTIVE ADMISSIONS MYTH

Graduate schools and graduate faculty believe in what Benkin (1984) calls the selective admissions myth. They believe that the admission process identifies the best students and that attrition is minimal and based on the student's *choice* not to continue. Seymour (personal communication, 1997; see also Seymour & Hewitt, 1997; Tobias, 1990) contends that this notion is rooted in the long-standing belief among faculty that talent is a scarcer commodity than it actually is and that selecting for it, rather than seeking to develop it, is their main job. Indeed, Professor Perkins remarked, "We select in such a way that it's unlikely they're going to fail to meet our expectations." At the same time, faculty hold the contradictory belief that if they could only make more informed admissions decisions they could reduce their department's level of attrition. The assumption underlying these views conveniently situates the problem not with the graduate school and dynamics of graduate study but with the students themselves. The data suggest otherwise.

THE SOCIAL-STRUCTURAL CONTEXT
OF GRADUATE STUDENT ATTRITION

Standard rates across time in any social process, be it attrition, crime, divorce, or suicide, reflect social structures and social forces that remain relatively unchanged from year to year. According to Durkheim (1897/1951), these forces must be independent of individuals because the force acts with the same intensity, achieving the same result, in the same numbers, on individuals who do not form a natural group and who are not in communication with one another. Thus, from a social-structural perspective, if the structures and processes of graduate education remain unchanged over time, one could expect not only a constant attrition rate for graduate students but also standard patterns of variation in attrition rates across disciplines because of systematic differences in the structure of the disciplines. To paraphrase Durkheim, the regular recurrence of identical events in proportions constant within the same discipline but very inconstant from one discipline to another would be inexplicable if each discipline did not have a similar structure that affected its members with a similar force.

If graduate students are responsible for their own departure, then there should be no discernible pattern in their attrition. The lack of a pattern would indicate that students' psychological dispositions and private experiences are the primary cause of attrition. By contrast, if the structure of graduate education is responsible for their attrition, then standard rates across time in the system should prevail.

Although no national data exist on attrition from graduate programs (National Research Council, 1996), data from studies on time to degree and persistence show a consistent pattern of attrition over time and by discipline, with a slight increase over time.[2] Table 2.1 presents attrition statistics for cohorts from 1950–53 to 1972–76. The data show an overall rate of attrition of roughly 40 to 55 percent from Tier I[3] institutions and roughly 50 to 60 percent from all other institutions by recipients of prestigious fellowships. The sciences have the lowest attrition rates and time to degree (time-to-degree data not shown; see Wilson, 1965), the humanities the highest rates and time to degree.[4] The data thus support the contention that systemic forces are operating over time and across disciplines and that the onus of responsibility for student departure lies with the university. However, as discussed later, neither the university nor the graduate student make the appropriate attribution.

ATTRIBUTION OF RESPONSIBILITY FOR GRADUATE STUDENT ATTRITION

The issue of assigning responsibility for students' departure from doctoral study has never been addressed directly. However, evidence from Berelson (1960) shows that graduate deans, graduate faculty, and recent Ph.D. recipients place the burden of responsibility for attrition more on the departing student than on the institution. Table 2.2 re-presents Berelson's data on reasons for doctoral student attrition and categorizes the responses in terms of liability: the departing student responsible versus the university responsible.

Graduate deans, who cite lack of financial resources as the primary reason for graduate student attrition, are the one major exception to the tendency to place responsibility for attrition on the departing students. This response reflects their location in the university's organizational structure. Given that a primary task of their job is the allocation of financial resources, it is not surprising that deans view the problem in such terms. This response, however, contrasts sharply with their nonacceptance of the possibility that graduate students quit their programs because they become disappointed with graduate study and, by implication, graduate school. Graduate faculty and degree recipients are more willing to concede this point, but not appreciably so. This nonacceptance suggests an unwillingness to consider the role that the structure and process of graduate education play in students' departure.

Conspicuously missing from Berelson's study are the departers, the actors themselves, and their reasons for leaving. The actor–observer model of attribution theory (Jones & Nesbitt, 1971) in social psychology is a theory about how people perceive events. It argues that actors and observers focus differently on the situation. Actors focus on the context (and tend to be more

Table 2.1. Attrition Rates over Time and across Disciplines (in percent)

Study/Cohort	Overall Attrition	Sciences		Social Sciences & Humanities		
		Physical	Life	Social Sciences		Humanities
Tucker (1950–1953)[1]	38.1	29.5	28.7	41.2		49.8
Berelson (1960)[2]	40.0	—		—		—
Woodrow Wilson Fellows (1957–1961)						
Tier I universities	55.0	42.0		57.9		65.0
All other universities	59.9	48.8		59.8		71.1
Woodrow Wilson Fellows (1962–1966)						
Tier I universities	49.0	37.3		50.9		58.7
All other universities	59.8	47.3		66.9		65.2
NDEA Graduate Fellows (1962)						
Tier I universities	41.7	28.6		43.8		52.6
All other universities	51.7	50.0		48.1		57.1
Ten-University Data Set (1967–1971)[2]	—	33.2			44.9	
NSF Fellows (1962–1976)	—	35.1		42.2		—
Ten-University Data Set (1972–1976)[3]	—	37.3			55.0	

—Data unavailable.

[1]The study was restricted to individuals enrolled as doctoral students in the traditional arts and science fields at twenty-four selected universities.

[2]The attrition figure is based on the estimates of graduate deans who were surveyed in June 1959.

[3]The data come from eight of the ten universities in the data set. No overall attrition rate is given. Data for the humanities and the social sciences are combined into a category called English, History, and Political Science.

Sources: Berelson (1960), Bowen & Rudenstine (1992), Tucker (1964).

**Table 2.2.   Attribution of Responsibility for Departure from Doctoral Study
(in percent)**

	Graduate Deans	Graduate Faculty	Degree Recipients
Departing student responsible			
Lack if intellectual ability to do the work	50	64	52
Lack of proper motivation	38	45	47
Lack of necessary physical or emotional stamina	33	33	49
University responsible			
Lack of financial resources	69	29	25
Disappointed in graduate study	1	12	21
Other			
Found the degree was not necessary for what they wanted to do	19	10	12

Source: Adapted from Berelson (1960, p. 169).

accurate in their judgments than observers), while observers focus on actors' dispositions. This leads observers to make what is known as the fundamental attribution error (Ross, 1977); that is, observers tend to overestimate the role of actors' dispositions and underestimate the situational causes of their actions. The reasons for attrition presented in the Berelson study come from observers only. Hence, there is good reason to believe that the graduate deans, graduate faculty, and Ph.D. recipients have overestimated the departers' responsibility for their attrition. In doing so, they remove the need to seek a situational explanation for departure and, thereby, exonerate the university.

Faculty's Attributions for Graduate Student Attrition

To explore their attributions, the thirty-three graduate faculty and the eighteen directors of graduate study (most of whom also were faculty) were asked two complementary questions: "What do you think are the primary reasons doctoral students leave before completing their degrees?" and "What do you think contributes most to degree completion?"

Few faculty (graduate faculty and directors of graduate study combined) gave only one reason for attrition, perhaps recognizing, as did Professor Cromwell, that "it's always a constellation of reasons," about which he further stated that "it's even hard for the student himself or herself to realize what the main reason is." The profound truth of this statement will be explored in chapter 8.

All told, the faculty offered more than ninety reasons for attrition. Consistent with attribution theory, two-thirds of the reasons held the students responsible for their attrition. The remaining third were situational. However, the majority of these reasons focused on contexts external to the university, while only a handful focused on situations internal to the university.

One of the most notable things about the student-responsible reasons is how infrequently lack of academic ability and poor academic performance were mentioned. Only three faculty cited academic failure as a primary reason for attrition. When academic reasons were given, they tended focus on the student's relationship with research or on things that happened during the dissertation stage. Their research-related comments are about prior socialization; that is, they believe that students leave graduate school because as undergraduates they were inadequately prepared to do research or entered graduate school with inappropriate expectations about what research is really about.

The emphasis many placed on the dissertation stage further highlights faculty's blindness to predissertation stage attrition. Once again, the faculty placed the onus of responsibility on the student. Their reasons included the student not being able to find a faculty member to work with, the student not getting the right dissertation topic, the student not being able to focus on a single topic or issue, and problems writing the dissertation, about which one faculty member commented was "a long, lonely job."

Two faculty, both low producers, mentioned the role a student's adviser may play in his or her attrition. Both cited conflicts with the adviser. At first blush this appears to be a situational reason. Closer analysis shows that it is not.

> *Burr*: The other [reason] would probably be discovering that you can't really get along with your thesis director.

> *Stephens*: Students also leave because of conflicts with their advisers. We have some that just could not get along with their adviser for one reason or another and they leave, too.

What is noteworthy about these remarks is the belief that it is the student, not the adviser, who is responsible for the nature of the relationship. If the student and the adviser do not get along, then it is the student's fault. These remarks also reveal a lack of corporate responsibility for the student; that is, there is no sense in these remarks that the department or university has any responsibility for seeing these students through.

More common were responses that could be characterized as a lack of understanding of the nature of graduate education—for instance, the student not knowing what he or she was in for when starting; not realizing the level of effort or dedication required; and not being informed about the type of work one might do with the Ph.D., including not knowing what the academic profession is really like. Another common response was that students find out that "it" is not for them or that they lose interest. This response, however, raises the question, Why? Why do students decide that it is not for them? Why do they lose interest? Or, in other words, what happens to students after they arrive at the university that brings about this change?

As noted earlier, when the faculty gave situational reasons for attrition, they cited situations that are primarily external to the university, such as emotional entanglements in another geographic location or conflicts over being in a two-Ph.D. marriage. Other external personal reasons cited shade into financial reasons, such as pressure to improve the family's standard of living or the poor state of the job market. Another commonly cited situational reason focused on financial support, which in some cases is internal or partially internal to the university. This factor included not having fellowship support; not being able to continue because support was cut off; and not having financial support in the dissertation stage, thus requiring the student to get a job, which in turn leads to insufficient time and energy to devote to the dissertation. By contrast, Professor Tomlinson stated, "In my experience, . . . it [attrition] has not been [due to] things like lack of money, although I'm sure some do leave for those reasons."

Finally, the faculty cited only one situational reason that was exclusively internal to the university: the nature of graduate student life. Five faculty mentioned the difficulties and contradictions inherent in this situation. Two are worth quoting:

> *Forrest*: The passivity of the graduate student life is deeply stultifying . . . . [T]here's a contradiction in your disposition toward the profession, which is the way I always understand Howard Bloom's *Anxiety of Influence*. . . . He came up with a theory that writers are in a Freudian relation with their predecessors, and they're always struggling to overcome them or get around them. . . . I think it has a lot to do with being a graduate student . . . because your disposition toward the field that you're working in is one of evasion, overcoming, finding the way through. "Oh, no! someone's just come out with a book on that subject," and, of course, it's the subject that you're interested in. You think you would be happy about that, but, of course, it takes up a space in a world as you imagined it, that you could imagine yourself filling. . . . There is something deeply contradictory about the very idea of contributing to the displacement of other people and of being in a relation, of feeling displaced to other people who have done work like what you do before [you]. So, this whole . . . obsession with the original contribution is a bit of a problem. . . . The passivity and the internal contradiction. . . . This sense that the field itself is contradictory as an enterprise or can feel that way when you're a graduate student.

> *Lee*: Well, various kinds of depression. I think psychologically it's a hard status to be in. You're old enough to be an adult but you are still in a kind of student situation. I think that's stressful. People want to get on with their lives, feel depressed. They are not moving on quickly enough. . . . [I]t's not like law school where you just move along and it's three years and you're out. . . . With luck it's five years and you're out and into a job, but often it's six years or seven years, and it's not necessarily a job waiting there. So I think people get depressed.

Although the question posed to faculty about factors that contribute to completion is essentially the opposite of the question about reasons for attrition, the nature of the faculty responses were markedly different. Again, most faculty cited more than one contributing factor, resulting in close to one hundred factors. Also, again consistent with attribution theory, two-thirds of their responses focused on factors related to student dispositions. The most frequently mentioned ones were drive, passion, curiosity, love of the subject and one's research, dedication, and perseverance, perseverance, perseverance. The faculty also mentioned intelligence, academic ability, talent, creativity, and sometimes even luck.

In contrast to their situational reasons for attrition, when they cited situational reasons for completion, the faculty were twice as likely to cite factors internal to the university as they were to cite external factors. While the faculty continued to mention such external factors as funding and the state of the job market, fully one-third of the faculty stressed the importance of a good adviser and good advising. Good advice and encouragement, and moral and intellectual support were among the adviser attributes the faculty felt contributed to degree completion. They also felt that students were more likely to complete when the adviser made regular contact with students, promoted enthusiasm for the dissertation project, enrolled students in the excitement of the profession, and consistently pushed and pulled students over the obstacles of getting the dissertation done—all things that require the adviser to take some responsibility and initiative. Professor Burr, a low producer, highlights the role of the adviser in the success of "lesser"-quality students:

> *Burr*: Having a supportive director who is determined that you will get through. I've seen quite mediocre students complete because their director always assumed that they would and had absolutely no compunction about encouraging them to continue—these students that I personally would have felt very uneasy about sending to the outside world. . . . These other people—for one reason or another, they march those students through. Clear and repeated expectation of performance by the thesis director is the single most important thing.

A few faculty cited the role that peer support and interaction can play in completion. In other words, they addressed the role of supportive community structures.

> *MacIntosh*: I think community makes a lot of difference. I think the students who are most likely to complete it are those that are involved with other students in a community of one kind of another.

> *Stuart*: It helps for students to have circumstances with which they can succeed by means of the communities in which they interact. The university here has had what I think is an ideal program in this workshop program that follows on

students' years in seminars in the classroom, which really is a way for students and faculty from different programs to get together around commonly defined areas of interests, provide [feedback], read to one another chapters of unfinished work or work in progress; get feedback from a community, et cetera, and have a sense of being part of an intellectual community that is supportive of students completing their work.

In sum, the faculty's responses to the attribution-related questions support the contention that observers commit the fundamental attribution error when asked to explain why graduate students leave without completing their degrees. They penalized students for their failure to complete by attributing it to student dispositions and behaviors, yet they gave partial credit to themselves for students' success by highlighting the role that they, as advisers, play in retention and completion—and none were cognizant of the contradiction inherent in their responses. This differential mode of responding is, however, consistent with the actor–observer model of attribution theory in that when it comes to attrition, faculty see themselves as observers only, but when it comes to retention, they see themselves as actors or coactors—hence, the partial shift from dispositional to situational explanations. In short, by blaming students for their own attrition, faculty exonerate themselves of any role they or the structure of graduate education may play and thus remove the need to seek explanations in the nature of graduate education.

Noncompleters' Attributions for Their Attrition

Contrary to the actor–observer model of attribution theory, the argument to follow contends that departers (actors) will place a higher degree of blame on themselves for their attrition than would normally be predicted by attribution theory. Research (Serge, Begin, & Palmer, 1989) suggests that a strict psychological orientation to the actor–observer model of attribution theory is too narrow and that the complexity of the context in which attributions are made must be considered. In particular, the theory contends that self-blame and system-blame attributions result from socialization and that socialization in a complex setting may lead actors to make more internal (self-blame) attributions than would normally be expected.

Graduate school is a complex setting. It provides intense socialization and resocialization experiences (Baird, 1972, 1992; Bess, 1978; Bucher, Stelling, & Dommermuth, 1969; Egan, 1989; Gerholm, 1990; Goodman, 1989; Green, 1991; Heiss, 1970; Katz, 1976; Piliavin, 1989; Rosen & Bates, 1967; Wright, 1967). Graduate students often find themselves at the bottom of a status hierarchy and in a dependent relationship with their professors. Despite their efforts to please, they often do not fully understand what their professors want.

Consequently, many students come to feel inadequate and attribute this inadequacy to themselves instead of the situation. Indeed, in his discussion of anomic suicide, Durkheim (1897/1951) argues that persons abruptly cast down below their accustomed status in situations in which they thought themselves in control either blame themselves or someone else for this turn of events. Regardless of the object of blame (self or other), Durkheim argues that the individual will revolt against the cause, real or imaginary, to which he or she attributes his/her downfall and seek solace in the act of self-destruction (suicide/attrition).

As a means of tapping students' attributions for their attrition (self or system), the noncompleters who were interviewed were asked two related questions, one indirect and the other direct: "Did you ever feel that if you had done things differently you might not have left?" and "Did you ever feel responsible or blame yourself for your own leaving?" Regardless of how the question was phrased, the interviewees were twice as likely to take responsibility or blame themselves for their leaving than they were to attribute their leaving to the system in which they were embedded. In addition, self-blame-related statements are sprinkled throughout the interviewees' discussions of their experiences in graduate school.[5]

In response to the indirect question, several interviewees took explicit responsibility for their decisions, asserting that they were not forced out, that they made a conscious decision to leave. Others implied personal responsibility. They felt that they should have been more forceful or assertive in dealing with faculty or that they should have had more knowledge about the program before they enrolled. Those who attributed their leaving to the system felt that there were problems with the department (it was not honest about its expectations for students; it was not receptive to students' interests) or problems with the faculty (they did not provide proper guidance, support, or advice).

In response to the more direct question, the modal self-blame response is summed up best by Boyd, who was enrolled in a rather dysfunctional department with a very high attrition rate:[6] "I feel completely responsible for deciding to go there, [for] what I did when I was there, and [for] leaving," indicating that he, like others, did not see the decision to leave as something brought about by the social structure of his department. Similarly, Beatrice's response is illustrative of the way in which some students blame themselves, at least initially, for things that are beyond their control. Beatrice, who left after four years when her funding ran out, had an adviser who was out of the country more than he was in and did not go to bat for his students; yet Beatrice blamed herself for her attrition:

Interviewer: Did you feel responsible for your leaving? Did you ever blame yourself for it?

Beatrice: Sometimes. Like I say, I didn't play the politics. It might have made a difference. Maybe if I had really fought for [funding] more, but I don't know. At first, I mostly blamed myself, and then I thought, No, it wasn't entirely my fault.

Interviewer: What did you blame yourself for?

Beatrice: Well, like I say, for not being streetwise, you might say.

Interviewer: What made you think it might be your fault?

Beatrice: Well, just the fact that I didn't get any [funding], and then I realized it had nothing to do with me. Not entirely. It wasn't a personal thing because a lot of people like, I got some sympathy, "Oh, I'm so sorry you didn't get funding," but I didn't have anybody pulling for me to get it for me, and maybe I should have pushed a little harder myself.

The students' responses to questions about responsibility and blame support the contention that given the complex environment in which they are embedded, rather than blaming the situation as attribution theory suggests they should, some take full responsibility for their decision and/or blame themselves for not being able to complete even when the cause of their attrition stems from things beyond their control. This self-blame not only inhibits students from realizing that some of their difficulties lie within the system and not within themselves but also prevents them from voicing their discontents because they have internalized the locus of responsibility.

Noncompleters blame themselves for their attrition, in part, because the structure of the graduate school leads to a high degree of pluralistic ignorance[7] among graduate students. The competitive environment does not encourage students to admit that they are having difficulty understanding what is expected of them or fulfilling expectations that are often unrealistic. Thus, when graduate students who are struggling see other students putatively thriving, they come to believe that they are the only ones having problems and attribute their difficulties to their own inadequacies rather than the situation in which they are embedded.

India's statement, which follows, is illustrative of the degree of pluralistic ignorance among graduate students and the way in which pluralistic ignorance leads to inappropriate attributions. Her remarks show that students who understood things about the program that are often not made explicit to graduate students assumed that everyone else understood them, too, and that students who did not know these things assumed they were the only ones who did not. Consequently, they were reluctant to let on and blamed themselves for their "ignorance."

Interviewer: Did you ever feel that other graduate students knew or understood things about the program or being a graduate student that you didn't?

India: Yes. They seemed to understand. Some of the people who came in when I did already knew what their thesis was going to be on and had already picked out an area they were going to hone in on when they did their Ph.D. They were already that far ahead, and they were already working toward that. And it never occurred to me that I had to be that far ahead because nobody had ever mentioned it.

Interviewer: How did you feel about knowing that other graduate students knew or understood things about the program or being a graduate student that you didn't?

India: It made me feel stupid. It made me feel like I should have known all that, and yet I don't know how anybody could because the school I went to [as an under-graduate] did not have graduate students on campus. There was no graduate pro-gram, so I had never been exposed to it before. . . . But yet, you felt rather stupid asking the questions [at Rural University] because people looked at you like you should have already thought about that, not faculty but some of the other gradu-ate students.

Interviewer: What did you do about it?

India: What did I do about it? I took a leave of absence.

Interviewer: What did you do about feeling stupid or not knowing what other stu-dents seemed to know?

India: I talked to other students in our office and some of them were having the same experience and some of them really and truly had thought about some of [these things] beforehand or were much better prepared for it than I was. So, they didn't seem to see it as a major problem. So, if at least you talked to someone, now, you didn't feel quite so ignorant. . . . I think that a lot of us didn't really understand how the program worked. [T]here was an orientation, but, to be honest, it didn't tell you that much about the school. A lot of the kids that I was in with had gone to Rural for undergrad so they already knew some of the professors and knew the campus and they knew the building and knew how things went 'cause they'd had graduate students in their classes the whole time and things. So they had a better exposure to it, and it was different for them than it was for us.

Thus, the high and persistent rate of attrition can be partially explained by the failure of the university and the individual to make the appropriate attribution. This argument is further supported by the following chain of reasoning: If stu-dents take personal responsibility for their failure to complete their degrees, they should exit without giving voice to their discontent. However, if students place responsibility for their failure on the university, they should voice their discon-tent with the system. If departing students were expressing their discontent, then one would expect universities to take notice and take appropriate self-corrective actions (Hirschman, 1970). If this were the case, then one would expect to see both a far lower attrition rate than that which prevails and a decline in the attri-tion rate over time. However, the constant and high rate of attrition indicates that students are departing in silence, and this silence is a strong indicator of self-blame. The next section combines attribution theory with the theory of exit, voice, loyalty, and neglect (Hirschman, 1970) and that of greedy institutions (Coser, 1974) to further explain the high and persistent rate of attrition.

WHY AREN'T UNIVERSITIES MORE
RESPONSIVE TO STUDENT ATTRITION?

Stifled Voices, Silent Exit

Graduate students, like consumers or members of an organization, can express their discontent with the system in two ways. They can stop purchasing the university's product (i.e., education) and leave the university (exit), or they can express dissatisfaction to some authority or engage in some general protest (voice) (Hirschman, 1970). Given the amount of personal and financial investment graduate students make in their programs, one would expect them to exercise the voice option vigorously. Yet, as data from a survey question based on exit, voice, loyalty, and neglect (EVLN) theory (Barry, 1974; Birch, 1975; Farrell, 1983; Hirschman, 1970, 1974, 1976; Kolarska & Aldrich, 1980; Spencer, 1986; Withey & Cooper, 1989) indicate, noncompleters tend to exit in silence.

The students were asked what they did when they experienced periods of dissatisfaction with their graduate program. They were provided with two response options for each EVLN behavior. Exit behaviors involved actively exploring options outside the university (e.g., investigating other graduate schools or graduate programs, looking for a job), whereas neglect involved passively allowing the situation to deteriorate (e.g., missing classes, not completing assignments). Voice behaviors involved actively attempting to improve conditions (e.g., talking to people to make the situation better, seeking help and advice), whereas loyalty involved passively waiting for conditions to get better (e.g., waiting and hoping the situation will improve, passively assuming the problem will work out).

A higher percentage of students responded affirmatively to the voice options than any of the others, though completers were more likely than noncompleters to exercise it. Even though there were no significant differences between completers and noncompleters with respect to loyalty, the trend was in the predicted direction. By contrast, noncompleters were more likely than completers to engage in exit and neglect behaviors (see table 2.3).

Although expressing dissatisfaction to administrators was not, but should have been, included as one of the voice options, two other voice-related questions in the survey provide support for the contention that graduate students do not share their discontents with people in power. One question asked the students how often they discussed their feelings about being a graduate student with a variety of people, including university administrators. Although more noncompleters (19 percent) spoke with administrators than completers (12 percent), both percentages are low, as was the mean frequency of interaction (1.17 for completers vs. 1.28 for noncompleters on a five-point scale [1 = never to 5 = often]). The second voice-related question asked noncom-

Table 2.3. Students' Exit, Voice, Loyalty, and Neglect Behaviors during Periods of Dissatisfaction with Their Graduate Programs (in percent)

Behaviors	Completers	Noncompleters	p
Voice[1]	86	74	**
Talk to faculty and try and make things better	54	50	
Seek help or advice from other graduate students	79	63	**
Loyalty[1]	61	55	
Wait and hope the problem would solve itself	58	53	
Say nothing to others and assume things would work out	29	24	
Exit[1]	22	49	**
Explore other graduate schools or graduate programs	15	28	**
Start looking for a job	12	30	*
Neglect[1]	16	35	**
Miss classes or stay away from the department	10	26	**
Stop doing readings, research, or other graduate work	11	21	**

[1]Percentage of students who responded *yes* to one or both options.
$*p < .01.$
$**p < .001.$

pleters with whom they discussed their leaving. Only thirty-three (11 percent) of noncompleters indicated that they had discussed their leaving with an administrator. However, neither question asked what type of administrator they spoke with. It is not clear whether they spoke with administrators who could change the structure and process of graduate education such as the president/ chancellor, provost, or dean of the graduate school or whether they spoke with more powerless administrators such as financial aid officers, registrars, deans of students, or departmental administrators.

The interview data, however, lend support to the contention that when departers speak with administrators, they do not speak with the most powerful ones. Only one of the thirty interviewees indicated that he spoke with an administrator, "one of the higher administrative people in the math department," who he assumed was a dean. He, and other students in his department, felt that a professor came to class unprepared and talked about his research instead of the topic of the course. Although the complaint was looked into, James was not satisfied with the outcome. According the James, the "dean" investigated the problem and "felt that it was probably on the lower end of quality of courses being offered," and "the response seemed to be, 'Well, we can't do much about it.'" This was one of the things that "really soured" James on the "whole stance of academia."

Most of the other interviewees with whom this topic was discussed had never even considered the possibility of talking to an administrator— including the department chair—or chose not to for political reasons (e.g., the department chair was their adviser). Thus, despite the deficiencies in the voice question, it does not appear that key people in university administration are privy to students' concerns about, and discontents with, their graduate programs, and, consequently, they lack the information necessary to make appropriate attributions about attrition and take appropriate remediative actions.

Students' silent exit raises two questions: Why don't students exercise voice? and Why don't universities respond to their exodus? The answer to both questions lies in the organizational culture of doctoral education. The culture is premised on norms, values, and beliefs about how to train graduate students and about the nature of the interactions that take place between and among faculty and graduate students. Its compliance system is coercive; superiors exert a high degree of control over subordinates (Etzioni, 1961, cited in Austin, 1990). As such, graduate schools—like utopian societies, seminaries and monasteries, secret police or criminal organizations (Coser, 1974), kibbutzim (Talmon, 1972), journalism schools (Parry, 1990), and the military and the family (Segal, 1986)—can be conceived of as greedy institutions (Coser, 1974; Goodman, 1989). As coercive organizations, greedy institutions make great demands on their members in terms of commitments, loyalty, time, and energy. Whereas total institutions (e.g., jails, mental hospitals, concentration camps) use external coercion to achieve their ends (Davies, 1989; Goffman, 1961), greedy institutions rely on voluntary compliance—commitment and loyalty. They maximize compliance by appearing as highly desirable places to be, by proffering selective admission and membership, and, in the case of graduate schools, by promising highly desirable rewards (high-paying, high-status, prestigious jobs) to those who make it through.

Within greedy institutions, newcomers hold low-status positions (Coser, 1974). In these types of cultural systems, newcomers are expected to acknowledge the authority of the socializing agents and submit themselves to it. In the graduate school context, graduate students hold low-status positions relative to the faculty who are the socializing agents. As several commentators point out (Egan, 1989; Goodman, 1989; Rosen & Bates, 1967), this arrangement has a paradoxical quality to it: Graduate students are expected to perform as mature, independent (though fledgling) scholars in an authoritarian social structure where they are in a subordinate and dependent position socially, intellectually, and financially. The status asymmetry between graduate students and graduate faculty leads students to believe that they have no alternatives to their present state of dependence; hence, they acquiesce to the demands placed on them because they feel they have no opportunity for choice—or voice. To express discontent represents one's inability to handle a situation into which one has voluntarily placed oneself, a personal shortcoming. It is also a sign of disloyalty. Consequently, graduate students react to the system by keeping their discontents to themselves.

Furthermore, graduate students know they are highly selected, chosen for their intelligence, ability, and competence. They are aware that they are in a system where the most desirable rewards (fellowships, assistantships, faculty sponsorship, and subsequent job placement) go to the best and the brightest. Consequently, they are always in competition with one another, and they each play the role of the graduate student who is everything the system selected him or her to be: brilliant, self-assured, confident, and making it through without any major problems.

This competition and role playing leads to pluralistic ignorance among graduate students about how they are really faring in the system and how the system is affecting them. The system and its reward structures create an environment that prevents students from sharing their concerns about their current status in, and progress through, the program. This barrier contributes to a lack of socioemotional integration among students because the cause of their discomfort is so linked to their identities and such an admission of "inadequacy" is highly self-threatening. As a result of the structure of the situation, graduate students become isolated from one another on critical issues and do not band together to complain because they cannot identify a common problem to rally around.

Any student who attempts to break through the atomism created by the pluralistic ignorance risks exposing him- or herself as an impostor,[8] a person who does not have "the stuff" that it takes to be a member of "The Select." Consequently, forces in the system prevent graduate students from discovering that many of their problems lie within the system and not within themselves. As a result, graduate students do not band together and complain. Those students who are having trouble with the system wallow in their ignorance, blame themselves for their "failings," and exit in silence.

Power and Complacency

Graduate schools have a relatively high degree of monopoly power over graduate students. They provide a good for which few readily available substitutes exist. The more prestigious and specialized a graduate department or program, the more power the department or program has. This power reduces competition with other schools for quality students, restricts enrolled students' options and freedom of movement, and leads to a growing complacency or "laziness" in the institution itself.

Hirschman (1970, p. 60) argues that "those who hold power in lazy monopolies may actually have an interest in *creating* some limited opportunities for exit on the part of those whose voice might be uncomfortable" (emphasis in original). To allow students to voice discontent would force the university to confront the deterioration of its product and force it to change. Furthermore, to allow students voice would potentially challenge the university's control over them and upset the social order.

In addition, universities have few, if any, formal mechanisms in place that allow graduate students to voice their complaints cheaply and effectively. Thus, by stifling voice and permitting exit, universities can persist in a state of "comfortable mediocrity" (Hirschman, 1970, p. 59). Deficiencies need not be exposed, deadwood need not be rekindled, and dissatisfied and discontent students need not be accommodated.

Another reason that graduate schools do not respond to exit is because the demand for admission to graduate school is highly inelastic. Graduate schools face a steady pool of quality applicants from which they continuously attempt to select the best. A student who leaves can be always be replaced. As will be discussed later, exit actually benefits the university and helps perpetuate false assumptions about graduate education.

Unlike organizations in which consumers purchase the product supplied, graduate schools frequently pay their consumers to attend: the better the perceived quality of the consumer, the higher the price universities pay in fellowships, stipends, and assistantships. Yet, as Seymour (1995) points out, faculty and administrators ignore their customers because students do not behave like customers. And unlike "normal" organizations in which the investments made in members contribute immediately and directly to the functioning of the organization, investments made in graduate students only benefit the organization indirectly and in the long run in the form of reflected glory—and only if the now-former student makes important contributions to his or her field.

Because students who obtain degrees reflect on their alma maters, graduate schools have a vested, though latent, interest in seeing that only "the best of the best" get through. This interest often leads graduate schools to the false and tautological conclusion that those who make it through are the "The Best" and that those who leave before completing their degrees are of lesser quality—a contemporary trial by ordeal.

The assumptions underlying this conclusion create a tolerance for exit. The assumptions also allow the university to maintain the illusion that it was not responsible for the exodus of half its students and that all it has to do to reduce exit is make better, more informed admissions decisions. Consequently, when students leave, resources in the form of financial aid and faculty time and effort are freed up. The university can now invest in new, hopefully, higher-quality students in whom it would have been unable to invest had other students not left. In fact, one faculty member said as much to an interviewee when she told him she was leaving.

> *Solange*: I . . . had a tuition waiver and $2,000 stipend, and he said something to the effect that, "Well, it's a good thing you're leaving instead of wasting money that could be used on someone who deserved it."

The university thus benefits from attrition, or, more accurately, believes that it does.

CONCLUSION

The high rate of graduate student attrition persists because universities have focused on student characteristics at the time of admission rather than on the organizational culture of graduate school and the structure and process of graduate education itself. This emphasis has been ineffective and, possibly, counterproductive. Evidence presented in chapter 1 shows that little or no difference exists between completers and noncompleters in entering academic ability and that even students admitted to doctoral programs with low undergraduate GPAs complete the Ph.D. at almost the same rate as those with high undergraduate GPAs. This indicates that criteria currently in place to select students based on academic achievement are not good predictors of success. Indeed, the more selective graduate schools become in their admissions processes, the more pressure graduate students may feel to maintain the illusion that everything is fine; that they completely understand the structures, processes, and expectations of their graduate program; and that sharing concerns, doubts, and uncertainties is a weakness to be avoided at all costs. As a consequence, universities cannot learn about the true causes of student discontent and cannot take proper remediative actions.

The data on faculty and students' attributions as well as those on students' exit, voice, loyalty, and neglect behaviors also help explain the persistently high rate of doctoral student attrition. They show that all the relevant actors (administrators, faculty, and students—completers and noncompleters) place the burden of responsibility for attrition on the student who departs: If the student is at fault, then the university is not, and nothing needs to change. In addition, when departing students experience dissatisfaction with their programs, they frequently leave without expressing their displeasure. Thus, people who can change the structure and process of graduate education are denied the important feedback they need to reform graduate education and to correct their thinking (attributions) about the causes of attrition.

NOTES

1. In addition to altering their recruitment and admissions policies, universities have responded to high attrition rates among racial and ethnic minorities by instituting retention programs (financial support, academic support or advising, and sometimes cultural support programs). These programs are premised on the assumption that the problem lies with the student and not with the system, and are thus designed to treat the symptom and fix the student (Ibarra, 2000).

2. Bowen and Rudenstine (1992) contend that attrition rates have increased over the last three decades. According to Durkheim (1951/1897), patterned changes in rates over a long period of time indicate that the structural characteristics of society have simultaneously undergone profound changes. This finding for graduate student attrition suggests that conditions surrounding graduate education have deteriorated.

3. Tier I institutions are universities whose programs received top ratings from one or both of two graduate program quality rating systems: Jones, Lindzey, and Coggeshall (1982) (Bowen & Rudenstine, 1992) and Roose and Andersen (1970).

4. Further support for a consistent pattern of attrition comes from Benkin's (1984) study of the 1969 to 1971 entering cohort at UCLA who indicated either a master's or a doctorate as their degree objective. Benkin found that approximately 31 percent of this cohort received no degree, while 24 percent completed the Ph.D.; the remaining 46 percent either received a master's as their highest degree (40 percent) or were ABD (6 percent). Benkin's data by discipline are consistent with those presented in table 2.1 (life sciences: 24 percent, no degree; 48 percent, Ph.D.; physical sciences: 26 percent, no degree; 35 percent, Ph.D.; social sciences: 31 percent, no degree; 23 percent, Ph.D.; and humanities: 42 percent, no degree; 16 percent, Ph.D.).

5. Golde's (1994) transcripts of doctoral students' descriptions of the attrition process contain a large amount of self-blame. Similarly, Seymour and Hewitt (1996) find a high degree of self-blame among undergraduates who switched out of science, mathematics, and engineering majors for their attrition/switching. The self-blame was greatest among vulnerable groups, women and students of color.

6. This department weeded out at the master's level. Both interviewees characterized it as very competitive and hostile. Between 1981 and 1993, the department also had a very high faculty turnover rate, indicating that something was fundamentally wrong. When confronted with the data on faculty turnover, my contact in the Graduate School acknowledged that during the time period in which the study's cohort was enrolled, the department had a lot of problems.

7. Pluralistic ignorance is a situation in which most members of a group (the plurality) do not know or understand something. Those members who do, assume that everyone else does too. Each member who does not assumes that he or she is the only uninformed member of the group and each is embarrassed to admit this ignorance. Consequently, no one speaks up and everyone remains ignorant of the issue and of each other's ignorance.

8. Many high achievers experience "imposter phenomenon," an intense, subjective self-perception of phoniness and a secret belief that they are actually less competent or intelligent than their peers. They concomitantly fear eventual discovery and unmasking by professionally significant others. See Clance and Imes (1978); Harvey, Kidder, and Sutherland (1981).

Chapter 3

Explaining Departure

Although it is true that roughly 50 percent of those who enter doctoral programs leave before completing the Ph.D., it is also true that 50 percent *do* achieve it. These consistent rates indicate that factors in the structure and process of graduate education contribute to attrition and that other factors contribute to retention. The key to improving graduate education and reducing attrition lies in exposing both sets of factors.

As we have seen in chapter 2, atomism and pluralistic ignorance appear to be key factors in attrition. They separate students from each other and from faculty. They interfere with the development of clear understandings of the nature of graduate education. They prevent students from finding moral support within the departmental community and student subcultures, and from giving voice to their concerns and discontent. In short, they throw students onto their own resources for survival.

If the forces that divide and separate students encourage attrition, then it stands to reason that forces that unite and assimilate students encourage retention. This chapter explains persistence (retention and attrition) through a theory of community membership. It shows how bonds that tie an individual to a community develop through interaction and how they provide individuals with support structures that promote retention. It also shows how information about the structures in a community facilitates bonding with the community and how participation in the community provides individuals with the knowledge they need to negotiate its systems. These explanations for persistence are developed within the context of the departmental community and then are generalized to explain differences in attrition rates between domains of knowledge and between departments within a discipline. However, before an explanation for persistence is offered, a brief discussion of the process of graduate education and the characteristics students bring with them—and which interact with the structures they encounter there—is in order.

INSTITUTIONAL AND INDIVIDUAL
CONTEXTS OF GRADUATE EDUCATION

Graduate schools are complex organizations. They have a large number of relatively autonomous departments. Power over and decision making about graduate education is largely decentralized and located in individual academic units. The university sets minimum criteria and requirements for graduate students and programs, while departments control admissions, curricula, degree requirements, and student training.[1] This structure enables departments to organize graduate education to fit their disciplinary cultures, models of thought, and styles of interaction.

The typical graduate program consists of three years of coursework, which usually progresses from general, moderate-sized, lecture-style classes to small, advanced, special-topic seminars and culminates in independent research. Some graduate programs require students to pass preliminary examinations at the end of their first year, while others may require them to write a master's thesis. Some programs require students to show proficiency in one or two foreign languages. After students complete their coursework and other requirements, they must pass qualifying examinations, usually in two to four specialty areas. The examinations may be written, oral, or a combination of both. After passing qualifying examinations, graduate students usually prepare a proposal for their dissertation research and defend it in front of their dissertation committee. Once the proposal is approved, graduate students spend several months to several years researching their topics and writing up their findings in standardized dissertation style.[2]

The manifest goal of this process is to instill a large body of general and specialized knowledge in fledgling scholars with the aim of turning them into competent academic professionals (Baird, 1992; Rosen & Bates, 1967). The latent goal of this process is to socialize them to the norms, values, ethics, thought processes, and modes of verbal and written discourse of their chosen disciplines (Gerholm, 1990) and sometimes even to a new vision of the self (Egan, 1989), such that graduate students leave their programs ready to fulfill the role of academic professional.

The process of graduate education is not continuous or unchanging; rather, it can be divided into stages that mark key transition points in students' progress toward the Ph.D. Each stage has its own characteristic structures, requirements, and socialization processes that students must negotiate successfully—academically, socially, and emotionally—to attain the Ph.D. Although other conceptualizations are possible, the literature on graduate student education (see especially Bowen & Rudenstine, 1992; Tinto, 1991, 1993) typically uses the following three-stage model:

Stage 1: Entry and adjustment (the first year)
Stage 2: Development of competence (second year through completion of all requirements except the Ph.D.)
Stage 3: The research stage (completing the dissertation)

Student Characteristics and Their Interaction with the Structure and Process of Graduate Education

Students enter graduate school with a variety of background characteristics. These characteristics include family background (socioeconomic, marital, and parental status, as well as values and expectations), individual attributes (sex, race, ethnicity, age, ability), and prior schooling (grade point average and a variety of social and academic experiences and achievements). They also enter graduate school with different goals and intentions and different levels of commitment to their universities, departments, and disciplines and to achieving their goals (Bean, 1980, 1982a, 1982b; Spady, 1970, 1971; Tinto, 1975, 1987, 1993). Their background characteristics, their external commitments and responsibilities, their socialization as undergraduates, and the clarity of their understanding of the system of graduate education in general and their own program in particular, as well as their adaptive capacities, interact with the structures they confront in their programs to determine their persistence outcomes.

When they enter graduate school, new students are subjected to socialization processes that are intense and influential. The department presents them with a new culture and new identities. Graduate students often have to replace many of their old values with something approaching a departmental model. The level of awareness of this socialization process is varied: Some students automatically internalize the values being espoused; others are more ambivalent yet not fully cognizant about what is happening to them; still others are aware that they are being assimilated into a distinct culture that requires a new vision of self. Some students accept the changes, whereas others do not and elect to leave rather than conform (Taylor, 1975).

To the extent that the student acquires an identity that includes the norms, values, beliefs, and thought processes of the discipline, the student has become a part of the collective conscience of his or her department and can be regulated by it. Such control prevents the student from breaking with the community. Students who do not internalize the values and norms of the department are less likely to be controlled by it and are more likely to experience anomie, a sense of normlessness. This anomie allows them to remove themselves from the community.

INTEGRATION INTO THE
DEPARTMENTAL COMMUNITY

The departmental community is composed of two subsystems, an academic system and a social system (see Spady, 1970, 1971; Tinto, 1975, 1987, 1993). Each system has its own characteristics and methods of integration. Integration into the academic system (academic integration) is the primary purpose of graduate education. It is influenced by interactions with faculty and fellow students that are academic in nature as well as by students' perceptions of their intellectual and professional development (Tinto, 1987, 1993). Failure to integrate into the academic system can undermine a student's reasons for being a member of the community and thus lead to exit. Integration into the social system (social integration) is an unintended consequence of academic interaction. It results from informal socializing with faculty and fellow students in academic and nonacademic contexts. Because obtaining a Ph.D. does not require social integration, failure to integrate into the social system of a department does not undermine a student's reasons for attending graduate school. However, failure to integrate into the social system can lead to dissatisfaction with the community and influence attrition decisions.

Integration into each subsystem is brought about by different mechanisms. Academic integration develops through task integration, working together on the intellectual and professional tasks of graduate education: learning, teaching, researching, and publishing. To achieve these ends, students interact with faculty, other graduate students, and even undergraduates in a variety of formal contexts.

Social integration is brought about through socioemotional integration, supportive interactions inside and outside the department with members of the departmental community. Socioemotional integration arises from the need for affiliation and from close proximity with members of a tight and closed community who share common interests and common problems. It develops through informal, casual interactions between and among graduate students and graduate faculty in a variety of informal contexts.

In the graduate school environment, academic and social integration are closely intertwined. Events such as colloquia, brown bag lunches, on- or off-campus social hours, and sports or other recreational activities that bring students and faculty into regular, casual contact are more likely to foster an esprit de corps. Departmental traditions such as holiday parties, picnics, and the like, heighten socioemotional integration between and among the graduate students and graduate faculty who participate.

The programmatic structure of a graduate department is related to the structure of the discipline. Some disciplines, such as the sciences, are often structured around research teams. Students and faculty are in almost constant interaction all day long and sometimes late into the night. In such situations, the line between formal academic interaction and informal social interaction becomes blurred. Other disciplines, such as history and English, are structured around individualized research that takes place in isolation in libraries, archives, and the field. Opportunities for social interaction to develop as a consequence of academic tasks is reduced.

How a department's physical space is structured has implications for both types of integration. Graduate lounges provide opportunities for students, as well as faculty who use them, to meet and interact informally. Group, as opposed to individual, offices for graduate students bring students into prolonged, casual contact. The frequent, and sometimes chance, meetings and exchanges that take place in hallways and around mailboxes and coffee pots help students develop a sense of community membership.

When task-related and social interactions are cooperative and supportive, students are likely to become integrated and persist. Their participation in their programs and their daily interactions in their departmental community become well scripted and taken for granted. However, when the interactions are competitive and divisive or characterized by benign neglect, students are likely to become factioned and atomized. The separation of the individual from the community leads students to see themselves as figures against a ground of which they are not a part, causing them to question whether they are achieving their intellectual, professional, and personal goals and to examine their reasons for being a member of that community. When students become doubtful and begin to question their participation in the community, their daily interactions become effortful and their desire and willingness to persist are compromised. They start looking up and out at other communities and begin to weigh the costs and benefits of persisting.

Although most attrition results from lack of integration and regulation,[3] some attrition may result from too much integration and regulation, as depicted in table 3.1.[4] Graduate students who are overly task oriented may not integrate adequately or at all into the department's social systems and, consequently, fail to establish bonds which tie them to the community. Overly task-oriented graduate students are best characterized as workaholics. They are likely to devote

Table 3.1. Predicted Persistence Outcomes by Degree of Task and Socioemotional Integration

Degree of Socioemotional Integration	Degree of Task Integration		
	Too Low	*Appropriate*	*Too High*
Too low	Detached	Persist	Workaholic
Appropriate	Persist or depart	Persist	Persist
Too high	Party out	Persist	Persist or depart

almost all of their time to academic pursuits and may often be dissatisfied with the quality of the work they produce. Consequently, excessively task-oriented graduate students are likely to burden themselves with incompletes. Those who persist are likely to exhibit long times to degree in their effort to turn every assignment—papers, thesis, and dissertation—into a magnum opus. Those who leave are likely to exhibit irritation and disgust with themselves and graduate school and depart in the later stages of their programs.

Some graduate students may become overly integrated into the social systems of their departments or universities at the expense of academic integration. They are likely to put fun before coursework and other requirements and, ultimately, party themselves out of graduate school. These students may be asked or encouraged to leave and are likely to depart in the early stages of their programs. Some may complete because they are carried along by the social support they receive from their peers, but they will exhibit long times to degree because they are unlikely to complete assignments and requirements in a timely fashion. The timing of the decision to leave for these students is likely to interact strongly with finances. Students with low or inadequate levels of financial support should leave earlier in their programs than those with high or adequate levels of support.

Finally, graduate students with appropriate levels of both task and socioemotional integration are likely to be well adjusted and persist unless some exogenous factor such as finances, health, or family matters forces them to leave. These students are likely to exhibit short or normal times to degree. By contrast, graduate students low in both task and socioemotional integration are likely to exhibit melancholy detachment and apathy and leave quickly.

In sum, integration/community membership is more than simply social support. It is also a mechanism for success. By providing people with resources that are more extensive than their own, the collective force of the community makes people function better—academically, socially, and emotionally.

COGNITIVE MAPS: KNOWLEDGE AND UNDERSTANDING OF THE GRADUATE SCHOOL PROCESS

Cognitive maps are mental models that are created jointly by members of a community and give coherence to perceptions of events, people, and objects (Howard, 1995; Morgan & Schwalbe, 1990). They help people make sense of what they are experiencing, providing them with a conceptual understanding of the environment, a plan of action, and platform for informed decision making.

The accuracy and clarity of students' cognitive maps of the graduate school terrain facilitate their passage through the system.

Graduate students need two kinds of cognitive maps to get through their programs: a global map and a series of local maps. The difference between a global map and a local map is analogous to the difference between a state map and a street map. The former illustrates a large bounded region and the major highways and features of the terrain; the latter provides the minute details needed to get around in a specific locality.

The global map provides the graduate student with a picture of the larger, formal system and its requirements. Students who have read graduate school catalogs and handbooks or discussed graduate education with knowledgeable sources are likely to possess a global map that contains the following features: coursework, master's thesis, qualifying examinations, and dissertation.

Graduate students need at least two kinds of local maps of their programs— maps of the academic system (tasks) and maps of the social system (socioemotional relationships)—and possibly one of department politics as well. These maps provide students with an understanding of informal expectations. Much of this knowledge is tacit and contained in, and passed along by, the graduate student subculture.

Although no research has been done on graduate students' cognitive maps per se, some evidence exists that indicates that first-year students do not have well-constructed global or local maps and that ill-structured maps create obstacles that hinder students' progress through the system. Heiss (1967) found that new students have only vague notions what the doctoral program intends, involves, or includes. Some students regard the program as a set of hurdles that they must jump; others wander through a diffuse program of courses without seeing their relevance to each other or to their degree goals. When personal contact with advisers is missing, first-year students tend to select courses illogically, be unaware of aids and facilities at their disposal, or lack a clear conception of the various options in their fields. Heiss concludes that students' survival or nonsurvival is closely related to the nature and degree of orientation (a map creating and clarifying process) students receive during their first year. Similarly, Rosen and Bates (1967) found that entering graduate students often have a great deal of difficulty determining what they are supposed to be learning and how it is related to the goals of socialization.

Students' mental models provide them with predictions about events and sequences of outcomes. Each time students make a transition between stages in their graduate programs, the academic requirements and social interactions change. Behavior thus becomes largely unscripted and therefore guided by thinking and sense making (Louis, 1983). When predicted outcomes do not occur, the students' cognitive consistency is threatened. This threat produces a state of tension and need to return to a state of equilibrium. One way to alleviate the strain is to eliminate the stress that caused it, which for the newcomer or person making the transition can mean leaving the stressful situation.

The literature on the dissertation stage (see especially Heiss, 1967) supports the contention that students who have survived this far often lack coherent cognitive maps for traversing this juncture and are thus thrown back on their own, often deficient, strategies and resources. Many students do not have a clear sense of how to select an adviser or a research topic, and many have an even less clear sense of how to cope with the style required in thesis writing. In addition, dissertators' interactions with fellow students tend to decrease while their interactions with faculty increase (Sherlock & Morris, 1967). As a result, they may become disconnected from the student subculture and the knowledge contained in it that they need to construct a viable cognitive map for hurdling this phase of their program. Their mental models thus become heavily dependent on the quality of advising they receive.

The relationship between cognitive maps and integration can be conceived of as mutually causal (see figure 3.1). Good cognitive maps result in integration, and integration results in good cognitive maps. Students who enter graduate school with good cognitive maps should integrate into the academic and social systems with relative ease. By contrast, students who do not have good cognitive maps at the time of entry, but who become integrated into the academic and/or social systems, will develop those maps because they are in close and frequent contact with people who can provide them with the requisite information.

In sum, well-structured cognitive maps of the academic and social terrain come from high-quality academic advising and from formal and informal interactions with faculty and fellow, usually more senior, graduate students. Well-structured cognitive maps provide students with guides that can help them predict and gain a degree of control over a highly complex and ambiguous

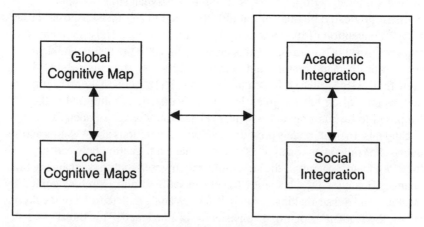

Figure 3.1.   The Relationship between Cognitive Maps and Integration

environment. They can illuminate the most direct route to achieving one's ends as well as highlight and help students avoid potential pitfalls. However, when cognitive maps are vague and inaccurate or when they are read incorrectly, students are likely to stumble and fall.

EXPLAINING DIFFERENCES IN ATTRITION RATES BETWEEN DOMAINS OF KNOWLEDGE AND BETWEEN DEPARTMENTS WITHIN A DISCIPLINE

The theory of community membership developed earlier can be used to explain characteristic patterns of attrition between domains of knowledge and to explain the variability in attrition rates between departments in a discipline. Data presented in chapter 2 showed standard patterns of variation in attrition across domains of knowledge. The sciences had the lowest rates of attrition and the humanities the highest, with the social sciences falling in between. These systematic differences suggest differences in the strength of community across disciplines.

The intellectual organization of the discipline structures the academic and social interactions of its members and is responsible for the characteristic and stable patterns of attrition across disciplines that have been observed for several decades. Intellectually, the sciences are highly structured disciplines. Their subject matter is vertically integrated, and graduate students focus on mastering one or a few contemporary theories. Consequently, students in the sciences are able to develop a coherent understanding of their intellectual trajectories through their programs. In addition, graduate students in the sciences often choose, or are chosen by, an adviser by the end of their first year, if not by the end of their first term, and begin work on research projects that will serve as the basis of their dissertations. This arrangement usually provides stable funding for the student and a stake in completed research for the adviser. Much of this research is done in teams, which ensures that graduate students in the sciences are in frequent academic and social contact with faculty and fellow graduate students during their entire graduate careers (Bowen & Rudenstine, 1992; Wilson, 1965).

By comparison, the humanities and many of the social sciences are more loosely structured. Their subject matter is horizontally integrated, and graduate students are required to develop a deep understanding of a broad range of classical and contemporary theories, which often inhibits their ability to see the discipline as a coherent whole. Students in these disciplines frequently do not select an adviser or commence dissertation-related research until they have passed their qualifying examinations. Moreover, their research is often

conducted in isolation in libraries, archives, or the field (Bowen & Rudenstine, 1992; Wilson, 1965). Consequently, graduate students in these disciplines do not receive the same amount of academic and social support as their
counterparts in the sciences.

Departments are organizations that have (or, more accurately, are) cultures,
which are independent of the parent discipline. These cultures, by definition,
are enduring patterns of deeply embedded norms, values, beliefs, and behaviors that are difficult to change (Peterson, & Spencer, 1990). Departmental
cultures are passed down to new faculty and students through apprenticeship
and the enactment of written and unwritten rules (Ibarra, 2000), and they are
manifested in formal and informal practices and in cultural forms such as traditions, rituals, and physical arrangements (Martin, 1992). Indeed, differences in departmental cultures are evident the moment one physically enters
the building(s) in which a department is housed. Some departments (or programs or research groups within departments) are friendly and welcoming.
They showcase individually labeled photos of faculty and/or currently enrolled graduate students in different culturally relevant formats: formal black-
and-white portraits, color photos with informal poses that reveal the subject's
interests and personality. Bulletin boards are carefully arranged and well
maintained, and important events and notices are highlighted. Faculty and/or
student publications and research results are on display. Comics, news clip-
pings, and photos of social and academic events, weddings, and births are
posted on faculty and graduate student office doors and on hallway bulletin
boards as well. Office doors are open, and students and faculty can be observed interacting. Lounges are cozy and inviting; some vend fresh food and
contain daily newspapers and other reading materials. These departments provide frequent opportunities for their members to interact by holding regularly
scheduled events such as colloquia, brown bags, and happy hours.

Other departments, by contrast, are austere. Bulletin boards are either
empty or splattered with haphazardly arranged notices. Few personal affects
are in evidence, and lounges do not exist or the doors are locked. Faculty and
students are hard to find, and, when they are around, they are working in isolation. Academic and social events are held infrequently or not at all.

These differences in cultures and their value systems shape the nature of
the relationships between and among the members of the departmental community and, in the process, influence persistence outcomes. Departments that
are collegial and that provide structures and opportunities for interaction and
intellectual and professional development, should and do (see chapter 5) have
lower attrition rates than departments that are less collegial and that offer few
opportunities for integration.

CONCLUSION

Regardless of unit or level of analysis—student within department (intradepartmental), department within discipline (interdepartmental), domain of knowledge within the graduate school enterprise (institutional)—the theory developed in this chapter argues that graduate student attrition is a function of the differential distribution of structures and opportunities for integration into the prevailing community. The more structures and opportunities a community provides its members to interact and engage in the professional tasks of the discipline, the more bonds the members will have with each other and with the community, and the less likely its members will be to leave.

The next four chapters explore issues related to cognitive maps and integration, with an emphasis on where things go wrong. Departments' policies and practices along with faculty's views on the various processes of graduate education and their assumptions about graduate students are juxtaposed with students' views and assumptions about the same processes to highlight weaknesses and breakdowns within the community.

NOTES

1. See Berelson (1960, p. 120) for a discussion of how the major policies and practices in graduate study are "actually determined, regardless of formal regulations."

2. Some departments accept a combination of three published or submitted journal articles in lieu of a formal dissertation.

3. See Durkheim (1897/1951) on egoistic suicide.

4. This conception of academic and social integration and its relationship to attrition was inspired by Durkheim's (1897/1951) fourfold conception of suicide (egoistic, anomic, altruistic, and fatalistic), which, he argues, results from too little or too much integration and regulation.

Chapter 4

The Lack of Information

The understandings students have about the nature of graduate education shape their global and local cognitive maps of their programs. These understandings include the relationships among people, policies, and practices at each stage of their graduate careers. The quality and accuracy of their understanding depend heavily on the type of the information they have access to and the sense they are able to make of it.

This chapter explores the opportunities that departments and faculty provide for cognitive map development and the ways in which information is disseminated to students. It also examines the nature and quality of the understandings that result. In the process, it highlights the lack of congruence in assumptions and the breakdowns in communication between departments/faculty and students. It shows that persistence outcomes for those who leave without the Ph.D. are closely related to the quality of their mental models.

The discussion starts with stage 0, prior and anticipatory socialization, because students do not enter their programs as tabula rasa. Their prior socialization as undergraduates and their models of graduate education influence how they cope with graduate school. The discussion moves across stages and culminates in an analysis of the relationship between persistence outcomes and students' cognitive maps of their departments' formal requirements and informal expectations.

STAGE 0: PRIOR AND ANTICIPATORY SOCIALIZATION

Application and Selection Decisions

A *two-way* effort to achieve "fit" between the student and the program begins before the student arrives. Long before entry, most prospective students use a variety of strategies to gain information about graduate school and choose a program. These strategies include getting recommendations about programs from undergraduate faculty; knowing the reputation of a university; reviewing a university's, department's, or program's materials; reading faculty's papers or knowing their reputations; and actually visiting the graduate school. Graduate programs send prospective students the university's catalog as well as department materials and brochures. In addition, faculty may write to or call the student, and the department may even invite the student to visit the campus and underwrite the student's expenses.

Yet, graduate students—completers and noncompleters—nonetheless appear to be relatively uninformed about the programs to which they apply. As shown in figure 4.1, regardless of status, more students used the university's general reputation than information about the department or program, and more students used information about the department or program than information about individual faculty or a campus visit. The data also show that the closer the source of information to the most interpersonal interactional level (faculty), the larger and more significant the difference between completers and noncompleters becomes. The survey data thus indicate that while most students' application and selection decisions are uninformed, noncompleters' decisions are even more uninformed. This is one of the very few statistically

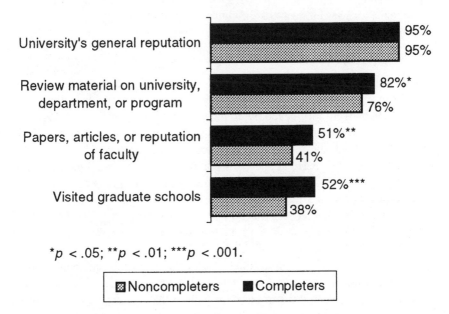

$*p < .05; **p < .01; ***p < .001.$

Figure 4.1. **Sources of Information Students Used to Select Graduate Schools to Apply to**

significant prior-to-entry differences found between completers and noncompleters, and it is not something that can be readily detected on students' applications for admission.

The noncompleter interviews reinforce just how uninformed many students' graduate school application and selection decisions are. Many of the interviewees had little genuine prior knowledge of the university, department, program, or faculty—and this includes two of the three Rural University students who attended Rural as undergraduates. Urban University students chose Urban because of its reputation and/or because it was the best school they got into, whereas Rural University students premised their choice on the financial aid package they received. A few students chose to attend their universities based on advice and encouragement from undergraduate faculty. However, those who mentioned this method of selection were often unhappy with the advice they received. They felt the advice reflected the faculty's interests rather than their interests, as exemplified in Pauline's experience. Pauline was a graduate student in psychology and wanted to go into clinical practice, not clinical research.

> *Pauline:* The most important thing [that would have prevented my leaving] probably would have been, starting in undergrad, better guidance there in terms of picking my program. I feel some resentment. The people there [at my undergraduate school] knew me really well. They knew me very well, and I think they should have probably been able to direct me a little bit more instead of, you know, I think it was almost like I was vicariously fulfilling desires of theirs to go to this hot-shot research program. I think they knew exactly what I wanted to do with my career, and I think that, frankly, they should have given me more guidance in terms of how to pick a program other than go to the most prestigious one you get into.

Four students indicated some prior knowledge of the department, although in three of the four cases, the knowledge was rather abstract. These three students' choices were influenced by an *awareness* of the department's superior *reputation* or by knowing the university's particular *approach* to the discipline. By contrast, the fourth student, Gerald, seems to have had more concrete prior knowledge. He applied to Rural because "there were people doing the type of work I was interested in." In fact, Gerald is a noncompleter only with respect to Rural University because he followed his adviser to another university and completed. Advance knowledge of the type of work one will be doing in graduate school—and having that in common with the faculty (see chapter 7)—seems to make a difference.

Although familiarity with graduate faculty appears to contribute to persistence, the interviews reveal that selecting a graduate school because of a particular faculty member can backfire *if* the selection decision is made in the absence of information about the professor as a graduate adviser. Three interviewees selected their programs to work with a particular professor. They either were familiar with that person's research and writings or were aware of that person's academic reputation. However, after they arrived on campus, two of these students learned that the person they went there to work with did not have a reputation for getting graduate students through their programs.

Visiting the campus and interacting with faculty and other graduate students prior to entry is a means some students use to assist in the selection process. It also helps students begin developing a global cognitive map of the campus, the department, and life as a graduate student. The survey data show that completers were more likely than noncompleters to have visited the campus. However, the interview data indicate that when campus visits occur, the visits are not always optimal.[1]

Approximately half of the students interviewed visited the campus. Overall, these students were about equally split as to whether they interacted with faculty. Interactions, when they occurred, tended to be brief, and the students typically met with only one person. In addition, the students often did not obtain the information they needed to determine whether the program was the right one for them. This impaired their ability to develop appropriate mental models of their upcoming graduate school experience.

Despite having somewhat lengthy interactions with faculty, two students failed to establish that their interests were at variance with the primary orientation of the department. Even though Ellen, who hated theoretical mathematics, spoke with the "curriculum counselor," she did not find out how theoretically oriented the department really was until after she enrolled. Pauline, who enrolled in a research-oriented clinical psychology program, did not mention her interest in going into private practice during her campus visit because she "knew it wasn't the right thing to say."

Students who visited the university but did not meet with faculty took themselves on self-guided tours of the campus and the surrounding neighborhood; a few interacted with currently enrolled graduate students. Katie, who visited the campus before enrolling, talked with the "staff director" but not with the faculty, and had a particularly bad experience at the university, remarked wistfully, "I probably should have [met with faculty], and I wish now that I had." Reflecting upon not having visited Urban before enrolling, Philip commented, "It's one of my lessons learned from life."

As already mentioned, the effort to achieve fit is a two-way process. Universities and departments send out materials and brochures advertising the attractive features of their programs. Faculty court prospective students over the phone and make special overtures to students who make formal campus visits, often arranging lunches and/or housing with other students or taking them out to lunch or dinner themselves. Several students who relied on the university's materials or who had these experiences reported that these solicitations were false advertising. James felt that his department was resting on its reputation and that the current program was "not what it was advertised to be" in the catalog in terms of course offerings. Upon entry, Letty, who chose her university because of its receptivity to doing interdepartmental studies, found that it was more "lip service" than reality. Pauline was deceived by the recruitment process.

> *Pauline:* The interview process was very reassuring. They told me what wonderful credentials I had, and how highly qualified I was, and how much they'd love to have me there. And I'll tell you, when I went there to interview, it felt like this was one big happy family feeling in the department. It seemed like it was going to be very warm and supportive. That is not what I found when I got there.

If students follow the general advice to go to the best graduate school they can get into, regardless of fit, many graduate programs admit the best applicants they can, regardless of fit. Professor Sherman addressed this issue at three separate points in his interview. The first time, he mentioned his department's tendency to admit the best students without attending to the match between the department's mission and students' interests and career projections: "[W]e just have not done a very good job of matching up what we're about with what students who apply here say they want to achieve when they come here." The second time, he discussed his department's recent attempts to take fit into consideration for the benefit of the student and the department: "[W]e cannot be all things to all persons who would like to have a Ph.D. from Rural University in sociology. But we can be all things to those who want to do what we do well." The third time, he considered the advantages of selection based on fit to students in terms of retention and job placement: "Here's what this faculty's about. If you're interested in doing this and learning to do research about these kinds of things, then we welcome you to come into our department and we'll try to get you through and we'll try to get you a job." Longitudinal data from his department suggest that recent reforms—focusing on the department's strengths and admitting students in those areas only—has led to a decrease in attrition.

Anticipatory Cognitive Maps

Graduate programs and entering graduate students make a number of assumptions about each other that are often incongruous. Graduate programs assume that entering students have achieved a modicum of socialization to the norms, values, and experiences of graduate training prior to admission (Bucher et al., 1969). As we shall see, this assumption is especially faulty when applied to students who attended small, liberal arts colleges and who have had little or no exposure to graduate education. A number of programs hold contradictory assumptions about students' prior training. They admit students who they feel have mastered the undergraduate curriculum, yet they may administer exams to identify students' weaknesses and then use these exams to eliminate students from the program.[2] This practice, according to Letty, can be very off-putting:

> *Letty:* There were a whole series of exams you had to take, and if you didn't pass them, you weren't allowed to continue in the graduate program. And . . . that seemed sort of contradictory because you should have already mastered the material, or you shouldn't have been admitted to the program. . . . I felt pretty good about who I was coming in, and it seemed there were a lot of things set up to try to undermine [how you felt about yourself] and just sort of weed people out.

Prior to entering graduate school, prospective students develop expectations about their social and academic lives as graduate students, often based on their experiences in college. Research in the area of organizational socialization indicates that such anticipatory socialization is usually idealistic and inaccurate (see Baird, 1976; Bess, 1978; Green, 1991; Wright, 1967). Thus, the degree of fit between expectations and reality frequently determines who stays and who leaves.

Survey respondents were asked whether, in retrospect, they felt they had enough information about the department, the amount of work required, and program/degree requirements when they applied to graduate school. Completers, especially *on-track* completers (i.e., completers who never seriously considered leaving without finishing), were more likely than noncompleters and *at-risk* completers (i.e., completers who seriously considered leaving without finishing) to feel they had enough information about the department at the time of application (67 percent of completers vs. 55 percent of noncompleters; 73 percent of on-track completers vs. 58 percent of at-risk completers). On-track completers also felt more informed about the amount of work than at-risk completers (66 percent vs. 58 percent). These results suggest that completers, particularly on-track completers, were better prepared for the challenges of their programs than noncompleters and at-risk completers.

Analysis of the student interviews reveals that students whose initial experiences in graduate school met or exceeded their expectations had longer durations than students whose initial experiences did not meet their expectations. Most of the students who expressed satisfaction (or were neutral about their initial experiences) had prior graduate experience and/or left for reasons external to the university (i.e., departure of their adviser, health or financial reasons). By contrast, most of the students who expressed disappointment left by the end of their first year; none made it to the dissertation stage. Indeed, studies of newcomers' experiences in organizations (Louis, 1983) indicate that coping with differences between expectations and experiences typically occupy the newcomer for the first six to ten months. In the graduate school setting, this coping duration would fill the entire first year. Thus, feelings of commitment or alienation and the decision to stay or leave often follow from the sense new students make of their situation early in their encounters with their programs.

Unlike premed and prelaw students, undergraduates who desire to purse graduate education and an academic career receive little or no pregraduate advising. Thus, when asked what they hoped to get out of their graduate experience and how their actual experience compared with their expectations, several students indicated that, in retrospect, they were very naive about what graduate school was all about and about what it would be like to be a professor. This stands in contrast with faculty's assumptions that new students understand the structure and process of graduate education and the intricacies of being a professor.

> *Cade:* The interesting thing was I had no idea what it was all about. I had no idea that it involved research and that the Ph.D. was given for an original contribution to the field.

> *Emmie:* I had this very vague idea that I was going to somehow be a researcher, and I did not give a whole lot of thought on what would be involved, and I don't think that I had a very good road map that showed me how to become a researcher.

Several students entered graduate school expecting it to be more of what it was they liked about studying their disciplines as undergraduates and that coursework would be stimulating. However, many quickly became disillusioned with what they encountered. The contrast between the undergraduate curriculum and the graduate curriculum was most acute for English students (close textual analysis vs. literary criticism). However, students from other disciplines also expressed surprise at the difference.

> *Boyd:* I think I assumed it was going to be a continuation of what I had liked about studying literature in college . . . a lot of free exchange of ideas, and people were really encouraged to think creatively and think originally. . . . I think, I had expected that I was going to continue in the same vein I had been working as an undergraduate. . . . Unfortunately, . . . [in graduate school] I felt like I was being hammered into this kind of predetermined mold for academics: somebody who spends most of their time sifting through what other people have written about literature and very little time actually engaged with literature itself.

> *Charlie:* What'd I hope? I guess a continuing sense of . . . wonder and awe, and a sense of enlightenment, if you will, that [it] would be fun and fulfilling. . . . [I]n graduate school, I felt the joy and fun of learning was missing.

Some students entered graduate school not knowing that the process of graduate education is different from that of undergraduate education. Philip did not know "[y]ou don't go to graduate school; you go to school to work with some people." Ashley was unaware of the degree of self-motivation required: "Graduate school is different from undergraduate school in the sense that you have to be completely self-motivated. Nobody is going to tell you to do anything. . . . I didn't completely understand that at the time." Katie entered—and apparently left—not understanding that graduate education entailed a greater degree of independence and a different type of engagement with the material than undergraduate education. She attributes the differences she encountered not to the difference in level of education but to differences between universities:

> *Katie:* I worked harder [in college] at State University than I worked there, because . . . at Urban you may have six or seven books assigned to you and the professor has no idea whether you've read them or not. . . . [The professor] never gives you a test, like a true/false, multiple-choice test, or any type of test to ascertain whether or not you know that material. And then, I guess, to make life easier on you, he'll assign one paper at the end of the class. . . . and the whole grade is riding on this paper. . . . You can BS on the paper, and you can still not have read the books. . . . You can BS your way through the whole program. At State University you couldn't do that. The professor would give you an objective test where you're answering facts from the story; you're identifying characters; you're talking about plot, events, things that happened.

Although most students expected to work harder in graduate school than in college (see Baird, 1976), they often found that the work was more rigorous and demanding than they anticipated. The students also expected faculty to be more supportive and more interested in them as people and in their interests and ideas. Indeed, these expectations seem to be grounded in a prior experience.

> *Stuart:* The [problem] with my experience, there wasn't quite as much attention paid to the progress of the graduate student, the first-year graduate students, as I would have expected. . . . I was under the impression that Urban University focused on its graduate students and provided . . . quite a bit of guidance on their course of study, their academic pursuits, and so on. . . . [I got that impression from] talking with professors and advisers at my undergraduate institution . . . [and] perhaps, from some of the university's materials. . . . My expectations were that my primary adviser would take a little more of an interest in my interests or, at least, in guiding my interests along a line that would be academically challenging.

> *Irene:* In general, it was not what I expected it to be. . . . I expected the sort of environment that I had experienced [elsewhere] as a master's student. . . . I guess I was hoping that the faculty as a whole would maybe be interested in my progress . . . [T]here just wasn't the level of interest on the part of the faculty in the doctoral students that I had hoped for.

In sum, many graduate students appear to select and enter their graduate programs possessing too little information about the program and about the nature of graduate education and the graduate school experience. Graduate schools, for their part, also appear to be less than optimal in their selection decisions; that is, some appear to place too much emphasis on prior achievement and too little emphasis on the fit between the student's interests and the program's strengths. In addition, they assume that all entering students are equally knowledgeable about the nature of graduate education, and they sometimes appear to misrepresent themselves to prospective students. Thus, when students' and graduate programs' assumptions and expectations about each other collide, students are less likely to feel comfortable in or satisfied with their programs, and the chances of their successfully completing the program or even persisting beyond the first year diminish.

STAGES 1 AND 2: FIRST YEAR
THROUGH ATTAINING CANDIDACY

Stage 1 is the entry and adjustment stage. It encompasses the first year of graduate education, the period in which the student is making the transition between outsider and insider (Tinto, 1988, 1991, 1993). Stage 2 is the development of competence stage. It encompasses the second year through the attainment of candidacy. These stages have been combined in this chapter for several reasons. The retrospective survey methodology employed in this study did not allow students' cognitive maps to be assessed over time, although some stage-specific information could be gleaned from the interviews. Instead, the discussion of what information departments do and do not provide to students to help them develop cognitive maps of their programs, and the information students do and do not possess about them, is divided into two sections—formal requirements and informal expectations.

Formal Requirements

Along the road to degree completion, students must pass through a number of gateways. These gateways include completing coursework; getting programs approved; constituting supervisory committees; and passing preliminary, qualifying, and, sometimes, foreign language exams. Studies that have explored how students traverse these junctures indicate that the road to degree completion is "rocky" at best (see Baird, 1969, 1972; Girves & Wemmerus, 1988; Heiss, 1967; Rosen & Bates, 1967; Tinto, 1991, 1993; Weiss, 1981). To understand what makes the path so difficult, the DGSs were asked how their departments helped students learn about the formal requirements. The faculty were asked about the type of advice they gave students on these matters. Similarly, the survey participants were asked about their access to such information, and the interview participants were asked about their understanding of these aspects of their programs.

Information before and after Arriving

Invariably, all students are sent a brochure that provides an overview of the department. The brochure usually describes degree requirements, although the amount of detail varies by department. When students arrive on campus, most departments provide them with a handbook that describes the requirements in detail. It may illustrate the various patterns of courses available for different degrees as well as discuss the character of the examinations and what it means to make normal progress. Some of the handbooks lay out the department's policies and procedures. Some departments simply reissue the materials that were sent to students upon admission. Students are expected to read and understand the materials, which, in some cases, are an inch thick.

Two students mentioned the advance materials. They indicate that a complete understanding of what was expected of them—the informal, unwritten aspects of graduate education—could be obtained only by interacting with an adviser or with more advanced graduate students, something that underscores the importance of integration for cognitive map development.

> *Katie:* There were forms explaining what to do as far as how to register, how to get an ID [card], how to get library privileges, where to go to get books, and how to get them, et cetera, et cetera. . . . And then there was a form explaining how many credits you needed to have the degree and how you should distribute it and that kind of thing; . . . [and they] left the rest to, I guess, your adviser or whatever.

> *Beatrice:* We got the general outline of what students are supposed to do. We got the student handbook and all that kind of thing. And talking with other students . . .— the one's that were more advanced—you knew what they were doing, and you just expected you were going to be doing the same thing. So . . . it wasn't necessarily formally said, but everyone just seemed to know from everyone else.

Orientation

Orientations serve a number of functions. Although their primary purpose is (or should be) to help students develop an understanding of their programs, they also begin the process of integrating students into the academic and social systems of the department.

Interviews with the DGSs reveal great variability among departments in the quality and duration of their orientations. The greatest emphasis is placed on orienting students with TAs to their roles and responsibilities. When academic orientations do occur, they are conducted by the DGS and last for a half day to one full day. First-year students are generally welcomed by the department chair. Sometimes members of the graduate committee will be

present, although two DGSs said that the committee members had to be "cor-
ralled" into attending, and their attendance depended "on their timing and
how much they want to sleep that day and so forth."

The manner in which departments characterize themselves to students
during orientation begins the process of integration. One Urban DGS tells
students, "It's sort of like Quantico. You're going at the Marine Boot Camp,
and this is it, gang." He commented, "We pride ourselves on what is probably the toughest first-year graduate program in the country. And we tell
them it's tough." The militaristic, combative metaphor gives students the
message that they are going to have to struggle and prove themselves. By
contrast, the chair of one particularly eminent department at Urban tells students about the background and history of the department. Students get the
message that they are at an important place, will be working with important
people, and are among The Chosen. Some students find this message intimidating. Emmie, who was a graduate student in this department, remem-
bers the orientation this way:

> *Emmie:* I know that they also had some kind of evening orientation by the faculty
> where all of us sat very quietly and the various faculty talked to us about the
> school and the prestige and how important the research there was. And you just
> got the sense that, boy, you were becoming a part of this very elite group.
>
> *Interviewer:* How did that make you feel?
>
> *Emmie:* Well, you know, it's kind of a thrill, but then it's kind of like, gee, can I do
> this?

At its best, the academic orientation involves the DGS going through the
program step by step and discussing the different requirements from coursework through the dissertation, with plenty of time for students to ask questions. Frequently, the DGS or a preassigned temporary adviser will meet with
students individually and help them select courses. One department at Rural
University simply gives students an elaborate list of requirements and courses
and leaves it to the students to figure out how what they have taken as undergraduates corresponds with what is being offered.

Most orientations involve some sort of informal reception that begins students' social integration into the department. The receptions often take place
during orientation week or during the first week of the term. They are held on
campus or in the department chair's home and include the faculty and often,
but not always, advanced graduate students. One department introduces new
students to the faculty one by one, and the DGS states a few things about their
backgrounds and interests. This type of introduction facilitates interaction between students and faculty because it provides information that can serve as
the basis for academic contacts and conversation.

Student responses to the survey question "Did you attend an orientation for new graduate students?" show a high degree of variability in participation by department and university. Few of the interviewees remembered participating in an orientation, and those who did recalled mainly its social aspects.

The absence of a high-quality academic orientation coupled with the assumption that students understand everything in the materials given to them can have deleterious effects on students' understanding of their program, as revealed by Jim, who did not remember attending an orientation.

> *Jim:* They have literature and materials, but . . . as I said, I didn't feel like I had an orientation, and no one really went over it with me, and I hadn't had any kind of experience comparable to that in my previous academic career. . . . I guess I had gotten a bit jaded not to read things more carefully and ask more questions earlier on. The important thing was to me that whatever was required of me, I knew that if I just stuck to it and I had the support I needed and affirmation, I would succeed whatever it was. But I had no idea that what the catalog was talking about when it said things like oral or written exam and comprehensive oral and written examinations. I don't even know if that's the language that was used; it might have been. I'm just saying, I didn't know anything about that at all. In fact, I went through the whole year at Rural University without knowing about that or understanding what that was all about. In fact, it wasn't until the summer of my first year [after I transferred to another university] that I started to understand what this qualifying examination thing was all about. I never knew that one had to go through that kind of stuff.

By far, the greatest emphasis during the orientation is placed on TA training. The survey data indicate that having a TA position increases the likelihood of attending an orientation[3] (63 percent of students who received TA positions attended an orientation compared with 51 percent of those who did not). At these orientations, which last from two days to two weeks, TAs are usually familiarized with the curriculum they will be teaching and often engage in practice teaching and test development. Consequently, prior to the start of classes, students who enter with TA positions have more opportunities to interact and develop a sense of community with other entering TAs, to interact with faculty and advanced graduate students who assist with the TA orientation, and to become familiar with the department than students who do not receive TA positions. Thus, the TA orientation facilitates the development of an understanding of the department and the academic profession. It also facilitates the academic and social integration of those who receive TAs relative to those who do not.

Program Planning

The first two or three years of most graduate programs involve taking a combination of required and elective courses. In some programs, required courses culminate in preliminary or qualifying examinations. Elective courses are generally taken in areas in which students plan to specialize, and they determine which qualifying examinations students will take. Areas of specialization are key to selecting a dissertation topic as well as a dissertation adviser. Constructing a coherent program and getting through it in a timely fashion therefore entail some understanding of, and foresight in, the selection and sequencing of courses—something that, as will be demonstrated later, not all graduate students know how to do.

The DGSs were asked how students go about planning their programs—the sequencing of courses. Most of DGSs characterized the first year of graduate study separately from subsequent years. In most departments, the first year of coursework is very structured, and students get few, if any, choices. Those who have choices receive assistance in course selection.

After the first year, the process becomes murky. In some departments, students are "left pretty free to take whatever advanced courses they might wish," but "what advanced courses are available in the given year depends very much on the whims and fancies of the faculty." The departments rely on student judgment of what will enhance their understanding of their fields; many students confirmed this lack of assistance. In fact, all six interviewees who made it to stage 3 said that they put their programs together on their own. Two of these students complained about the lack of structure and guidance they received, as did students who did not make it that far.

In some departments, students develop a program of study with advisers in their area of stated interest. In others, students are provided with generic guides. Courses are often offered in two-year rotations, and students are supposed to know this. Regardless, most DGSs assume that most students will have found an adviser by the end of the first year. If not, they assume that the students will talk to faculty or more advanced graduate students about course selection. However, when faculty were asked about the advice they provided to their students about getting through the formal requirements, most resisted. Several faculty deferred to the DGS or other formal advising structures, stating either that students knew about these structures or that they referred students to them. Others asserted that by time they started working with students, most of the formal requirements were already gone, so there was no need to advise them on these matters. In other words, graduate faculty do not see themselves in the role of adviser prior to the dissertation proposal stage; consequently, they offer little, if any, advice about program planning. Interviews with students confirm this lack of guidance in both the first and subsequent years of course taking.

Students who were assigned to advisers reported that their interactions about coursework occurred only once a term. They stated that the interaction was often formalistic and perfunctory and that the adviser generally rubber-stamped the set of courses the student had selected. Even when students consult with advisers it is not clear that they always get good advice, as demonstrated by the experience of John, a graduate student in history who was assigned to an adviser and who left after one year. His narrative also illustrates how lack of prior socialization to the graduate school experience leads to cognitive map deficits about important components of graduate education. In addition, it hints at the assumptions faculty make about what students know and understand about graduate school and at their over-reliance on the handbook to convey important information.

> *John:* I don't think I got the advising that I really needed because one of the problems was I took too heavy a class load, I realize in retrospect. I hadn't had any experience with graduate study. I really didn't know what a normal class load was or what an extraordinary one was, and it turns out that mine was a little bit too heavy. And I think that's one of the main reasons that I wound up not completing it.
>
> *Interviewer:* What kind of advising did you receive?
>
> *John:* Well, not really very much. I told them what I was interested in studying, and, basically, they told me what courses were available and also what requirements there were, what courses I had to take. They were clear as to what the requirements for graduation or for getting a master's and a doctorate were. It was like they told me what was in the guidebook, but they didn't really give me any guidance as to what was a typical experience for a graduate student, I mean, as to how many courses I should take, which courses would be good to take this semester, which courses would go better if I waited a semester or two to take and that sort of thing.
>
> *Interviewer:* So, how many classes did you take your first semester?
>
> *John:* Five.
>
> *Interviewer:* Didn't somebody have to sign off on that?
>
> *John:* Yes, but nobody said, "Well, this is a heavy load," or "Maybe you should reconsider," or "Maybe you shouldn't take this many."

John also took five courses his second semester, while holding a part-time job for the entire year. Later in the interview, he mentioned that some of his professors knew he was taking five courses but that "I think they might have assumed that I had been told about it or that I had been advised about it. . . . They never said, 'That's an unadvisable course of action.'"

Analysis of the faculty interviews confirm the students' reports that when faculty dispense advice about program planning, they place emphasis on structure rather than process—that is, on telling students *what* they have to do, rather than on *how* to do it. The most common type of advice faculty said they give is about what course(s) they think students should to take. This advice, however, is often less about developing a coherent program of study geared to meeting departmental requirements than about taking courses, often outside the department, which would broaden them and be good for their careers. High producers showed more interest in and concern about individual students and what courses they took and with whom than low producers. Compare Professor Slattery, a low producer, with Professor Ashburn, a high producer:

> *Slattery:* The choice of courses—primarily it would be the academic adviser who does that. If students ask me would I recommend a particular course or another, I give them my opinions.

> *Ashburn:* I do desire and—insist, really, I should put it—insist on seeing each one of my graduate students before they register so that I know exactly what courses they're taking. And I try to exert some control. Now we have graduate advisers that they have to go visit, who talk to all of them, but I insist on seeing my students so that I can keep a handle on what they're taking.

Although the typical advice faculty dispensed on programs, fields, and minors emphasized concentrating on fields that are in demand and not specializing too early, the high producers were more likely to encourage students to be adventuresome and to take intellectual risks. Again, compare the style and the content of the advice given by a low producer (Perkins) with that of a high producer (Prudhomme)—incidentally, they are in the same department. Professor Perkins focuses on meeting requirements, Professor Prudhomme on helping students develop a vision of their intellectual careers in the department and beyond.

> *Perkins:* I will talk to them about the planning of their programs so that they can be sure to meet our particular course requirements, our core of course requirements, our divisional requirements, our minor requirements.

> *Prudhomme:* I get them to pay attention to [the department and distribution requirements] and have a plan early on, vary the plan as much as is useful, but not wait until their fifth year to discover that they haven't built something that they then can't vary easily. I like to try to help students prevent surprises of that kind. In terms of minor . . . I encourage students to build minors that they think will be interesting and fun to get into and . . . encourage them to be imaginative. With some frequency, my students put together packages which I help them petition and get approved because I think to put together a package that makes sense for that student is more valuable than taking two of these and two of these that somebody else set up as a fixed curriculum.

Students who are affiliated with high producers thus appear to receive more and better advice about their programs of study than students who are affiliated with low producers.

Most students who did not have advisers or whose advisers did not take an active interest in their programs[4] turned to the graduate student subculture for advice; the rest were left to their own devices. Cade, who made it to stage 3, illustrates the taken-for-granted transfer of information by the student subculture. India, who had a superficial relationship with her adviser and left after one term, demonstrates the benefits of sharing an office with other, usually more advanced, graduate students.

> *Cade:* [W]hich classes to take and all that kind of stuff? . . . I think I figured out all the informal stuff.
>
> *Interviewer:* How did you go about figuring it out?
>
> *Cade:* Gosh, I don't know. Mostly from talking to the other graduate students, I guess.
>
> *India:* There really wasn't that much contact [about your program] with faculty on that level. . . . The older graduate student, he was a Ph.D. candidate who was my like direct adviser, he helped probably more, and so did some of the other . . . grad students. . . . We had offices together. There was like ten of us in one office, so if you had questions . . . there was a lot of interaction there.

Finally, Hugh is a case of program planning in isolation. He relied on his own judgment about what courses he needed to take to succeed in the program and to pass his qualifying examination. (He didn't pass.)

> *Hugh:* I tried to take courses that were in my areas of weakness so that I would be prepared to pass on to the next level—at least ones that sounded interesting, if nothing else. That didn't always happen, but I tried to take ones that would fill in gaps or be interesting.

Choosing an Adviser

Choosing an adviser is probably the single most important decision a graduate student makes during his or her graduate career. Who a student works with can often spell the difference between completion and noncompletion. This person also influences the nature and quality of the student's graduate experience, the student's socialization as a researcher and academic professional, and the student's subsequent job placement. Some programs, the laboratory-based disciplines in particular, expect students to find an adviser by the end of the first year. Most programs want students to have an adviser by the end of the second year, and all require students to have an adviser either shortly before taking qualifying exams or by the time they start working on a dissertation proposal. Yet, like so many other aspects of graduate education, students are given very little formal advice about how to choose an appropriate adviser.

Although most of the laboratory-based disciplines (biology, chemistry, psychology) have structures in place to help students choose an adviser, by and large the DGSs commented that graduate students typically get attracted to particular faculty by taking advanced-level courses with them and that by talking to each other they find out who has a good reputation, who seems to take good care of students, and who does not. In a tone of exasperation, one DGS remarked, "How do graduate students get informed about anything? The biggest answer is scuttlebutt. . . . There's nothing like scuttlebutt to get them informed." Susan's remarks about adviser selection support those of the DGS. Susan was a biology student who selected her adviser based on having taken classes with her and having rotated through her laboratory. Yet, she felt that it was not clear whose laboratory students should go into, that it was "pretty much up to you," and that selecting laboratories was done by word of mouth: "'Oh, he's a nice guy,' or 'She is a good person.'"

If the process is not clear to graduate students, it is apparently not clear to senior graduate faculty, either. When asked how they come to be a student's adviser, two high producers used the term *mysterious* to describe the process. One was resigned to the mystery: "It's a bit mysterious the process to me, and I guess I'm inclined to live with the ambiguity and mystery of the experience." The other expressed some concern and tried to explain it: "That's perhaps more mysterious than it should be. The reason it's mysterious, it seems to me, has to do with social lubrication. Some students might feel dissonance about singling out one member of their committee for chairmanship. It is probably something we need to do a little better than we do."

The following remarks show that some faculty are aware that students do not know how or even when to ask a faculty member to be an adviser. The process resembles a mating dance composed of codes, signals, and indirection.

> *Bonnell:* A student may come into my office and just blurt out, "Will you be my major adviser?" . . . and then other students are reticent about the whole thing, and they'll often take you through the whole process without ever asking you to be an adviser. Usually I leave it to the student to bring it up, figuring that it's probably better to wait till they're comfortable. I've had students actually go through the entire process of formulating a research plan and so forth and never ask me to be their adviser, sort of leaving it up in the air.

> *Bedford:* [Working with a student on the special field exams is] usually a good signal that the students are interested in the topics you hold yourself available for. And then they come back and would initiate a conversation about who their, the usual way they do this is sort of by indirection because they don't know whether I would be available or interested in it.

Cade's experience highlights students' lack of understanding of the process, faculty's assumptions about students' understandings, and the concomitant feelings of discomfort:

Cade: I took a class from him in the first term. . . . [W]e were supposed to be finding a research adviser, and I guess I didn't feel like I knew or if I was interested enough in many of the research projects that were going on. This subject that he was working on interested me, and so I got up the courage to ask him, which took some courage. You know, what do I say? Is it just sort of automatic that if we want to work for somebody that they'll take us in, or do we have to sell ourselves or what? I knew already that he had a lot of students at the time, and so I knew that he might be reluctant to take on more. But I asked him anyway, and oh, this is another thing that I didn't really know, but he explained to me, is what you do is if you're interested in working for somebody, you take a [reading and research] course with him.

Although some students come in knowing who they want to work with, many do not and, consequently, are either assigned to or must choose an adviser. In cases in which students are assigned to an adviser, many do not know that the assignment is temporary or that they can change advisers without penalty.

Other Formal Requirements

In addition to coursework, graduate education involves a series of hurdles that students must surmount to receive the Ph.D. While the concept of coursework is familiar to all students, the nature of master's theses, preliminary and qualifying examinations (especially orals), and the dissertation are often vague and alien concepts. They are also complex processes with which students have had little, if any, prior experience.

When asked about how students acquired information about their department's formal requirements, the basic response from the DGSs was that the requirements are in the graduate handbook and are stated during orientation. Referring to the handbook in his department as a "thick mass of information," one DGS commented, "All the students know what's in it—at least I hope so," indicating less than full confidence in the assertion he was making. The experience of Jim (quoted earlier) belies the assumption that all students understand what is in the handbook. Some DGSs commented that students could get the information from the administrator for graduate studies or the department secretaries: "They know the details, and they counsel students in this regard as to deadlines and when they have to do what and so forth and so on," thereby deferring responsibility for this important aspect of graduate student advising to support staff.

Overall, the DGSs' responses focus on the nuts and bolts of the requirements—that is, when the requirements need to be fulfilled and what the prerequisites are. By contrast, students who are approaching the requirement are less concerned about the timing and the prerequisites (because, presumably, they have fulfilled them) than they are about how you actually *do* the requirement—that is, what it means to fulfill it success-fully. Graduate students know that failure to fulfill the prerequisites and failure to hurdle the requirements in a timely fashion is likely to lead to ter-mination from the program. They also know that fulfilling the prerequisites and meeting the requirement on time does not guarantee their retention in program unless their *performance* meets a certain *standard of quality*, and it is this standard of quality—how to prepare oneself to meet it and how they will be judged—that they need information about. For example, Hugh, a graduate student in English, thought that he had to read all three hundred books on the master's exam reading list before he could take the exam.

> *Hugh:* The kinds of things that we were asked to do became sort of daunting, espe-cially something like reading over three hundred works of literature in a year and a half and then taking an exam on them.
>
> *Interviewer:* Did they really expect you to read all three hundred?
>
> *Hugh:* Yes.

Hugh took three years off, got a full-time job, wended his way through the list, and then failed the exam by one point.[5]

In response to a question about the advice they gave students about for-mal requirements, some faculty focused on the process of getting through the program rather than on meeting the department's standards. They said they talked with students about the place of the masters' thesis and qualify-ing examinations in the great scheme of things—and their relative lack of importance—and about understanding examination and dissertation com-mittee politics. High and low producers were equally likely to encourage students to get the formal requirements out of the way as soon as possible. However, high producers were more likely to say that they *work with* stu-dents and help them get through, whereas low producers were more likely to say that they give students *advice on how* to get through. Compare Pro-fessor Johnston, a low producer, with Professors Tomlinson and Sherman, both high producers:

> *Johnston:* My advice is this . . . I say, "Hey, get through with it! Get through with it! Follow the rules! Get it over with so then you can form your independence and carve out your own career" . . . I tell them, "Hey, get through with it. If necessary, work on somebody's project. The more you know about that project, the more in-teresting it becomes. But get out of here and get on your own."
>
> *Tomlinson:* I sit down with them and have long talks with them about what we need to do. . . . I've tried to be very explicit with my students about what they have to do to get done and what their job likelihoods are.

Sherman: I try to figure out ways with them that they can meet those requirements in a way that serves their own education and gets them through the hoops or over the hurdles as quickly as possible.

In sum, graduate students need to be provided with local cognitive maps of the department's formal requirements individually as they approach them. Providing students with a handbook and discussing the individual requirements for the Ph.D. during orientation is important for developing a global cognitive map of the graduate program. However, students are barraged with information during orientation at a time when they are also making a major life transition. It is too much to expect that students will hold a deep understanding of distant requirements over an extended period of time, especially when they are preoccupied with fulfilling the more immediate ones. By the time they approach the more distant requirements, most of what was said about them during orientation is likely to have been forgotten. High producers seem to work with students on hurdling the requirements in a manner that is tailored to their individual needs and interests, whereas low producers seem to dispense advice on simply getting through.

Informal Aspects of Being a Graduate Student

All formal organizations have expectations that are not codified, yet members of the organization must learn them and conform to them if they are to fit in and be successful. Graduate schools, like other organizations, have their share of informal, unwritten expectations. The DGSs were queried about how their department helped students develop cognitive maps of a variety of them. The faculty were asked how they helped their students deal with their department's unwritten expectations.[6] The interviewees' understandings of informal expectations were revealed throughout their interviews.

Quality of Work

All graduate programs require doctoral students to maintain at least a B average. However, A is the most common grade given to graduate students, and graduate students are frequently exhorted to write papers of publishable quality. Given the high expectations and the small range of variability in grading, how do students find out about the quality of the work they are expected to produce?

Many of the DGSs were initially taken aback by the question. Some simply restated the program's grading policy and indicated that the handbook tells students what grades are necessary in required courses and what the minimum grade point average is. A number of the DGSs, however, were aware of vast differences among professors in the quality and quantity of work they demanded. Some made spontaneous remarks about faculty resistance to instituting department-wide standards. At the time of the interview, one department had recently undertaken a self-study and discerned that fifty to seventy different adjectives were used to register students' performance on oral examinations and dissertations. The Graduate Committee in that department had also undertaken a review of the grading of seminar papers because there "is no department-wide standard." The Graduate Committee circulated a draft of a seminar paper grading score card. The score card clarified the meaning of A's, A–'s, B+'s, and so on. However, the DGS reported that the faculty were resistant to any kind of interference by the Graduate Committee.

Overall, the DGSs' answers indicate a failure to convey information about standards of excellence. They commented, "The message is just there," "They pick it up being around, talking, reading, and so forth," and "Ultimately, it is the graduate student scuttlebutt that does some of these things." In other words, the departments do not objectively define what they mean by "high-quality work." Students who maintain a B or better average or even get straight A's may not necessarily be producing the type of high-quality scholarship the department expects of graduate students.[7]

Even when "standards" exist, they may be part of an oral tradition. One department that weeds at the master's level has a long-standing tradition that "an A means this person is definitely doctoral material, a B means this person is not doctoral material, an A– means I think this person is doctoral material, and a B+ means I'm not sure this person is doctoral material—I probably think not." Although the DGS felt that this system gave graduate students a pretty good reading of grades as a predictor of their ability to go on to the doctorate, he was not sure how long the department had been making the criteria explicit and said he had heard students say they did not understand it. Indeed, Katie, a black woman who intended to get a Ph.D. in that department, was unaware of the criteria.

Katie: See, with my grades, I really should have been admitted into the doctoral program, and there's no reason why I should not have gotten in there because I had, out of eight classes, I had maybe four A's and four B's, and the letter they sent to my house didn't say anything at all. Basically, what it said was, "We decided not to admit you, but many people who are not admitted go on to fulfill their goals in life." I still have it in my room somewhere. It says something to that effect, and so I had to find out through the grapevine [why I was rejected]. . . . I had to find out through the grapevine exactly what went on at this meeting [where faculty evaluate applicants for the Ph.D. program]. And, well, anyway, afterward I got this sense of relief emanating from the faculty and staff because I did not file a lawsuit against them or enact some other kind of arbitration. . . . But I could have made waves. I could have made trouble for them, especially with the grades.

Although a great deal of variability exists among graduate faculty with respect to their expectations of quality, what is meant by quality is neither standardized nor conveyed to graduate students in a coherent or objective manner. Students are, as the DGSs indicate, left to pick up the information from the graduate student subculture. Those students with rich social networks and strong connections to advanced graduate students and faculty are more likely to find out what high-quality work is and produce it than students who are not. Katie, who was socially isolated, was disconnected from communication channels that might have provided her with a better understanding of her chances for acceptance into the doctoral program and a better understanding of the reasons for rejection.

Basis of Judgments

Graduate students are often judged on a wide variety of tacit factors over and above timely progress and GPA. Although the DGSs were asked, "How do students obtain information about the basis on which they are being judged as graduate students?" they responded as if they were asked, "How do you judge graduate students?" The most common response was that faculty review students' performance and progress every year, and students, depending on the department, get a letter indicating whether they are making satisfactory progress. The second most common response was that students know whether they are doing well. Only one DGS came close to answering the substance of the question. She stated, "We try to explain to them that it's not exactly like undergraduate school where if you get A's, it necessarily means that you're doing well. But ultimately, you're going to be judged by the quality of your research and your publication record."

Most graduate students, however, feel that they are judged on more than just the quality of their work and timely progress. For instance, they often feel that they are judged on the quality of the questions they ask or the amount of time they put into their research assistantships (RAs) beyond that which they are being paid for. They feel that these judgments have implications for their future in the program and for subsequent job placement.

How Best to Become a Professional in the Discipline

Most students enter graduate school with the intention of becoming an academic professional, yet, as noted earlier, their understanding of what professors really do and what the alternatives to academic jobs are for Ph.D.'s are vague and often idealized. Learning "how to become a professional in the discipline" occurs through a process of tacit socialization that begins upon entry into the program and is concentrated in stage 2—the development of competency stage.

The DGSs were asked how students obtained information on how to become a professional in their discipline. Many answered that students learn by emulation and imitation: "We more or less teach them to be the way we are ourselves." Indeed, a few faculty indicated that they modeled the behavior, although the word *modeling* was rarely used. These behaviors include defining problems and asking questions in such a way that students are given a sense of the discipline's expectations, exposing students to research problems, jointly planning and critiquing research designs, spending time in the laboratory doing menial jobs, and simply presenting themselves as models.

Differences in the way high and low producers help students become professionals emerged in their discussions of the "critical transition"—the transition from being a course taker to an independent researcher/scholar. Three high producers talked about *modeling* and *scaffolding* the behaviors and thought processes necessary to make the transition, such that their relationship with their students evolved from master/apprentice to genuine peer by the time their students finished. By contrast, the one low producer who mentioned this transition said he simply *encouraged* students to move from the structured, passive classroom note-taking mode to being creative scholars who think, create, and do work on their own. Thus, students who work with high producers may have better models of, and better role models for, becoming an academic professional.

STAGE 3: THE RESEARCH STAGE

The research stage is the final phase of graduate education. It involves finding a dissertation topic, constituting a dissertation committee, completing a research project, and writing and defending a dissertation. These are complex processes with which most students have little familiarity or prior experience. Students who reach this stage know (or discover) that they must conduct research that distinguishes them from their peers. Most feel inadequately prepared to do this type of research and find themselves unprepared to cope with writing in the style required for a dissertation (Heiss, 1970). Indeed, as we have seen, some students entered graduate school not knowing that they would be expected to conduct original research and having only a vague concept of what a dissertation is and what writing one entails.

The DGSs and the faculty were not asked specific questions about the research stage, nor were issues related to the dissertation tapped directly by the survey instrument. Few students who participated in the interviews made it this far.[8] Consequently, although some insights about this stage can be gleaned from the DGSs' and faculty's comments and from the interviewees' experiences, reliable generalizations about cognitive map issues cannot be made.

The first task in the research stage involves finding a research question or dissertation topic. Very few faculty mentioned the advice they gave students on these matters. However, to the extent that the issue was discussed, differences emerge between high and low producers. Low producers focused on the mechanics of choice. They advised students to choose topics that overlapped with other materials and to build on what they already knew, to select topics that were ambitious enough to be challenging but not so ambitious as to fall flat, and to find the literature on the topic and begin reading and developing an outline. High producers focused on the relationship between the dissertation topic and their students' careers. They advised students to choose topics that were current, of interest to others, and that would help them get established in their field. Students working with high producers seem to be encouraged to conduct research that is exciting and intellectually engaging and that provides optimism about career prospects. This type of advice may give students of high producers the motivation necessary to see a dissertation project through to completion.

Some of the interviewees who reached stage 3 discussed the strategies they used to find a dissertation topic. Beatrice found a question for which there seemed to be no answer and talked it over with her adviser. Cathleen had one general discussion with her adviser about her interest in a particular area and was sent off to put a bibliography together. Tom's topic emerged from research he had been doing with his adviser as an RA. By contrast, Elinor did not come up with a dissertation topic because she discovered that she had many interests and could not commit to focusing narrowly on one. Only Tom actually began a dissertation project.

No DGS or faculty member mentioned helping students understand how to conduct dissertation research. Their silence on this issue suggests they assume that students know how to proceed. However, as noted earlier, a few faculty acknowledged the difficulty of making the transition from course taker to independent researcher/scholar. However, very little concrete advice appears to be dispensed about how to make this transition.

Rhett and Cade began their dissertation research, and each persisted for seven years. Rhett's progress was obstructed because he did not know how to proceed: "It somehow never became clear to me where to begin. . . . I did not get a grasp of what I had to do to make progress with the dissertation, and I felt really awful about it." (Rhett cried at this point in his interview.) Cade's research involved conducting a critical experiment, but, after several years of repeated equipment failure and the desire "to get on with his life," he abandoned his project.

Tom is the only interviewee who started writing a dissertation. Therefore, no insights can be gained on problems students have with this aspect of the graduate school experience. His dissertation was undermined by taking a nonacademic job in another city that removed him physically and intellectually from the departmental community. However, Irene's encounter with a dissertation early in her career provides some insight into students' feelings about the genre. One of her professors gave her a copy of a dissertation, saying "This was written by a [student in your area], and this is about what you could be expected to produce." She read it, handed it back to him, and said, "This is the most boring piece of literature that I have ever read."

Students' Assessments of Their Cognitive Maps

Student assessments of the quality of their cognitive maps was probed by the survey and in the interviews. Before exploring the results, a few methodological issues need to be addressed. In retrospective studies, questions about experiences need to be anchored in time. This constraint, combined with limitations on survey length and the amount of detail students could reasonably be expected to recall ten or more years after the fact, meant that questions had to be framed in terms of "at the time of entry" and "when you started graduate school." This time anchor limited the ability to assess students' cognitive maps of stages 2 and 3 as well as changes in the quality of their cognitive maps over time. However, the discussion that follows shows that the quality of students' entering cognitive maps reaches forward and affects their experiences across all stages as well as their persistence outcomes.

The survey asked two two-part questions about students' understanding of their departments' formal requirements and informal expectations at the time of entry. It also asked about their perceptions of *other* graduate students' understandings of these things. The latter questions were included to tap the existence of pluralistic ignorance—that is, believing that you are the only one who does not know or understand something, when in fact that thing is neither known nor understood by the plurality. Table 4.1 summarizes completers' and noncompleters' assessments of their own and other graduate students' cognitive maps.

During the telephone interviews, students were asked two separate but related questions: "When you started graduate school, how well did you understand what was expected of you as a graduate student?" and "Did you ever feel that other graduate students knew or understood things about the program or being a graduate student that you didn't?"

Understanding of Formal Departmental Requirements

The survey data show that completers felt they understood the formal requirements much better than noncompleters (see table 4.1). Among the

Table 4.1. Comparison of Students' Assessments[1] of Their Cognitive Maps at Time of Entry by Status and Completer Type

	Status			Completer Type		
	Completers	Noncompleters	p	On-track	At-risk	p
When you started your graduate program:						
How well did you understand the *formal departmental requirements?*	3.99	3.73	*	4.04	3.90	
How well did you understand the *informal expectations of your department* for completing the program?	3.15	2.74	*	3.33	2.89	*
How well do you think *other graduate students* understand the *formal departmental requirements?*	3.89	3.90		3.86	3.92	
How well do you think *other graduate students* understood the *informal expectations of your department* for completing the program?	3.12	3.25		3.18	3.02	

[1] 5-point scale: 1 = *not well at all* to 5 = *very well.*
*p < .001

interviewees, most who believed they understood the formal requirements
had durations of three or more years, had prior graduate experience, or left for
reasons external to the university such as marriage.[9] Many of these students
asserted that at a pragmatic level they understood what they needed to do to
succeed, and a few rattled off the requirements—required courses, seminar
paper, qualifying exams—or, in other words, elements of a global cognitive
map. Either the formal requirements had been explained to them early on, or
they figured them out by observing more advanced graduate students.

Many who did not understand the formal requirements came from small,
liberal arts colleges[10] and had little prior exposure to graduate education.

> *Elinor:* I didn't understand what was required of a Ph.D. program. . . . At the under-
> graduate level I certainly wasn't prepared, or I was not told, or I wasn't com-
> pletely informed of what getting a Ph.D. in musicology was all about.

Others focused on them at a more local level. Although they understood
such things as required coursework, they initially did not have a good understanding of how to get through their classes. They were surprised by the
amount of reading and did not understand that they would not, in their opinion, be given a reasonable amount of time to get through the material. One
student was surprised that she could turn in papers late and take incompletes.

Understanding of Informal
Departmental Expectations

The survey data show that completers felt they understood the informal expectations much better than noncompleters (see table 4.1), as did on-track
completers relative to at-risk completers. The interview data provide insight
into students' problems with the informal expectations. Some interviewees
described discovering that they had to do things they did not know they had
to do, such as going to conferences, subscribing to journals, networking,
working overtime (unpaid) on research assistantships, and even conforming
to a departmental persona.

> *Boyd:* As I learned about the local culture throughout that year, I began to understand
> there were other unwritten expectations. To sort of keep your head down. To sort of,
> it's really hard to even explain . . . to remember that you were engaged in something,
> a discipline that . . . exists as separate from literature, in that literary criticism views
> itself as a discipline or art form or something like that, that is equal to, if not, even,
> I think in some ways, . . . superior to the art form of literature. So that if you want
> to succeed in that environment you have to conform to a kind of academic, a sense
> of what an academic is—I guess that's it. I guess there was an unwritten sense that
> you have to become a kind of person as well as perform certain academic functions,
> . . . [become] kind of a company man, business, extremely conformist.

Several interviewees mentioned how they learned about the informal expectations. Their responses highlight the importance of integration with an adviser and the graduate student subculture. Most felt that it just happened through "osmosis," by being there, by observing the more advanced students, and by talking to, and asking questions of, other graduate students. They stressed the importance of latching onto an adviser and having a very good working relationship with him or her. John, who was isolated and atomized, was not sure whether he even knew that there were informal requirements or expectations because, in his words, "I didn't really get into the graduate student culture. . . . And I didn't have a lot of contact with faculty outside the classroom."

Students' Understandings Compared with Their
Perceptions of Other Graduate Students'
Understandings

Table 4.2 shows what happens when the students' understandings of the formal requirements and informal expectations were compared with their perceptions of other students' understandings. Completers and on-track completers felt they understood the formal requirements much better than other graduate students. Completers believed that other graduate students understood the informal expectations as well as they did, while on-track completers believed that other graduate students understood them less well. At-risk completers felt they understood the formal requirements as well as other graduate students, but thought that other graduate students understood the informal expectations better. By contrast, noncompleters thought that other graduate students understood the formal requirements and the informal expectations far better than they did.

These results suggest that either completers have good entering understandings of their programs' formal requirements and informal expectations or they experience an illusion of knowing. Either way, these beliefs facilitate their progress. By contrast, either noncompleters either do not have good entering understandings or they are suffering from pluralistic ignorance.

The interview data provide insight into what noncompleters thought other graduate students knew or understood that they did not and how they knew it. Some said other students entered with a clear vision of the end state of their graduate education and of how they were going to get there (global cognitive map of system). They noted that their peers knew who they were going to work with, what their areas of specialization were, and what the subject of their dissertations were going to be. Some thought other students possessed a good understanding of departmental politics. They mentioned that successful graduate students were good politicians; that is, they knew how to find an

Table 4.2. Comparison of Students' Assessments[1] of Their Own Cognitive Maps with Their Perceptions of Other Graduate Students' Cognitive Maps at the Time of Entry

	Formal Requirements			Informal Expectations		
	Own Understanding	Others' Understanding	p	Own Understanding	Others' Understanding	p
Status						
Completers	3.99	3.89	**	3.15	3.12	
Noncompleters	3.73	3.90	***	2.74	3.25	***
Completer Type						
On-track	4.04	3.86	***	3.33	3.18	**
At-risk	3.90	3.92		2.89	3.02	*

[1] 5-point scale: 1 = *not well at all* to 5 = *very well.*
*p < .05.
**p < .01.
***p < .001.

adviser, how to design their programs of study, how to select and make progress with a dissertation topic, and how to network and get known. Commenting on these students' political savvy, Hugh remarked, "Obviously, some of them had been groomed or taught something about what it takes to survive in academics and get a job when they finished."

Finally, a number of interviewees pointed to the role that integration into the graduate student subculture plays in understanding the informal expectations. Katie, who never felt especially welcomed and lacked a lot of information about the program, believed that she was on the outside looking in on the "in-crowd." Philip believed that there were natural categories of people that served as informal channels of mentorship and information, of which he, too, was not a part.

The interview data reinforce and extend the survey data. They indicate that when graduate students are struggling to develop cognitive maps of their programs and see other graduate students thriving and confident in their knowledge of the system, they come to believe that they are the only ones in the dark. They attribute their difficulties to their own inadequacies and not to the structure of the situation. The interview data suggest that cognitive map deficiencies can be rectified through interactions in the student subculture. However, this works only if the student has good powers of observation or is willing to break through his or her atomism and admit that he or she does not know or understand aspects of the graduate school experience that everyone else seems to understand.

CONCLUSION

Graduate students do not get the information they need to develop clear and coherent cognitive maps of almost every aspect of their graduate programs. For many students, this deficit can be traced back to program selection and preview and to their exposure (or lack thereof) to the graduate school experience as undergraduates. Indeed, the type of information they used to select graduate programs, in addition to the presence of a preenrollment campus visit, are two of the few prior-to-entry characteristics that distinguish completers from noncompleters. These differences are not easily captured on applications for admission. Even were this possible, they should not be used to reject a student. Rather, these differences suggest that prospective graduate students need more advice and guidance about how to pick an appropriate program and better information about the nature of graduate education and the graduate school experience.

Although graduate students should be responsible for reading materials provided by the department, departments make the unwarranted assumption that students understand all the concepts, policies, and procedures described therein. As we have seen, this can be a fateful assumption. General orientations do contribute to students' understandings of the department's formal requirements, but most are too short and cover too much information too superficially. Faculty often view the general orientation as a burden and of secondary importance to the TA orientation. Students who enter with TA positions receive longer, more extensive, and more informative orientations, which also begin the process of academic and social integration with faculty and other graduate students. Those who do not enter with TA positions are therefore disadvantaged relative to students who do.

Graduate departments also appear to defer too much information about too many important and complex matters to the graduate student subculture. This works well for some, especially full-time students who are well connected with the subculture. It works less well for students who are less integrated with their peers, including part-time students, commuter students, students who hold off-campus jobs, students with weaker social skills, and students who are marginalized for other reasons, including race or ethnicity. Thus, graduate departments inadvertently set some of their students up for failure.

Regardless of their cause, cognitive map deficits create a sense of discomfort and unease that is detrimental to persistence. These feelings lead to a need to find comfort and security, which for some students can be achieved though casual interactions in the student subculture. For others, it can be achieved only by breaking through their isolation and atomism and revealing their "ignorance" or by leaving the program.

Finally, students who work with high producers seem to have qualitatively different access to information about their graduate programs than students who work with low producers. Low producers offer advice about formal requirements upon request. By contrast, high producers socialize students to their programs and to the profession by modeling and scaffolding behaviors and intellectual processes, such that much of the requisite *how* information may be dispensed during taken-for-granted interactions. High producers also take a more long-term view of their students' information needs; that is, the advice they provide appears to be tailored to the individual student and takes his or her intellectual and professional goals into consideration. Students who work with high producers appear to receive more of the kinds of information necessary for developing accurate cognitive maps of the formal and informal aspects of their graduate programs than students of low producers.

NOTES

1. Because interviews were not conducted with completers, it is not possible to determine how optimal their campus visits were.

2. Golde (1996) finds that some programs are inadvertently structured to eliminate students who were not exposed to graduate education as undergraduates (e.g., came from liberal arts colleges and did not have research experience).

3. The evidence is supporting rather than confirmatory because the survey did not collect data on *when* students received a TA. Students who entered with a TA could not be separated from students who received a TA at later points in their graduate careers.

4. Because no matching of students with advisers was done, I cannot assert that these advisers were low producers, although the evidence suggests that they probably are.

5. The high producer in this department was queried about this expectation. He indicated that at the time Hugh was in the department, the qualifying exam had short identification questions and answering them correctly required being familiar with the corpus.

6. Many of the faculty did not really understand the question even when prompted, and some even denied that there were unwritten expectations. Yet, in responding to questions about whether they encouraged students to join professional organizations and subscribe to professional journals, several faculty indicated that they never mentioned it to students because graduate students "know" that it is expected of them.

7. One DGS said that he has informally encouraged students to talk to professors after a course is over to get an interpretation of the grade and to find out what the professor really thought of the student's ability to proceed to the doctorate.

8. See Benkin's (1984) study of ABDs for a more detailed discussion of factors related to attrition at the research stage.

9. Comparisons of noncompleters who, on the survey, indicated that they had prior graduate experience (65 students) with those who did not (195 students) reveal no differences between groups in terms of duration or any of the cognitive map factors. This lack of difference may be due to self-selection on the part of the interview sample, a closer analysis of the cognitive map factors and their relationship to prior experience and duration in the interview data set, or the inability to control for external factors on attrition in the quantitative data set.

10. The undergraduate institutions that the students in the sample attended were coded using a modified Carnegie classification scheme (doctoral university, comprehensive university, liberal arts college). Analyses were conducted on the relationship between type of undergraduate institution and the four cognitive map factors. The main factor that distinguished students who attended liberal arts colleges (completers and noncompleters) from students who attended other types of institutions was the quality of their cognitive map of the department's informal expectations. Students who attended doctoral degree-granting universities as undergraduates had the best cognitive maps of their department's informal expectations, students who attended liberal arts colleges had the worst. This finding suggests that organizational structure affects students' prior socialization to the informal, unwritten aspects of the graduate school experience.

Chapter 5

The Absence of Community

Communities, and the bonds that tie an individual to them, are created through formal and informal interactions among members. The nature of these interactions are shaped in large part by the beliefs, values, and norms of the cultures in which they are embedded and affect how well integrated their members become.

This chapter explores the relationship between interaction and persistence at the interdepartmental and intradepartmental levels. It shows that differences in departments' student—and faculty—attrition rates are a function of the number of opportunities they provide for academic and social integration. In addition, within departments, who persists and who does not is a function of how such opportunities are distributed to students. It also assesses the relationship between "chilly climate" factors (e.g., sexual involvement with faculty, sexual harassment, discrimination) and attrition decisions.

DIFFERENCES BETWEEN DEPARTMENTS

Data on department structures and opportunities for integration come from the director of graduate study (DGS) interviews and from my site visit notes. The DGS interviews explored the nature of their departments' academic and social activities. Data on students' engagement with department opportunities for integration come from their responses to survey questions asking about their participation (yes/no) or frequency of participation in the same basic set of activities about which the DGSs had been queried. My field notes include information on the material culture of the departments. Table 5.1 lists these data points.

The Absence of Community 83

Table 5.1. Sources of Data on Departments' Structures and Opportunities for Integration and Students' Engagement with Them

	Department Structures and Opportunities		Student Engagement
Type of Integration	Director of Graduate Study Interviews	Site Visits	Graduate Students' Survey Responses
Academic Structures and Activities	Sources of financial support Colloquia Brown bag lunches Study groups Dissertation support groups Graduate student government Graduate students on department committees Encourage participation in professional activities	Student lounges Graduate student offices	Sources of financial support[1] Share an office[1] Subscribe to journals[1] Belong to a professional association[1] Attend professional meetings[1] Participate on departmental committees[1] Attend colloquia/brown bag lunches[2]
Social Structures and Activities	Social hours on campus Social hours off campus Departmental picnics Sports activities Other departmental traditions		Socialize with faculty and students on campus[2] Socialize with faculty and students off campus[2] Participate in departmental sports activities[2] Participate in other departmental activities[2]

[1] *Yes/no* items in the questionnaire.
[2] Scaled items in the questionnaire.

Structures and Opportunities for Integration

Financial support is a factor in integration less because of its monetary value than because of the obligations inherent in the award. Some forms of support (especially teaching assistantships [TAs] and research assistantships [RAs]) require students to spend time on campus interacting with faculty and other students who have TAs and RAs. Students who receive full fellowships often do not have to come to the department to perform professional tasks; consequently, they are not forced, and may have less opportunity, to interact. Students who receive no support at all have little reason to spend time in the department and may have to spend time off campus because of employment obligations. Therefore, students with TAs and RAs should be more academically integrated than those without assistantships or with no support at all.[1]

Rural University and Urban University have different practices for awarding teaching assistantships. At Rural University, TAs are the main form of support. Almost all students get TAs, most in their first year of graduate study. By contrast, TAs at Urban University tend go to advanced students (except for chemistry, where almost all entering students receive a TA). Survey results confirm the differential distribution of TAs by university: 84 percent of Rural students reported receiving a TA, whereas only 36 percent of Urban students did. These differences are inversely related to Rural and Urban's overall attrition rates (33 percent and 68 percent, respectively).

RAs are invariably awarded at the discretion of faculty who have research support. Outside funding is more common in the sciences and social sciences, especially the laboratory-based disciplines (biology, chemistry, psychology), than in the humanities. Furthermore, 76 percent of students in the laboratory-based disciplines reported receiving an RA, regardless of university. Students in the sciences are more likely to receive RAs in their first year than students in other disciplines.

Although some students enter with fellowships from outside sources, university- or department-based fellowships are typically offered to the best students and are often used as a recruiting device. "Best" is determined by a vote of the full department or the department's admissions committee. The awards are generally for the first three or four years of graduate study. Fellowships are sometimes awarded to students admitted without support who "prove themselves" during the first year. Some departments have dissertation fellowships, which, again, tend go to those students considered to be the "best."

With respect to the 1982–84 cohort, most departments at both universities admitted students without support. However, according to the DGSs, more students at Urban did not receive support than students at Rural, and a higher percentage of students in the humanities at both universities did not receive support than students in the sciences and social sciences. Again, analysis of the survey data confirms the DGSs' reports. Almost one-fourth of Urban students but less than one-tenth of Rural students did not receive financial support. Similarly, 25 percent of the humanities students (14 percent at Rural, 40 percent at Urban) did not receive support, compared with 5 percent of the science students (6 percent at Rural, 0 percent at Urban) and 5 percent of the social science students (1 percent at Rural, 14 percent at Urban).

Analysis of attrition rates by type of financial support confirms predictions about persistence outcomes relative to the integrative nature of support type. Overall, students who received TAs and RAs had the lowest attrition rates (24 percent and 17 percent, respectively), followed by students who received full fellowships (31 percent, university fellowship; 39 percent, private fellowship) and students who received no support at all (80 percent).

Table 5.2.   Attrition Rate and Type of Support by Race/Ethnicity (in percent)

	White	*Asian*	*Black*	*Hispanic*
Attrition rate	*25*	*38*	*57*	*45*
Type of support				
TA	71	66	43	55
RA	48	49	21	36
University fellowship	14	12	43	46
Private fellowship	14	14	50	46
No support	12	8	0	0

Although the number of racial and ethnic minorities in the sample is quite small (fourteen blacks and eleven Hispanics), table 5.2 shows that their attrition rates track with the integrative nature of the support they received. Whites and Asians, who had the lowest attrition rates, were more likely to receive TAs and RAs than blacks and Hispanics. By contrast, blacks and Hispanics who had the highest attrition rates were more likely to receive fellowship support than whites and Asians. No black or Hispanic was unsupported, although some of the whites and Asians were. These data suggest that fellowships were used to recruit minorities into graduate programs, but because these forms of support are not integrative, they did not lead to the completion outcomes they were designed to achieve.

Integration through Sharing an Office

Having a desk in a "gang" office can facilitate and deepen students' academic and social integration. It provides them with a place to work and hang out and an incentive to spend more time on campus and in the department. This prevents isolation and increases the probability of formal and informal interactions with faculty and other graduate students. Students who share office space also have more access to the tacit knowledge contained within the graduate student subculture, and they can more easily share concerns and obtain the information they need to succeed.

Access to office space varies by university, discipline, and type of financial support. According to the DGSs, all Rural University students in the laboratory-based disciplines get a desk in their research group's laboratory, and every student who receives a TA gets an office for its duration and sometimes beyond. By contrast, according to the DGSs at Urban University, few TAs get offices. The only students who receive offices are those in mathematics and the laboratory-based disciplines and some RAs in nonlaboratory-based disciplines. It is unusual for graduate students at Urban University in nonlaboratory-based disciplines to get an office during their first year.

Consistent with the theory of integration, which predicts an inverse relationship between degree of integration and attrition, the distribution of office space for universities (84 percent, Rural; 38 percent, Urban) is inversely related to their attrition rates (33 percent, Rural; 68 percent, Urban), and the distribution of office space for discipline collapsed into domains of knowledge (83 percent, sciences; 78 percent, social sciences; 49 percent, humanities) is inversely related to their attrition rates (41 percent, sciences, 45 percent, social sciences; 52 percent, humanities). The survey data also confirm that students with TAs and RA are more likely to share an office (88 percent and 59 percent, respectively) than students who receive full fellowships (13 percent regardless of type) and that students with no support are the least likely to share an office (3 percent). These office-sharing rates are inversely related to attrition rates by type of support. Moreover, within support type, sharing an office further reduces the amount of attrition. The attrition rate for students with TAs drops form 24 percent to 22 percent, that for students with RAs from 17 percent to 14 percent. More significantly, the attrition rate for students with full university fellowships drops from 31 percent to 13 percent, that for students with private fellowships from 39 percent to 18 percent, and that for students without any support from 80 percent to 24 percent. Sharing an office thus increases students' integration in the department and decreases the likelihood that they will leave without completing their degrees.

Integration through Informal Activities and Structures

In addition to having formal requirements, graduate departments host informal activities and events that bring graduate students and faculty into academic and social contact. Participation serves to further integrate students into the academic and social systems of the department and enhances their intellectual and professional development. The DGSs were queried about activities and events commonly found in graduate schools. Student reports of their participation (or frequency of participation) is noted where data allow.

Although colloquia may involve presentations by faculty or advanced graduate students from the university's own department, they typically entail presentations by outside speakers. They thereby provide opportunities for faculty and students to learn about research on other campuses or research centers. Colloquia are typically preceded or followed by receptions at which participants mingle, discuss the speaker's research, and make professional contacts.

Most of the departments in the study held weekly or biweekly colloquia, although some held them infrequently and on an ad hoc basis. Most colloquia were reported to have very good student turnout, although for the colloquia in the vertically integrated disciplines (mathematics, chemistry, and economics), where topics tend to be more specialized, the attendance of the more advanced graduate students was reported to be better than that of less advanced graduate students.

Brown bag lunches serve a function similar to that of colloquia, although the talks are usually more casual and limited to presentations by faculty and students in the department. There was wide variability among the departments concerning the existence, frequency, structure, and even the intended participants.

The survey asked students how frequently they participated in "colloquia/ brown bag lunches." Because of the phrasing, students' participation in these events cannot be assessed separately. However, analysis of this item shows significant variability in student participation between universities and across departments, as well as a university-by-department interaction effect. Students in the social sciences at Rural University and in the sciences at Urban University participated most frequently. Students in the humanities participated least frequently.

Social hours are a good way for graduate students and faculty to get to know each other outside their academic roles. An off-campus location separates the academic world from the social world, allowing students to see faculty without their academic hats and in roles other than professor. With the exception of the two mathematics departments, which hold daily social hours, where social hours existed, they happened on Friday afternoons. The departments at Urban University were much more likely to have weekly or biweekly social hours on campus than those at Rural University. On-campus social hours at Rural University are infrequent and tend to occur at the students' discretion. However, faculty and students from several departments at Rural University meet at local bars.

The survey data show that students at Urban University participated as frequently in on-campus social activities as did students at Rural University. However, students at Urban University participated in off-campus social activities more frequently than did students at Rural University.[2] Despite this, great variability in both types of socializing was noted across departments. Students in Urban's Mathematics Department did indeed participate the most frequently of all departments at Urban (and in the sample) in on-campus socializing, but students in Rural's Mathematics Department participated the least frequently of all departments at Rural (and the second least frequently in the sample).

Fall and spring picnics, like social hours, facilitate informal interaction between faculty and students, and they often include faculty's and students' families, thereby allowing faculty and students to see each other in a broader family, as opposed to individualistic, context. Most departments at both universities had fall and spring picnics. The survey did not query students about participation in this activity.

Sports activities involving students and faculty are another form of informal socializing that can foster social integration and relieve some of the stress and tension of graduate student life. Many of the departments at both universities have sports activities—softball, basketball, volleyball, soccer. Where they occurred, their frequency and composition varied. Some departments had formal teams on which both faculty and students played regularly, some had teams of graduate students only, and in some departments both faculty and students played sports together occasionally and usually in conjunction with some other event (e.g., the department picnic). The students reported participating in sports activities with equal frequency at Urban and Rural. However, students in the humanities participated less frequently than did students in the sciences and social sciences.

The DGSs were asked about the existence of a graduate student government in their departments because it can serve several integration-related functions: increase the academic and social contact of those who hold office; provide nonoffice-holding students with an outlet for sharing concerns about the department along with the expectation of action; organize academic and social events, thereby increasing the probability of their occurrence; and provide students with input into departmental policymaking. Almost all of the social science and humanities departments at Urban and Rural have a student government, while very few of the science departments do. The survey did not query students about this activity.

Inclusion of graduate students on departmental committees can also serve a number of integration- and cognitive map–related functions: integrate the students with the faculty on the committees; enhance students' professional development by exposing them to the less visible roles and responsibilities of faculty members, as well as to the nature of the decisions they have to make and the criteria they apply (e.g., search committees, admissions committees); and add the voice of the graduate students to faculty deliberations. Moreover, in providing feedback to other students in the department, the student representatives demystify departmental practices and help other students develop an understanding of committee work.

Many departments at both universities have graduate student representatives on departmental committees, and those that do not indicated that they were moving in that direction. Some departments have a graduate student on most major committees; others have a representative only if an issue involves graduate students in a direct way. In general, the practice does not appear to have been widespread in the early 1980s. However, one DGS commented that since her department increased student input into what goes on in the department, relationships have loosened between faculty and students. The survey data show that 21 percent of students participated on departmental committees; students in the social sciences were the most likely to serve.

Student lounges are places where students, especially those who do not have offices, can interact informally. Whether or not a department had a lounge appeared to be a function of the size of the department. Departments that occupied more than one building (biology and chemistry departments, in particular) or that were housed in buildings that were several stories tall were less likely to have a central graduate student lounge than departments housed in a single, smaller building. Lounges that vended food (fresh food, in particular), had kitchen areas, or made available newspapers and periodicals were more likely to be used than lounges that did not.

No students were observed in many of the lounges during the admittedly brief observation periods; in fact, some were locked. When lounges were used, the most typical use was by individual students who sat quietly reading either a book or a newspaper. However, a few dyadic and one small-group interaction were observed. The interactions tended to be conversations that were academic in nature.

Integration through Engaging in Professional Activities

Subscribing to journals, joining disciplinary associations, and attending annual meetings are rites of passage into the professional world. They are also indicators that the student wishes to become, or believes him- or herself to be, a member of the discipline's community. Therefore, it is a sign of actual or attempted academic integration. Receiving a journal and an association's materials and attending conferences not only keeps students informed but serves to reinforce a student's sense of community with the discipline.

The DGSs were asked whether their department encouraged students to subscribe to journals or attend professional meetings and whether the department subsidized these activities. The responses about journal subscription varied widely. The most common response was that although students were encouraged to read the journals, they were not encouraged to subscribe to them because of the cost and their availability in the department's reading room or the university's library. One DGS pointed to the importance of academic integration with faculty for journal subscription when he commented that subscribing to journals "depends on what faculty contact the students had and how much advice they would get on the issue." Indeed, when asked whether he encouraged his students to subscribe to professional journals, one high producer's response acknowledged the importance of subscribing to journals for professional development:

> *Hilton:* Definitely, particularly once they have a particular area that they're working in and there are one or two journals that are really specific in that area. Then my standard advice is the best way to see what you might write for a particular

journal is to be continually reading that journal and get a feeling for what its on-going discourse [is], and what issues come, and who is cited in it and how the articles feel and all that sort of thing. And that if you have a really good sense of that for the couple of key journals in your field, it makes it a lot easier to publish. And, really, going to the library is just not as good as getting it in the mail and opening it up and getting a sort of ongoing relationship with it.

Graduate students in both mathematics departments receive free memberships to the American Mathematical Society and, as a natural sequelae, receive the society's journal. The humanities disciplines were more likely than any of the other disciplines to encourage students to subscribe to journals, but no department subsidized journal subscriptions.

Whether students actually did subscribe to journals varied between universities and among departments. Despite (or perhaps because of) their free subscriptions, far less than 100 percent of mathematics students reported subscribing to a journal (57 percent, Rural; 75 percent, Urban). And despite allegedly being encouraged to subscribe to journals, humanities students were significantly less likely to do so than science and social sciences students (64 percent for humanities vs. 73 percent for both science and social sciences).

The DGSs were not asked whether their department encouraged students to join professional societies. However, a few DGSs volunteered information on this topic. As indicated earlier, students in both mathematics departments automatically receive professional memberships, and Urban's English department encourages students to join the Modern Language Association.

Like subscribing to journals, the percentage of students who joined professional associations varied considerably between universities and among departments. More mathematics students reported joining professional organizations than subscribing to journals (69 percent, Rural; 83 percent, Urban), but their engagement was still not 100 percent. Urban's English students, despite department encouragement, were less likely than students in any other department to belong to a professional association (38 percent), as were humanities students compared with science and social sciences students (62 percent, humanities, vs. 77 percent, sciences, and 75 percent, social sciences).

Virtually all departments encourage students to attend professional meetings. Some departments provide support for students, but that support is often contingent on working with a faculty member who has a grant. In fact, there is a strong and significant correlation ($R = .64$) between having an RA and attending professional meetings. Some departments provide support for students who have had a paper accepted for presentation. However, these students are likely to be in the advanced stages of graduate education and, consequently, are already fairly well integrated in their departments.

Once again, the percentage of students who attended professional meetings varied considerably by university and department. Like many of the other activities discussed, humanities students were less likely than science and social sciences students to attend professional meetings (60 percent, humanities, vs. 77 percent, both sciences and social sciences).

Students' Overall Integration in Their Departments

A score for students' integration in their departments was calculated for each student by summing student responses to the survey questions using the academic and social integration factors displayed in table 5.1.[3] The overall student integration score was subdivided into an academic and social component. There was significant variability between universities and among domains of knowledge, disciplines, and departments with respect to how integrated their students were. Rural students were more integrated than Urban students, overall and academically, but not socially. On all three measures of integration, students in the sciences and social sciences were significantly more integrated than students in the humanities. Chemistry students were the most integrated, overall, academically, and socially. English students were the least integrated overall, but music students were the least integrated academically; history students were the least integrated socially.

Departmental Environments for Integration and Attrition

Using information reported by the DGSs or observed during the site visits, an overall integration score was calculated for each department.[4] The overall scores were subdivided into academic and social integration scores based on the factors depicted in table 5.1.

When the departments' three integration scores were compared with their student attrition rates, two correlated negatively and significantly: overall ($R = -.41$) and academic ($R = -.54$).[5] These results indicate that the more opportunities a department has for integration, academic integration in particular, the lower its student attrition rate.

An aggregate score for students' integration into each department was calculated by summing individual student responses to the survey questions depicted in table 5.1 and obtaining averages for each department. The overall integration score was subdivided into an academic and social component. The three aggregate student integration scores were compared with their departments' attrition rates. Although none of the correlations were statistically significant, the signs of all the correlations were negative, as would be expected if the hypothesis "The more integrated students are in the department, the lower the department's student attrition rate" were true.

To assess the relationship between the departmental environments for integration and actual student integration in the department, the departmental integration scores were correlated with the aggregate student integration scores. The correlation between the academic integration scores achieved significance in the predicted direction ($R = .48$), indicating that the more opportunities a department has for academic integration, the more academically integrated its students become. The correlation between the social integration scores also achieved significance, but not in the predicted direction ($R = -.42$).

Faculty are also members of the departmental community. Consequently, the opportunities the department provides for interaction with other faculty and students should influence their persistence decisions as well. When the departments' faculty retention rates[6] were compared with the three departmental integration scores, faculty retention correlated positively ($R = .34$) and marginally with the overall departmental integration score. This result suggests that the more opportunities a department has for integration, the more integrated its faculty are, and the more likely they will be to remain in their departments.

More important, the data reveal a strong and very significant negative relationship ($R = -.60$)[7] between faculty retention and student attrition; that is, the higher the faculty retention rate, the lower the student attrition rate. This finding, combined with the previous one, suggests that the more integrated a department is, the more likely it will be to retain both its faculty and its graduate students and that the relationship between faculty retention and student attrition is a function of the environment in which both groups reside.

In sum, differences in departments' environments for integration help explain the observed variability in attrition rates (student and faculty) between departments and between departments within disciplines.[8] They help explain why, for instance, even though chemistry as a discipline may have a low attrition rate, the Chemistry Department at Urban has a higher attrition rate than the Chemistry Department at Rural. Differences in departments' attrition rates relative to their environments for integration lend support to the contention that graduate student attrition has less to do with what students bring to the university than with what happens to them after they enroll, as departments' attrition rates can be, and were, assessed and explained solely in terms of departmental factors and without recourse to student characteristics. In short, graduate student attrition appears to be a function of the department's social organization. The more structures and opportunities a department provides for integration, especially academic integration, the more likely its students (and faculty) will take advantage of those opportunities, the more integrated they become, and the less likely they are to leave.

DIFFERENCES WITHIN DEPARTMENTS

In assessing differences within departments, we begin to consider differences between completers and noncompleters, as well as differences between on-track and at-risk completers and between men and women. However, before doing so, it is worth determining whether completers and noncompleters were differentially integrated into their undergraduate programs and the profession prior to entering graduate school, and whether these differences influence their persistence outcomes.

Prior Professional Socialization

The survey contained a nine-item question designed to capture students' academic integration as undergraduates while at the same time capturing their prior socialization to the graduate school experience and to the profession. The items asked about such integrative or professional experiences as being mentored by faculty, working as part of a team, publishing journal articles, presenting papers, subscribing to journals, attending professional meetings, belonging to professional associations, serving on departmental committees, and belonging to campus organizations.

Although one would expect a higher percentage of completers to have had these experiences than noncompleters, as figure 5.1 shows, the reverse was true. As undergraduates, noncompleters were significantly more likely than completers to have attended professional meetings and to have served on departmental committees. Although not statistically significant, on four of the remaining seven items (received mentoring, presented a paper, subscribed to a journal, and belonged to campus organizations), a higher percentage of noncompleters engaged in the activity than completers. When the nine items are collapsed into an index and completers are compared with noncompleters, the result is statistically significant and favors the noncompleters.

As undergraduates, on-track completers were more likely than at-risk completers to have presented a paper outside the classroom (24 percent vs. 14 percent), whereas at-risk completers were more likely than on-track completers to have belonged to campus organizations (71 percent vs. 57 percent). Women were more likely than men to have served on departmental committees (21 percent vs. 11 percent). The latter two effects suggest that at-risk completers and women may have broader interests and a greater degree of social involvement in the departmental and university communities than on-track completers and men, an issue that will be explored in greater detail in chapter 6.

In sum, noncompleters were more integrated and engaged in the profession as undergraduates than completers. Therefore, on paper predictors of success such as applications for admission, noncompleters are likely to appear as well

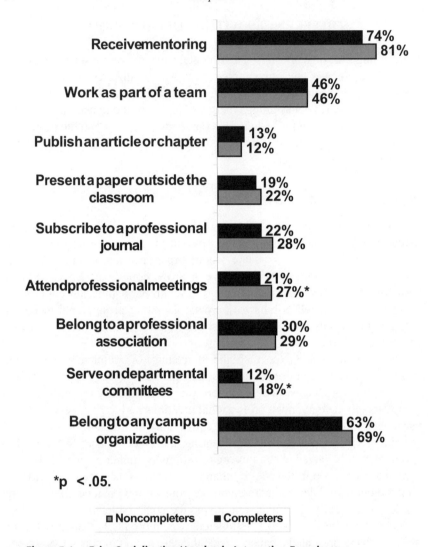

Figure 5.1.   Prior Socialization/Academic Integration Experiences
as Undergraduates

or better prepared for graduate school and for entry into the profession than completers. More important, these results combined with data that show no differences in self-reported undergraduate GPA between completers and non-completers (see chapter 1) suggest that universities *are* making appropriate selection and admissions decisions. They also indicate that attrition is more a function of what transpires after the student enrolls in graduate school than a function of the aptitudes and experiences that the student brings to the graduate program. We now turn to what happens to students after they enroll.

Structures and Opportunities for Integration

In the first part of this chapter, we looked at how resources for integration were distributed between departments as well as between universities, domains of knowledge, and disciplines and how the differential distribution affected attrition rates. In this part, we examine how the same basic set of structures and opportunities for integration are allocated differently to students within a department and how the difference in the distribution of resources helps determine who stays and who leaves.

Integration through Type of Financial Support

Teaching and research assistantships are the most integrative forms of support, so it should not be surprising to discover large differences in attrition rates between students who receive these forms of support and students who do not. Table 5.3 shows that completers were, in fact, almost twice as likely as noncompleters to have received a TA and three times more likely than noncompleters to have received an RA. At-risk completers were as likely as on-track completers to have received a TA, but they were significantly less likely than on-track completers to have received an RA, suggesting that among completers, the RA, which gets students involved in research projects, has a greater influence on progress toward the degree than the TA, because the TA may force students to take time away from their research. In addition, women were significantly less likely than men to receive a TA (63 percent vs. 74 percent) or an RA (41 percent vs. 52 percent), despite the fact that assistantships are awarded on the basis of academic merit and that the women in the sample entered graduate school with higher undergraduate GPAs than the men.[9] This difference in the allocation of assistantships is, however, consistent with the gendered rate of attrition (48 percent, female; 31 percent, male).

Students who receive full fellowships are denied important opportunities for academic integration and professional development that students who

Table 5.3. Type of Support by Status and Completer Type (in percent)

Type of Support	Status			Completer Type		
	Completers	Noncompleters	p	On-track	At-risk	p
TA	85	45	**	84	87	
RA	64	21	**	68	60	*
University fellowship	16	13		17	14	
Private fellowship	15	16		15	14	
No support	4	25	**	3	5	

*p < .05.
**p < .001.

receive RAs and TAs benefit from in the process of fulfilling their assistant-ship obligations. Consequently, students who receive full fellowship support should be as likely to stay as they are to leave; the data support this hypothesis. Completers were as likely as noncompleters to have received full university fellowships and private outside support. On-track and at-risk completers were equally likely to have received each type of fellowship support, as were men and women (15 percent for each sex for each type of fellowship).

No support at all detracts from integration and should increase attrition because, like fellowship support, no support denies students the integrative benefits that derive from the obligations attached to an assistantship. In addition, lack of support may force students to take jobs outside the department, which further decreases their ability to interact with members of the departmental community. Indeed, noncompleters were six times more likely than completers not to have received support, and they were significantly more likely than completers to report income from a job on campus (27 percent vs. 20 percent) or off campus (35 percent vs. 26 percent). On-track and at-risk completers were equally likely to report not having received financial support and equally likely to report having a job on campus (18 percent vs. 22 percent). However, at-risk completers were significantly more likely than on-track completers to report having a job off campus (34 percent vs. 20 percent), suggesting that this pull had a negative impact on their full integration in the department and thus on their thoughts about leaving. In keeping with their higher attrition rate, women were significantly more likely than men not to have received support (16 percent vs. 9 percent), but they were as likely as men to have had a job on campus (23 percent vs. 22 percent) or off campus (27 percent vs. 30 percent).

Integration through Sharing an Office

Office space provides students with a place to work and interact with other graduate students. As such, it is an important factor in integration, and, consequently, one should expect to see differences between completers and noncompleters with respect to their access to this resource. Indeed, not only were completers almost twice as likely as noncompleters to have shared an office, but they were also more likely than noncompleters to have shared an office when the type of financial support they received is controlled (see table 5.4). Completers who received TAs, RAs, and university fellowships were significantly more likely to have shared an office than noncompleters who received the same forms of support. However, completers and noncompleters who received private fellowships or did not receive any support were equally likely to have shared an office. So, not only are completers more likely than noncompleters to receive the types of financial support

Table 5.4. Percentage of Students Who Shared Office Space Controlling for Type of Support by Status and Completer Type

	Status			Completer Type		
	Completers	Noncompleters	p	On-track	At-risk	p
Shared an Office	85	46	***	85	86	
Type of Support						
TA	90	81	**	84	85	
RA	67	36	***	66	56	**
University fellowship	15	8	*	17	12	
Private fellowship	14	9		15	15	
No support	3	3		3	5	

*$p < .05$.
**$p < .01$.
***$p < .001$.

that contribute to integration and persistence, but they are further advantaged because they are also more likely to be given a desk in a gang office.

Although on-track and at-risk completers were equally likely to share an office, when type of financial support is controlled, the data show that on-track completers with RAs were significantly more likely than at-risk completers with RAs to have shared an office. Finally, women were significantly less likely than men to share an office (64 percent vs. 74 percent). However, this effect disappears when type of financial support is controlled. Women were less likely to share an office than men because they were less likely to receive the types of support (TAs and RAs) that are associated with being given a desk in an office. In other words, within support type, office space is distributed equitably by gender.

Integration through Informal Activities

Participation in informal academic and social activities can increase the integration among those who participate. Thus, one should expect to find differences between completers and noncompleters in their frequency of participation in such departmental activities as colloquia/brown bag lunches, sports activities, socializing on campus, socializing off campus, and other social activities involving faculty or students.

Overall, completers participated significantly more frequently than noncompleters in all informal departmental activities except off-campus socializing. However, the question arises as to whether these differences are due to differences in students' dispositions or to differences in the social situations in which students find themselves. In other words, given what we know about the role of financial support in integration, students who have integrative forms of support may be more likely to participate in departmental activities because they are more likely to be on campus when these activities occur and are therefore more likely to be carried along by peers and colleagues. To separate dispositional effects from social structural effects, differences between completers' and noncompleters' participation in departmental activities were analyzed controlling for type of support.

The results show that regardless of support type, completers were more disposed to attend colloquia/brown bag lunches than noncompleters. But, when controls are applied to the social activities, the differences between completers and noncompleters' disappears, indicating that the social-structural situation in which students find themselves influences their participation. On-track completers participated significantly more frequently than at-risk completers in colloquia/brown bag lunches only, but the effect disappears when type of support is controlled. The only gender difference was for sports. Men participated with much greater frequency than women under all circumstances.

Perhaps more interesting is the frequency of students' participation in departmental activities when assessed against the integrative nature of the type of support they received. Figure 5.2 shows that activity for activity, students (completers and noncompleters) who had TAs and RAs participated more often than students with fellowships, and students with fellowships participated more often than students with no support at all. The effect is stronger and more consistent for noncompleters than completers.

Integration through Engaging in Professional Activities

Subscribing to journals, joining disciplinary associations, and attending professional meetings are signs of integration. Students' engagement in these activities may also be influenced by dispositional and contextual factors. Indeed, the data show that while there appear to be dispositional differences between completers and noncompleters, the social-structural context also influences noncompleters' engagement.

Although as undergraduates noncompleters were more likely than completers to subscribe to a professional journal and attend professional meetings, as graduate students completers were much more likely than noncompleters to engage in all three professional activities (subscribe: 82 percent vs. 50 percent; join: 86 percent vs. 47 percent; attend: 87 percent vs. 45 percent). The differences between groups persist across types of financial support, suggesting dispositional differences. However, these differences can be explained, in part, by duration, because these activities are things students are more likely to do in the later stages of their graduate careers. Noncompleters who persisted four or more years were significantly more likely to engage in each professional activity than noncompleters who left after three or fewer

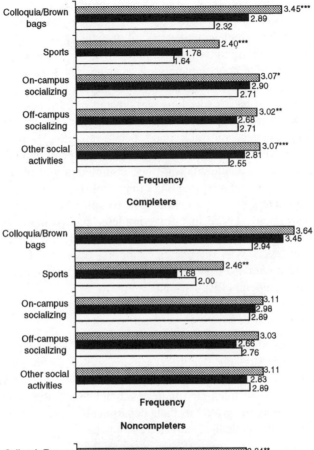

Whole Sample

Colloquia/Brown bags: 3.45***, 2.89, 2.32

Sports: 2.40***, 1.78, 1.64

On-campus socializing: 3.07*, 2.90, 2.71

Off-campus socializing: 3.02**, 2.68, 2.71

Other social activities: 3.07***, 2.81, 2.55

Frequency

Completers

Colloquia/Brown bags: 3.64, 3.45, 2.94

Sports: 2.46**, 1.68, 2.00

On-campus socializing: 3.11, 2.98, 2.89

Off-campus socializing: 3.03, 2.66, 2.76

Other social activities: 3.11, 2.83, 2.89

Frequency

Noncompleters

Colloquia/Brown bags: 2.84**, 2.57, 2.14

Sports: 2.17**, 1.83, 1.54

On-campus socializing: 2.97, 2.89, 2.67

Off-campus socializing: 2.97, 2.69, 2.69

Other social activities: 2.95*, 2.80, 2.45

Frequency

*p <.05; **p < .01; ***p < .001.

☐ No Support ■ Fellowships ▨ RA and TA

Figure 5.2. Frequency of Participation in Department Activities by Support Type

years (subscribe: 61 percent vs. 41 percent; join: 63 percent vs. 40 percent; and attend: 64 percent vs. 37 percent). When the later-leaving noncompleters are compared with completers, they are still less likely to engage in these activities, even controlling for type of support. However, as shown in figure 5.3, a higher percentage of noncompleters who had TAs and RAs engaged in each activity than noncompleters who had fellowships, and a higher percentage of noncompleters who had fellowships participated in each activity than noncompleters who had no support at all, suggesting that context plays a role.

As undergraduates, on-track and at-risk completers, and men and women, were equally likely to engage in these professional activities. However, as graduate students, on-track completers and men were more likely to attend professional meetings than their counterparts (90 percent on-track completers vs. 79 percent at-risk completers; 75 percent men vs. 66 percent women). The effect for completer type disappears when all forms of support except having a TA are controlled, and it disappears for gender within every type of financial support. These results indicate that social structure exerts a greater influence on integration and persistence outcomes than students' dispositions.

Students' Integration in Their Departments

Using individual student integration scores based on factors depicted in table 5.1, differences in students' overall, academic, and social integration in their departments were assessed. For each type of integration, completers were overwhelmingly more integrated than noncompleters.[10] By contrast, at-risk completers were as integrated in their departments as on-track completers. Women were as academically integrated as men, but they were less integrated overall and socially.

In sum, there appear to be some dispositional differences between completers and noncompleters with respect to participating in informal academic activities (colloquia/brown bags) as well as with respect to engaging in professional activities. However, the latter is partially a function of early-stage attrition as graduate students are increasingly likely to engage in these activities as they progress through their programs. Also, as we shall see in chapter 7, these differences may be due, in part, to the type of adviser the students had. Despite these dispositional differences, a large part of the variability in persistence can be explained in terms of the distribution of structures and opportunities for integration, particularly type of financial support and office space. In general, the more opportunities for integration a student received, the more integrated the student became and the more likely the student was to complete. This finding reinforces the contention that graduate student attrition is less a function of what students bring to the graduate program in

Whole Sample

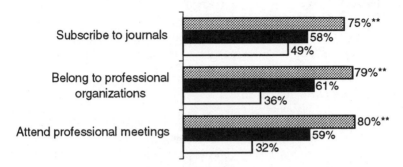

Completers

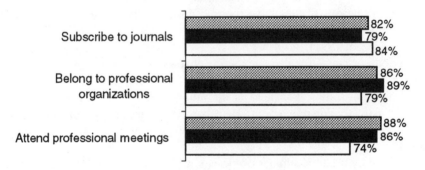

Noncompleters

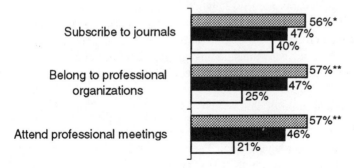

p = .06; **p* < .001.

□ No Support ■ Fellowships ▨ RA and TA

Figure 5.3. Percentage of Students Engaging in Professional Activities by Support Type

terms of background and dispositions than a function of what happens to students after they arrive. Indeed, as undergraduates, noncompleters appear to have been more integrated and more professionally socialized than completers, but their fates in graduate school appear to have been altered by their graduate programs' differential allocation of resources for integration.

Chilly Climates and Attrition

Climate can be defined as the current pattern of important dimensions of organizational life, including patterns of interaction and participant behaviors (Peterson & Spencer, 1990). It is a barometer of culture, an indicator of current attitudes, beliefs, and behaviors. Departments' climates shape and are shaped by the nature and quality of the interactions that take place within them. Among other things, climates can be warm or cold, hospitable or hostile. Numerous studies have focused on the chilliness of the academic climate for women (see especially Hall, 1985; Hall & Sandler, 1982, 1984; Sandler, 1986, 1991). They have assessed the degree to which interactions in various organizational contexts are characterized by discrimination or harassment. High levels of discrimination, harassment, or even sexual involvement indicate a weakness in the moral code of the organization and should indicate a disintegrated rather than an integrated environment. Disintegrated organizations should have higher attrition rates than integrated organizations.

The survey asked a number of climate-related questions: (1) whether the students had ever been sexually involved with their adviser or another faculty member; (2) whether the students had ever experienced unwanted sexual comments or contact (harassment); (3) whether the students were ever pressured for sexual favors; and (4) whether the students experienced discrimination because of race/ethnicity, gender, or sexual orientation. The survey also asked who the perpetrator was: the students' adviser, a faculty member in the department, a nondepartmental faculty member, or another graduate student.

Racial/Ethnic Discrimination

Overall, 5 percent of the students said that they had experienced racial/ethnic discrimination while in graduate school. There is variability among racial/ethnic groups in terms of the amount of discrimination they experienced and who committed it. Because the number of racial/ethnic minorities in the sample is quite small, the number of each racial/ethnic group who experienced it is given with the percentage.

Blacks experienced the greatest amount of discrimination (71 percent, ten students), followed by Asians (23 percent, fifteen students), Hispanics (9 percent, one student), and whites (2 percent, fifteen students). The blacks felt equally discriminated against by their adviser, departmental faculty, nondepartmental faculty, and students. The Asians felt discriminated against most by other students, followed by departmental faculty. The one Hispanic who reported discrimination felt discriminated against by other students. By contrast, whites felt most discriminated against by departmental and nondepartmental faculty.

The experience of racial/ethnic discrimination did not have a large effect on noncompleters' decisions to leave or on at-risk completers' thoughts about leaving. Of the at-risk completers who experienced discrimination, two blacks (20 percent) and one white (6 percent) said that it influenced their thoughts about leaving. Of the noncompleters who experienced discrimination, two blacks (20 percent), two Asians (13 percent), and three whites (20 percent) said that it influenced their decision to leave. No minority noncompleter who responded to an open-ended survey question asking them to state in their own words the most important reason for their decision to leave reported that racial/ethnic discrimination was a factor in their leaving. Furthermore, neither of the two Hispanics nor the two Asians who participated in the noncompleter interviews reported experiencing racial/ethnic discrimination. In fact, Cathleen, an Asian, stated, "I think one aspect I really felt good about was that they were very nondiscriminatory. I have heard . . . stories of a lot of harassment, either sexual or perhaps on a ethnic basis at other prestigious institutions. That was never the case at Urban University." However, Katie, a black woman, experienced extreme racial discrimination by faculty and students.

> Katie: I was resented. I felt a sense of resentment and hostility on both the parts of professors who were there and also on the part of other students who were there. It was thought that anyone who was black and a graduate student at the English Department had to also be a fellowship student. . . . I feel that they had this certain stereotype of all blacks who should have been inarticulate, illiterate, stupid, unable to read or write beyond, say, a sixth-grade level, and certainly not qualified to be a part of their graduate program and definitely not qualified to get a fellowship. . . . [The professors] would say things like, "I'd be very interested to know what your background is." I'm quoting one English professor who said that to me. And the students themselves would not want to be seen talking to me or speaking to me at all. There was one who was brave enough to tell me this; but others—I know when I'm being avoided. . . . They didn't want to say hello to you, and they didn't want you to say hello to them either, because, according to the story, the only reason the black person was there is so that there could be diversity in the classroom and they weren't there for any academic reason.

Gender Discrimination

The women in the sample were seven times more likely than the men to have experienced gender discrimination (22 percent vs. 3 percent), bringing the total amount of gender discrimination to 10 percent. These students reported that more than half the discrimination was committed by a faculty member in their department (55 percent), about a fourth by the student's adviser (24 percent), and slightly less than a third by other students (31 percent).

Of the students who experienced gender discrimination, 48 percent (forty students) were noncompleters and 30 percent (twenty-four students) were at-risk completers. Gender discrimination influenced 38 percent of these noncompleters' decisions to leave (fifteen students) and one-third of these at-risk completers' thoughts about leaving (eight students).

Gender discrimination does not turn up as a factor in a search of the noncompleters' open-ended responses about their reasons for leaving, although two women in the interview sample mentioned it.

> *India:* I felt that as a married woman graduate student there was definite discrimination. We were not given the same sort of leeway that men who were married . . . were. If one of them had something going on at home, it was . . . not a problem. . . . But if you had anything going on, it was [that] you had divided loyalties.

> *Solange:* Three of the guys [in the class] just seemed not to listen at all to what I said, no matter what I said. . . .That was the first time that I was really aware of feeling somewhat discriminated against. . . . [I]f I made a remark, a couple of these people would like look at me, turn away, and then make their own comment that might be paraphrasing what I said.

Sexual Orientation Discrimination

Two percent of the students (fourteen) felt discriminated against because of their sexual orientation. Because the survey did not ask students about their sexual orientation, this statistic cannot be put in perspective. However, all the students who experienced this form of discrimination were either noncompleters (eight) or at-risk completers (six), and it influenced two noncompleters' decisions to leave and four at-risk completers' thoughts about leaving. Most of the discrimination was perpetrated by other students, followed by departmental faculty; few students (three) had problems with their adviser. None of the interviewees mentioned their sexual orientation, but one noncompleter did implicate bias against gays in his written remarks about his reasons for leaving: "Race/gender issues had to do with anti-white-male attitudes & English faculty & students. Curiously, some of these people were remarkably insensitive to gay issues. I feel I was ignored by right and left alike."

Sexual Harassment and Pressure for
Sexual Favors

Stories of lecherous professors harassing students and pressuring them for sexual favors abound in graduate student folklore and reality (Dziech &

Weiner, 1984). This study's cohort confirms its existence. One out of five female students, and one out of twenty-five male students, reported being sexually harassed (10 percent of the total sample), but only 2 percent of the sample reported being pressured for sexual favors (one man, twelve women). Faculty in the students' department were responsible for more than half the harassment (63 percent) and sexual pressure (54 percent), followed by faculty outside the students' department (25 percent harassment, 38 percent sexual pressure). Advisers appear to be relatively well behaved on this score. They were implicated in only 12 percent of the harassment reports (ten students) and 8 percent of the sexual pressure reports (one student). Although completers and noncompleters were equally likely to have experienced each form of misbehavior, at-risk completers were more likely to have been sexually harassed than on-track completers.

Despite the prevalence of these forms of misbehavior, they do not appear to be strong factors in students' attrition decisions. Only six (22 percent) of the noncompleters who were sexually harassed indicated that it influenced their decision to leave, while only five (16 percent) of the at-risk completers indicated that it influenced their thoughts about leaving. Similarly, three (38 percent) of the noncompleters who experienced pressure for sexual favors indicated that it influenced their decision to leave, while one (33 percent) of the at-risk completers reported that it influenced their thoughts about leaving. None of the interviewees mentioned having these problems with faculty. However, one noncompleter wrote on her survey, "My junior faculty member had a very sexual manner with me at times, which made me uncomfortable. . . . I never felt comfortable with him."

Sexual Involvement

Although a relatively high percentage (25 percent) of female clinical psychology students in the 1970s reported having had sexual contact with their graduate educators (Pope, Levenson, & Schover, 1979), only two female students in this study's sample, a noncompleter and an at-risk completer, reported having been sexually involved with their adviser. Both were in Rural's Biology Department. However, nine students declined to answer this question. An additional thirteen students (two male, eleven female) reported having had a sexual relationship with a faculty member in their department (four from Rural's Biology Department); four were noncompleters, and four were at-risk completers. Despite the high percentage of attrition or thoughts of attrition among students who were sexually involved with their adviser (100 percent) or another faculty member (62 percent), only two noncompleters (40 percent) and one at-risk completer (20 percent) indicated that it was a factor in their decision to leave or thoughts about leaving.

Boyd, whose department had the most reports of inappropriate sexual behavior of all departments at Urban, demonstrates students' awareness of the
sexual goings on in a department and the general impact these trysts had on
the community. He talked about a "repressed sexual overtone" and discussed
the dysfunctional sexual relationships between faculty and students. He described how faculty and students would get drunk at the department's happy
hours, and "you would start to see the faculty members sort of stroking the
heads of the other graduate students" and how this would lead to short lived,
one-night stands. He said if you went to one of the local diners early on Sat-
urday or Sunday, "you could see who'd been sleeping with who by which
people were paired up in booths that morning." He also talked about the impact these affairs had on relationships between people in the department.

> *Boyd:* By the end of the year, so-and-so would have had a one night-stand with so-
> and-so, and then they would not be talking. By the end of the year, if you went to
> one of these happy hour things, there would be these unbelievably complicated
> lines of tension between this person and this person, and that person and that per-
> son, and this person and this person.

Climate and Attrition

Two climate scores were computed for each department, one that reflects
the number of reports of discrimination, harassment, pressure for sexual favors, and sexual involvement with advisers and department faculty (*faculty
climate*—a barometer of faculty culture) and another that includes the number of reports of discrimination by other students (*overall climate*—a barometer of departmental culture). Rural's faculty and overall climates were much
chillier than Urban's. There were 130 negative reports involving faculty at
Rural compared with 49 at Urban. When negative reports involving student
perpetrators are included, Rural's climate score climbs to 160, Urban's to 67.
All told, four departments at Rural had overall climate scores above 20 (Music, 36; Biology, 34; Psychology, 26; English, 21); with the exception of
Chemistry (17), the rest of the departments had scores under 10. Only one department at Urban had a score over 20 (English, 38); the next closest score
was for Sociology with 8 reports.

The departments' faculty and overall climate scores did not correlate with
their attrition rates. However, because Rural has a lower attrition rate than
Urban but a higher occurrence of negative reports, the correlations were re-
run separately by university. The relationship between each university's departments' climates and their attrition rates were all strong, and most were
significant.[11] These findings support the contention that climate is an indicator of culture and hence of integration: the chillier or more hostile the department's climate, the less integrated the community, and the more likely

students will leave. Conversely, the warmer or more hospitable the climate, the more integrated the community, and the more likely students will complete. Indeed, the strength and significance of these correlations are a testament to the influence of a department's climate on its attrition rate. Given that the analyses were conducted on samples with only nine cases, the power of the analyses was greatly reduced, as was the probability of seeing a significant result.

CONCLUSION

In contrast to most studies of graduate student attrition that have sought to explain the phenomenon in terms of students' personalities, dispositions, and background characteristics, this chapter focused on social-structural causes. In particular, it looked at the role that community—as measured by the distribution of structures and opportunities for integration—plays in attrition at the interdepartmental and intradepartmental levels, and it found strong effects.[12]

At the interdepartmental level, departments' student attrition rates can best be explained by differences in their environments for academic integration. In addition, within universities, the chilliness of their climates also accounts for a respectable proportion of the variance in attrition between departments.[13] Even though direct contact with chilly climate factors may not cause all of the "victims" to leave or to think seriously about leaving, the prevalence of these negative factors has a chilling effect on the departmental environment as a whole and impacts its members' willingness to persist.

At the intradepartmental level, differences between completers and noncompleters can best be explained by differences in their access to resources for academic integration. Although some dispositional differences between completers and noncompleters appear with respect to their participation in their departments' informal academic activities and in professional activities, much of the difference in these behaviors can be explained in terms of the distribution of opportunities for integration: completers received greater quantities of these resources than noncompleters.

The theory and data put forth in this chapter do not warrant the claim that individual differences play no role in attrition or that interactions between the individual and the institution play no role in persistence outcomes either. Rather, this chapter provides solid evidence that a large proportion of attrition can be accounted for by how resources for integration are distributed between and within departments. These findings imply that graduate student attrition rates can be reduced considerably by a more equitable distribution of resources.

Strong, bonded graduate communities are characterized by the existence of numerous opportunities for supportive academic and social interactions between and among their members—faculty and graduate students. In the absence of these community structures, departments will have high attrition rates. Similarly, students who are strongly bonded to their communities are the ones who have been provided with resources that enable them to interact frequently with other members of the community and to engage in the intellectual and professional tasks of the discipline. When students are not provided with these resources, they leave in large numbers. In a nutshell, noncompleters' graduate school experience is best characterized by the absence of community.

NOTES

1. A number of students in the sample had more than one form of support during their graduate careers.

2. This difference may be a function of differences in the way the questions were asked. The DGSs were asked specifically about social *hours*; the students were asked about social *activities* or socializing in general. Although social hours create opportunity for interaction, a lot of socializing takes place in other contexts as well.

3. Weights were applied to some yes/no items relative to their contribution to integration. For instance, having a TA or an RA received more points than having a full fellowship because these forms of support contribute to integration, while having no support at all received a negative weight because it detracts from integration. Weights were built into the frequency of participation items.

4. Each structure or activity a department had was weighted relative to its contribution to integration. For instance, a department that had weekly colloquia received more points than a department that had monthly colloquia, and a department that had monthly colloquia received more points than one that had them "occasionally" or "rarely." Similarly, because TAs enhance integration, departments that gave all entering students a TA received more points than departments that admitted only some students with TAs. Admitting students without support cost departments points, because lack of support detracts from the full integration of all students in the department.

5. These analyses were run using one-tailed Spearman correlations.

6. The faculty's deviation from expected retention rates were used as a measure of faculty retention (see chapter 1).

7. A one-tailed Pearson correlation was used for this analysis. It was significant at $p = .004$.

8. This research on department environments for integration is novel and highly exploratory; consequently, the resulting indices are very crude. For instance, it is not clear how much weight responses from nonanchored verbal protocols should receive. It is also not clear that things like encouraging students to subscribe to journals should receive the same weight as having a graduate student lounge or providing students with office space. In addition, the sample size was very small. Only eighteen departments were included in analyses of between-department differences, and data for a few departments came from a single program or area within the department, thus weakening the relationship between departmental environment and student outcomes for those departments, as students' pro-

grams or areas within those departments could not be controlled. Given these problems with the data, the fact that a number of the analyses were significant or nearly significant is an important finding. It suggests that departmental environments for integration exert a strong effect on the departmental community and students' actual integration in that community. It also suggests that measures and weights for the nature of departmental environments and opportunities for integration should be developed and refined further.

9. Graduate deans have been aware of the problem with the distribution of TAs (and RAs) for some time and have made efforts to rectify the situation. So, while this gender effect exists for this cohort (and for cohorts that preceded it), it may no longer hold for contemporary cohorts.

10. The results for each analysis were significant at $p < .001$.

11. Rural: faculty climate: $R = .67, p = .025$, overall climate: $R = .73, p = .013$; Urban: faculty climate: $R = .69, p = .019$; overall climate: $R = .51, = .080$.

12. Indeed, effects were also found at the university, disciplinary, and domain of knowledge levels.

13. The variance accounted for is as follows: faculty climate: 65 percent at Rural, 21 percent at Urban; overall climate: 54 percent at Rural, 18 percent at Urban.

Chapter 6

Disappointment with the Learning Experience

Students who pursue graduate education care deeply about their intellectual growth and development. Indeed, intellectual development is the means to the end, the Ph.D., and it has been defined as a component of academic integration (Tinto, 1975, 1987, 1993). Consequently, the more satisfied students are with their level of intellectual development and the components of their education that contribute to it—their program of study, the faculty in their department, their fellow graduate students—the more likely they should be to complete.

The previous chapter focused on the relationship between the quantity of interaction and attrition. This one focuses on the quality of the learning experience. It explores the nature of the academic and social interactions in the surrounding learning environment and how disappointment with those experiences contributes to attrition. It starts with students' discussions of their programs and then moves on to their discussions of the quality of the interactions they had with faculty and fellow graduate students.

THE PROGRAM

The central locus of intellectual development is a student's program of study. At its core, a program of study includes not only the individual courses that comprise the curriculum but also their content and the materials and teaching styles used to impart knowledge. Surrounding this core is the department's or faculty's approach to the discipline and treatment of ideas as well as the intellectual interactions that take place between faculty and graduate students in formal and informal settings.

Overall, the survey data show that noncompleters were less satisfied with their intellectual development and their program of study than completers, as were at-risk completers relative to on-track completers. The less satisfied the noncompleters were with their intellectual development, the faster they left. Differences in academic performance do not completely account for these findings. While completers had higher graduate GPAs than noncompleters (3.75 vs. 3.62) and were more satisfied with their academic performance than noncompleters, the noncompleters certainly were not doing poorly. In fact, their 3.62 grade point average indicates they were getting more A's than B's, and, as argued in chapter 4, the truncation of the range of grades available to graduate students makes graduate GPAs relatively meaningless. In addition, there were no differences in the undergraduate or graduate GPAs of noncompleters who left by the end of their first year compared with those who persisted longer, suggesting that something other than academic ability and grades contributed to their dissatisfaction and attrition.

The only interviewees who were uniformly positive about their program of study and its contribution to their intellectual development were two students who made it to stage 3 (both persisted seven years) and ones who left for external reasons such as marriage or an injury. The satisfied students said that their programs matched their intellectual orientations and met or exceeded their expectations for growth and development. Their delight with their programs bubbles forth in their characterization of their learning experiences and the ways in which they contributed to their educational and professional goals. Cade left after seven years, and Tony left because of an injury.

Cade: It was a wonderful place to be because, in general, the university and the department—because there were a lot of seminars going on that I took full advantage of. . . . I had a good group to work with because it was both chemists and astronomers. One of the most positive things about it was that I got a wide variety of experience in a wide variety of fields, not just chemistry and not just my own research group. It was a huge diversity. . . . [It] was nice to have my own [research project] and be able to work at my own pace and to take diversions at times [that] wouldn't necessarily be productive but that I learned a lot from. . . . Except for the fact that I was frustrated by my research . . . everything else was really wonderful.

Tony: It was a great experience, and it was overall what I wanted to do. I was happy at the department, and I was doing significant research. It was fine. I was on time. The professors were worldly ranked and outstanding, and the school of thought was what I was pursuing.

These students' experiences and positive feeling stand in stark contrast to the characterizations by those of students who were less than fully satisfied with their programs.

Whether or not the graduate program they enrolled in was their first choice, most interviewees felt honored to have been accepted and looked forward to being supported in their intellectual endeavors. However, this is not what many encountered. Shortly after entry, some students confronted the reality that their program was designed to weed them out. This expectation permeated the learning environment, and the students picked up the message loudly and clearly as early as their department's orientation. Students in "sink-or-swim" programs felt the system was trying to undermine them rather than support them and help them achieve their goals. And, if the students' perceptions are correct, one unintended consequence of the weed-out process is that graduate programs often lose some of the very students the practice intends to retain—the best and brightest.

> *Emmie*: [W]hat I sensed, and it was almost conveyed by the faculty, is that the first term or first year is actually a weeding-out process. So, the idea is really not to keep you on . . . but the idea is to really get rid of a lot of the student body, so that it was just only a few who were kept on and then would apparently get paired off with the researcher [who] decided that they wanted to have you work on their project. And I got that message pretty clearly, that this was a sink-or-swim [program]. . . . It was a boot camp.

> *Philip*: The whole first year is a "Fuck you" year, and the whole approach to the [preliminary qualifying] exams is "We won't talk to you till you pass the exams." . . . I think it might be argued that the department accomplished what it was seeking to accomplish, which is a particular type of economist. . . . [T]hey just had a very open door and anyone who was reasonable could walk in, and the winnowing occurred in the program. And that's just a very expensive way to do it. It's very expensive for our lives. . . . [T]here are a lot of people who suffered . . . people taking exams the fifth or sixth time. . . . A lot of people didn't give up. . . . [S]ome of the really smart people gave up early and just got out. I'd say of my year, three of our brightest people left early at the end of the first year.

Students' first and most direct learning experience in graduate school takes place in the classroom. It is here that the knowledge and ideas that serve as the basis of their future research, and often their careers, are first encountered. Based on positive classroom experiences they had as undergraduates, the students expected their graduate courses to be stimulating and intellectually challenging and to contribute to their professional growth and development. Yet, many interviewees were deeply disappointed with what transpired in the classroom. Many said that their classes were not of the caliber they expected. They found many of their courses disorganized and poorly taught, with haphazard coverage of the material. Some remarked that classroom discussions were competitive, if not combative, and that they sometimes never got around to the topic of the course. A number of interviewees provided specific examples of classroom experiences that they felt were a complete waste of time and that often undermined their desire to continue.

Ashley, a mathematics student who persisted for four years, described several bad classroom experiences during his first year at Urban. He talked about how halfway through the term a professor realized he was not going to get tenure and from that point on would "come in and mumble some things and then walk out." He discussed another professor who was relatively famous and terminally ill and was, according to Ashley, interested in teaching his favorite subjects one last time. "So instead of teaching the standard course of material in a standard way, he went right into his area of specialty and talked about things he liked talking about, which wasn't that helpful to me [because] I had a weak background in the area." The last experience he described as bad involved a professor whose field of specialty was geometry but who decided that it would be fun to teach the third-term algebra class because he wanted to remind himself about all the things he had forgotten. As Ashley put it, "It was like he had no greater knowledge of complex analysis than we did, so it was like a survey class." Ashley summed up his first-year experience by stating, "Overall . . . seven out of nine classes were a complete waste."

English students' descriptions of their classroom experiences were not much better. Boyd, an English student at Urban, used a classroom experience to sum up his first and only year of graduate study. During that year he had a class with a teacher who he felt was "the biggest blowhard" that he had ever encountered. "The guy had absolutely nothing to say, and it was a complete waste of time." Boyd remembered writing a paper for this professor's class that he felt was one of the most interesting things that he had ever done. The paper involved analyzing a connection he had not noticed before between two of the *Canterbury Tales* and was based on close reading and original thinking. He got a B+ on the paper with a note that said, "This certainly would have been an A if you had cited outside sources." From this experience, Boyd got the message that "thinking for yourself or thinking originally was okay, but what was really important was to keep flogging the library." It ultimately dawned on him "that this is not leading me where I wanted to go."

While individual courses are the basic threads of graduate students' learning experience, the department's general approach to graduate education and the discipline are the cloth that shrouds that experience. It is at this higher, more abstracted level that students begin to see the bigger picture. Several students expressed disappointment and frustration with this aspect of their experience.

Philip, who persisted for four years and whose department, as we have already seen, used preliminary and qualifying exams to "weed out" students, stated that his department's approach was "structured to create chaos and confusion." He felt that there was a lot of "loose course work, loosely tied to what was the basis of work, which was to pass the exams." He described a situation in which the only way to pass exams was by studying old exams and boning up on the questions. By his third year he found himself "just taking exams, not reading, not discussing other [things], not discussing economic controversies, not really being in seminars, but taking exams." His intellectual frustration is evident in his request to "put yourself in a situation where none of the people around [you] are reading journal articles; they're just studying old exams." Philip ultimately gave up his quest to pass exams and get the Ph.D. because "I just chose not to compromise how I studied what I studied. I studied to learn things, not to pass exams, and I didn't pass exams, but I learned a lot."

Several students critiqued the intellectual orientation of their program and its relationship (or lack thereof) with their orientation and goals. Of particular frustration and disappointment was the perceived irrelevance of what they were learning to the world outside the academy. Cathleen, a music student, was "quite disappointed" in her experience at Urban. She felt that most of the work being done there was "extremely academic and arcane" and that "much of the theoretical work was very irrelevant . . . to any actual music making." She expressed frustration at "the total bookishness of it."

In a similar vein, James (mathematics) became "disenchanted with the level of abstraction." He began to feel that what he was doing was "not very useful" and that he was not "solving any relevant problems." Rather, "What I was doing was proving one definition equals another definition. . . . I don't think it was internally very satisfying."

Urban's emphasis on research about serious social issues excited and stimulated Emmie (sociology), but the fact that it was divorced from "anything that's really practical in real everyday life" helped her "clarify in my own mind that I really wasn't prepared or even interested, really, in continuing a career in academia." Finally, Irene, a music student at Rural, started feeling "disillusioned about the program" because she was "asked to do things that didn't really seem relevant to the program."

Another aspect of their programs that came in for criticism was the way ideas were treated, the whole critical, debunking nature of the academic enterprise in particular. The following interview exchange with Charlie not only addresses how graduate students are socialized to deal with ideas but also touches on students' motivations for pursuing graduate education—"the joy and fun of learning"—and how that motivation becomes compromised by the way knowledge and ideas are treated in graduate school.

Charlie: I felt the joy and fun of learning was missing.

Interviewer: What do you mean by "the joy and the fun of learning was missing"?

Charlie: Hard to express, very hard to express, to articulate in a more definite way, except that I felt less, less something. Whereas earlier as an undergraduate, when I learned some new ideas and stuff, it was like I felt an aha! experience and I was seeing the world in new ways that I hadn't seen before. Whereas in graduate work, even when that was the case, somehow just the excitement, the spirit seemed different. It just seemed more like just shoveling information at us as well as concepts. There was just too much, and all were treated somehow as equal and equally valid or, I'm sorry, it's better to put it, equally invalid, okay?

Interviewer: What do you mean by "equally invalid"?

Charlie: What do I mean by "equally invalid"? I mean the tremendous intellectual skepticism about each and every idea that was presented and the debunking tendency on the part of the faculty which was also expected of us. While intellectually I can understand the importance of that skepticism, at the same time it made me less excited about what I was learning.

Interviewer: How did you feel about all the debunking?

Charlie: I felt it quite often veered into having these little axes to grind and posturing on the part of both the faculty members and . . . the authors of the readings they would assign.

Although the ultimate goal of graduate education is to produce independent, creative scholars, several students felt that the experience had just the opposite effect; that is, they felt positively stifled. Indeed, several used the word *stifled* or such synonyms as *stultifying, constricted,* and *calcified* to characterize how they felt. These feelings were most prevalent among, but not limited to, students in the humanities. Boyd and Hugh were English students at Urban and Rural Universities, respectively. Both enjoyed doing close textual analysis, had a love of language, and believed themselves to be talented writers. They describe what they perceived to be a bias against creative expression and the impact it had on them.

Boyd: I felt like the whole process of being there was calcifying that part of me that I drew on to do other more creative kind of work. So as opposed to creating a nurturing bed from which other things could spring, I felt that I was lying at the bottom of a poured concrete foundation while the cement was hardening.

Hugh: One of my talents is that I'm very good at writing . . . and what I saw happening is that all of the kind of creativity that I thought was so important seemed to be blanched out of the work that we were required to do. We weren't really encouraged to use any kind of creativity in our presentation of papers, for example. It was all very academic. . . . It took not only the love of the language out of the text we were studying, but it also did not allow one who was writing about that literature to display his or her own love of language.

In sum, most students were inspired to pursue graduate education because of the fun, joy, excitement, and challenge of exploring new ideas in creative and original ways they had experienced as undergraduates. They entered graduate school expecting it to be at least as intellectually invigorating as college and to further their intellectual development. However, this is not what they encountered. Many were quickly "disappointed," "disillusioned," and "disenchanted" by programs designed to weed them out; classes that were poorly taught; curricula that did not address the topic of the course; attitudes that did not reward originality or creativity; intellectual orientations that had little relevance to things that were happening in the real world; and a constant cutting down and tearing apart of the work of other scholars, the very people many of these students one day aspired to become. Consequently, many students ended up feeling that their courses were a waste of time; that they were not learning new, important, or interesting things; and that their learning experiences were not supporting their intellectual growth and development. It was at this point, the point where students realized that they were not getting the education they went to graduate school to obtain, that many lost their interest, motivation, and desire to continue.

THE LEARNING ENVIRONMENT

Environments, by definition,[1] are the physical and psychological conditions that influence growth and development as well as the social and cultural circumstances that surround and affect an individual or a community. Learning environments include the programmatic elements discussed earlier. They also include the social relations and cultural expectations that surround those experiences. In the students' minds, their departments' learning environments were very real entities, and as such, they exerted integrative and disintegrative forces on the community, which, in turn, influenced their willingness to persist. Indeed, eighteen of the twenty-nine interviewees used the word *environment* or *atmosphere* to describe, characterize, or critique explicitly or implicitly the academic, social, and cultural situation in which they found themselves. Two interviewees directly implicated their department's environment in their attrition decisions. One left because "I didn't like the environment"; another stated, "It wasn't really an environment I wanted to be part of." And the department's environment was a clear though not necessarily decisive factor in many other students' attrition decisions.

Only two of the interviewees characterized their department's learning environment in a positive way. Gerald, whose department had the lowest attrition rate in the sample and who left with his adviser, thought his department had a "nice atmosphere." By this he meant that the people were friendly, open, and enthusiastic about what they were doing. In discussing her relationship with other graduate students, Elinor, who left because she realized that academics was not something she wanted to do, commented that there was a "very supportive atmosphere, especially when we weren't taking our qualifying exams."

The remaining sixteen interviewees stated or implied that their departments (and sometimes universities) had a negative environment, which often interfered with their intellectual development. The students' critiques fall into two overlapping categories. One category emphasizes the feeling in the air—a weighed-down, heavy, almost choking feeling. In addition to feeling too competitive, not friendly, not collegial, and not nurturing or supportive, these environments were also described as too serious and pretentious, as well as conservative and repressive. A number of students found the environment artificial and intellectually stifling in that "the environment did not really demand original or creative thinking from its students" and that "if you wanted to succeed in that environment, you have to conform" to a certain model of what an academic is and does. Katie, a black woman, described the atmosphere in her department with respect to minorities as "circuslike" and "hysterical."

The other category focuses on people, their traits and interactions, and the effect of the environment on people. Boyd found the environment in his department "unhealthy" because of the characteristics of the people in it. He felt "surrounded by people who were using the university as a place to hide out from real life" and who were "misfits" and "one-dimensional." Hugh became discouraged by "overbearing" professors who had "so little self-confidence that they had to project themselves extra strongly on the atmosphere." The rest of the students described environments in which the student body was "unsociable" and "too competitive," where the faculty were not supportive or collegial, and where people were unable to step back and look at the larger picture. One student even felt that the environment so damaged people that they were not able to work normally and complete their degrees in a reasonable amount of time.

INTERACTIONS WITH FACULTY

The interactions students have with faculty inside and outside the classroom constitute an integral part of their learning experience. In their capacity as teacher, mentor, colleague, and friend, faculty play an important role in students' intellectual development as well as in their integration in the departmental and larger disciplinary community. They help students come to see how the field is defined and how the role of academic professional is enacted.

The nature and quality of interviewees' interactions with faculty were investigated by asking students to "Tell me about the faculty in your department." If the students did not address or differentiate between their academic and social interactions, they were asked more direct questions. In addition, in an effort to discern what students perceive as a good experience with faculty and what they perceive as a bad one, and how these experiences may influence persistence decisions, the interviewees were asked to talk about a particularly good experience they had had with a faculty member as well as a particularly bad one.

General Overview

Most of the interviewees reported that they had had minimal interaction with faculty and, when they did interact, the interactions were limited. The survey data support this lack of interaction. They show that at all stages of graduate education, noncompleters spent less time interacting with faculty than completers, and they suggest that within each stage, the quantity of noncompleters' interactions with faculty was more likely to decrease over time than completers'. Two interviewees talked about this change. Ashley, who left after four years, stated that his interactions decreased over time from "a very low level" such that by the time he left, he was probably not interacting with faculty at all. By contrast, Pauline, who left after one year and was initially "friendly with quite a few of them," talked about becoming alienated from the faculty and the mutual distancing that ensued when the faculty became aware that she was unhappy with the program.

Despite the lack of interaction, the interviewees were generally impressed with the faculty and noted how hardworking, intelligent, and dedicated they were to their disciplines. However, the survey data show that the noncompleters were much less satisfied with the faculty than the completers. At-risk completers were also much less satisfied with the faculty than on-track completers even though they had the same quantity of interaction with faculty over all three stages of their graduate careers.

Based on the little interaction they did have, the interviewees found the faculty to be cordial and civil, but not terribly open or warm. They characterized the faculty as being completely indifferent to students, more interested in their own research than in students, or preoccupied with their own students. Some of the interviewees were bothered by what they perceived to be a wall between faculty and students, and the faculty's lack of interest in developing any sort of personal relationship with students. Indeed, Cathleen, who left after five years, captures the essence of the typical faculty–student relationship: "They were all very good about finding time when we asked time of them, but they certainly did not go out of their way to look after any of us or to inquire after any of us." Cathleen foreshadows a theme that emerges more clearly in subsequent discussion with the interviewees about the nature of their relationship with faculty and their adviser; that is, the onus of responsibility for creating and sustaining a relationship with a faculty member lies with the student.

Academic Interaction with Faculty

Students' academic interactions with faculty are a critical component of their intellectual development. Faculty can fan or smother the flames of intellectual passion by the enthusiasm that they show for the discipline and for students' work, ideas, and classroom contributions as well as by the quality of their teaching, the nature of the material they assign and the degree of respect with which it is treated, and their own professional achievements.

In discussing their academic relationship with the faculty, the interviewees addressed the following aspects of their interactions: frequency, location, content, and accessibility. In addition, many were asked how much interest the faculty took in them and in their ideas and research.

Most of the interviewees commented that they did not have much interaction with faculty outside the classroom. This was a source of disappointment for some; two students remarked that they had more interaction with faculty as undergraduates. All of these students left within two years. Students with RAs, TAs, or work-study appointments had more interaction with faculty than those who did not. Students who made it to stage 3 or left for external reasons (injury, marriage, left with adviser) had a "fair amount" of interaction with faculty, ranging in quality from mostly professional to "decent."

A small handful of students interacted with faculty at talks, seminars, project meetings, or on a departmental committee. Most of these students had somewhat longer durations. A few students mentioned having casual interactions with faculty in the hallway. Office hours were mentioned only by one student who used them to find out what she was doing wrong in class and for help with a particular problem or theorem. She characterized the interaction as "always down to business." Indeed, the content of the students' academic interactions with faculty tended to focus on coursework, and they described the interactions as being assertive and to the point.

In terms of accessibility, the faculty were characterized as being "around" and "approachable." However, the following remarks indicate that students bore responsibility for initiating interactions with faculty: "[They were accessible] in the sense that they were available to be seen and could be asked about what they were doing"; "If you stopped by and wanted to ask a question, they were always willing to devote some time"; "I found them willing to help when I sought help"; and "I really didn't tend to pursue big academic discussion with them."

Not only were the students disappointed in the amount of interaction they had with faculty, but they also were disappointed by the lack of interest faculty took in them. Most of the students felt that the faculty took "none" to "very little" personal interest in them. One student reported feeling "lost in a sea of people" and "not feeling like an individual anymore," while another student felt that he was just "another student among a huge parade of students they see all the time." Several expressed disappointment about not getting to know faculty well and about not being able to find a mentor. It was these disappointments and this lack of connection that caused some students to question their commitment their programs.

Other interviewees talked about the faculty's lack of caring, support, or helpfulness. Jim and Pauline are illustrative. Jim stated, "I had more than one professor [who] just didn't really care enough about me to help me and support me so that I could have some assistance in doing my best." Pauline said, "I think that they knew that I was not happy, and they certainly didn't go out of their way to find out why or to ask . . . or give me encouragement. They certainly didn't do anything to help me out."

When faculty took the initiative and showed interest in a student, the student viewed the experience favorably. For example, Stuart, who left after one year, indicated that a couple of faculty members would occasionally ask him how things were progressing. He commented, "I was flattered that these faculty members were taking enough of an interest to ask and a little disappointed that I never got that kind of interest from my adviser."

Although a number of students felt that the faculty took "zero" interest in their ideas and research, in general, they thought that the faculty showed more interest in them professionally than personally. When faculty showed interest in their ideas and their research, the faculty's interest was typically characterized very passively, in that the professor might take an interest in a paper the student had written as exhibited by comments written on the paper. But again, it was up to the student to follow through with the professor if an interaction were to ensue. Only two students, students who made it to stage 3, indicated fairly strong faculty interest in their ideas and research. Cade, a science student who spent several years working on a research project, felt that the ones he talked to about his research were quite interested. But his comment is phrased as faculty "he talked to," not as the faculty who "talked to him." By contrast, Cathleen, who had received the highest ranking in her cohort on her qualifying exams, showed much greater ambivalence and highlighted both faculty passivity and the burden on the student to take the initiative. When asked, "How much interest did they take in you?" she replied:

> That's not clear. I'm hearing a lot more in hindsight that professors did like my work. But at the time that wasn't terribly apparent to me. I know they did not dislike my work. And I felt they basically respected my work and my ability, but no one was demonstrating that they wanted to take me on as an advisee or take me under their wings, so to speak. I suppose it was up to me to ask that of them, but at the same time, [I was] not really getting a clear indication from anyone. You were kind of left to flow.

What emerges from this analysis is that academic interactions with faculty were quite limited, impersonal, and businesslike. Those that did occur were often initiated by the student; revolved around a particular, usually course-related, question or problem; or pertained to the faculty's, not the students', interests. The students appear to have desired ongoing, high-level academic discourse and more personal contact with faculty and to have been very disappointed by the structure and content of the little interaction they did have.

Social Interaction with Faculty

If the students' academic interactions with the faculty were limited, their social interactions with them were even more so. The survey data show that noncompleters spent less time socializing with faculty than completers. Those interviewees with profiles similar to that of completers (dissertators and those who left for external reasons) had more and better social interactions with faculty than the rest of the interviewees. For example, Tony, who was in what appears to have been a well-integrated department and who would have completed but for an injury, was the only interviewee who reported a lot of social interaction with faculty. His interactions ranged from attending brown bag lunches and seminars to playing sports and sharing a cigar. Three interviewees, two of long duration, mentioned that the amount of social interaction they had with faculty decreased over time. Cathleen provides insight into how the structure of disciplines like the humanities contributes to diminishing interaction and the negative consequences of such a change. When asked why she participated less frequently in departmental social events after her first couple of years, she replied:

> I think, in part, feeling more disconnected after the first two years. It probably had to do with the amorphousness of after you've finished your comprehensive [exams], then what? As you took less classes after the first two terms, you were just around the department less and . . . definitely feeling less and less of a connection where ironically we should have been feeling more of a connection. We should have been feeling more of a connection. We should have been tying directly with someone who would be our adviser and feeling more upper level and more special.

Student–faculty social interactions occurred in four different contexts: department-organized social events, as part of an academically oriented departmental event, events at faculty homes, and student-initiated interactions. Department-organized social events included daily or weekly social hours as well as occasional parties. Students who were in departments with daily social hours and who commented on them seemed to feel that the social hours were a waste of time unless they had something specific they needed to talk to someone about, and their participation in them dropped off over time. Departmental parties, which did not happen very often, were generally mentioned without additional comment, although one student felt that the secretaries enjoyed them more than anyone else.

Students cited seminars and colloquia as academic-oriented events at which social interactions occurred. Tom, who abandoned his dissertation after taking a job, went out for meals with faculty and students after seminars with relative frequency. But, with the exception of Tony, who found colloquia occasions at which to share "wine and economics, cheese and statistics," a number of the students said that faculty and students just milled around and had nontechnical, mindless discussions.

A few students reported that some faculty members would have a class or students who were working for them in some capacity to their homes at the end of the term. Elinor highlights the humanizing, integrative effects of such interactions, but she was wistful about the lack of social connection with faculty on a more ongoing basis:

> *Elinor:* [Dinners at faculty homes were] always lots of fun because at least you got to see these people outside of their work environment, so to speak. At least it was an opportunity to see their homes and their spouses and children, if that was the case. And I personally enjoyed that very much. But in terms of continued social interactions with particular faculty members, there was none of that, at least for me.

Student-initiated, faculty–student social interaction was commented on more often, and more favorably, by students of long duration than by students of short duration. One student noted that there were a couple of faculty who would come to parties thrown by students and that sometimes a professor would join a group of students downtown. Two students mentioned inviting faculty to dinner. Tom, who left after five years, had professors over for dinner on a number of occasions. Boyd, who left after one year, tried having coffee with faculty or inviting them to dinner. The faculty would come, "but every time it was just so stiff."

Thus, on what appears to be the rare occasions during which the interviewees interacted socially with faculty, the interactions tended to take place in structured, group settings. In general, the students found these interactions to be uncomfortable and inconsequential, although there is clear evidence that some students desired more frequent, closer, and better social interaction with faculty. However, the students were less disappointed by these interactions, or lack thereof, than they were by the lack of academic interaction, because social interaction with faculty is not the primary reason that students attend graduate school.

In sum, the student interviews suggest and the survey data support the contention that noncompleters have less social interaction with faculty than completers. When social interaction does occur, it often does not occur until the later stages of graduate education when students have entered into an advisee relationship with a faculty member, and most of the students interviewed had left before they entered into such a relationship.

Faculty with Whom Students Had
Good Experiences

Students' remarks about the faculty member with whom they had a particularly good experience provide insights into the qualities of people and characteristics of interactions that undergird integration in the graduate school setting. Of the twenty-one interviewees asked this question, three Urban and one Rural student could not think of a faculty member with whom they had a good experience. Only five students cited their adviser; all but one of these students left for reasons external to the university. In addition, three Urban but no Rural students cited a faculty member outside their department. Two of these students came from the same department that both characterized as very serious and the faculty intimidating. All of these students had short durations; two left by the end of the first year, the other made the decision to leave at the beginning of the second year.

The students provided four different types of reasons for why the experience with the chosen faculty member was a particularly good one. The reasons, in descending order of frequency but not discussion, are as follows: the way the faculty member treated them, the quality of the faculty's teaching, the faculty's personality, and a personal bond between the student and the faculty member.

The students described the faculty with whom they had particularly good experiences as people who were friendly, warm, open, and human. They were people whom the students found interesting and easy to talk to, and they were often described as having interests that were not limited to the department or discipline.

Good-experience faculty were faculty with whom the students had a fair amount of interaction and from whom they often took several classes. These faculty were interested in the students' interests and academic progress. They helped them develop intellectually and professionally, and they were nonjudgmental. The students also felt that these faculty cared about them and took a personal interest in them. In these relationships, the line of demarcation between faculty and student was often blurred, with the faculty treating the students like colleagues.

Several, predominantly shorter-duration students commented on the quality of the chosen faculty's teaching, presumably because they were not there long enough to develop relationships. These faculty were characterized as being interested in and concerned about their teaching and their students. They taught with enthusiasm, making the material seem relevant and important. As a result, the students enjoyed their classes and learned a lot.

Finally, four students (all from Urban University) either developed or perceived there to be a special bond between themselves and the chosen faculty member. Even though most of these students enjoyed that person's classes, the bond was not centered around the students' academic or professional development, and, in three of the four cases discussed here, the chosen faculty member was not even in the student's department.

Two female students had perceived bonds with their chosen faculty member. One music student, Elinor, frequently saw the professor in nonacademic contexts such as concerts, plays, and operas, and she liked the fact that he was active in playing an instrument himself. The other female student, Emmie, a Hispanic, bonded to someone whom she perceived to be a role model because the professor was also a minority female who she felt was "able to hold her own in this environment and still be very feminine and very kind."

Two male students developed a bond with their chosen faculty member. Charlie cited a visiting professor. They went drinking a couple of times and had "light-hearted interaction" that "seemed so rare to me between myself and faculty." Stuart cited a visiting professor in another department from whom he took a course. They had running in common and could discuss it.

Despite the existence of a bond, none of these bonds were integrative. They did not serve the primary purpose of graduate education—intellectual and professional development—and consequently, they did not contribute to persistence. Two of the students left after one year; the other two remained longer but made their attrition decisions early on. However, what characterizes the bond the student had with the faculty member is a human element.

Faculty with Whom Students Had Bad Experiences

Students' remarks about the faculty member with whom they had a particularly bad experience provide insights into the qualities of people and characteristics of interactions that inhibit or undermine integration. Three Urban and two Rural students could not think of a faculty member with whom they had a particularly bad experience. These students fall into two distinct groups. One group is composed of students with long durations and students with short durations who left for external reasons. The other group is composed of students with short durations who either found the "whole environment distasteful" or who were so unintegrated that they did not have "any experience [with faculty] at all." The following analysis uses the same basic categories as the previous one, except "personal bond" is replaced with "undermined development."

The students often found the bad-experience faculty to be cold and intimidating. Some found them to be completely disconnected from everyone around them, never lifting their faces out of books, and unwilling to entertain or tolerate different points of view.

In some cases, the student and the faculty member simply did not "click." The student felt that the professor did not like him or her, or the student did not feel comfortable around the professor. Some students objected to being treated as if they were still in high school, and two women felt they were treated poorly because they were married.

A number of students made comments about the bad-experience faculty's teaching. These students found the professor's approach to the subject to be out-of-date, the professor to be pedantic and unoriginal or ill prepared for class. Some students found their lectures to be useless, and a few stopped attending classes because they were not getting anything out of them.

Finally, a number of students related an incident or characterized an ongoing interaction with a professor that undermined their intellectual or professional development. These experiences included a professor trying to kick the student out of graduate school by grading a five-person class on a curve and giving her a D; advising a student to read a book for his qualifying exam that was exactly the opposite of what the student was interested in and asking questions during the exam on chapters they had agreed to exclude; and receiving a teaching assistantship and being told that instead of being allowed to teach her own section, the student would be the paper collector and record keeper. These types of incidents were often pivotal in students' decisions to leave the university.

In sum, with the exception of personal bonds, the students had particularly good experiences with faculty members who in some way aided their intellectual or professional development, be it in an interpersonal relationship or simply in the classroom setting. However, facilitating intellectual or professional development is not sufficient for being chosen as a faculty member with whom one had a particularly good experience. The relationship also requires a human dimension, one characterized by interest, openness, concern, and respect on the part of the faculty member toward the student. By contrast, the students had bad experiences with faculty who in one way or another stymied or undermined their intellectual and professional development. And this type of experience was often sufficient to cause students to rethink their reasons and motivations for being in graduate school. What this analysis highlights is not only the importance of relationships and interactions that contribute to students' sense that they are achieving their intellectual and professional goals, but also relationships and interactions that demonstrate to students that professors can be both excellent scholars and warm, caring, human beings.

INTERACTIONS WITH OTHER
GRADUATE STUDENTS

Other graduate students make an important contribution to individual students' learning experiences. They are a significant source of intellectual stimulation and social support both inside and outside the classroom. At a formal level, they assist with homework, assignments, and preparation for tests and qualifying examinations, and even with the dissertation, often in the context of an organized study group. At an informal level, they share knowledge, ideas, and opinions about faculty, course work, assignments, books, journal articles, and teaching and laboratory techniques. Graduate students often become close friends, lovers, and spouses. They are also each others' future competition for jobs and future professional colleagues.

Like the nature and quality of their interactions with faculty, the nature and quality of interviewees' interactions with other graduate students were investigated by asking the them to "Tell me about the graduate students in your department."

General Overview

Most of the interviewees liked their fellow graduate students and had good relationships with them. Many said they became friends with students in their department. However, the survey data show that noncompleters had less interaction with other graduate students during the first two stages of graduate education and that they were much less satisfied with their relationships than completers. On-track and at-risk completers had the same quantity of interaction with other graduate students, but at-risk completers were less satisfied with the quality of their relationships than on-track completers.

Although the interviewees thought that their colleagues were serious, hardworking, and committed students, a number were disturbed by their single-mindedness and lack of interest in or involvement with things besides the discipline. These interviewees felt that some of their fellow graduate students were completely oblivious to the outside world, that nothing in life besides the discipline mattered to them, and that this lack of balance in their peers' lives was not normal and not healthy.

A number of the interviewees talked about having or pursuing other interests and activities in addition to their graduate work. This made them feel different from other graduate students. Boyd, in particular, felt sanctioned because of it.

Boyd: [There] was actually almost a kind of hostility or skepticism from . . . other students around the fact that I had a part-time job, and it was almost like, "Well, such a serious intense program—how could you assume that you have any time to do anything else?" or "If you're doing something else, you're obviously not taking it very seriously," which I thought was kind of a bizarre attitude. . . . [I]t turned out to be the narrow end of a wedge, and one of the things that drove me really crazy about the place was that my fellow students . . . felt the need to buy into it, that the program was incredibly intense, . . . incredibly difficult. And I, frankly, found the work no more difficult . . . than what I had done as an under-graduate. . . . [I]t wasn't difficult to organize my time and do other things outside the academic stuff that I was doing and to have a more well-rounded life.

Academic Interaction with Graduate Students

The interviewees interacted with other graduate students for the purpose of accomplishing academic tasks and achieving a variety of academic goals. Many of the interviewees had study groups with which they met on a regular basis; others met irregularly on an as-needed basis. Although a few students mentioned interacting with other graduate students in the classroom or the laboratory, these locations were mentioned less frequently than more casual settings. For those students who had offices, the office seemed to be the central locus of academic interaction. A number of interviewees said that their academic interactions happened by chance, such as running into each other on campus, in the library, or walking down the hall. One Rural student, who was self-supporting and had very little academic interaction, commented that he never bumped into graduate students because the campus was so big. Two students mentioned having academic interactions at departmental colloquia, at the receptions, in particular.

Two students discussed their lack of fit in the prevailing graduate student culture. Awareness of this lack of fit can start a student down the slippery slope of increasing alienation and isolation from the primary community, and ultimately to breaking all bonds with the community.[2] Indeed, both students who were conscious of their lack of academic integration left after one year. Pauline is worth quoting:

> *Pauline*: We [my office mates and I] just had such different mentalities. . . . I was sort of a work-hard/party-hard person. Psychology was not my life. I just wanted to get my degree. I saw graduate school as a means to an end. . . . They saw it as like their being. [Their being] was in being graduate [students], and they loved hanging out there. I mean, they'd stay there till forever. And . . . I wanted to get the paper written and get the hell out.
>
> *Interviewer*: So why did you stop hanging out in the department?
>
> *Pauline*: Well, I think just because I felt very alienated, because I felt very different from them, and because I felt like I really am a malcontent. I'm really discontent with this and they're okay with it. And so, frankly, I started to really have self-doubts about who, if they're all happy, if ten of them are happy, and I'm not, I really started to think this is me—Is this just me? This is me. . . . I'm obviously not enjoying this process, and if this is the process that's going to last five or six or seven years, this is a problem, because I'm not happy.

Interviewer: Did you discuss your discontent with anybody?

Pauline: I did, initially, at the beginning. Again, over a period of time, I just really withdrew from that whole group of people. I discussed it with some of my colleagues, but then it was very clear that I was the only one who felt that way. And I really didn't feel like they even understood what I was talking about. . . . So I stopped really talking about it with people.

Social Interactions

When asked about the kind of social interactions they had had with their fellow graduate students, the interviewees focused on who their friends were, how the friendships were formed, and how their relationships changed over time. While most of the interviewees had socialized with other graduate students in their department, not all had.

A few of the Rural students commented that their interaction with fellow graduate students had been primarily professional; all left after one year. Interviewees at both universities who were in or entered into romantic relationships either did not socialize or socialized with people in their significant others' department or social world. Most of the interviewees who were married lived off campus and tended not to see other graduate students socially. With few exceptions, those interviewees who were married or were in relationships *and* who did not socialize in the department left after one year. Thus, their leaving was not impeded by having to break social bonds.

Students who socialized with other students in the department tended to socialize primarily with members of their entering cohort "who were in the same boat." Friendships were formed in study groups and in graduate student offices, as well as in dormitories. Indeed, one student who had received a TA and an office commented that she did not get to know graduate students who were there only for classes, further highlighting the importance of the TA and offices for bringing and keeping students on campus and fostering social cohesion. A few remarked that there was not a lot of time for socializing, which led to feelings of isolation.

One thing that distinguishes noncompleters from completers is a decreasing quantity of interaction over time. Three interviewees, all who were at Urban and all whose durations were greater than one year, mentioned this change. Perhaps most interesting is the difference between Tom's experience and that of Ashley and Charlie. Tom's profile resembles that of a completer. He received an RA early in his graduate career and was working on his dissertation when he took a nonacademic job. His interactions with other graduate students increased after the first year. By contrast, neither Ashley nor Charlie had RAs or TAs and neither made it to stage 3. Their interactions decreased after the first year, a year in which "everyone's taking the same classes."

Although graduate students play an important role in each others' learning experiences, they play a less critical role in attrition decisions than the other factors discussed in this chapter—program, learning environment, and faculty. Indeed, the nature and quality of the interviewees' interactions with other graduate students do not appear to differ from those one would expect completers to have had. However, both the interview and survey data show that the quantity of noncompleters' academic and social interaction with other graduate students decreased over time. This decrease is, in part, a function of their lack of access to formal social structures—RAs, TAs, and offices—that facilitate formal and chance interaction and, in part, a function of realizing that they did not fit in with the prevailing graduate student culture, which weakens whatever integrative bonds they have with the community. In addition, the interviewees' criticisms of their fellow students' single-mindedness and their remarks about their own broader interests and extracurricular involvements suggest that graduate programs may be losing, if not selecting against, some of their more well-rounded students. This raises important policy questions about the types of people graduate programs are producing as well as the nature of the research questions completers ask over the course of their professional careers relative to the types of questions the more well-rounded noncompleters might have asked had they completed. This latter difference is particularly salient in light of noncompleters' complaints about the lack of relevance of the academic enterprise to the world outside the university.

CONCLUSION

What emerges clearly from the interviews is that persistence is related to students' achieving their conscious, and sometimes even unconscious, needs and goals for intellectual and professional growth and development. All of the aspects of the learning experience discussed in this chapter—the program, the learning environment, faculty, other graduate students—are vehicles for intellectual and professional growth and development. When these vehicles do not serve students' needs; when students are "disappointed," "disillusioned," or "disenchanted" with the learning experience; when they realize that "this isn't leading me where I wanted to go"; and when they feel they are not being intellectually supported or, worse, are being intellectually stifled or undermined, they are less likely to persist than students whose intellectual needs and goals are being met.

The interviews also provide insight into students' views of, and their reactions to, their socialization to the world of academe. Most of the interviewees were inspired to pursue graduate education by the love of their disciplines, the positive experiences they had with faculty and fellow students as undergraduates, and the desire to instill that love and those values in others as it had been instilled in them. However, their encounters with one-dimensional faculty and peers, and with people who embodied many of the negative stereotypes of academic professionals and who appeared to lack important human(e) qualities, caused many to question whether they wanted to become members of that type of community. Indeed, some, like Hugh, left, partly out of fear that the socialization process would ultimately cause them to pick up characteristics of people they viewed as negative professional role models. In fact, by the time he left, Hugh felt he was changing in ways he did not want to change. He felt he was becoming arrogant. He is quoted here because of his insight into the relationship between personality and social structure, and because his insight suggests that some of the negative aspects of the learning experience that cause students to leave can be corrected by changing the larger social structure.

> *Hugh*: There seemed to be a lot of people who needed to project that ego. And that's not how I want to live my life. I didn't want to become part of that larger structure. I was even afraid finally of what academia would do to people, because I don't think people necessarily were always like that or always had those sort of overbearing egotistical qualities. I think that something about the structure of higher education in this country . . . can develop those kinds of personality traits in people, and that became scary because I don't want those.

Finally, the most critical aspect of the learning experience—the adviser–advisee relationship—was not discussed in this chapter. Because that relationship is so central to success or failure in graduate school, it warrants its own chapter. It is to that relationship that we now turn.

NOTES

1. See *environment* and *atmosphere* in *Webster's II New University Dictionary* (1984).

2. Ebaugh (1988, p. 10) calls this process "disengagement." She defines it as a process of mutual withdrawal. It occurs when an individual's decreased association with a group is accompanied by the group's decreased demands on and involvement with the individual, such that as the group expects less from the individual, the rewards of belonging decrease to the point where withdrawal from the group becomes an increasingly viable option.

Chapter 7

The Quality of the Adviser–Advisee Relationship

The adviser is often the central and most powerful person not only on a graduate student's dissertation committee but also during the student's trajectory through graduate school. The adviser influences how the student comes to understand the discipline and the roles and responsibilities of academic professionals, their socialization as a teacher and researcher, the selection of a dissertation topic, the quality of the dissertation, and subsequent job placement. Consequently, integrative experiences with one's adviser are critical for helping students develop cognitive maps of the program, the discipline, and the profession, as well as for having a positive and fulfilling graduate school experience. Affiliation with the proper adviser can often spell the difference between completion and noncompletion (Baird, 1969, 1972, 1992; Girves & Wemmerus, 1988; Heiss, 1967; Rosen & Bates, 1967; Weiss, 1981).

This chapter explores the nature and quality of the adviser–advisee relationship from the perspective of both the student and the faculty. It starts with an analysis of how students become affiliated with an adviser. It then examines the types of academic and social interactions the interviewees had with their advisers, drawing on survey data to assess differences in completers' and noncompleters' experiences. Next, it investigates differences in the way high- and low-Ph.D.-productive faculty interact with graduate students and concludes with an analysis of why completers and noncompleters were or were not satisfied with their advisers. Along the way it posits a relationship among satisfaction, adviser type, and persistence.

SELECTING AN ADVISER

Selecting an adviser is probably the single most important decision a graduate student makes during his or her graduate career for all the reasons already mentioned. Yet, as demonstrated in chapter 4, a large number of interviewees did not understand the process. To explore the relationship between method of adviser selection and persistence, the survey asked students, "Did you have an adviser?" and, for those who responded affirmatively, "What was the main reason you selected your *last* adviser?"[1] The results, which will be discussed here, reveal large differences between groups.

If having an adviser is critical to understanding and getting through a graduate program, then not having one should be detrimental to persistence. Indeed, noncompleters were seven times more likely than completers to report that they did not have an adviser (23 percent vs. 3 percent). Similarly, women were twice as likely as men to report not having had one (14 percent vs. 7 percent).

Having an adviser has implications for duration in a program. Noncompleters who had an adviser persisted about a year longer than noncompleters who did not (3.3 years vs. 2.2 years).

Many graduate programs assign provisional advisers to entering students so that students have someone to turn to for advice and guidance. The assignments are often but not always made on the basis of the closeness of students' expressed interests to faculty expertise. Given the widespread nature of this practice and the expectation that students will ultimately find a suitable adviser on their own, one would expect roughly equal proportions of completers and noncompleters to have been assigned to their last adviser. This, however, was not the case. Noncompleters were six times as likely as completers to have been assigned to an adviser (44 percent vs. 7 percent). A similar pattern is found for completer type and gender: At-risk completers were four times as likely as on-track completers to have been assigned to an adviser (12 percent vs. 3 percent), and women were about one and a half times as likely as men (24 percent vs. 15 percent).

Changing advisers does not account for why completers were less likely than noncompleters to have been assigned to their last adviser. Student responses to the survey question "Did you ever change advisers?" revealed no statistical difference in the percentage of completers (31 percent) and noncompleters (26 percent) who did. In addition, there was effectively no difference between completers and noncompleters in their reasons for changing advisers. Only one of seven items in a question that asked students why they changed was significant: Completers were more likely than noncompleters to change advisers because they had found a better one (60 percent vs. 39 percent).

Being assigned to an adviser is associated with short durations. Noncompleters who were assigned to their last adviser persisted an average of 2.5 years. Of the noncompleters who persisted one year or less, 76 percent had been assigned to their adviser. By contrast, only 33 percent of the noncompleters who persisted for two years or more had been assigned to their adviser. The noncompleter interviews provide deeper insight into these processes.

Almost one-third of the students interviewed (nine) reported that they had been assigned to an adviser. More than half (five) left by the end of the first year; the rest trickled out. All were gone by the end of four years, and none started dissertation research. Some of these students believed that the pairing had been done randomly, while others thought that they had been matched with the specialist in their area. Two students complained that they had had absolutely no say in the matter.

With the exception of one student who left after three years, students who had been assigned to advisers felt no connection with them. Indeed, four of the five who had left after one year could not remember their adviser's name; one commented that she could not even visualize talking to him. Students assigned to advisers typically met with their adviser only once a term to discuss the courses they would be taking and to have their adviser sign-off on their registration forms. Hugh, who left after two years, summed up the perfunctory nature of the relationship experienced by many: "I didn't feel he was in any way trying to guide my course of study or give me any practical tips or good advice or anything like that." Hugh's and others' perceptions of the relationship with an assigned adviser may reflect the true reality of the situation. The faculty interviews reveal that most professors have little identification with their role as predissertation adviser and almost no sense of connection with their predissertation advisees, so little identification and connection that they frequently underestimated their and the department's attrition rate.

Given the general dissatisfaction with assigned advisers, several of the students were queried as to whether they had ever considered changing advisers. The basic reply was that it had never occurred to them—they did not know it was an option. Reflecting on the question, Ellen, who left after one year, commented that, in retrospect, "that might have been a good choice." Only one student, Pauline, did, in fact, change advisers. Her comments reveal both how uninformed graduate students are about how best to choose an adviser and how politically sensitive they believe the change process to be.

Pauline: I was given an adviser, was assigned to an adviser with whom I had no interest. It was just a random thing. We had no interests in common and I switched. I picked somebody else who I thought, purely on paper—and this was within the first couple weeks—and I really didn't know. But somebody who, on paper, looked like they had similar interests with me.

Interviewer: How did you go about changing advisers? What gave you the motivation to do that?

Pauline: I think because I didn't like the first guy either, and I remember having a conversation with the director with whom you discussed these things, that how am I going to do this because I don't want to piss this guy off. And he just said, "Oh, it's no big deal. You just tell him it's based purely on your academic interests." And that's what I did.

Interviewer: You were concerned about changing advisers?

Pauline: Oh, yeah, I remember being very concerned about it.

Interviewer: Why was that?

Pauline: Just because I thought this guy's going to be insulted. I thought he would be insulted or pissed or something, I don't know. I thought he would be angry about it. Plus, I didn't want to make anybody mad. I didn't want to get blackballed early on.

Selecting or being selected by an adviser suggests that the student and the adviser had some form of interaction prior to deciding to work together. It also suggests a higher degree of integration between the adviser and the advisee than that likely to be found between advisers and advisees who are assigned to each other. Consequently, students who select or are selected by an adviser should be more likely to complete than those who are assigned to an adviser. Similarly, noncompleters who select or are selected by an adviser should persist longer than those who do not. The survey data support these conjectures.

Ninety-three percent of completers compared with only 57 percent of noncompleters selected or were selected by their last adviser. Of the seven reasons provided to survey respondents for basis of selection, the one that most distinguished completers from noncompleters was "adviser's intellectual interests closest to yours." Completers were twice as likely as noncompleters to have selected their adviser for this reason (47 percent vs. 23 percent). Similarly, on-track completers were more likely than at-risk completers to have chosen their last adviser based on closeness of interests (52 percent vs. 40 percent) as were men relative to women (42 percent vs. 35 percent).

Noncompleters who had not been assigned to their last adviser persisted about a year and a half longer than noncompleters who had been assigned to their advisers (4.1 years vs. 2.5 years). Of the noncompleters who persisted for three years or less, 44 percent had selected their last adviser, whereas 73 percent of the noncompleters who persisted for four or more years had done so.

The majority of the interviewees selected their advisers. However, the method of selection varied, often with implications for duration in program. Three students selected an adviser based on some form of prior knowledge, and all had positive experiences. Solange had been a visiting undergraduate at Urban and had taken courses with her adviser; Irene was familiar with her adviser's reputation and writings and had used one of his books in a course she taught; and a professor at her college had told India that her adviser was wonderful in her area of interest, and she had met him during a campus visit. Despite this, two left after one term, and one left after a year. This rapid rate of attrition tends to contradict the survey data showing that completers are more likely than noncompleters to have prior knowledge of the faculty, until reason for leaving is explored. Solange's adviser became seriously ill with a degenerative disease before she started graduate school, and she was also weighed down with family and financial stresses. Irene suffered an injury, but to this day she remains in contact with her adviser. India liked her adviser very much, finding him friendly, talkative, and supportive. He made her feel special, and she learned a lot from him. Despite this experience, India found the whole graduate school environment so distasteful that her adviser's positive attributes could not overcome other forces.

Four students acquired their advisers by default. (A few actually used the term *default* to describe the process.) Default takes two forms. One form, *field*, is when the adviser is the only person in the department working in the student's area. If the student wants to pursue his or her interests, then he or she has no choice but to work with that person. Students who defaulted to their advisers based on field did not did not find their advisers supportive or helpful. In fact, as discussed in chapter 4, shortly after arriving at the university, two of the three students who "chose" their adviser this way found out that their adviser did not have a reputation for getting their students through their programs. Of the three students who selected their adviser based on field, two left after one year, and the third endured until her funding ran out.

The other form, *true default*, happens when the adviser is the only one willing to take a student on. Although there was only one instance of true default in the student interviews, this situation may occur more often in the laboratory-based disciplines in which students are required to find an adviser well before the end of the first year, before they have had a chance to get to know the faculty and their interests. Indeed, Letty entered graduate school expecting faculty to be looking for students and was surprised when she found that she had to go around and talk to faculty and convince them to take her on. She describes feeling very pressured to find an adviser, lack of assistance from the department, and a feeling of competition with other first-year students who entered the program knowing with whom they were going to work. She ended up with an adviser who was the "only person that was at all friendly" and who seemed to want to work with her. She later found out that he was a very close friend of a friend of the family, and she had gone to see him because the family friend encouraged her to. She took a master's and left after a year and a half.

The remaining interviewees engaged in some form of purposive action to establish their relationship with their advisers. These methods were structured by the department, and all of the students who mentioned these methods came from the laboratory sciences.

In one chemistry department, each faculty member gives a brief presentation or seminar on his or her current research. Students identify several faculty with whom they might be interested in working and then meet with them in small groups to find out what, specifically, they have to offer. After the interviewing process is complete, the students submit their top choices to the department chair who, with the faculty, tries to accommodate the students' wishes. This method is highly structured and explicit. Consequently, it not only provides students with a clear understanding of the process but helps them develop cognitive maps of faculty interests and even starts the process of integration by facilitating interaction with faculty prior to final selection. Although meeting with faculty in small groups is probably done for expediency, this procedure reduces the fear and uncertainty some students may have about approaching a potential adviser. Even though both students interviewed from this department left within a year, both left for reasons external to the university.

Rotating through faculty laboratories and interviewing faculty were methods mentioned by biology students. Susan selected her adviser after having rotated through her laboratory. Although she ended up in a good lab and had a good experience with her adviser (she left after two years because of marriage), Susan thought it would have been better if the department had given graduate students a clearer idea of how to go about choosing a lab. By contrast, Melanie, who had prior graduate experience, interviewed faculty and made her selection based on the nature of the professor's research and the degree to which people in the lab seemed happy and stimulated. She left at the end of her first year after she found out that her adviser had taken a job at another university, and following him there was not an option she could consider. Given her efforts to choose wisely, she, somewhat bitterly, remarked, "Evidently, I chose poorly because he did not have the integrity to quit taking graduate students when he realized he was leaving."

Finally, approximately one-fourth of the students interviewed (seven) chose their adviser because they felt that their adviser's interests were closest to their own. This method of selection is associated with long durations. Indeed, five of the seven students who chose their adviser this way made it to stage 3 and had durations of four to seven years. Of the students with shorter durations (one to two years), one student left because of an injury, and the other, who found his department too serious, transferred to another university.

In general, students who chose their advisers based on close interests pursued the adviser–advisee relationship after having taken one or more classes with him or her or after hearing the professor give a talk they found interesting. In most cases, the student simply went to the professor and indicated an interest in working with him or her, and the professor agreed. Most of the students who chose advisers on the basis of close interests had good relationships with them. And most of the students who made it to stage 3 entered into the relationship with their adviser years before they began work on their dissertations.

Thus, despite the importance of the adviser in a graduate student's educational and professional career, the interview and survey data show that few noncompleters enter graduate school knowing who they want to work with and that they have a poor understanding of how to select an adviser—and many departments do not seem to provide much help or guidance in this regard (see chapter 4). In situations in which students are assigned to an adviser, they do not seem to know that the assignment is temporary or that they can change advisers. When students do know that they can change advisers, they fear they are placing themselves in political jeopardy and fear reprisal from the jilted faculty member. Even those students who select their adviser do not or cannot always select wisely. Although they may have chosen a department and/or adviser based on a professor's area of research or reputation in the field, they sometimes learn too late that this professor's renown does not extend to helping graduate students complete degrees.

Finally, the interviews and the survey data indicate that having interests that are close to a faculty member's *and* establishing the adviser–advisee relationship early in the graduate career based on firsthand knowledge and interaction contribute most to duration and to commencing work on a dissertation. By virtue of the criteria used to select interviewees (noncompletion), it is not possible to determine whether this configuration of interest and interaction does, in fact, contribute most to completion. However, the survey data and the theory undergirding this study indicate that it should.

STUDENTS' INTERACTIONS WITH THEIR ADVISERS

The nature and quality of interviewees' interactions with their advisers were investigated by asking students to "Tell me about your adviser." If the students did not address or differentiate between their academic and social interactions with their advisers, they were asked more direct questions. If necessary, the interviewees were probed about the frequency and duration of their interactions, the quality of the relationship, assistance provided in developing a coherent program of study, and the amount of interest their adviser took in them as people and in their ideas and research.

Twenty-two of the interviewees participated in this component of the interview. Five were not included because it was clear from their response to a question about how they chose their adviser that they did not have a relationship with him or her; two interviewees did not have an adviser.

Before addressing students' academic and social interactions with advisers, it is worth noting two other aspects of interviewees' relationships with their advisers: comments about their advisers' personalities and comments about things they wished had been different. Two personality types emerged. One type was described with a neutral to good tone. These professors were characterized as shy, reserved, polite, modest, and unassuming. The other type was described with an ambivalent to negative tone. These professors were characterized as not appealing, moody, rigid, inflexible, and spacey. This category contains two familiar negative stereotypes of academics: the head-in-the-clouds type and the hard-nosed-bully type.

Quite a few interviewees spontaneously mentioned things they wished had been different in their relationship with their adviser. The term *wish* was used by a few students, and it carries with it the sense that if their relationships with their advisers could have been magically transformed, things would have turned out differently. They wished for more of a mentor–student relationship, more time to talk at more length, and more encouragement on and greater involvement in "my work"—this last wish was made most frequently by those in stage 3. One student even wished that his adviser had been less intimidating.

Academic Interactions

When they met with their advisers, the meetings typically lasted twenty to thirty minutes. Several interviewees noted that these meetings were brief and to the point. A few Urban students mentioned how busy their advisers were, that it was difficult to meet with them, and that their advisers did not have much time for students.

The survey data show that completers had a greater quantity of interaction with their adviser than noncompleters at all three stages of graduate education. On-track completers had a greater quantity of interaction than at-risk completers during stage 2. Men had a greater quantity of interaction than women during stage 3. Consistent with Urban University's students' complaints about their advisers, the survey data show that Urban students did indeed have less interaction with their adviser during their first year than did Rural students. In addition, regardless of status, students who were assigned to their advisers had significantly less interaction with them at all three stages than students who selected their advisers.

Given the pivotal role the adviser plays (or should play) in helping students develop a coherent program of study and facilitating their progress through it, the interviewees were queried about this issue. Students who had been assigned to an adviser did not feel that they got much advice or guidance. They typically presented their adviser with a list of courses and the adviser generally approved or disapproved. Ellen, who remembered the interaction as follows, highlighted the impersonal nature of the interaction combined with the desire for a more personal one. In fact, the structure of her description, "this is the way it was/this is the way I would have liked it to be," was a discourse pattern used by a few interviewees.

Ellen: It was basically what courses am I going to take, not "How are you doing." It was "Here are the courses you've got to take to stay on track. You've got to take your preliminary exams here and qualifying exams there, and pick a thesis topic at this point." It was very mechanical, as far as I can remember.

Interviewer: Did you get the information from him that you felt you needed?

Ellen: In terms of the mechanics of the program?

Interviewer: Um-hm.

Ellen: Yes.

Interviewer: What about other aspects of the program?

Ellen: Absolutely not.

Interviewer: What other aspects didn't you get that you needed?

Ellen: Well, there were so many students there I guess it's only reasonable to think that as a first-year graduate student there is not going to be a lot of personal touch to the program. And maybe that happens after year 2 of a master's program and year 3 when you are assigned a Ph.D. counselor or whatever. But there was nothing personal there.

Several students who reached stage 3 commented that by the time they established their relationship with their adviser, the program requirements were behind them. In general, the rest of the students said that no one helped them put their programs together, sometimes because the program was so structured there was no need for advice or because they did not feel that talking to their adviser "was a very efficacious route to take to figure out how to get through." Indeed, one student even described his relationship with his adviser as characterized by a failure script:

Jim: I did understand in talking about it [the program] some with him that if I didn't do this, this, and this, or I didn't take this approach, I was going to be in big trouble when I got to my qualifying exams; I'd never make it through them. And it became, at that level of the kind of thing—unfortunately, that happens between a parent and a child, that the parent tells them they'll never amount to anything or just sort of talking to them in a way that's not encouraging but rather produces a failure script. I just didn't get any kind of affirmation or support that "This is how I can help you get through this," that "You'll be all right; you'll do fine." All I got were these threatening ominous reports of how tough these exams are, and there was this big mystery that surrounded the exams.

Amount of Interest Students Felt Advisers Took in Them as People

Very few interviewees felt that their adviser took any personal interest in them, regardless of duration or method of selection. When asked about this, they made remarks such as "None. Zero," "I really didn't feel he took very much interest," and "I didn't feel like he took a personal interest in me." Only one student, Tony, who left because of an injury, indicated any strong personal connection with his adviser. He thought his adviser was "very, very concerned and very, very attentive." In fact, for a period of time after he left, his adviser would call and say, "We're waiting for you." Tony regrets that the relationship dwindled over the years, but he still "remember[s] him with much appreciation, warmth"[2]—a strong contrast with how many of the other interviewees remembered their advisers.

Survey data on how much interest the students felt their advisers took in them as people, their research or ideas, and their professional development support the interview findings. Overall, completers felt that their advisers took considerably more interest in them as people than did noncompleters (see table 7.1). Regardless of status, students who had selected their advisers felt that their advisers took more interest in them as people than did students who had been assigned to their advisers (3.64 vs. 2.39). The survey data also show that the more interest noncompleters felt their advisers took in them as people, the longer they persisted.

Amount of Interest Students Felt Advisers
Took in Their Research, Ideas, and
Professional Development

How much interest the interviewees felt their advisers took in their research or ideas varied by duration. Three distinct patterns emerge, one for short duration, one for moderate duration, and one for those who made it to stage 3. Few of the short-duration students talked about their adviser's interest in their research or ideas, probably because few had started research or begun developing ideas. Those who did comment on it felt that their adviser "did not take a great deal of interest in my academic success"—a sentiment that appears again and again on noncompleters' questionnaires as a reason for why they were dissatisfied with their adviser.

Table 7.1.   Degree of Interest[1] Students Felt Their Adviser Took in Them by Status and Completer Type

Type of Interest	Status			Completer Type		
	Completers	Noncompleters	p	On-track	At-risk	p
You as a person	3.68	2.89	*	3.75	3.63	
Your ideas	4.09	3.10	*	4.25	3.89	*
Your professional development	3.92	3.06	*	4.11	3.68	*

[1] 5-point scale: 1 = *none at all* to 5 = *a lot.*
*p < .001.

Students of moderate duration indicated that their advisers showed some interest in their ideas, but either the adviser was the one generating the ideas or the adviser's interest was limited by virtue of the fact that the student's interests and ideas were not the adviser's interests or ideas. A paradox, if not a double bind, is thus set up in that doctoral students are supposed to be trained to think independently and a Ph.D. is supposed to be awarded for an original contribution, yet many graduate students found that having interests and ideas that diverged from their adviser's was not wholly acceptable to the adviser.

Brent: He was interested in the ideas that I wanted to develop, but they weren't his ideas and they weren't exactly his area of interest, and, consequently, we got along just fine as long as I didn't attempt to push what it was that I really wanted to work on. So I think we got along well, just not fabulously.

Interviewer: Can you tell me a bit about the nature of your interaction about academic things?

Brent: Well, I think he liked my input, when I had input on studies that he proposed. I think I have a pretty good eye for what makes a study work and for what makes a study not work. And he accepted that, approved that, and liked that. So, I think that my input to his studies was something that he valued. And he was a real nice guy. I liked him. I got along well with him on a purely social basis. [We were] just not entirely intellectually in synch because what I wanted to do was not what he wanted to do, and it wasn't what he wanted me to do.

Interviewer: Was there a conflict about that?

Brent: No, no, there wasn't a conflict. It was just that he'd say, "Well, I really would like for you to do this." And I would do it. Then I'd try to do my own work on the side.

Not surprisingly, lack of intellectual support is one of the reasons Brent cited when asked why he left graduate school without completing the Ph.D.: "I didn't feel that I was being intellectually supported because I wasn't getting input that was actually relevant to what I wanted to work on from the faculty on the research that I was attempting to do."

By contrast, students who made it to stage 3 indicated that their advisers had seemed or actually had been interested in their dissertation research. Rhett, a mathematics student, said, "He always was quite interested in what I'd done, . . . [and] he gave me other ideas and things to work on." Cade, a chemistry student, stated, "He was extremely interested in the research, and he was very interested in seeing that I carried it out successfully. I don't feel like he took a very personal interest in me, except to the extent that he was interested in my work being successful."

The survey asked the students how much interest their adviser took in their ideas and their professional development. Table 7.1 shows that completers and on-track completers felt that their advisers took much more interest in their ideas than their comparison group. Consistent with research on women's interactions with their advisers (Kjeruff & Blood, 1973, cited in Adler, 1976), women felt that their adviser took less interest in their ideas than men (3.56 vs. 3.91). Regardless of status, completion type, or gender, students who had selected their adviser felt that their adviser took considerably more interest in their ideas than students who were assigned to their adviser (4.05 vs. 2.43). Finally, the more interest noncompleters felt that their advisers took in their ideas, the longer they persisted.

The survey data on students' perceptions of their advisers' interest in their professional development are similar to those for their perceptions of their advisers' interest in their ideas, except that there was no effect for gender, and noncompleter's perceptions of their advisers' interest in their professional development did not affect their duration. However, Rural students felt that their advisers were more interested in their professional development than Urban students (3.79 vs. 3.27), as did students who selected an adviser relative to those who were assigned to an adviser (3.88 vs. 2.55).

Social Interactions

Of the seventeen interviewees asked about social interaction with their adviser, eight had no social interaction whatsoever, and the rest had infrequent, limited, or occasional interactions. Neither duration nor method of adviser selection appears to make a difference for the quality or quantity of the interactions. When social interactions did occur, they were primarily in group settings, and, even then, the students were more likely to share physical space with their adviser than to interact with them in a substantial way.

A number of the interviewees did, however, comment on the social nature of their advisers. They characterized them as not extroverted or gregarious, not open to socializing with students or even with other faculty, and never or rarely showing up at faculty–student get-togethers. This profile suggests, as we shall see in the next section, that their advisers were probably low producers.

ADVISERS' INTERACTIONS WITH
THEIR STUDENTS

A picture has emerged of noncompleters as students who had quantitatively less interaction with their advisers than completers and who quite probably had a different qualitative experience with their advisers, too. This, however, raises the question as to whether these differences stem from differences inherent in the students themselves (their personalities and dispositions) or whether noncompleters had different experiences with their advisers because they were working with different types of advisers. Without direct one-on-one matching of students with advisers, the question cannot be answered conclusively. However, differences in the way high and low producers interact with their students can provide evidence for or against such a supposition.

The interviews conducted with the faculty asked them a series of questions about how they acquire and work with their graduate students as well as a series of questions about their social interactions with graduate students, including their participation in their departments' activities and events. To complement the questions in the student interviews about faculty with whom the students had particularly good and bad experiences, the faculty were asked to talk about one of their most and least successful adviser–advisee relationships. Analysis of this component of the faculty interviews is contained in the appendix.

Establishing the Adviser–Advisee Relationship

If selecting an appropriate adviser is a critical decision for students, then agreeing to be a student's adviser indicates (or should indicate) that the adviser is committed to seeing the student through to completion. In chapter 4, we saw that faculty are aware that students do not know how or even when to ask a professor to be an adviser and that the courtship often involves a mating dance of codes, signals, and indirection. The question arises as to whether there are differences in the courtship rituals among high and low producers.

One difference is that high producers (HPs) enumerated more ways in which their adviser–advisee relationships were established than low producers (LPs). It was not uncommon for HPs to state two or three means. By contrast, LPs typically stated only one. Another difference between adviser types is in their openness to taking on students. Although faculty, in general, do not actively recruit advisees, two LPs prefaced their remarks by stating that they did not seek out students. By contrast, one HP mentioned that he recruited students from overseas, while another one remarked that he smoothed the way for students to ask him to be their adviser by writing encouraging comments on papers of students with whom he was impressed, along with the suggestion that "If you want any future help from me, feel free to come and ask." In addition, two LPs, but no HPs, said that they reviewed students' records before agreeing to work with them.

The three most commonly cited methods of establishing the adviser–advisee relationship are similar to the ones mentioned by students. These methods include the student taking a class or seminar from the professor and then expressing interest in working with him (seven HPs, four LPs), having common interests (six HPs, four LPs), and the student simply indicating he or she wants to work with him (two HPs, three LPs). Five other methods of establishing the adviser–advisee relationship were mentioned by both high and low producers in roughly the same low numbers—that is, by one or two of each type of adviser. These methods include the student applying to work with the professor at the time of admission, the student taking a reading course with him or her, the student being referred to the professor by an undergraduate faculty member, the student going through the department's formal faculty interview and selection process, and the student having been the professor's RA or TA. There were, however, differences in high and low producers views of their RAs or TAs. The HPs expected that most of their RAs and some of their TAs would ultimately ask them to advise their dissertations and that they would accept the invitation. By contrast, the one LP who mentioned this method had been less accepting and more judgmental of his TAs.

> *Burr*: Well, they were both TAs for me. I had them both in classes the first year they were here. I think I probably, in both cases, kept a slightly arm's-length approach to it because I thought that possibly they wouldn't succeed in the program. And I didn't want a lot of emotional baggage already wrapped up in them.

In fact, Professor Burr was one of the LPs who reviewed students' records before agreeing to work with them.

High and low producers also had some nonshared methods of acquiring students. Two HPs acquired students who took qualifying exams in their area. One said that he retained many of the students who were assigned to him because they were paired on the basis of close interests, whereas another reported that students came to him because he has a reputation for being conscientious in reading and returning students' work in a timely fashion. Four LPs, on the other hand, stated that they acquired students by default; that is, they became students advisers because the students' initial adviser left or they did not get along, or because the students were in some way orphaned in the department.

In general, the faculty's responses indicate that HPs were more interested in and receptive to taking on new students than LPs. They also suggest that HPs had more shared interests and a greater quantity of interaction with their advisees before establishing the relationship than LPs and, consequently, were more academically integrated with them prior to the start of the adviser–advisee relationship.

Academic Interactions

While the survey data demonstrate that completers spent more time interacting with their advisers than noncompleters, the question remains as to whether these differences are due to differences between the students themselves or whether they are a function of the type of adviser the students were working with. Differences in the amount of time high and low producers spend with their students suggests that noncompleters may, in fact, have been more likely than completers to have been advised by LPs than by HPs.

The faculty were asked how much time they gave to each of their graduate students in a typical week. Although the question was fairly straightforward, their answers were not. Some faculty provided estimates of the amount of time they spent with individual students, some with graduate students collectively, and some gave estimates of both. Overall, on an individual basis, which includes working together on research projects, high producers estimated that they spent 4.85 hours a week with their advisees, compared with 4.50 hours for low producers—a difference of roughly twenty minutes a week. This difference when summed over a several-year relationship adds up to a considerable amount of time. On a collective basis, which includes classroom, seminar, and workshop contact as well as laboratory group meetings, the HPs estimated they spent 7.4 hours a week with their graduate students compared with 4.8 hours for LPs. However, the number of faculty whose responses focused on the collectivity was small, so the difference should be considered with caution.

More interesting differences between high and low producers are contained in the gloss surrounding their responses here and elsewhere. High producers showed a greater sensitivity to the nature of the advising process and to individual student needs. They were more likely to preface their remarks with "it depends" and then go on to draw distinctions about variation in students' needs for advising and/or variations in the amount of time spent advising students during different stages of their graduate careers.

High producers were also more likely than low producers to say that they initiated interactions with students. For instance, Professor Wheeler, a LP in the sciences, said that he was always available, but contact was "something they initiate." By contrast, Professor Clayton, an HP in the same department, talked about a free, two-way flow of interaction, "Students also come into my office and I go into their lab on a daily basis." Similarly, Professor Hilton, an HP in the humanities—a domain of knowledge where students tend to work off campus and in isolation—commented, "If a long time goes by without their producing something, I'll call them up and say, 'What's going on?' just to make them aware that I'm still thinking of them." This difference in initiative taking suggests that noncompleters who described having to take the initiative with faculty (see chapter 6) were more likely to have been working with low producers.

In addition to the amount of time they spend with their students, how advisers work with their students and the advice and encouragement they give

them affects both their intellectual development and professional socialization. In an effort to discern factors leading to differential academic integration
by adviser type, the faculty were asked a series of questions that had bearing
on various aspects of academic integration and how they fostered it. The topics included whether they worked collaboratively with their students; issues
of coauthorship; whether they encouraged their students to become active
participants in the discipline by subscribing to journals, joining disciplinary
associations, and attending professional meetings; and whether and how they
helped their students launch their careers.

Collaboration

Professional socialization takes place most effectively through collaboration.
When students apprentice to a master they learn the formal and informal art
of the trade. Thus, advisers who work closely with their students not only will
have a higher frequency of interaction with their students but also will facilitate their students' intellectual development and professional socialization to
a greater degree than those who do not.

Although collaboration was discipline-specific (chemistry, biology, psychology, sociology), HPs were almost twice as likely as LPs to say they engaged in
collaborative research with their students. Faculty in the humanities, regardless
of productivity, were more likely than other faculty to say they have collaborated
with their students, but only after their students finished their degrees.

Professor McLure, a high-productive chemist, provides a detailed discussion of how he works with his students and scaffolds their development. His
comments contrast sharply with those of Professor Wheeler, a low-productive
chemist, who pretty much simply gives students projects and leaves them to
their own devices.

> *McLure*: What we often will do is talk over an idea together. . . . We'll talk through some
> ideas and come to a consensus about what the next steps should be. Usually outline
> what things need to be known, need to be done to carry those out and then the stu-
> dent will go off and do them. . . . As they get further along the proportion of ideas
> that they contribute goes up, the amount of detail in how to carry out the ideas goes
> down; that is, they can walk out of the discussion with the ideas still at a conceptual
> stage and not necessarily a nitty-gritty, this-is-the-mathematical-tool-you-need stage,
> because they'll know that by then. But I very much like to have them heavily in-
> volved and increasingly involved in shaping the ideas that they are working on, so
> that by the time they're ready to write their thesis, they're contributing very signifi-
> cantly, essentially as a peer, to shaping what's actually happening in the research.

> *Wheeler:* No [I don't work collaboratively with my students]. Mostly what happens
> here, and I think this is pretty much true throughout the Chemistry Department, the
> student kind of indicates they want to work with you. And usually when you talk to
> them, you give them three or four areas within a larger subarea where you're doing

research and they usually will pick one of these and you try and select a problem that seems promising. . . . I think at times, I've had four or five different students, they would all be working on their own, individual projects. It doesn't mean they wouldn't be talking to each other or that we wouldn't have group meetings where each one in turn would discuss what they'd been doing and try and get advice from outside. They tend to be individual projects that the student is working on.

Writing papers, articles, or chapters with graduate students would seem to flow naturally out of collaborative research, even in disciplines like the humanities in which students, as part of an RA, are involved in doing library or archival research for faculty. Writing papers with faculty also helps students advance their careers by introducing their names and work to the broader community, and it helps them build their vita. Yet, graduate student folklore is rife with horror stories of faculty "ripping off" student work or students not being credited properly, or at all, for the work they have done on faculty projects. This lore raised the question as to whether there were differences between high and low producers with respect to producing papers with students and whether there were differences between the types in allowing students to be first author on jointly produced papers.[3]

Like collaboration on research, collaboration on papers, articles, and chapters varied by discipline.[4] Within the norms of their disciplines, HPs were more likely to collaborate on papers with their students than LPs. High producers in chemistry and biology said that their students were always first author. By contrast, LPs in chemistry and biology, and high and low producers in the social sciences, tended to have policies or philosophies about first-authorship that involved the quality of the paper, the amount of work contributed, and the alphabetical order of authors' names. Compare the responses about coauthorship of two biology faculty from the same university.:

> *Tomlinson (HP):* Oh, yes, [I collaborate on papers with them], but they publish on their own, too. I tell them if they do something that's really their own, I'm not going to [put my name on it]. I know it's not good for my funding, I suppose, but I let my students publish things entirely on their own, out of the lab, as long as they acknowledge the grant.

> *Cromwell (LP):* My rules on coauthorship, if you will, are that the person who made the greatest intellectual contribution to the work is the first author, and if that's the student, then the student is first author. Anybody who didn't make any intellectual contribution to the work doesn't warrant authorship. Now usually I work closely enough with my students on not only the project but on the preparation of the project for publication that I would normally expect to be an author.

Integration into the Disciplinary Community

Joining professional associations, subscribing to journals, and attending professional meetings not only integrate students into the discipline but often serve as an important nexus to the broader disciplinary community. Students who participate in these activities should have not only a broader knowledge of their fields but a larger network of professionals with whom they can interact about intellectual matters and job openings. Given the importance of these activities to students' careers, one would expect all advisers to take particular interest in this component of their students' development. This, however, was not the case.

Almost three times as many HPs as LPs encouraged students to join professional associations, and they often linked such membership with professional socialization and the networking requisite for finding a job. Low producers, by contrast, tended to abdicate responsibility for such encouragement, deferring instead to the student subculture to communicate its importance. The general position of LPs is captured in Professor Cromwell's response. Professor Prudhomme represents the extremes that some HPs will go to to get their students integrated into the discipline and the profession.

> *Cromwell*: That's something that we don't really talk about. I think that comes when students see the advantage of being connected to a professional network. It would be surprising to me if an American science student, for example, didn't want to join the professional society or whatever organization would be appropriate to their particular work.

> *Prudhomme*: I encourage them to either join either one of two associations. . . . I encourage them to join the regional. I encourage them to join a specialty division. . . . In fact, the association has . . . a gift membership thing, where you can give somebody a one-year membership, which gets them the journal and membership for a year and then they either stay on it or they don't. And, in fact, if you do several of them at a time, it's very cheap. . . . So, sometimes you use those essentially as gifts.

> *Interviewer*: So, you give your students gift memberships?

> *Prudhomme*: Yeah, for a couple of reasons. One is that there are students that I think would like to, probably would be interested in those issues. . . . It's [also] a very good recruiting thing because people tend to stay in the organization and pay regular dues. So, as far as I'm concerned, I'm helping both sides and it makes me feel good. So, I do that.

Although a few faculty, regardless of productivity, cited journal subscription as an unspoken expectation, twice as many HPs as LPs encouraged students to subscribe to journals. Low producers were much more likely than high producers to cite their expense as a reason for not encouraging students to subscribe and to mention the quality of the department's or university's library, encouraging students to use it instead.

All faculty said that they encouraged their students to present at professional meetings. However, there were differences in the enthusiasm with which high and low producers encouraged students. Low producers were more qualified in their encouragement, often saying "when funding allows," whereas high producers frequently paid for their students to go or managed to guide their students successfully through departmental competitions for department funds. Some also mentioned that they helped their students prepare their papers and presentations. In addition, HPs seem to get their students out on the conference circuit earlier in their graduate careers and more often than LPs. Finally, a few faculty, regardless of productivity, recognized the importance of having students attend and present at conferences from the standpoint of their professional development. While LPs simply made the statement, HPs articulated what students learned from the experience:

> *Hilton*: I think, what you can prove by doing that, when someone is looking at you as a job candidate, is that you are capable of doing it. Capable of organizing a paper, showing up, and presenting a paper. You can certainly get a little bit of professionalization by going through the process. . . . If during the course of your graduate studies, you do three or four, I think that you've done all that you can actually can get any benefit from. But I encourage them to attend more meetings than that. You can learn a lot by watching how other people field questions, by how they deal with controversy, by the way they read papers. There's a lot of learning about the codes of the profession that can take place by watching other people perform. So, I encourage them to do that a lot.

In chapter 5, we saw that differences between completers' and noncompleters' participation in their department's social activities disappeared when the type of financial support they received was controlled. This indicated that the difference between groups was due to the structural context in which they were embedded. However, differences in completers' and noncompleters' engagement in the professional activities discussed earlier persisted when these controls were applied, suggesting that the effect was due to differences in their dispositions. The preceding analysis showed that high and low producers interact differently with their students about these activities. The question arises as to whether the differences between completers' and noncompleters' can be accounted for by the type of adviser with whom they were affiliated.

Evidence is presented in the next major section that suggests that the more satisfied students were with their adviser, the more likely it is that their adviser was a high producer. Thus, degree of satisfaction with adviser was used (cautiously) as a proxy for adviser type to help sort out situational effects from dispositional effects. Table 7.2 shows that the more satisfied students were with their adviser, the more likely they were to engage in each professional activity, and that satisfaction played a greater role in noncompleters' behaviors than completers'. In addition, there was no statistical difference for subscribing to journals between completers and noncompleters who persisted for four or more years *and* who were very satisfied with their adviser, although the differences remained for the other activities. These results suggest

Table 7.2. Students' Engagement in Professional Activities as a Function of Satisfaction with Their Adviser (in percent)

Activities	Whole Sample				
	Not at all Satisfied	*Not too Satisfied*	*Somewhat Satisfied*	*Very Satisfied*	*p*
Subscribe to journals	51	58	75	81	***
Belong to professional associations	51	47	79	84	***
Attend professional meetings	54	56	79	84	***
	Completers				
	Not at all Satisfied	*Not too Satisfied*	*Somewhat Satisfied*	*Very Satisfied*	*p*
Subscribe to journals	73	76	82	85	
Belong to professional associations	82	78	87	89	
Attend professional meetings	86	76	89	90	
	Noncompleters				
	Not at all Satisfied	*Not too Satisfied*	*Somewhat Satisfied*	*Very Satisfied*	*p*
Subscribe to journals	39	46	60	66	*
Belong to professional associations	34	42	61	62	**
Attend professional meetings	37	42	61	60	*

*$p < .05$.
**$p < .01$.
***$p < .001$.

that students' engagement in professional activities may be partially a function of dispositions and partially a function of the type of adviser they had.

Assistance with Job Search

The final way in which advisers can integrate students into the discipline and the profession is by helping them find jobs. Consequently, the faculty were asked whether they helped their students find jobs and, if so, how they went about doing it. Overall, the faculty mentioned eleven different means by which they assisted students. As a group, HPs used almost twice as many means as LPs. Indeed, several HPs but no LP prefaced their remarks by stating that helping students find jobs was one of the most important things they do. Many asserted that it was an important part of their role and responsibility as an adviser. High producers also appear to work much harder than low producers at helping their students get jobs. Many said that they help "as much as I can" and that they "put in a tremendous amount of time" assisting students with their job searches.

More than half the faculty interviewed said that they called colleagues at other universities either to alert them about a student going on the market or to talk up one of their students. High producers were slightly more likely to make such calls. As one high-productive sociologist put it, "I try to serve as a kind of a loose tie[5] with those folks even if I'm not a strong tie with them. . . . It's a fact of life: sponsored mobility in the contest of getting jobs." In addition, two faculty (one HP and one LP) forthrightly said that they did not make such calls—the HP because he did not like receiving them, preferring to rely on his own judgment of student application packages, and the LP because "I'm not that aggressive."

The second most common means of helping students find jobs was writing letters of recommendation. Almost twice as many HPs as LPs mentioned writing them. They were also more likely to discuss the time, care, and effort that they put into such letters.

More HPs than LPs said that they networked with colleagues to find out what jobs were coming up and alerted their students about them. By contrast, more LPs than HPs simply handed job notices to their students and left the rest up to the student. Several HPs, but no LP, mentioned introducing graduate students to colleagues at professional meetings and helping them prepare for job interviews.

Humanities faculty were the only ones to mention helping students prepare their vita and supporting materials, as well as themselves, for the job market. High producers were more likely to provide this form of assistance than low producers. Indeed, they were more proactive in making sure that their students came across in the best possible light, as the actions of Professor Hilton demonstrate:

Hilton: I do put a lot of time into writing letters of recommendation, and for any student whose dissertation I'm directing, I will go look at their file [and] read all of the letters that are in the file. If there's a letter by someone else that I don't think should be in there, I tell them we should take it out. I won't give them a lot of detail. I'll just say, "Look, it's my judgment this letter doesn't belong in there. It's not strong enough," whatever. I will also go to my colleagues and ask them or insist—it varies—that they revise a letter. If I think that they haven't put what they might put into a letter, then I will pressure a colleague to revise it. And I've also sometimes done that for students where I'm just on the committee, not directing [it]. If it might be a case, let's say the student's in a different field, . . . but the [director] is not the sort of person who's going to take the trouble to read other people's letters or get involved in that way, then they can ask me to do it. As long as they've asked me, I'll go ahead and do that for them.

In summary, regardless of what dimension of academic integration they were queried about, HPs seem to be more engaged with their students than LPs and to engage with their students with a greater degree of enthusiasm. High producers see developing their students as professionals and helping them build their careers as among the most important components of their jobs. By contrast, low producers seem to take more aspects of the graduate training experience for granted. Consequently, their students are more likely to have to take the initiative with them to get the same type of entrée into the discipline and the profession that students of high producers automatically get. However, this assumes that students of LPs know that they need to take the initiative and that they know what questions to ask or what advice to seek, and this is a big assumption. Such students must either enter graduate school with good cognitive maps of graduate education or become well integrated into the graduate student subculture to acquire the same know-how that is given freely to students of HPs. However, even if they do this, they still are less likely to get their names on papers and to be introduced into important career-building networks than HPs' students.

Social Interaction

Graduate school provides a number of opportunities for faculty to interact with graduate students informally. Consequently, the faculty were asked a series of questions about their participation in activities that afforded opportunities to interact with graduate students. Their interviews were tailored to include only those activities that their department's DGS said took place in their department. The faculty were also asked a series of questions about their extradepartmental interactions with graduate students.

All but one HP said he attended at least half of his department's colloquia; the majority said they always attended when they were in town.[6] One high producer noted that he leaned on his students to attend; two others said that they made a special effort when their students were presenting. By contrast, less than half of the LPs always attended their department's colloquia; the rest attended occasionally, often only when the topic interested them.

The faculty were further queried as to whether they participated in the department's social function that either preceded or followed the colloquia. High and low producers were about equally likely to participate. However, there is some evidence that HPs view the social component of colloquia as an opportunity to interact with colleagues and students. One "religious" colloquium-goer who worked in a different building from most of his colleagues stated, "I'm usually the first person there because I count on talking to people at that meeting because I don't run into them in the halls." Another mentioned that he often went out to dinner with the graduate students and out-of-town speakers after the colloquium.

High and low producers were about equally likely to attend their department's brown bag lunch and with the same relative frequencies, which for both groups was not often. Within the same department, the HP was more likely to attend than the LP, but there was a high degree of variability.

More than half the HPs and only about a third of the LPs said that they participated in regularly scheduled on-campus social events such as happy hours. Of the HPs who attended, the majority attended more than half the time. One remarked that he thinks of the happy hour as half pleasure, half responsibility. By contrast, most of the LPs who attended social hours attended only occasionally. One recognized that his infrequent participation in his department's daily social hour was a limitation, that it restricted him to interacting only with students who were interested in his area.

Very few faculty said that they participated in off-campus social hours. In the one instance where two members of the same department provided an answer, the high producer said that he occasionally went to the graduate student Friday afternoon bashes and would buy a pitcher of beer for the students. By contrast, his low-productive counterpart did not even know that the department had social hours.

Four times as many HPs as LPs attend departmental picnics regularly. Several of the LPs were unaware that their departments had a picnic.

Most of the faculty interviewed who once played sports with students no longer did, because, in their words, they are "too old now." However, twice as many HPs as LPs said that they played sports with students in some capacity. One HP plays racquetball with his students, but only with his male students. He talked about recruiting them to play and about taking them out for drinks afterward, which, in his view, helped them develop a close ongoing relationship. Although the integration advantages of such a relationship are obvious, when queried as to whether he played racquetball with his female students, he drew a strict line. Thus, when it comes to sports, his female students—and probably the female graduate students of many other male advisers—are not afforded the same integration opportunities or experiences as their male counterparts.

In addition to interacting with graduate students in departmentally structured contexts, faculty may also interact with students informally outside the department on their or their students' initiative. About an equal number of high and low producers said they socialized with their graduate students outside the department. There do not appear to be any differences between adviser types as to whether the socializing was with individual students or with groups of students. However, HPs socialize with their students with greater frequency and in a wider variety of contexts than LPs. High producers were more likely than low producers to go with or take students out to lunch or dinner. By contrast, LPs said that if they bumped into their students in the cafeteria, they might sit with them.

The two adviser types also viewed their relationships with their students differently. Several HPs but no LP used the word *friend* to describe the relationship: "I socialize with them and they are friends," "In most cases, I have become fairly good friends with my students and maintain that friendship over the years," and "Usually there are one or two students in a given period of time that I become quite close to and are social friends."

High and low producers were equally likely to say that they attend student parties to which they are personally invited and that they accept students' dinner invitations. Several faculty, particularly LPs, noted that their involvement and participation has dropped off as they have gotten older. As one LP put it, "I used to. I mean, I'm over fifty now, and I don't think I look like as likely an invitee. . . . I guess as I've gotten older. Also I felt a little more hesitant, a little less sure that my company would be welcome."

Virtually all the faculty said that they have had graduate students to their homes at one time or another. However, there were large differences between adviser types in the nature and frequency of the events. High producers typically had students to their homes at least once a year. Many had students to their homes once a term, some up to five times a year; a couple had students over monthly for dinner or musical evenings. Low producers, by contrast, typically had students to their homes once a year or less. No LP mentioned having holiday parties or having students over for the holidays, whereas three HPs did. Indeed, one made it a point to identify students in his research group who were likely to be "orphaned" for Thanksgiving or Christmas.

High producers were also more likely than low producers to have students to their homes individually and to do so earlier in the students' graduate careers. When low producers had students to their homes individually, it was often to celebrate the completion of their dissertation, thereby obviating any integration benefits that having students to their homes earlier bestows.

Finally, a couple of HPs in the laboratory sciences, but no LP, referred to their research groups as part of their family or blurred the distinction between family and students:

Clayton: Generally, in the late fall, we'll have a party, Thanksgiving or Christmas, and then again in the summer we'll have a get-together. The last few years it's been on July 4th. . . . [A] good research group, which I hope my group is, is very much like a family. And it's like a family affair.

Bedford: Every summer I have a field project, a long-term field project, and so we camp out there for usually two weeks, sometimes as long as a couple of months. And since a lot of my wife's family and mine live nearby, they come up and visit. And we usually have present, past, and sometimes prospective students up there as well. And we get our families to help the students with their projects. So it's kind of a giant two-week field soirée in which there isn't really a distinction between family and academics.

Using students' satisfaction with adviser as a proxy for adviser type, the students' frequency of participation in departmental activities was assessed against their degree of satisfaction with their adviser. Table 7.3 shows that the more satisfied students were with their adviser the more frequently they participated in colloquia/brown bags, sports, and other social activities involving faculty and students. The effect holds for the whole sample, but not for completers and noncompleters as separate groups. Large differences in participation in colloquia/brown bags persist between completers and noncompleters who were "not too satisfied," "somewhat satisfied," and "very satisfied" with their last adviser, but not for those who were "not at all satisfied." There were

Table 7.3.　Frequency of Students' Participation in Departmental Activities as a Function of Satisfaction[1] with Their Adviser

	Whole Sample				
Activities	*Not at all Satisfied*	*Not too Satisfied*	*Somewhat Satisfied*	*Very Satisfied*	*p*
Colloquia/brown bags	2.91	3.00	3.36	3.57	***
Sports	1.94	2.04	2.20	2.40	**
On-campus socializing	2.95	2.81	3.15	3.08	
Off-campus socializing	2.95	2.77	3.06	2.98	
Other social activities	2.81	2.98	2.91	3.13	*
	Completers				
Activities	*Not at all Satisfied*	*Not too Satisfied*	*Somewhat Satisfied*	*Very Satisfied*	*p*
Colloquia/brown bags	3.05	3.56	3.58	3.71	
Sports	1.67	2.22	2.28	2.56	*
On-campus socializing	2.95	2.75	3.13	3.13	
Off-campus socializing	2.86	2.78	3.09	2.99	
Other social activities	2.78	2.97	2.99	3.18	
	Noncompleters				
Activities	*Not at all Satisfied*	*Not too Satisfied*	*Somewhat Satisfied*	*Very Satisfied*	*p*
Colloquia/brown bags	2.82	2.58	2.84	2.90	
Sports	2.10	1.88	2.00	2.05	
On-campus socializing	2.95	2.86	3.18	2.87	
Off-campus socializing	2.95	2.77	2.94	2.96	
Other social activities	2.84	2.98	2.73	2.89	

[1] 5-point scale: 1 = *not at all* to 5 = *a lot.*
*$p < .05$.
**$p < .01$.
***$p < .001$.

also significant differences in degree of participation in sports and other social activities between completers and noncompleters who were "very satisfied" with their adviser, but not for other levels of satisfaction. These results
suggest that the propensity to participate in department activities is partially
a function of dispositions and partially a function of adviser type.

In sum, for each of the activities explored here, more HPs engaged in it,
and engaged in it more often and with greater enthusiasm than LPs. Indeed,
HPs appear more committed to social involvement in their departments and
with their graduate students and are more likely to take the initiative to insti-
gate and sustain social interaction than LPs. As a result, HPs appear not only
to facilitate their students' academic integration into the department and discipline but also to facilitate their social integration into the department, the
adviser–advisee relationship, and even colleague/peer relationship as well.

The good feelings that come from the sense of belonging created by positive academic and social interactions should make it harder for students to
break bonds with the community and, thereby, prevent their attrition. Indeed,
the survey data show that completers participated more frequently than noncompleters in the same informal department activities the faculty were
queried about. This finding indirectly supports the contention that they had
more interaction with the faculty who attended. Consequently, they become
more socially integrated with those faculty—and those faculty are more likely
to be high producers. Thus, completers may end up working with high producers because of the interactions they have with them in these contexts. Or,
because they are working with high producers, students, in general, are encouraged to participate in departmental activities and, as a result, become
more integrated and complete. Finally, to the extent that social integration is
intertwined with academic integration, students of high producers receive the
added (multiplicative) benefits that informal interactions bestow on their intellectual development and professional socialization.

SATISFACTION WITH ADVISER

Based on numbers alone, because high producers produce more Ph.D.'s than
low producers,[7] completers are more likely than noncompleters to have
worked with them. Additional support for this contention comes from the students' responses to an open-ended survey question about why they were or
were not satisfied with their last adviser. As we shall see, students who were
satisfied with their advisers wrote about them in terms that are consonant in
the attitudinal and behavioral patterns of HPs. By contrast, students who were
dissatisfied with their advisers wrote about them in terms that are consistent
with the attitudinal and behavioral patterns of LPs. And, not surprisingly,

Table 7.4.   Students' Degree of Satisfaction with Their Adviser by Status and Completer Type (in percent)

	Status		Completer Type	
Degree of Satisfaction	*Completers*	*Noncompleters*	*On-track*	*At-risk*
Very satisfied	60	31	68	48
Somewhat satisfied	29	29	26	33
Not too satisfied	7	23	5	11
Not satisfied at all	4	18	2	8

as demonstrated in table 7.4, more completers, on-track completers in particular, were more satisfied with their last adviser than noncompleters and at-risk completers.

Before filling out the open-ended question, the students were asked to rate their level of satisfaction with their adviser. As shown in table 7.4 completers were twice as likely as noncompleters to be very satisfied.[8] Similarly, on-track completers were more likely to be very satisfied than at-risk completers. Although males were more likely to be very satisfied than females (54 percent vs. 47 percent), the effect for gender was not significant. By contrast, noncompleters and at-risk completers were about four times more likely than their counterparts not to be at all satisfied with their adviser. Women were also less satisfied than men (12 percent vs. 7 percent).

Method of adviser selection plays a large role in students' degree of satisfaction. Students who had selected their adviser were more than three times as likely to have been very satisfied with him or her than students who had been assigned to their adviser (58 percent vs. 16 percent). Among students who had selected their adviser, completers and on-track completers were much more satisfied with them than their counterparts, as were the men relative to women. By contrast, regardless of status, completer type, or gender, less than a fifth of students who had been assigned to their adviser were very satisfied.

Six dominant types of reasons for satisfaction or dissatisfaction with their adviser emerged from the analysis of students' open-ended survey responses.[9] The categories, in declining order of the frequency with which they were mentioned by the whole sample (some students' responses spanned more than one category), are as follows: intellectual/professional development, interest in me, professionalism, personality, advising style, and accessibility (see table 7.5). Each category is discussed in turn by degree of satisfaction. It is important to note that students who were very satisfied were uniformly positive about their advisers, whereas students who were not too satisfied and not at all satisfied were uniformly negative. By contrast, those who were somewhat satisfied frequently made both positive

Table 7.5. Major Reasons for Satisfaction with Adviser by Degree of Satisfaction and Status (in percent)

	Degree of Satisfaction							
	Very Satisfied		Somewhat Satisfied		Not Too Satisfied		Not at All Satisfied	
Reason	Completers	Noncompleters	Completers	Noncompleters	Completers	Noncompleters	Completers	Noncompleters
Intellectual/ Professional development	51	25	35	28	9	19	6	28
Interest in me	61	23	22	20	9	36	7	20
Professionalism	66	56	31	41	3	4	0	0
Personality	54	32	32	20	8	24	6	24
Advising style	80	86	20	14	0	0	0	0
Accessibility	31	8	62	60	8	24	0	8

Note: Row percentages for completers and noncompleters may not add to 100 due to rounding.

and negative comments about their advisers, often in the same sentence. In fact, roughly one-third of the students who were somewhat satisfied used or implied the word *but* in their statements. In other words, they were satisfied with some things about or aspects of their relationship with their adviser, but dissatisfied with others.

Intellectual/Professional Development

Students' greatest satisfaction and greatest dissatisfaction with their advisers centered on their advisers' involvement in their intellectual and professional development. Roughly 35 percent of both completers and noncompleters who were very satisfied with their adviser made comments about this aspect of their relationship. By contrast, 53 percent of the completers and 29 percent of noncompleters who were not too satisfied and 55 percent of both completers and noncompleters who were not at all satisfied with their advisers wrote about this component of their relationship.

Twice as many completers as noncompleters were very satisfied with the contribution their adviser made to their intellectual and professional development. These students reported a high degree of intellectual compatibility with their advisers and found them to be strong mentors who were very helpful and supportive—academically, financially, and emotionally. They described their advisers as demanding and as people who challenged them to think harder and more imaginatively. Many commented that they learned a great deal from them. They also described their advisers as attentive, willing to listen, and enthusiastic about their (the students') work. Their advisers provided quick, helpful feedback. Completers, by virtue of having finished their degrees, credited their advisers with teaching them how to research or think scientifically and with being responsible for many of their good professional qualifications and for the success they had achieved in their careers.

Completers who were somewhat satisfied with their advisers were equally likely to say positive things about their advisers' contribution to their intellectual/professional development as they were to say negative things (16 percent, positive, vs. 19 percent, negative). By contrast, noncompleters who were somewhat satisfied with their advisers were twice as likely to say negative things as positive things (19 percent, negative, vs. 9 percent, positive). The students' positive comments are similar to those made by students who were very satisfied, but they are less glowing and unconditional. These students were more likely to state specific ways in which their adviser helped them—choosing courses, preparing for preliminary exams, improving their dissertation. Students who made negative comments did not find their advisers particularly helpful, encouraging, or intellectually stimulating. Some felt their advisers had not pushed them hard enough or given them enough direction. Others did not think their adviser had been particularly interested in their work. None of the noncompleters both praised and criticized this aspect of their relationship with their adviser, although several of the completers did. In general, these completers were pleased with their advisers' contribution to their intellectual development but displeased with their advisers' contribution to their professional development; that is, they were dissatisfied with their advisers because their advisers did not help them find jobs or assist them in getting their research published. Regardless of whether or not they had positive things to say about their advisers, one-third of the somewhat satisfied completers who made negative remarks made them about these issues.

Noncompleters were twice as likely as completers to be not too satisfied with their adviser's contribution to their intellectual/professional development and almost five times more likely than completers to not be at all satisfied. Students who were not too satisfied did not find their advisers helpful, did not receive enough guidance or intellectual support, and felt their advisers had shown little interest in their work. Some noted that they did not share the same interests with their adviser and had poor communication with him or her. Students who were not at all satisfied found their advisers to be uninformed about the program and the discipline; uninterested in advising; and uninterested in them as people, in helping them through their program, in their professional development, or in students in general. In fact, two noncompleters wrote that their advisers did not like them: "He made it clear that he could not be bothered with me—I was beneath contempt"; "Also made it clear he did not care for me." Several students—completers and noncompleters—felt that they had been "lied to" or "misled" by their advisers about time and work requirements and when they could expect to complete the program.

Interest in Me

Fifteen percent of completers and 16 percent of noncompleters were very satisfied with their advisers because of the degree of interest they took in them. By contrast, 19 percent of completers and 33 percent of noncompleters were not too satisfied with their adviser for this reason, as were 25 percent of completers and 27 percent of noncompleters who were not at all satisfied with their adviser.[10]

Students who were very satisfied with the degree of interest their adviser took in them reported that their adviser had been interested in them as people and in their needs, plans, goals, and general success. Completers, who were almost three times as likely to be very satisfied with this aspect of their relationship with their adviser as noncompleters, wrote about how their adviser had been interested in their ideas, research interests, academic progress, and professional development. In fact, at least one completer was aware that the amount of interest his adviser had taken in him was not the norm: "I received a great deal of attention, a situation not enjoyed by all of my colleagues." The completers described their advisers as having been "dedicated" and "devoted" to getting them through their programs and in helping them negotiate the job market. A few commented about how their advisers promoted them at conferences and noted that their advisers' interest in them, their research, and careers had continued beyond degree completion.

Completers and noncompleters were about equally likely to be somewhat satisfied with their advisers' interest in them for positive and negative reasons (positive reasons: 12 percent, completers, vs. 9 percent, noncompleters; negative reasons: 10 percent, completers, vs. 11 percent, noncompleters). Students who made positive comments wrote that their advisers had been "interested in me and my work," whereas those who made negative comments indicated that their advisers had not been truly interested in them; that the relationship was strained, formal, or declined over time; or that the relationship was not as personal as they would have liked.

Students who were not too satisfied with their advisers felt that their advisers had not been particularly interested in them or their work: "He seemed disinterested"; "He was not much interested in the success or failure of his students." By contrast, students who were not at all satisfied with their advisers felt that their advisers had taken *no* interest in them: "Paid no attention whatever to me"; "Took zero interest in me; made me feel unwelcome"; "Seemed to have no contact or interest in me." A few of these students—both completers and noncompleters—noted that they had been assigned to their adviser.

Professionalism

Slightly less than one-fifth of completers and about one-fourth of noncompleters who were very satisfied with their advisers praised them for being excellent, brilliant, inspiring, and dedicated teachers, researchers, scholars, advisers, and mentors. They described their advisers as not only competent, knowledgeable, and enthusiastic but as highly ranked and active researchers in their fields. They also noted their advisers' excellent skills and integrity. Several completers wrote or implied that their advisers were good role models: "Very willing to help, serious dedication to research, was a very good role model & [model] to what research can be & should be"; "He was committed to teaching, protecting his students, and excellence in research & clerical work."

Students who were somewhat satisfied with their adviser for positive reasons made similar remarks about the quality of their adviser as a teacher, researcher, or scholar. However, over half of these students' remarks were qualified with a "but" statement. More than half of these completers, but none of these noncompleters, had negative things to say about their advisers' personalities, while roughly an equal number of completers and noncompleters complained that despite their advisers' brilliance and/or reputation, their advisers had not contributed to their intellectual/professional development or had been inaccessible.

Ten percent of completers and 3 percent of noncompleters who were somewhat satisfied with their adviser cited negative reasons concerning them as teachers, researchers, or scholars, as did 6 percent of completers and 2 percent of noncompleters who were not too satisfied. These students criticized their advisers for not having kept up with current research and methodological approaches, for having been out of touch, and for having shown general incompetence. None of the students who were not at all satisfied with their advisers cited professionalism as a reason.

Personality

Overall, 13 percent of the students were either satisfied or dissatisfied with their advisers because of their advisers' personalities. Approximately 13 percent of completers and noncompleters who were very satisfied with their adviser cited this reason, compared with 20 percent of completers and 16 percent of noncompleters who were not at all satisfied with their adviser.

Students who were very satisfied and those who were somewhat satisfied for positive reasons noted that their adviser had been friendly, caring, kind, honest, moral, nurturing, and easy to talk to. Others simply noted that their adviser had been a "great person" or "personable," or had had a "great personality." One completer went so far as to state, "Exemplary model of scientist and person."

By contrast, students who were somewhat satisfied with their advisers for negative reasons or not too satisfied complained that their advisers had had rough edges to their personalities; that they had been remote, hard to approach, difficult to talk to and work with; and that they had been intimidating or had made the student feel intimidated. Students were who not at all satisfied with their advisers found them to have been abrasive and abusive. Two completers commented that their advisers had belittled students; another wrote that his adviser had been a "hypocrite and a liar."

Advising Style

Although the percentages are small, completers were three times as likely as noncompleters to cite their advisers' advising style—the balance between freedom and guidance—as a reason for their degree of satisfaction (9 percent vs. 3 percent). Overall, 94 percent of these students were "very satisfied" or "somewhat satisfied" with their adviser for positive reasons; the remainder were "somewhat satisfied" for negative reasons.

Students' positive remarks reflect how their advisers scaffolded their development as researchers/scholars. They credited their advisers with having been flexible and having given them the proper amount of freedom and independence to explore their ideas while at the same time having provided appropriate advice and guidance when needed. By contrast, the students who were less than fully satisfied with their advisers criticized them for having been too controlling and not having given them enough independence. One student referred to his adviser as a "slave driver."

Accessibility

Their advisers' accessibility was a greater source of dissatisfaction than satisfaction among the students who commented about it. Indeed, 75 percent of the responses concerning accessibility were negative. Students who were dissatisfied with their adviser repeatedly remarked that their advisers had been too busy in general, or with their own work in particular, and that they (their advisers) had spent very little time interacting with them. Some noted that this lack of availability and involvement with their work either slowed down their progress toward the degree or impeded their completion. One noncompleter who was not at all satisfied with his adviser wrote, "He was too busy—and I didn't matter." By comparison, students who were very satisfied or somewhat satisfied for positive reasons noted that their advisers had been accessible, always available for them, and generous with their time.

In sum, analysis of the students' reasons for their satisfaction or dissatisfaction with their advisers indicates that the one thing that contributed most to these feelings was their adviser's contribution to their intellectual and professional development. Indeed, every type of reason that students gave for their satisfaction or dissatisfaction with their adviser, except personality, was in some way directly related to their adviser's contribution (or lack thereof) to their intellectual and professional development. Students were most satisfied when their advisers had supported and advanced their learning and professional goals and challenged them intellectually; when their advisers had been genuinely interested in them as people and in their ideas and research; when they had been positive role models of competent, enthusiastic, and inspiring teachers, researchers, and scholars who were actively engaged in the discipline; when they had been flexible and able to scaffold students' learning and research by providing the proper amounts of freedom and guidance; and when they had been readily accessible. By contrast, students were dissatisfied with their advisers when their advisers had come across as uninformed and uninterested in helping them through their programs and in achieving their professional goals; when their advisers had taken little or no interest in them as people or in their ideas and research; when they had been out of touch with the current research and methods of their fields or displayed general incompetence; when they had controlled them and had not given them enough independence or advice; and when they had been too busy to interact with them.

CONCLUSION

Whether graduate students have a positive and successful graduate school experience (and sometimes even a successful professional career) is in large part determined by the quality of the relationship they have with their adviser. The quality of this relationship is influenced by two main factors: method of adviser selection and adviser type.

Like so many other components of graduate education, access to advising is not distributed equally to all students. Some students do not have advisers; others are assigned to advisers with whom they have not established a relationship and with whom they may have little, if anything, in common; while others select or are selected by an adviser with whom they have common interests and some type of interpersonal relationship. Students who work with advisers by mutual choice are more likely to get the advice and guidance they need to progress smoothly through their programs and into their careers, to be academically and socially integrated with their adviser, to be very satisfied with the relationship, and to complete the Ph.D. than students who have little or no say in the matter.

Contrary to Benkin (1984; see also Dolph, 1983), who found that Ph.D.'s were more satisfied with their relationship with their advisers than ABDs (all but dissertation) and who posits that this difference in satisfaction derives from differences in the way faculty treat students based on a subjective assessment of student quality (basically a Pygmalion effect; see Rosenthal & Jacobson, 1968), evidence from the survey and interview data suggests that noncompleters and at-risk completers are more likely to work with low producers than completers and on-track completers. And, as we have seen, low producers are less forthcoming with information and advice, less academically and socially engaged with their students, less engaged in department activities, and less engaged in cutting-edge research than high producers. Thus, the nature and quality of noncompleters' and at-risk completers' interactions with their advisers, and, consequently, their fates in graduate school and the labor market, may be different than those of completers and on-track completers because they are interacting with different types of advisers.

NOTES

1. *Adviser* was defined in the survey as "the person most responsible for guiding you through your graduate work." Students were asked to respond in terms of their *last* adviser to control for the possibility that some students had more than one adviser during the course of their graduate career and because the last adviser should be more influential in getting a student through his/her program than prior ones.

2. Tony mentioned his adviser by name, so it was possible to look up his adviser's productivity in the data complied from *Dissertation Abstracts International* on the number of dissertations chaired per faculty member between 1987 and 1994. Tony's adviser was in the top half of the department in terms of Ph.D. productivity.

3. Although these phenomena are real, the faculty in this sample were purposively selected by their chairs, so for a variety of reasons, the chairs may not have selected faculty who engage in such practices. In addition, the faculty themselves are unlikely to admit it.

4. Joint authorship appears to be almost standard operating procedure in chemistry and psychology. Most of these faculty said they did almost all their publishing with their students. Sociology faculty did a fair amount of publishing with their students, while mathematics, economics, and humanities faculty rarely or never did.

5. Loose or weak ties are formal, professional relationships. In a job search, loose ties offer job seekers a chance to contact someone of rank outside the status range of their social network. Strong ties are informal, intimate social relationships. They offer job seekers the opportunity to contact persons of higher prestige within their social network (Granovetter, 1973).

6. High producers were more likely than low producers to be the recipients of large grants and to be more productive and acclaimed in their disciplines than low producers. Consequently, they were also out of town more often than low producers.

7. The high producers estimated that they produced more than twice as many Ph.D.'s as low producers (39 vs. 17). Data compiled from *Dissertation Abstract International* on numbers of Ph.D.'s produced by the faculty in the sample from 1987 to 1994 confirm the high producers to be more productive than low producers.

8. Dolph (1983) found a similar degree of satisfaction among the completers and noncompleters in his sample of educational administration doctoral students at Georgia State University: 69 percent of the completers felt their relationship with their adviser was "totally favorable," compared with 37 percent of the noncompleters.

9. Crosstabs, which controlled for status, were run in SPSS for satisfaction rating by case identification number. The open-ended responses, which were sorted by status and case identification number, were then matched with the SPSS output, coded with the satisfaction ratings, and entered into NUD*IST for sorting by status and level of satisfaction. No coding or sorting was done by completer type or gender. However, using the student's case identification number, the gender of a student was occasionally looked up so that the proper pronoun could be ascribed when quoting a student directly. Not all students who gave a rating provided a reason, and it appears that some students gave reasons without giving a rating.

10. Students' satisfaction with their adviser correlates .67 with the degree of interest they felt their adviser took in them as people, .75 with the degree of interest they felt their adviser took in their research and ideas, and .76 with the degree of interest they felt their adviser took in their professional development.

Chapter 8

The Decision to Leave

The decision to leave a Ph.D. program is not a casual one or one made overnight. Yet, little is really known about the decision-making process. Few studies have asked the departers, the actors themselves, why they abandoned their programs, and most of those that have have been institutional self-study projects sponsored by the universities from which the students departed. Most of these studies provide students with only forced-choice response options, thereby limiting the field of possibilities.[1]

This chapter focuses on what made students consider leaving their programs and on their actual attrition decisions, the types of people students turned to for support and advice during the decision-making process, and the type of support and advice they received. It concludes with interviewees' policy-relevant views on what could have made their graduate experience better and prevented them from leaving, and what could be done to improve the experience for others.

FIRST THOUGHTS ABOUT LEAVING

In an effort to discern critical periods in the attrition process, the interviewees were asked when they first started to think about leaving. Different patterns emerge for students who persisted for different amounts of time, but the pattern does not fit neatly into the three-stage model. Rather, patterns emerge for students who left after one term, one or two years, three to five years, and seven years.

Students who left after the first term started to think about leaving within the first couple of months. However, they did not make the final decision until the very end of the term. Most students who left after one year first began

166

thinking about leaving in the middle of the second term, and most who left after two years first entertained thoughts about leaving early in the second year. These students' thoughts about leaving were triggered by negative experiences in the academic domain. By contrast, many of the students who persisted for three to five years (including some who failed qualifying exams) had considered leaving one or more years before they actually departed. They persisted because they saw no alternative to the path they were on—"you feel like you're stuck." Finally, the students who left after seven years first started to think about leaving during their sixth year when their time to completion started to become an issue for them.

REASONS FOR LEAVING

The noncompleter survey contained three separate questions that asked the students whether they left for academic, financial, or personal reasons. Students who responded affirmatively were then asked how strongly a series of factors in those categories affected their decision to leave. These forced-choice questions were followed by a request to state in their own words the most important reason for leaving. At-risk completers were not asked the yes/no questions but were asked how strongly the same series of factors had affected their thoughts about leaving.[2] The interviewees were asked why they left their university without completing their degrees and what had been the deciding factor. The interview data were analyzed with respect to duration and the order in which the reason was given. Order was included based on the assumption that the higher up in a student's response sequence the reason was given, the more salient the reason was.

Overall Results

Both the survey and interview data show that when students leave, it is usually not for a single reason but for a constellation of reasons. In fact, of the noncompleters who responded to the yes/no questions,[3] 26 percent responded affirmatively to both academic and personal reasons for leaving, 20 percent to both personal and financial reasons, 10 percent to both academic and financial reasons, and 7 percent to all three reasons. The twenty-eight interviewees for whom responses were available[4] gave a total of sixty-two different reasons for leaving.[5] Most gave two to three reasons, and a few gave up to six.

Contrary to popular assumptions that students leave primarily for financial reasons or because they are not doing well academically, the survey results show that more students leave for personal reasons than for any other reason. All told, over two-thirds (70 percent) of the noncompleters cited personal reasons for their attrition, while less than half (42 percent) cited academic reasons, and less than a third (29 percent) cited financial reasons.[6] The interview data follow a slightly different pattern, mainly because of a change in the way the interview responses were categorized: Items categorized as "personal" reasons in the survey (e.g., too much work, burned out, too much stress/pressure) were reclassified as "academic" reasons because the noncompleter's open-ended responses on these issues made it clear that they are rooted in the academic domain. Thus, of the sixty-two reasons given by the interviewees, 53 percent were classified as academic, 21 percent as personal, and 25 percent as financial. The financial category in the interview data was subdivided into career-related reasons (19 percent) or purely financial reasons (6 percent). This low percentage for financial reasons further supports the contention that finances in and of themselves are not the most important factors in students' attrition decisions.

A few gender and institutional effects were noted among noncompleters in the survey sample. More men left for academic reasons than women (57 percent vs. 43 percent). This result is consistent with men reporting lower undergraduate and graduate GPAs than women, regardless of status. Almost three times as many Urban students left for financial reasons as Rural students (73 percent vs. 27 percent). This is consistent with Urban admitting more students without support than Rural.

Academic Reasons

Table 8.1 shows the relative importance of the academic factors on noncompleters' decisions to leave and on at-risk completers' thoughts of leaving. Noncompleters and at-risk completers were very similar in the importance played by academic reasons in their leaving. However, each reason was of slightly more importance to noncompleters than to at-risk completers.

Academic reasons for leaving appear to fall into four distinct categories by salience. The first category focuses on dissatisfaction with the academic environment (dissatisfaction with program of study, dissatisfaction with the faculty in your department, dissatisfaction with your adviser). The second category contains a single item focusing on lack of or loss of interest in the discipline. The third category contains items related to unsatisfactory academic performance or academic failure (did not pass qualifying exams, did not maintain satisfactory GPA, faculty or adviser advised you to leave). Finally, the fourth factor involves the loss of one's adviser.

Two things are noteworthy about these results. First, when faculty and directors of graduate study (DGSs) were asked why graduate students leave

Table 8.1. How Strongly[1] Various Academic Reasons Affected Students' Decision to Leave/Thoughts about Leaving

	Means	
	Noncompleters	*At-risk Completers*
Dissatisfaction with your program of study	2.78	2.22
Dissatisfaction with the faculty in your department	2.40	2.20
Dissatisfaction with your adviser	2.16	2.07
Not interested enough in your discipline to continue	2.11	1.70
Did not pass qualifying exams	1.68	1.25
Did not maintain satisfactory GPA	1.62	1.17
Faculty or adviser advised you to leave	1.56	1.23
Adviser left or died	1.27	1.25

[1] 4-point scale: 1 = *not strongly at all* to 4 = *very strongly.*

without completing their degrees, one of the most common responses was loss of interest in the discipline (see chapter 2). Although this appears to be a factor in some decisions, it is not among those cited by students as most important. In fact, the most important academic reasons cited by the students—dissatisfaction with program, faculty, and adviser—were never mentioned by the faculty or DGSs. These differences reveal a large discrepancy between the factors surrounding actual attrition decisions and faculty's beliefs about the causes.

Second, by common lore, students who leave are viewed as less academically able than those who complete, yet academic failure and unsatisfactory performance rate among the least important academic reasons for leaving. In fact, only five noncompleters indicated that failure to maintain a satisfactory GPA was a very important factor in their leaving, and only nine indicated that failing qualifying exams was a very important factor. Thus, academic failure is not a tenable explanation for the magnitude of graduate student attrition that exists.

Noncompleter's duration is affected by the ordeal of graduate education. The more strongly the volume of work influenced their attrition decisions, the faster they left; and the longer they persisted, the more strongly burnout influenced students' decisions.[7] This latter finding suggests that students endeavor to complete until they simply cannot take the pressures of graduate student life anymore.

Academic reasons represent over half the reasons for leaving given by the interviewees. More than half the students (fifteen) gave an academic reason as their first, most salient reason. The thirty-three academic reasons given fall into nine categories, and there is variation in the categories by duration. Interviewees in stage 1 gave seven types of academic reasons (integration, ordeal, loss of interest, time to degree, academic performance, adviser left, inappropriate fit); those in stage 2 gave four types of reasons (integration, ordeal, academic performance, anomie); and those in stage 3 gave two types of reasons (academic performance, professional development undermined). The following analysis begins with categories that cut across stages and assesses differences by duration, and it ends with reasons that are distinctive to stage 1.

Academic Performance

Academic performance is the only academic reason for leaving that cuts across all three stages. When it was given as a reason, it was often the first (and sometimes only) reason. Failure to meet a performance standard prevented most of the students who cited it from advancing to the next stage or to completion. Although most people's first reaction to this reason would be to assume that the student did not have the ability to meet the standard, a deeper look at why some students failed suggests that the student was not always fully culpable. Rather, according to the students, failure to meet the standard was sometimes the result of poor advising, the structure of the program, or malice.

Of the students who left after one year, one student, John, would have been on academic probation had he continued. However, his poor performance resulted from having been allowed to take five courses a term and hold a part-time job as well. The situation of Katie, who was not admitted to the Ph.D. program, is less clear. However, she was so lacking in integration that she may not have received all the tacit information necessary to meet the department's standards, and she was one of the two interviewees who claimed not to have had an adviser.

Three of the four students in stage 2 who cited academic performance had failed their qualifying examinations. In at least two cases, the students were set up to fail, one by the structure of the program and the examination system, the other by the faculty.

Philip was in a weed-out program that, at the time he was enrolled, set the criteria for passing the exam so high that less than half the students passed. In addition, the courses necessary to pass the exam were taught by different faculty with different approaches to the discipline, and no attempt was made to coordinate a common course of study. According to Philip, passing the exam was often contingent on who was on the exam committee and whether the student had taken the requisite courses with them—something that could not be known several years in advance of the exam when the student was selecting courses.

Ashley, by contrast, was told in advance that if he did not pass his exam the first time, he should withdraw. When asked why he was not given the opportunity to take the exam a second time, he replied:

> Well, I'm not sure exactly what the circumstances were . . . I can tell you vaguely. This is all kind of absurd, but the director of the graduate program was having an affair with one of the graduate students, and I happened to know about it—not that I cared. And I think he was terrified that I might get mad or something and tell his wife. So he was sort of eager to get rid of me, I guess. I didn't know that until the person who failed me in the topic exam, after I confronted him with the idea that the whole topic exams were ridiculous and they didn't even ask me any questions—well, they actually did ask me one question on the application which I answered, and they said, "Oh, no, that's not right," and then we had about a twenty-minute argument about it until they agreed that I was right, and they really didn't understand it well enough to even discuss the most elementary parts of the subject. So when I confronted him with that, when I talked to him about it afterward, I said this whole exam is a joke. He essentially said that the graduate adviser had encouraged them to get rid of me.

Hugh was the third student who had not passed qualifying exams. He had been a graduate student in English who waited until the last possible testing period to take the exam—three years after completing course work—so that he could read all three hundred books on the exam reading list. He failed the exam by one point, and the exam committee would not reconsider the exam or let him retake the only section he had not passed. While failing by one point is clearly not a stellar performance, in a subjective discipline like English, neither does one point represent a monumental failure. The faculty may have been sending Hugh an unsubtle message expressing disapproval of his three-year hiatus from the program.

Finally, the fourth student in stage 2 who cited academic performance as an important factor was Brent. He had been unhappy with his performance in his classes, because, in his words, "I wasn't able to devote enough time to them." According to Brent, instead of spending twenty hours a week on his research assistantship, he was putting in forty to sixty hours.

Only two students who reached stage 3 had left for reasons related to academic performance. Neither, in their opinion, had been making satisfactory progress with their research. One could not get his experimental equipment to work properly; the other "wasn't getting anywhere." After seven years, both decided it was time to leave and do something else.

Integration

Reasons associated with integration (or lack thereof) were mentioned by students who left during stage 1 and stage 2. Regardless of stage, their reasons reveal a lack of integration in one or more domains: the departmental environment, the program, faculty, and graduate students. Students who mentioned the department's environment expressed dissatisfaction with the general atmosphere. These students found either the environment distasteful or the atmosphere uncomfortable. Either way, they did not feel that they fit in and did not want to conform to the prevailing departmental personae. Students who expressed dissatisfaction with the program essentially had put forward a referendum on the faculty on the grounds of insufficient intellectual support and incompetent teaching. Furthermore, the faculty's general attitude had caused them to become dissatisfied with their programs of study and their classes.

Finally, a number of interviewees were dissatisfied with the quality of their interactions with faculty and graduate students. Some were bothered by their lack of compassion toward them as individuals or to the world outside the department. Implicit here is a criticism of many faculty's and graduate students' single-minded devotion to the discipline to the exclusion of all else — something commented on by several students throughout their interviews.

By contrast, interviewees who had tried to devote themselves to their studies to the exclusion of all else (i.e., had become overly academically integrated) ended up experiencing anomie, a sense of detachment or normlessness. Charlie, who transferred to another university after two years, was one such student. He said, "I had a sense that I was becoming very distant from the rest of the working world and society. I felt what I was studying, devoting all my waking hours to, was somehow only of concern to a very, very small subset in society."

Ordeal

Several students in stages 1 and 2 provided reasons for leaving that evoke a view of graduate education as a painful, joyless ordeal that they were unable or unwilling to endure for very long. Some saw the pursuit of the Ph.D. as jumping through hoops, putting up with obstacles, and having to do things that were irrelevant to the program (see Hawley, 1993; Kerlin, 1995). Others found the experience too hard and lacking in fun, joy, and excitement. Without exception, they concluded that the ultimate outcome, the Ph.D., was not worth the personal and psychic costs of pursuing it.

Other Stage 1 Reasons

At least two students cited loss of interest in their discipline, time-to-degree concerns, and their adviser leaving as reasons for their attrition. As indicated earlier, loss of interest in the discipline is not as salient a reason for attrition as faculty believe, and loss of interest tends to mask other problems. Ellen was in a program with the wrong emphasis relative to her interests, and her loss of interest was, in part, a function of lack of fit. Although Stuart left because his field no longer excited him the way it once did, earlier in the interview he mentioned being disappointed by his adviser's lack of interest in him and his work and how greater interest by his adviser might have made a difference.

Time-to-degree concerns were never cited as the primary reason for attrition. Rather, they interacted with students' general discontent with, and lack of integration in, their programs. Students' pervasive unhappiness caused them to be disturbed by how long it could take them to complete their degrees and free themselves from the source of their displeasure. With no end in sight, time-to-degree became a weighted variable in their subjective cost/benefit analyses and influenced their decisions to cut their losses.

Finally, two interviewees left because their advisers left. While this is clearly beyond the control of the university, it does affect students' lives and careers. Melanie withdrew completely. Gerald transferred to continue working with his adviser and completed the Ph.D., but the upheaval cost him extra time.

Personal Reasons

Table 8.2 shows the relative importance of various personal factors on noncompleters' decisions to leave and on at-risk completers' thoughts of leaving. The factors fall into four relatively distinct (but nonparallel) categories. The first category (realized you were doing the wrong thing with your life and lack of proper motivation) emphasizes the inappropriateness of the program/graduate school for some students. This factor was the primary personal factor for noncompleters, but the secondary personal factor for at-risk

Table 8.2. How Strongly[1] Various Personal Reasons Affected Students' Decision to Leave/Thoughts about Leaving

	Means	
	Noncompleters	*At-risk Completers*
Realized you were doing the wrong thing with your life	2.70	1.82
Lack of proper motivation	2.53	1.91
Too much stress or pressure	2.26	2.48
Burned out	2.21	2.37
Too much work	1.77	2.01
Family pressures	1.57	1.51
Wanted/started a family	1.55	1.33
Illness or health problems	1.33	1.29

[1] 4-point scale: 1 = *not strongly at all* to 4 = *very strongly.*

completers. The second category (too much stress or pressure, burned out, too much work) is really an academic factor, emphasizing the ordeal of graduate school and its toll on students. This factor was of secondary importance to noncompleters but of primary importance to at-risk completers. The third category focuses on family factors (family pressures and wanted/started a family). This factor was of tertiary importance to both noncompleters and at-risk completers. Finally, illness or health problems were the least important reasons for both groups.

The interview data indicate that personal reasons (exclusive of stress, burnout, and too much work) affected students' decisions to leave primarily in the first two stages of doctoral study, and they exerted the most influence in the first year. The survey data support this finding for most of the personal factors. It may be that students of longer duration, who are also more integrated, have found ways to cope with personal issues and problems that students of shorter duration have not.[8]

Interviewees' decisions to leave at the end of stage 1 were influenced by factors external to the university (physical and mental/emotional health problems, and relationships), while the decisions of those who left during stage 2 were influenced by relationships. Physical health reasons were limited to an injury that occurred during the academic year and interfered (in the students' opinion) with their achieving to their fullest. Mental/emotional health reasons included an increase in depression as well as clinical episodes. Finally, relationships, usually with another graduate student, tended to push or pull students away from their programs. A breakup for females and an ongoing but unsatisfactory relationship for males tended to push them out of their programs. Marriage or a current boyfriend leaving the area pulled females away.

Financial Reasons

Table 8.3 shows the relative importance of various financial factors on noncompleters' decisions to leave and on at-risk completers' thoughts about leaving. The importance of factors to at-risk completers parallels that of noncompleters, with each factor being more important to noncompleters than at-risk completers. The fact that "unable to meet expenses" had the highest mean for all reasons for leaving across types of reasons is consistent with the fact that noncompleters were much less likely than completers to have received financial support (see chapter 5). In addition, the higher salience of poor future job prospects to noncompleters than to at-risk completers is consistent with noncompleters' greater propensity to go to graduate school because job prospects at time of entry were poor (Lovitts, 1997). This suggests that noncompleters may be more sensitive to, or more realistic about, the state of the job market than completers.

Table 8.3. How Strongly[1] Various Financial Reasons Affected Students' Decision to Leave/Thoughts about Leaving

	Means	
	Noncompleters	*At-risk Completers*
Unable to meet expenses	3.09	1.75
Prospects for future employment were not encouraging	2.51	1.73
Received a good job offer	1.85	1.43
Lost financial assistance	1.82	1.31
Spouse or significant other got a job	1.35	1.26

[1] 4-point scale: 1 = *not strongly at all* to 4 = *very strongly.*

Losing financial support was a more important factor in Rural students' than in Urban students' decisions to leave. This suggests that while Rural University may have used TAs and RAs to entice students to come, it did not maintain that support. In fact, only Rural interviewees mentioned losing support. By contrast, Urban at-risk completers were more influenced by their inability to meet expenses than were Rural at-risk completers, which, as discussed earlier, is consistent with Urban's higher tuition, its distribution of support, and the cost of living in Urban City.

The interview data show that when finances influence students' decisions to leave, its impact is greatest either very early or very late in graduate programs. The survey data do not support this finding,[9] but they do show that students who left for financial reasons persisted almost a year longer than those who left for other reasons (3.4 years vs. 2.6 years).[10] Interviewees who left after one year either entered without support or lost it. Those who left during stage 3 either did not receive dissertation support or had their funding run out.

Career-related reasons for leaving in the interview data follow a pattern similar to that of financial reasons; that is, they are most salient at the early and late stages of doctoral study. Students who left after one year gave three different types of career-related reasons for leaving: the need for a career with more financial security (cited by history students only), a change in career plans, and frustration with the job market. Change in career plans was never the first reason for leaving given by any student. Indeed, most of those who changed their career plans did so because of disappointment or disillusionment with their graduate programs and a lack of integration in them. By contrast, two interviewees in stage 3 gave the same type of career-related reason. Both were pulled into nonacademic careers, one before starting the dissertation, the other while working on it. These students also had concerns about their prospects in the academic job market. Indeed, noncompleters in the survey sample whose attrition decisions were very strongly affected by a good job offer persisted for an average of 4.7 years, suggesting that they were in stage 3 when they left and that their attrition was more a function of pull than push.

The Most Important Reason for Leaving

The forced-choice questions about reasons for leaving in the noncompleter survey were followed up with an open-ended question that asked the non-completers to state, in their own words, the most important reason for their leaving. A little more than half the noncompleters (61 percent) provided a written response. Although the interviewees were asked what clinched their decision to leave, the analysis here is limited to the survey responses because the interviewees are a subset of the noncompleters, and their (anonymous) written responses were easily matched with their verbal reports.

The students' open-ended responses were categorized using the same basic classification scheme as the survey with the following exceptions: As explained earlier, responses related to pressure, stress, and burnout were categorized as academic reasons. A few categories (integration, ordeal, transferred, children, and relationship related) were added to capture reasons not otherwise contained in the survey.

Despite the fact that students were asked to state the most important reason for their leaving, many gave more than one reason. Students' inability to cite a single reason supports the contention that attrition is brought about by a constellation of factors. In most instances, the first reason given was used to classify students into categories, but this was often contingent on the context of their other comments. Moreover, even when students were "cleanly" classified into a particular category, the extended response indicated that the primary reason was influenced strongly by a secondary reason that was often related to lack of integration. For example, this reason was classified as personal: "If I had been happy with my adviser, I would not have let the personal reasons make me leave."

Table 8.4 presents the frequency of students responses by category. Almost half the students left for academic reasons. About one-fifth left for either personal or financial reasons. A few students left for reasons classified as "miscellaneous." To shed new light on and obtain new insights into the factors that contribute most to attrition, the following discussion highlights only factors and issues not already addressed.

Academic Reasons

More students left their programs for integration-related reasons than for any other reason. Many found the environment too competitive or felt they did not receive adequate support, encouragement, or guidance. Some experienced discrimination based on religion, race/ethnicity, gender (including white

Table 8.4.   Most Important Reason for Leaving without Completing the Ph.D.

Reasons	Number of Students
Academic reasons	
Integration	26
Academic failure	21
Adviser left or died	8
Transferred	8
Problems with adviser	7
Lost interest	6
Dissatisfied with faculty	6
Dissatisfied with program	3
Total academic reasons	85
	49%
Personal reasons	
Wrong thing with life	18
Relationship-related	10
Children	5
Illness or injury	4
Family pressures	2
Lack of motivation	2
Total personal reasons	41
	23%
Financial reasons	
Got a job	13
Unable to meet expenses	11
Lost support	4
Job prospects not good	3
Spouse's job	3
Total financial reasons	34
	19%
Miscellaneous reasons	15
	9%
Total	175
	100%

males), sexual orientation, and marital status: "There was a strong feeling that married women students had to choose between their studies or their spouses. . . . My adviser . . . told me I had to decide between literature & my husband." The discrimination made them feel like they did not fit in or did not belong.

Feeling isolated was among the most frequently cited integration-related reasons. Several students actually used the term *isolated;* others wrote about the "lack of cohesion" in their department, having "too little contact" with faculty and graduate students, "too little contact" with people outside the departmental community (anomie), and being unable to cope with the "social deprivation." In the extreme, lack of integration in graduate school can lead not only to attrition but also to suicide, the act around which Durkheim's (1897/1951) theory of integration was developed.

> Isolation, little support in program, lack of inflated ego (essential in [my discipline]) all seemed to play a part in decline in my mental health. I developed depression & made 3 suicide attempts in second year, the last try landing me in the hospital. I was put on medical leave from the university.

Most of the students who cited academic failure were not making satisfactory progress in their programs or with their dissertations, or were denied admission to the Ph.D. program. Some of the predissertation students attributed their poor performance to dissatisfaction with their programs and lack of solid information on the requirements. Among those students who failed their qualifying exams, some commented that they had received little or no support or assistance from their adviser or the faculty in preparing for the exams. One student was overly integrated:

> Obsessing with perfection and unable to achieve closure on papers, I had many incompletes. I decided I was pouring my effort down a rat hole and that I would rather wrestle with creative writing than with academic writing.

Several of the students whose advisers had left the university and who had not gone with them were unable to find another professor who was willing to take them on as an advisee or who shared their interests. However, those who had followed their advisers completed their degrees at the new university.

Finally, several students transferred universities or entered professional programs in law or medicine. Many of the students who changed programs transferred to their first-choice institutions.[11]

Personal Reasons

Students who left because they had felt they were doing the wrong thing with their lives left for three primary reasons: They felt that they had been too young and immature when they entered graduate school and lacked sufficient life experience to make a commitment to their programs, they changed their career plans, or they decided the academic lifestyle was not for them. The latter two reasons raise the questions, What caused these students to change their career plans? and Why did they decide that the academic lifestyle was not for them? In other words, what transpired after they enrolled in graduate school to bring about these changes?

In addition to getting married or having a fiancé(e) or significant other who left or lived out of the area, getting a divorce was also a factor in attrition, principally because it interacted with the ordeal of graduate school: "I got divorced in my second year of grad school and could not handle the stress of grad school and divorce at the same time."

The five students who cited "children" as a factor in their decision to leave appear to be women: One had an unexpected pregnancy, took a leave of absence and intended to return, but never did; another with a new baby found that it was too difficult to continue full-time, switched to part-time, but realized she was not making adequate academic progress. The other three wanted to be "good mothers" and devote more time to their children.

Financial Reasons

Having a job or getting a great job offer caused a number of students to leave their programs. Most appear to have taken jobs in their fields; several took high school teaching jobs. Unfortunately, it is not possible to determine at what stage these students left their programs, although (based on the interview data) it seems that students in the early stages took jobs because of financial pressures, while students at the dissertation stage took jobs in their fields with the intention of completing but simply never did.

Students who were unable to meet expenses either entered without support or lost it. Some felt pressured by the size of the loans they had acquired first as undergraduates and then as graduate students. However, the following quote shows the lengths that some students will go to to get (or try to get) the Ph.D., combined with the lack of support they receive from faculty for their efforts: "Lack of funding & the corresponding stress of working 2 jobs & having faculty complain one is not 'serious' about their academics if working externally to the program."

Miscellaneous Reasons

Two students said that changes in departmental requirements had made it difficult for them to continue. One student realized that he had chosen the wrong graduate school. One student of unknown gender was unable to deal properly with his or her sexual orientation, and another student had had an "involvement" with a faculty member that, combined with feelings of inadequacy caused by the involvement, made it uncomfortable for her to continue.

SOURCES OF SUPPORT AND ADVICE

To discern who students turn to during the decision-making process, the noncompleters and at-risk completers were asked who they discussed their thoughts about leaving with. The question was asked with the expectation that such knowledge would yield information of value in intervening in students' attrition decisions.

Overall, 92 percent of the noncompleters and 96 percent of the at-risk completers discussed their leaving with someone. In descending order of frequency, these people were friends and family, departmental faculty, and professionals outside the departmental community.

Urban noncompleters were more than twice as likely to talk with a psychological counselor as Rural noncompleters (70 percent vs. 30 percent). This difference is consistent with Urban providing a less integrated, more stressful environment. Three times as many female noncompleters talked with a psychological counselor as males noncompleters (75 percent vs. 25 percent). By contrast, male noncompleters were almost three times as likely as female noncompleters not to discuss their thoughts of leaving with anyone (74 percent vs. 27 percent). This finding is consistent with the interview data, which show that men are more likely than women simply to announce that they are leaving after they have made the decision.

At-risk completers at Rural were far more likely to discuss their thoughts about leaving with their adviser, with other faculty, and with other graduate students than at-risk completers at Urban.[12] These university differences are consistent with data that show that Rural is a more integrated university than Urban and that Rural students were closer to members of the departmental community than Urban students. Finally, almost three-quarters (74 percent) of the male at-risk completers and less than one-third (28 percent) of the female ones discussed their thoughts about leaving with their adviser. This difference is consistent with data presented in chapter 7, which showed that men felt their advisers took more personal and professional interest in them than women did.

The interview data provide deeper insight into the decision-making process, the support system available to students, and the type of advice departing students receive when they share their thoughts about leaving.

Family and friends were used as sounding boards. They provided students the opportunity to think things out as well as understanding, encouragement, and support. No family member was reported to have tried to dissuade a student from leaving. Other graduate students functioned in much the same way. Laboratory mates encouraged Cade, a dissertator, to stay because he was the only one in a position to solve a particular problem. By contrast, Boyd's attempts to share his thoughts about leaving with other graduate students was met with noncomprehension and defensiveness to the point where he just stopped trying to discuss it with them.

Students often seek out professors' advice about academic- and careers-related matters. For this reason, they are in the best position to counsel and intervene in students' attrition decisions. Consequently, a deeper analysis was conducted of the interviewees' interactions with advisers and faculty concerning their departure. The analysis included looking at duration, the method of adviser selection (assigned, not assigned), the type of responses students received, gender, and whether the student talked with faculty before or after the final decision was made.

Interviewees who selected an adviser on the basis of shared interests were more likely to inform their adviser after the fact than before, although students who selected an adviser for other reasons were equally likely to talk to them in either time frame. Students who were assigned to advisers were more likely to talk to another faculty member than to talk to their adviser, probably because these students do not have a relationship with their advisers. This finding may also help explain why professors underestimate their own and their department's attrition rate.

Students who spoke with their advisers before making the final decision found their advisers understanding, supportive, and sometimes even helpful with getting the necessary paperwork in order. However, understanding sometimes took the form of the adviser simply shrugging his shoulders and saying, "Well, I can't argue with your decision." No adviser was reported to have tried dissuading a student. Faculty with whom students discussed leaving before making the decision were described as ranging from helpful and encouraging to cold and lacking in concern. In two instances, faculty encouraged students to stay: one told a male student that he did not think leaving was a good idea because he thought the student was good enough to make it; the other offered to let a female student into a different Ph.D. program in the department and provide financial support.

Students who informed their advisers after they had already made the decision said that their advisers accepted the decision. However, the advisers of students in stage 3 seemed to show more interest and engage in more follow-up discussions than did the advisers of students who left at earlier stages. Students who simply informed a faculty member that they were leaving reported reactions that ranged from understanding and helpful to cold and disinterested. Overall, the modal response to student's decision to leave was to be supportive and say, "Do what's best for you."

Men were twice as likely as women to make the decision independently and then inform their adviser or another professor that they were leaving. Women, by contrast, were twice as likely as men to discuss their thoughts about leaving with their adviser or another professor before making the final decision. This finding is not trivial. It represents an opportunity for professors to intervene in female students' attrition decisions. Indeed, when women share their thoughts about leaving with professors, they may really be seeking support and encouragement to stay. Thus, when professors nod their heads and agree with all the reasons women proffer for why they think they should leave—reasons that may simply be masking self-doubt or a lack of self-confidence—the professors may be missing an opportunity to provide women with the support and encouragement they are really seeking. Such support might have kept Elinor and Emmie in their programs. Elinor discussed her thoughts about leaving with a professor. Emmie did not discuss her leaving with faculty because she was intimidated by them but felt that they should have taken more interest in her departure.

Elinor: Well, everyone essentially told me to just follow my gut instinct. No one really dissuaded me and said you are destined for an academic career. . . . Everyone just said, "Well, you are old enough to make a decision of this nature, and you have to decide what it is that you wish to do with your life." And I thought about it long and hard. I mean, it's not something that I sort of decided from one day to the next. It took me a good six months to make that decision.

Emmie: I didn't feel that the university felt any sense of my loss, of me being lost. There was no sense that, "Gee, Emmie, we really want you to stay, and you're really important, and you have a lot to contribute to this institution and to the whole field of social science. Maybe some research concept that you come up with could be important." But, I mean, nothing like that. You know, it's like, "Too bad. You're gone!"

To understand the factors that contributed to at-risk completers' decisions to stick with their programs, the survey asked them who had the greatest impact on their decision to continue. Table 8.5 shows the sources of influence in declining order of importance. What is most noteworthy about the sources is that "Other" was the most frequently selected category. Analysis of the open-ended responses to "Other" reveals that 83 percent of those who selected "Other" referred to themselves (e.g., me, self, myself). Extended responses to "Other" emphasized these students' personal motivation and determination to complete, their resignation that they were too far along to "bail out," and their desire not to be a "quitter."

From a policy perspective, it would be difficult if not impossible to intervene in students' discussions with family and friends. However, to the extent that students talk to their advisers, departmental faculty, and university administrators, these people could be trained to discuss students' concerns with them in a more appropriate manner than currently appears to be the case. They need to be

Table 8.5.   People Who Had the Greatest Impact on At-Risk Completers' Decision to Continue

Person	Percent of At-risk Completers
Other	31
Spouse or significant other	19
Adviser	15
Graduate students	10
Friends	8
Parents	6
Other faculty	5
Psychological counselor	5
Undergraduate professor	2
University administrators	1

Note: Percentages do not add to 100 due to rounding.

less quick to say, "That's your decision. Whatever you think is best for you. Good-bye. Good luck," and be more willing to discuss the personal and professional pros and cons of completing and not completing the degree. They could also be trained to help students consider where and how the Ph.D. could be used in the nonacademic world, especially when students are academically able to complete their degree but are discontent with the academic lifestyle.

NONCOMPLETERS' POLICY-RELEVANT VIEWS ON DOCTORAL EDUCATION

A study of the causes of departure from doctoral study—one that ultimately seeks to reduce attrition—would be incomplete if it did not ask the departers for their ideas on how doctoral education could be improved. As departers, the interviewees have privileged insights into those aspects of graduate education that cause students to become discontent and leave. This section thus analyzes interviewees' responses to three policy-relevant questions: (1) What kinds of things could have prevented you from leaving Rural/Urban University? (2) What would have made your experience as a graduate student at Rural/Urban University a better experience? and (3) What could be changed to make it a better experience [for others]? Although, these questions are quite similar, the intent behind them is different, and phrasing similar questions in different ways does yield different responses (Converse & Presser, 1986) and new insights on the issue. Indeed, the same students often provided different types of responses to each question.

What Would Have Made the Experience Better and Prevented Attrition

By asking interviewees what would have made their experience better and what kinds of things could have prevented them from leaving, the interviewees were effectively asked to highlight the weak points in the structure and process of graduate education. Students' responses to these two questions fell into the same basic categories; consequently, analysis of their responses is combined into one discussion.

A small handful of the interviewees believed that nothing could have *kept* them in their programs because they were so dissatisfied with them. By contrast, the three students who said that nothing could be *changed* to make it a better experience did so because they had good experiences. These students include Caroline, who had mental health problems: "There was not a whole lot more they could have done. The professors were understanding"; Gerald, who had followed his adviser to another university: "It was a pretty good experience. I think if our lab did not move, I would have been happier at Rural"; and Tom, whose job subverted his dissertation: "I was very well trained. When people ask me about that versus other programs—I mean, you have to go in understanding that your odds of getting out are lower than if you go to other places—I have no trouble recommending it." Incidentally, Caroline and Gerald were in the same well-integrated department at Rural, which has a very low attrition rate.

The rest of the students' responses fell into five categories: integration, product quality, cognitive map, financial, and personal. All of the categories, except personal, suggest places where universities could make improvements.

Almost half the students asked about what would have made their experience better honed in on various aspects of integration, as did more than a third of the interviewees asked about what could have prevented their attrition. In one way or another, this set of students felt that had they been more integrated in their departments (i.e., if the department and the people with whom they interacted had provided a more integrative environment), their experience would have been better and they would not have left. In particular, the students felt that their experiences would have been better if they had had more interaction with the faculty and/or their adviser and if the faculty or their adviser had been more open, more supportive; given them a little more personal attention; been more sensitive to their interests and career goals; and provided them with appropriate professional socialization experiences. Cathleen highlighted the frustration felt by students when their intellectual development and professional socialization are stymied as well the feelings of isolation that result when academic interaction with faculty is lacking:

Cathleen: I think that being granted that teaching experience in the fourth year [that only involved grading papers]. It's hard to second-guess things, but it seems to me that being granted that responsibility [to actually teach] would have led to closer working with the faculty there in terms of teaching ideas and guidance in the field and being able to bounce that off of undergraduates, and testing your own level and your own ability and your ability to communicate it, and granting relevance to your own pursuit. Something like that that gave a more rewarding aspect to the work you are doing. That you weren't just sitting there and doing it all on your own in the deepest, darkest corner of the library only to emerge finally five years later with a document—which seemed to be the expectation of the place, and that seemed to be the only way anyone finished their dissertation—as opposed to that, being given outlets for engagement and communication, and testing and feeding out and feeding back and whether that be with faculty, on one hand, or with undergraduates, on the other hand, through teaching assistantships and, in the latter case, presenting you with the possibility of income and also experience for your job search in the future.

The interviewees also felt that if the department had been warmer, more sociable and collegial, and less hostile and competitive, they would have been more inclined to stay. In other words, they wanted a greater sense of community and a more integrated environment.

Over a fifth of the students said that their experiences would have been better and that they might have stayed if the quality of the product they went to the university to consume had been better. The faculty, the courses, and the department's requirements all fell short of their expectations. More specifically, the students expected the faculty to have been more professional and interesting and to have been better teachers. They expected their classes to have been more challenging and stimulating. They expected the department's approach to the field to have been more aggressive, and they expected the department to have placed greater emphasis on learning through paper writing rather than on hurdling exams. If these things had been different, the students said that they would have been happier with their education and would have been more inclined to stay.

Many students felt that their experiences would have been better if they had had more and better guidance about the nature of graduate school and the graduate student experience during both their undergraduate and graduate years. Their comments illustrate a lack of understanding of the formal requirements and informal expectations, and they suggest that these deficits could be fixed by making tacit policies and procedures overt through more personal advisement and by increasing the level of integration in the departmental community.

A number of students stated (here and elsewhere in the interview) that they should have gotten better guidance from their undergraduate institutions on how to pick an appropriate program and that the graduate school they attended should have done a better, more personal job of helping them determine whether their programs were best suited to their interests before admitting them. Pauline is illustrative of bad advising at the undergraduate level. Brent, who attended Rural as an undergraduate, is a plea for better screening.

Pauline: The most important thing probably would have been, starting in undergrad, better guidance there in terms of picking my program. I feel some resentment. The people there at [undergraduate school] knew me really well; they knew me very well. And I think they should have probably been able to direct me a little bit more instead of, I think it was almost like I was vicariously fulfilling desires of theirs to go to this hot-shot research program. I think they knew exactly what I wanted to do with my career, and I think that, frankly, they should have given me more guidance in terms of how to pick a program other than go to the most prestigious one you get into.

Brent: It would have been nice if prior to my application, prior to my admission, there had been somebody that I could have talked to that would have told me exactly what that program was like. Ideally that would have been somebody who could evaluate my interest and recommended something else for me to go into— either a different program or a different school. So, I guess I'm not really faulting the program, I am faulting the advisement.

Some students expressed the desire for a better orientation prior to and upon entry. Emmie's response highlights a broad range of things about the graduate school experience that are not transparent to entering students and for which there is need for greater clarity on the part of graduate schools:

Emmie: A better experience, hmm. I think a much more focused orientation on the academic requirements themselves. A real orientation even at the point of application. Even as I was applying to the school, an invitation—"Come on down, talk with our faculty. You're on the list of acceptance now. We want to make sure that this is the right fit for you, too. Don't worry about your being accepted. You're already there, but we want you to feel that this is the right investment of your time and effort and resources." And just really to be demystified, to take off that ideal, "Oh, boy! Wouldn't it be nice to be a professor" type of baloney. What are the nuts and bolts of research and analysis and how to construct a research design, and what are some important themes right now in the social sciences? Where is the leading literature going? What are the hot topics? What are the faculty doing? And to give us a list. Here is what Professor Joe Blow, distinguished lecturer and theorist, [is doing]. This is what he's involved with today. Perhaps biographies of the researchers and professors. Who are they? What have they done? What are they doing today? How many graduate students do they have under their tutelage? What are their graduate students doing? The students who are being advised by them, what are they doing? I think those kinds of connections could have made it a lot more real for me, and [I'd have] been able to say, "Hmm! Okay, this student is doing this research model. That's an interesting idea. Maybe I could talk to her and get some ideas and find out what she is doing." There was none of that kind of transparency. It was like I was not connected to other students; I didn't know who they were, or what their interests were, or what their research concepts were.

Several students felt that their experience would have been better had the program been clearer about its expectations and had they been given more guidance about what to expect.

Interviewer: What would have made your experience as a graduate student at Urban University a better experience?

Solange: I think maybe a little more guidance. It could have come from either older students or just what to expect in terms of some of the trials and tribulations . . . I think I felt like I kind of knew the requirements, but if I knew more of learning the informal things . . . I think having that from an older graduate student would have helped.

Interviewer: What do you mean by the trials and tribulations?

Solange: Not being sure of what's expected of you or feeling like a new person all over again when I didn't really expect that. Feeling like a stranger in a sense. It's being in a new place. I think [it] would be true anywhere.

Interviewer: What kind of informal expectations left you feeling that way?

Solange: Well, things like one of our classes had on its weekly reading list, had like seven books on it that were like two hundred to four hundred pages long. Now you know nobody expects you to read that many books for one class. But if somebody could have said, "Well, if you just pick a couple and get together and everybody take one book or something." Things like that. I guess informal study arrangements. That's what I think probably would have helped.

The students also felt that their chances of staying would have been better had they gotten more guidance from faculty on developing programs of study suited to their interests and career goals. They also desired concrete signs that they were making good progress and that there was an end to the program.

Ellen: Someone catching early on that maybe my path should be a little different in terms of coursework. I probably should have taken, if there was any hope for me to have been successful at all, there should have been a realization up front that I should have taken some, maybe even senior-level, undergraduate theoretical classes. I'd have felt more comfortable with that. That might have helped.

Interviewer: Anything else?

Ellen: Well, there are personal aspects. If someone had taken a more personal interest in me, then not only would either some of my decisions to leave [have] been accelerated, which would have been better, or there would have been even more intervention in terms of focusing, "Gee, what do you really want to do?" and maybe I could have stayed.

Other students said that their experience would have been better had they received more advice and counseling on how to choose an adviser. Some students decided early on that they did not want to pursue an academic career, but they felt they might have stayed to completion had they been provided with information (and encouragement) about alternative careers for people with Ph.D.'s in their disciplines.

Although money and the funding of graduate education are a perennial problem for graduate students and graduate schools, money rated last among changes that would make graduate school a better experience and/or prevent attrition. Only five students said money could have prevented their decision to leave, and it was often secondary to some other cause. Only two students felt that more money would have made their experience better. This lack of emphasis on money reinforces the contention that money simply is not the primary factor influencing attrition decisions. When students are content in their programs and feel they are making good progress toward their goals, they find ways to deal with, or compensate for, low levels of income. It is only when lack of money completely obstructs students' ability to continue that they withdraw for financial reasons.

Finally, personal problems that the student brought with them to the university (emotional/mental health problems, family stresses) or that developed during their tenure (marriage, injury) were the second most frequently mentioned things that could have prevented them from leaving. No student cited the absence of personal problems as a something that would have made their experience better.

What Could Be Changed to Make Graduate School a Better Experience

When asked what could be changed to make graduate school a better experience for others, approximately half of the interviewees' suggestions fell into the integration realm and half into the cognitive map realm. Two said, "Nothing," because they thought the situation was hopeless.

At one level, improving integration-related problems is more difficult than improving cognitive map–related problems because, in some cases, integration problems are a function of personalities. However, integration-related problems are also social problems that can be dealt with by departments by changing their conceptions of how best to interact with and train graduate students. In other words, departments can overcome some personality problems by taking collective responsibility for their graduate students.

The types of integration-related changes needed in departments are captured in the following recommendations from students: "more openness on the part of faculty," "a greater interest in students," and "a greater focus on the individual." What these things mean are subject to interpretation, but given students' repeated pleas for these types of understanding and interaction, faculties need to start exploring these recommendations and start developing ways to address them. The same holds for recommendations to be "more receptive to different kinds of students," to "do something about the competitiveness," and to provide "more professor contact in nonchallenging ways." Melanie suggested ways to commence the reconceptualization and ways to improve relationships. Note her emphasis on greater frequency of interaction:

> *Melanie*: I think encouraging the faculty to look upon a new graduate class as an investment, as part of the department that needs to be mentored along, and really encourage that.
>
> *Interviewer*: How do you think you could get faculty to change in that way?
>
> *Melanie*: I think that a department head has a lot to do with that, and I think that having occasions for faculty and staff and graduate students to interact is very important.

The students' cognitive map–related recommendations were fairly detailed. They focus on the need to clarify prerequisites, better orient students to the intricacies of the program, explain variability in time to degree, and provide more advice and guidance and more background information on the faculty and the relationships among them. The interviewees' comments on these things also include a discussion of feelings that result from a lack of these understandings.

> *Emmie*: Finding out clearly what the student wants to get out the experience. If a student is coming with some very vague ideas, perhaps not to discredit them necessarily but to say, "You know what, here are some ways to help you clarify that. This is some course work that may help you come to some of those ideas. This is some stuff you may need to read." Even if I still hadn't finished the program, I think I would have felt I understood much more of what I was getting into and it's just not working out for me rather than feeling down on myself, which is what I felt. Feeling, senses of inadequacy and, boy, I couldn't cut the mustard. . . . It would have been better to think, "They're going in this direction with this research path; that's not really my particular interests at the time, and I need to go this other way," and not have felt those personal feelings.

CONCLUSION

Although the decision to withdraw from a doctoral program is almost always an individual decision, and although some attrition decisions are clearly appropriate for the student (and the university), many such decisions appear to result from the structure of the program and could have been prevented had circumstances been other than what they were. These decisions include ones shrouded in a lack of integration. They also include ones motivated by the dissonance and unease resulting from a lack understanding of what the program is about (cognitive map of informal expectations) and from the belief that you are the only person in your program who does not understand the inner workings of the program (pluralistic ignorance). To the extent that attrition decisions are embedded in social contexts, the reasons students provide for their departure on forced-choice questionnaires cannot be accepted at face value. The social contexts surrounding and motivating those reasons must be explored.

Almost all the noncompleters (and many of the at-risk completers) discussed their thoughts about leaving with someone. Yet, very few people tried to dissuade them. Consequently, universities inadvertently allow capable students to leave who are merely expressing self-doubt, who are discontent with the academic lifestyle, and who are simply seeking support and advice. Such students might have stayed and completed their degrees had they received proper advice, guidance, and encouragement.

The fact that so many at-risk completers drew on their inner resources to continue suggests that at-risk completers and noncompleters may have different coping strategies and different degrees of resiliency. However, the circumstances surrounding their decisions are not identical. At-risk completers were provided with more structures and opportunities for integration than noncompleters. This means that they had more sources of support in place to sustain them, the presence of which helped give them the inner strength they needed to persist. This difference in the distribution of resources and support structures also points to the need to consider social contexts when assessing differences in outcomes between groups of students.

Finally, the students' policy-relevant views on what could have prevented their attrition, what would have made their graduate school experience a better one, and what could be done to make the experience better for others reinforce the contention that universities and departments need to create more integrative environments and that they need to do a better job of explaining the intricacies of the structure and process of graduate education to prospective, entering, and currently enrolled students.

NOTES

1 One exception is Golde (1994, 1996).

2. Even though the response categories for noncompleters and at-risk completers were identical, the questions leading into them were not (noncompleters: "How strongly did each of the following academic/financial/personal reasons affect your decision to leave?"; at-risk completers: "How strongly did each of the following academic/financial/personal reasons affect your thoughts about leaving?"). Consequently, no statistical tests could be conducted comparing noncompleter responses with at-risk completer responses.

3. Only 65 percent of the noncompleters responded to the yes/no questions.

4. One student's interview did not record, and the second half of another interview was lost when the tape was flipped.

5. Many of the students volunteered reasons for leaving at different points throughout the interview. Only their responses to the direct question about reasons for leaving are included in this analysis.

6. If the yes responses are calculated as a function of *all* noncompleters (i.e., by including nonrespondents), the percentage of noncompleters responding yes to each type of reason is as follows: 18 percent financial reasons, 27 percent academic reasons, 45 percent personal reasons.

7. The B for too much work is $-.60$, $p = .02$. The B for burned out is $.54$, $p < .01$.

8. In a study of field switching among undergraduate science, mathematics, and engineering majors, Hewitt and Seymour (1991) found that the primary difference between switchers and nonswitchers was that nonswitchers had found ways to deal with some of the problems they shared with switchers (e.g., feelings of discouragement and lowered self-esteem). The nonswitchers had learned to tolerate these discomforts, to judge them-

selves less by the letter grade they received and more by their own level of comprehension, and to circumvent competition by group study and mutual support, while many of the switchers sought to struggle alone.

9. Students in the survey sample were categorized into stages as follows: stage 1—duration of one year or less; stage 2—duration of two to three years; stage 3—duration of four or more years. The stage 2 and stage 3 categorizations are not entirely accurate because many students take more than four years to enter stage 3, and some enter sooner. However, the categorizations for the interview data are accurate because I knew whether the interviewee had entered stage 3.

10. When the importance of the five different financial reasons for leaving were regressed on duration, neither the omnibus F nor the individuals t-values were significant. However the sign of the B for lost financial assistance was negative, whereas the sign for all the other Bs was positive. This finding suggests that losing support leads to more rapid attrition, whereas the other financial- and career-related factors come into play later in noncompleters' academic careers. In addition, selecting only for students who rated each financial reason as affecting their attrition decision very strongly, students who lost support persisted an average of 3.0 years, those who were not meeting expenses persisted an average of 3.3 years, and those who felt that their future jobs prospects were not encouraging persisted an average of 3.5 years. These financial reasons appear to influence students' attrition decisions around the time they complete course work, a time when many lose assistantships and have to decide whether to write a dissertation. By contrast, those who received a good job offer persisted an average of 4.7 years, suggesting that they were working on dissertations at the time they left.

11. Completers and noncompleters were equally likely to have been enrolled in their first- and second-choice universities (first choice: 71 percent completers vs. 68 percent noncompleters; second choice: 20 percent completers vs. 22 percent noncompleters).

12. Adviser: 97 percent Rural vs. 4 percent Urban; other faculty: 93 percent Rural vs. 7 percent Urban; and graduate students: 90 percent Rural vs. 10 percent Urban.

Chapter 9

Personal Consequences of Departure

Leaving graduate school is not just changing a job. It often involves changing a culture and redefining deeply held concepts and images of who one is and hoped to become. Students who leave graduate programs without the Ph.D. are forced to make sense of their graduate school experience and of all the personal and financial sacrifices they made, while at the same time reconstructing their lives, career plans, and dreams for the future. Their emotional and psychological reactions to departure have implications for their subsequent personal and professional lives. Some departers adapt easily and find the unexpected twists and turns in their lives positive and rewarding. Others experience emotional and psychological distress and find life after graduate school difficult and unsatisfying. Many go through life wondering what life would have, could have, been like on the road not taken.

This chapter focuses on the short- and long-term personal consequences of departure. It starts with an analysis of the immediate emotional and psychological impact of the decision to leave. Next, it explores how students' initial degree goals and graduate school experiences influence their current lives and future plans by examining how the careers and lives interviewees imagined for themselves when they started graduate school compare with the careers they now have and the lives they are living. The chapter concludes with an investigation of what, if any, regrets departers' have about their decision to leave and the absence of the Ph.D., as well as what they miss about graduate school and the graduate student experience. In the process, it also explores factors that motivate some noncompleters to continue the quest for the Ph.D.

THE IMPACT OF
THE DECISION TO LEAVE

Once a student has left a doctoral program, the student is out of sight and out of mind. Consequently, universities and faculties know virtually nothing about how the decision to leave actually affects the student who has had to make it. However, the decision is often a difficult one and often fraught with both strong and mixed emotions that can plague students for a year or more, and possibly even a lifetime. This section develops a theory of emotional distress and uses it to explore different emotions departers experience and their correlates, and then models the underlying social-psychological processes that lead to the evocation of emotion. It also explores how, and for how long, students deal with negative emotions.

The Theory of Emotional Distress

In many ways, leaving graduate school is analogous to ending a romantic relationship. Like the end of a romance, attrition often involves a disruption of activities, plans, and goals. Theories of emotion combined with the investment model of commitment (Berscheid, 1983, 1986; Rusbult, 1980, 1983; Simpson, 1987) predict that emotional distress should be greatest in relationships characterized by high satisfaction, poor alternatives, and high levels of investment. Applying this model to graduate student attrition suggests that the more a student has invested in his or her graduate program—not only financially but also personally and professionally in terms of plans and goals—the more emotional distress the departure should cause. Similarly, the poorer the quality of alternatives (real or imagined) to graduate school and to the career they anticipated when they enrolled, the more emotional distress departers should experience.

The Emotions and Their Correlates

To assess students' emotional and psychological reactions to their departure, the survey asked noncompleters how strongly they experienced a variety of emotions when they decided to leave (positive emotions: relief, happiness; negative emotions: anxiety, depression, embarrassment, inferiority, anguish, a sense of failure). Similarly, interviewees were asked how their decision to leave affected them personally. In addition, both completers and noncompleters were asked to rate their level of self-esteem at the time of entry, time of exit, and now (i.e., when they were responding to the survey).

Table 9.1 shows that all students entered with the same, relatively high level of self-esteem. However, by the time they left graduate school, noncompleters' level of self-esteem had dropped considerably, while completers' remained the same. However, the completers' constancy masks differences by completer type: On-track completers' level of self-esteem increased, while at-risk completers' decreased. By the time they responded to the survey, all students' level of self-esteem had risen above their entering level, and there were no differences in current level of self-esteem between groups.[1]

Table 9.1.   Changes in Level of Self-Esteem[1] over Time

	Status			Completer Type		
	Completers	Noncompleters	p	On-track	At-risk	p
When you entered the university	3.70	3.63		3.64	3.77	
When you left the university	3.73	2.81	*	3.98	3.38	*
Now	4.07	3.01		4.11	4.01	

[1] 5-point scale: 1 = *low* to 5 = *high*.
*$p < .001$.

Noncompleters' emotional and psychological attachment to the Ph.D. and the distress resulting from its nonattainment were captured using measures of their degree intentions at time of entry (master's, Ph.D., not sure if wanted a Ph.D.), by the importance of a variety of reasons for wanting to go to graduate school, and by the importance of many of those same reasons when they left.[2] Noncompleters' emotional distress was unrelated to their degree intentions at the time of entry. However, the more committed they were to the Ph.D., the lower their exiting level of self-esteem.[3]

Of the eleven reasons provided to noncompleters for attending graduate school, only one reason—desire for the status and prestige of the Ph.D.[4]— evoked strong and consistent negative reactions: The more students desired the status and prestige of the Ph.D., the more depression, embarrassment, inferiority, anguish, and sense of failure they experienced, and the lower their level of self-esteem. Similarly, students who still had a strong desire for the status and prestige of the Ph.D. when they left experienced a greater degree of emotional distress than those to whom it was less important.

Going to graduate school because of poor job prospects and to gain greater control over one's work schedule increased anxiety at the time of exit. The less interested students were in their discipline when they left, the more distressed they were and the lower their level of self-esteem.

While the measures of commitment used here represent a psychological attachment to the Ph.D. and to career goals, measures of noncompleters' degree of integration represent a social-psychological attachment to the context in which the degree is pursued. This relationship was assessed using four integration factors: the department's environment for integration, the students' individual levels of integration in their department, the average level of integration of all students in the department,[5] and the adviser's interest in the student as a person and in his or her ideas and professional development.

The department's environment for integration had no effect on students' degree of emotional or psychological distress, nor did their own level of academic integration. However, the higher the average academic integration of students in their department, the happier, more embarrassed, more inferior, and the more like a failure they felt. By contrast, the more socially integrated the student was and the higher the average social integration of students in their department, the happier and less like a failure they felt. In addition, their own level of social integration correlated positively with their departing level of self-esteem.

Only one adviser-interest-in-student variable—interest in your professional development—was associated with distress. The less interested the student's adviser was in the student's professional development, the more depressed the student was and the lower the student's exiting level of self-esteem.

Although the theory of emotional distress predicts that the higher students' level of satisfaction, the more distressed they should be upon departure, the survey data show just the opposite effect. The more satisfied the noncompleters were with their adviser, their academic performance, their intellectual development, and the other graduate students in their department, the lower their degree of distress and the higher their self-esteem.

The extent to which students invested financial and personal resources in their graduate education and the relationship of these investments to distress was measured by type of financial support they received and by other sources of outside income. Type (or lack) of financial support, had no impact on students' degree of distress, except for students who had TAs; they experienced anguish.

Different forms of supplemental outside income were related to different emotional responses. Departers who had loans felt more anxiety and left with lower self-esteem than students who did not have loans. Students who received income from their spouse or significant other felt inferior, whereas students who received income from family members were depressed and embarrassed.

According to the theory of emotional distress, the longer noncompleters are in graduate school, the more distress they should experience when they leave. Contrary to predictions, neither the survey[6] nor interview data show a relationship between duration and distress.

Students' reasons for leaving without completing the Ph.D. should also reveal something about their degree of commitment to and investment in the degree and their program; hence, they should have implications for their degree of distress. Among the financial reasons for leaving, being unable to meet expenses evoked the most distress—namely, all the negative emotions except anxiety. Losing financial assistance from the university evoked anguish among students. Leaving because one's spouse or significant other got a job decreased anguish and increased self-esteem. Finally, consistent with the investment model, the less encouraging students found the prospects for future employment, the more depressed and embarrassed they were, and the more they felt like failures. Conversely, those who had good alternatives—those who left because they received a good job offer—did not experience much, if any, distress at all.

Four of the personal reasons for leaving (realized you were doing the wrong thing with your life, illness or health problems, lack of motivation to continue, family pressures) were associated with different distress reactions. Students who left because they realized they were doing the wrong thing with their lives felt happy and relieved but also embarrassed and anxious. By contrast, students who left because of illness or health problems were not happy about their leaving. They experienced depression, anguish, and a sense of failure. Despite this, they left with high levels of self-esteem. Students who left because they lacked the motivation to continue also experienced depression and a sense of failure. Those who left because of family pressures experienced anguish.

Finally, academic reasons for leaving evoked three different emotions. Students who did not maintain a satisfactory grade point average, who failed qualifying exams, and who were not interested enough in their discipline to continue experienced relief. Students who were not interested enough in their discipline to continue also experienced happiness. Students who left because the stress and pressure of graduate school were too great left feeling like failures, whereas those who left because they were dissatisfied with their program experienced little or no sense of failure.

Quality of alternatives (real or imagined) was assessed by looking at employment-related factors. The less satisfied the students were with their prospects for future employment, the more distressed they were and the lower their self-esteem. Departers who already had a job when they left[7] were happier than those who did not, whereas those who did not have a job were more depressed than those who did.

The interview data allow flesh to be put on the bones of the foregoing analyses and provide greater insight into the relationship between noncompleters' emotional and psychological reactions to their leaving and the causes of those reactions. In addition, the interview data reveal some emotional reactions not tapped by the survey instrument. They also show that women's negative emotional reactions were much stronger than men's. Women tended to qualify their feelings with "very, very" and "really, really," whereas men tended to qualify them with "a little."

Although the interviewees expressed many different and sometimes mixed emotions, their emotions can be classified into eight distinct categories by nature and cause (see table 9.2). Six of the categories represent negative emotions, and two represent positive emotions. The most prominent negative emotions fell into the categories "bad/disappointed/depressed" and "failure."

Feeling bad, disappointed, and/or depressed were frequently stated in combination by the same individual. Feeling bad also included feeling "really shaken up," "horrible," and "shell-shocked" or finding the experience of making the decision "gut-wrenching." Emotions in this category tended to derive from failure to attain a deeply held personal goal, from not finishing something they had started, and from the long-standing desire for the status and prestige of the Ph.D. Women were twice as likely as men to express these emotions.

Interviewer: How did your decision to leave affect you personally?

Emmie: Hum! I think I felt real bad. I felt real disappointed in myself. I guess I have this, again, this idealized goal in my life that I wanted to be a Ph.D. . . . I think I was just disappointed. I wanted to have the prestige. Just having that Ph.D. after your name. . . . I wanted something that had some status, and I didn't have that. I mean, I didn't even graduate with a master's degree from Urban University. And I was just depre[ssed]—I mean, I was just kind of disappointed.

Feeling like a failure or feeling inadequate also derived from not finishing something the student had started, often in the context of having always been

Table 9.2.   Interviewees' Emotions at the Time of Leaving and Their Correlates

Emotion	Reason	Situation After Leaving
Bad/disappointed/ depressed	Unfinished business Had been a goal in life Wanted the status and prestige	—
Failure/inadequate	Unfinished business Had always been successful	—
Embarrassed/ discomfort	Thought self diminished in the eyes of others (reflected appraisals)	—
Decreased self-esteem/ self-confidence	Slipped in own eyes Not satisfied with self	Took jobs that were elementary, low paying, and way below their qualifications
Upset	Rejected by the program Failed qualifying exams	—
Bitter/crushed	Had been treated poorly	—
Relief	A negative experience was over A source of stress was eliminated	A next move was planned
Good	Turned the experience into a positive Angry with the department	Already had a job or an alternative career plan

— Not applicable.

successful academically. These feelings were experienced about equally by men and women, often in combination with feeling relieved.

> *Interviewer*: Why did you feel like a failure?
>
> *Ellen*: Well, if you springboard off my previous comments about excelling in high school and excelling in college, and then seeing, particularly from an academic standpoint, and then going to a graduate program and basically doing a bellyflop, that's why I felt like I was a failure, because I had broken a string of excelling in academics. . . . Up to that point in my life, I measured success by having such and such a grade point average, or graduating in this ranking in the class, or being a Phi Beta Kappa, or whatever. They'd always been very concrete recognitions of excellence. Here at Rural, I was failing. And all of those things that had given me motivation and gratification—and so then, I mean, then it's soul-searching time.

Students who felt embarrassed or discomfort were reacting to reflected appraisals; that is, they reacted to what they thought other people thought or would think of them. They felt diminished in the eyes of others. They were afraid their friends who had gone on to graduate school would look down on them for quitting. They felt they had to explain their leaving to family members and others and make excuses and apologize for why they left.

Interviewees who slipped in their own eyes, and/or who were not satisfied with their performance in graduate school, experienced decreases in self-esteem and self-confidence. Several of these students' initial jobs were elementary, low paying, and well below their level of education and qualifications (e.g., farmhand, salesclerk, waitress). Beatrice's experience illustrates how decreases in self-esteem or self-confidence affects subsequent life and career choices.

> *Beatrice*: I really went into a slump after I left, big slump. I was working for minimum wage and felt I was lucky to do that. And, in my own eyes, I slipped down considerably.
>
> *Interviewer*: Why did you feel lucky to be working for the minimum wage when you had four years of Ph.D. study?
>
> *Beatrice*: Well, I really felt that at that time that it really wasn't worth doing anything else. That I was just so depressed about everything, but I just didn't feel that, you know, I didn't have the confidence in my ability to do anything.

Running up against an external barrier to persistence, such as not being admitted to the Ph.D. program or failing qualifying exams, caused students to be upset. By contrast, students who felt they had been treated unfairly or unjustly felt bitter or were crushed by the experience. Such experiences included faculty not giving due consideration to an injury and faculty gossiping about the student.

Relief was the most frequently mentioned emotion, but it was often mixed with other ones. About a third of the students who experienced relief experienced it in combination with emotions in every negative category except decreased self-esteem/self-confidence and feeling bitter/crushed. Feelings of relief emerged from the realization that an unpleasant experience was now over and from the elimination of a major source of stress. Most of the students who felt relieved already had jobs or had begun planning their next moves in life before they left the university.

Finally, students who felt good to wonderful about their leaving were students who either blamed the department or who managed to turn the experience into something positive and leave with a sense of accomplishment (e.g., by leaving with a masters' degree). Students who felt good about their leaving also either already had a job or had an alternative career plan at the time they left.

Social/Psychological Processes Mediating Emotional Well-Being

Figure 9.1 summarizes the relationship between the causes of the emotional and psychological reactions and the reaction themselves along with the social/psychological processes that likely mediated the reaction. Indeed, it is the way students processed their experiences relative to their commitments, investments, plans, and goals that determined their reactions.

Although the theory of emotional distress posits that the quality of alternatives is a direct cause of emotional reactions, the quality of alternatives appears to mediate between the social and psychological causes of distress and the experience of distress itself. Students who were committed to the degree experienced a high degree of emotional distress because they had to reconstruct a professional future for themselves. By contrast, students who left feeling good were either satisfied with their current situation or able to envision an alternative future that was as rewarding, or possibly even more rewarding, than the one they had hoped the Ph.D. would buy for them.

Social comparison, comparing oneself with others, appears to mediate between the desire for the status and prestige of the Ph.D. and distress, and possibly between being in an academically integrated department and distress. In the former case, the students compared themselves with some social other they desired to become and were distressed when they realized that not only would they not become a member of that elite group but that they would now have to go through life comparing themselves unfavorably with that group. In the latter case, students likely compared their academic performance and degree of integration with that of other students whom they believed (justifiably or not) were more successful than they were.

Students' perceptions of what they thought others did or might think about them (reflected appraisals) is likely the basis for the distress experienced by

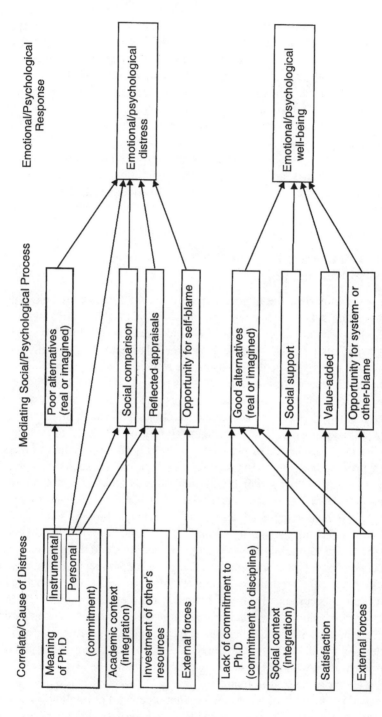

Correlate/Cause of Distress

Mediating Social/Psychological Process

Emotional/Psychological Response

Emotional/psychological distress

Poor alternatives (real or imagined)

Social comparison

Reflected appraisals

Opportunity for self-blame

Meaning of Ph.D
- Instrumental
- Personal

(commitment)

Academic context (integration)

Investment of other's resources

External forces

Emotional/psychological well-being

Good alternatives (real or imagined)

Social support

Value-added

Opportunity for system- or other-blame

Lack of commitment to Ph.D (commitment to discipline)

Social context (integration)

Satisfaction

External forces

Figure 9.1. Social and Psychological Correlates of Emotional Reactions to Departure

students whose relatives had invested financial resources in their graduate education. By not yielding the promised return on investment, these students may have felt that they had let down their relatives and that their relatives would judge them negatively for their "failure" to complete the degree. Reflected appraisals also appear to contribute to the distress experienced by students who desired the status and prestige of the Ph.D. Because they wanted the Ph.D. for the degree of esteem they believed it would attract, not only did these departers have to reconstruct an image of themselves as people without a Ph.D., but they also had to adjust to the idea that, in the eyes of others, they would be "just like everyone else."

Whether external causes of departure caused emotional distress appears to be mediated by the opportunity the students had to blame themselves or something else for the turn of events. Students who blamed themselves for their inability to complete the degree experienced much more distress than those who were able to blame the system (the faculty or department) or some other cause (injury, frustration with experimental equipment, fiancé living out of the area).

In addition to having good alternatives, social support and the value added by the education they received appear to mitigate distress and allow students to leave feeling good about themselves and their experiences. Students who were socially integrated and/or were in socially integrated departments had bonds with the community. Even though they had to break those bonds, the bonds provided them with support that eased their exit. Students who were satisfied with their academic performance and with their intellectual development also left feeling good about themselves and their experiences. Even though they did not obtain the Ph.D., they felt that they had accomplished something during their tenures or got what they came for in terms of knowledge or learning.

In sum, students' degree of emotional and psychological distress or well-being at the time of exit results from a complex interaction of the meaning and value of the Ph.D. to students, their experiences in graduate school, their reasons for leaving, and their situation or plans at the time of exit. The greater students' psychological investment in the degree; the more they internalized blame for their failure to attain it; the more they thought others would look down on them for this failure; the less social support they had; and the more reconstruction and redefinition they had to do in relation to their plans, goals, and images of self, the more emotionally and psychologically distressed they were at the time of departure.

Dealing with Negative Emotions

The decision to leave can have long-term effects on students' emotional well-being. Of the nine interviewees who mentioned the duration of their emotions, eight dealt with them for over a year; a few have been left permanently scarred. Two cried during the interview. Only Tom, who started but did not finish his dissertation and was gainfully employed when he quit, said that he got over his feelings of failure relatively quickly because, for him, it was not particularly a failure. It was just something he did not end up doing. He also felt that he has had a successful career. However, the others (even those who have experienced relative success in their lives and careers) had a much harder time dealing with their feelings.[8] Those who had overcome their negative feelings by the time of the interview said that they "struggled with it for about a year," experienced "two years of depression," or spent "several years apologizing for not having a Ph.D." Emmie was still affected by her decision to leave:

> *Interviewer*: How long did it take you to overcome those feelings?

> *Emmie*: (sighing) You know, I'm not sure I've overcome them at all. I mean, I have to a certain extent, but it's that type of thing where you look back and you go, what if? What if I'd done something a little different? Could I have done it? I don't know. Of course, I'm looking back on it ten years later, and I think I could have done it. I certainly know I have the abilities to do it. Plus I know other students, my friends from undergrad [who] . . . did complete a Ph.D. . . . [or] a master's . . . and I never felt that they were smarter than me or more competent than me. What I saw in their abilities was that they just have this kind of a stick-to-itness. . . . But not that they were smarter or brighter.

A common thread that unites most of those who struggled with their emotions for an extended period of time is that they would still like to get the Ph.D. Indeed, Ashley, who was "shell-shocked" and who felt "psychologically . . . completely useless for a couple of years," had just returned to graduate school at the time of the interview. When asked whether his feelings of failure were gone now, he provided a qualified response: "I think mostly."

The foregoing analysis of the students' emotional and psychological reactions to their decision to leave shows that many students experienced a great deal of distress upon departure, that they struggled with these feelings for an extended period of time, and that their feelings affected, and were affected by, their circumstances after departure. While some of their reactions are consistent with certain aspects of the theory of emotional distress, they are inconsistent with others. The differences result from limitations inherent in the analogy between the end of a romance and departure from doctoral study. Unlike a romantic relationship, which is often an end in itself, graduate school is a means to an end—the Ph.D. Students' primary commitment and investment of self is not in their programs or universities but in the attainment of the Ph.D. Similarly, their hopes, dreams, plans, and goals are more attached to life after the achievement of the degree than to the process of obtaining it. Consequently, students' emotional and psychological reactions to their departure are best understood in terms of their larger life plans and goals than in terms of their graduate school experiences, although these experiences do play a role.

DREAMS VERSUS REALITY

Possible selves (Markus & Nurius, 1986; Rosenburg, 1979, 1990) are components of the self-concept that govern how individuals think about their potential and their future. They are people's hopes, dreams, and ideas about what they may become, would like to become, and are afraid of becoming. They function as incentives for future behavior (selves to be approached or avoided) and provide an evaluative and interpretive context for the current view of the self. When students enter graduate school, they have dreams and images of their future selves. It is reasonable to believe that these images influence the direction their lives take after leaving graduate school, their retrospective assessment of the goals with which they began, their assessment of their current lives and careers, and their future plans.

To assess the relationship between, and influence of, noncompleters' dreams (past possible selves) on reality (their current selves), the interviewees were asked to compare their lives and careers with the ones they envisioned for themselves when they entered graduate school. The students' responses were analyzed along seven dimensions: (1) how they imagined their lives and careers, (2) the contrast between their dreams and their actual lives, (3) concrete images of their future lives and careers when they entered graduate school, (4) their current situation, (5) feelings attached to the discrepancy between dream and reality, (6) images of possible future selves, and (7) the continued presence of the past self in the current self.

Many of the interviewees conflated their images of their lives and careers. Most "thought," "envisioned," "expected," "assumed," or "saw myself as" becoming a college professor or doing some type of academic work in an academic setting; none realized this ambition. Even those who did not project an academic career did not envision their current careers. With respect to their future lives, several stated, "I don't know if I had any particular life goals mapped out," or "I never really thought that far ahead when I entered graduate school." Women, the stay-at-home mothers in particular, said that they always knew that they would have children but also thought they would have a career.

Of the twenty-two students who provided an assessment of how their current career compared with the career they envisioned for themselves when they entered graduate school, sixteen, regardless of whether they had a job that was related or unrelated to their discipline, felt that their current careers were "quite different," "diametrically different," "180 degrees opposite," or "not very close" to what they had imagined. Three felt their careers were similar to what they had envisioned. Solange, who was working in a completely different field, found continuities in that she was doing a variety of things and using a variety of talents. Beatrice, who was teaching in a field related to her discipline, felt that what she was doing was less scholarly than the career she had envisioned. Katie fell somewhere in between. By being a high school teacher in her field, she felt she had achieved half of what she set out to achieve. Two students perceived a "common thread" with or a "steady evolution" from the past. Only Gerald, who had followed his adviser to another university and completed the Ph.D., felt that his career was "almost exactly" what he thought it would be.

Similarly, most the of the interviewees thought that their current lives were very different from those they envisioned. In addition to assessing their lives along a similar/different dimension, many also assessed their lives along a better/worse dimension. Those who felt their lives were different stated, "much better," "financially more successful than I ever envisioned," "so far from it that it's unbelievable," "more complicated and going in a lot more directions," "more mundane than I hoped it would be," and "very unexpected." The few who felt their lives were similar stated, "similar in the sense that I'm not working for a boss," and "probably about the same in terms of what I have materially and where I am personally."

Three students, all men, provided concrete images of their perceptions of academia and how they saw themselves functioning within it. Their images fit with social and media-driven stereotypes of academic life. Stuart and James emphasize the lifestyle and costume associated with the role of professor. Brent emphasizes interactions with colleagues and students.

> *Stuart*: When I entered graduate school I thought I would go on get my Ph.D., study abroad before I did that. Think good thoughts. Live in the ivory tower. Wear cardigan sweaters. Get out [and] teach in a four-year college and be a professor. The whole thing. Have office hours. Write papers. Give lectures. Name it. I'm doing none of that now.

> *James*: I really saw myself as an academic. I saw myself as, when I'm fifty, I'll be teaching at some college and wearing the sports jacket with the leather patches on the sleeves. Your classic genteel academic lifestyle. I didn't see myself in the corporate world at all, and that's where I am.

> *Brent*: When I was entering graduate school, I was looking forward to academia. I was looking forward to being divorced from 95 percent of humankind, because the one thing in life that I really despised is people being stupid. And I wanted to be able to separate myself from that. And so I was looking forward to being in an elite group of people where the only people I talked to were intelligent, self-motivated people . . . that could tell me something I didn't already know. Now, what I'm doing now? If anything, I am living with the bottom 95 percent. In fact, I'd say I'm probably, for the most part, in the bottom half of that 95 percent.

A few interviewees provided concrete images of what they imagined their future lives would be like. Their images revolve around the type of community in which they thought they would be living as well as the nature of their social and intellectual interactions with people in the community.

Beatrice: A small college town with a lot of college people around. So, it's a lot different than where I live now. . . . In the area I'm living in right now . . . most of the people that are here are more blue-collar workers and, maybe, office workers, but not on the intellectual level that I had expected at the time I was working for my Ph.D.

Emmie: I think I envisioned living in an academic or university setting, near a university. I thought we would be living in an apartment and socializing with the upwardly mobile yuppie types. I thought that we would be doing a lot of real middle-class [things], just going to plays or going to this type of thing. I don't know, just this concept of what life must be like around a university. Going to wine and cheeses and going to interesting talks, because I really enjoy the academic environment. I think it's cool in a way. I'm so far from that now (laughter), it's unbelievable.

Tony: I was really geared to academic-type life. Go to baseball [games], basketball [games]. Summers free with the children. Take research in [the] summer. I haven't had a vacation since I left the university!

The students talked about their current careers in four different ways. One way was to simply state what they did: "I'm an executive in a finance department," or "I'm an at-home mom who freelances occasionally." A few highlighted the continuities between what they thought their careers would be like and their actual careers—for instance, a steady evolution from telling people what to do, to deciding what issues are relevant and taking an activist approach, or still worrying about policy problems but not to the extent envisioned ten or twelve years ago. Others emphasized the way in which their current careers were better than what they thought an academic career would have been like: "I've been exposed to a lot more people that are working in various professions associated with chemistry, various types of industries, and things, and so I have a lot better appreciation for the different things people do—and academics is pretty isolated"; "I now feel I have more control over my life than I ever had the sense I would have had I continued on in academics professionally." These three groups of students were satisfied with their current careers. By contrast, students who were dissatisfied with their careers highlighted the discrepancy between their dreams and reality: "I'm teaching at a high school level, and it's not as challenging academically"; "When I started graduate school, I envisioned myself being a full professor somewhere, and instead of that I'm working under one. . . . In terms of the money and the prestige factor, certainly nowhere near what I initially envisioned."

The interviewees also focused on three distinct aspects of their current lives: their career status, the source of the rewards in their lives, and the nature of their social/intellectual interactions. The only ones who mentioned their career status were women whose career status was lower than they had anticipated. Although they seem to have come to terms with it, for some, there is a tinge of ambivalence.

Katie: One of my biggest complaints with secretarial work [which I did after leaving graduate school] is that I wasn't respected as a professional. Now I'm quasi-respectable. People do give schoolteachers respect, but they don't give secretaries [respect]—not as much as doctors or lawyers or even college professors. But I have more respect than I did before. So, I have to say that I have fulfilled my goal maybe 60 percent or the life that I envisioned is 60 percent accomplished, maybe.

A source of reward in students' current lives appears to be unanticipated continuities between the way they function within their careers and the way they anticipated functioning. More specifically, many of the interviewees originally pursued an academic career to have control over their lives, to be autonomous and self-directed in their work, and to do something they found personally stimulating and gratifying.[9] As illustrated in the following quotes, the students were often surprised to discover these elements in the nonacademic world:

Solange: Well, I'm definitely moving into a happier phase of my life now. I think I'm finally getting the intellectual challenge back that I always wanted. . . . I'd always thought that if you're going to have an interesting job, the only way you could use your brain would be if you were in school. I had no idea how stimulating business could be, or anything besides law . . . or medicine, which I really wasn't interested in. . . . I thought, well, the academic life, there you get to think. It was just ignorance on my part, basically. I think that I find in business the challenge that I was looking for in graduate school.

Boyd: Well, it's similar in the sense that . . . I don't have a boss. . . . I'm self-directed and self-motivated and self-regulating, and that's one of the things that [was] mainly appealing to me about what I presumed to be the life of a professor.

Although possible selves are conceived of primarily as self-cognitions and as motivations to action, possible selves are also associated with self-feelings and affect (Markus & Nurius, 1986). The affect derives from conflicts or discrepancies within the self-concept. Thus, to the extent that individuals do or do not become who they desired to be, they are expected to feel positively or negatively about themselves and their situations.

Even though most students' current career self was very different from their anticipated career self, few had bad feelings about the discrepancy. Most were satisfied with what they were doing or, at least, were not dissatisfied with the way things had turned out. Few had any regrets. The strongest negative feelings came from Rhett, who had only recently withdrawn from doctoral study after two tries and who was effectively unemployed and looking for work in a related field. He somewhat angrily stated, "It makes a big difference not having the career you imagined having. Yeah, there's not much comparison." He stands in contrast with Gerald, who completed the Ph.D. at another university and whose career was almost exactly what he imagined: "I've been lucky in that things have worked out the way I had wanted them to." Few interviewees attached any affect to the discrepancy between their current life and the life they had envisioned. The two who revealed any feeling said that they were happy and content with their personal lives. Thus, for most of the interviewees, time and the actualization of a new career self appears to mitigate the dissonance associated with the discrepancy between a past possible career self and the current career self.

Critical aspects of past selves that remain within the self-concept represent an individual's enduring concerns. To the extent that they may define an individual again in the future, past selves can also be possible selves (Markus & Nurius, 1986). Indeed, a few of the students who still harbored the desire to complete the Ph.D. revealed the persistence of an academic possible self:[10] "Sometime, in the future, I do hope to rejoin academia"; "I'll go back to teach sometime later on. . . . when money constraints aren't a major factor. My first love is the classroom." Strongly held past selves not only can be desired future selves but can motivate behavior leading to the actualization or achievement of that self. After ten years in the business world, Ashley did return to graduate school, and, at the time of the interview, Cathleen was about to contact her university to explore the possibility of completing her dissertation. Thus, the discrepancy between the current self and an idealized past possible self can motivate people to reduce the tension it causes and guide the course of future action.

Several students who were content with their current careers highlighted the continuities between their past and current career selves and placed an emphasis on their desire to do something meaningful:

> *Philip*: The need to be socially active and the need to get things done were always part of my game plan. I had thought that a Ph.D. might be a good vehicle to do that. There was a drift toward more doing it, and a realization that economics was more not doing it. But I've been pretty consistent.

> *James*: I think it was maybe a little less of a transition because this profession initially solves the exam side of it, because when you move over you still have this studying emphasis. In fact, getting my certification I felt was more rigorous than anything I ever did in Ph.D. work. . . . I certainly felt myself, as someone who could compare both, that the work I had to do to get through the exams and what I had to learn in the process was more rigorous and more worthwhile obviously than my Ph.D. work. I think that made it a little less strange in terms of just going from an academic environment where you set your own hours to one where you work 9 to 5, cause people in this profession really don't work 9 to 5 . . . The company gives you time to study. You study at home at night, that kind of thing. . . . But this really satisfies my need to just sort of be interested and do things and at the same time do something that's meaningful.

Finally, although some students highlighted the ways in which their lives were different from what they had anticipated, elements of past academic selves are revealed in a way that indicates that this part of their self is still present in, and still influencing, their current lives.

> *Emmie*: I live in a very middle-class type of community. Actually, the community here is very ethnically diverse. We own a home, and we do gardening, and we do hiking. We do activities that would have been impossible to do in Urban City. We are much more outdoorsy now. Our lifestyle is very relaxed and, yet, we still go to bookstores, and we still do some things, but very, very different than the urban academic life I thought I was going to lead.

> *James*: Well, as I said, [my life is] drastically different. . . . [But] we seem to do a lot of things on our time off or on evenings . . . that other professionals don't do. A lot of them seem to do more what I call the normal . . . American lifestyle: You go home, have dinner, watch TV for two hours, that kind of thing. We generally do things that are more in trend with what you would think of as an academic background, like reading. We try to keep up on movies, music, things like that . . . We still have a lot of the values and the level of learning that we had, that we saw, we liked in academia. It's just that we've gotten out of the academia part itself, which I viewed as just another job and not a very good one.

These quotes reveal that the continuity between the past and the present is less the role the individual is playing than the key activities embodied in the role. In the past, the student projected these desired activities onto a future, usually academic, career. If in the present, the core of a past possible self can be actualized in the life a person is living, the continuity reduces the degree of dissonance.

In sum, whether noncompleters are happy with their lives and careers roughly ten years after leaving graduate school is a function of a complex interaction between their current life circumstances and their ability to resolve the discrepancy between their dreams of who they wanted to become and the reality of who they have become. Figure 9.2 depicts the relationship between noncompleters' satisfaction with their lives and careers, life circumstances, and changes in their self-concepts, along with the psychological processes influencing those changes across four dimensions. The dimensions above the line represent students who were satisfied with their lives and careers; those below the line, students who were dissatisfied. Similarly, the dimensions left of the center line represent students who thought their lives and careers were similar to what they had envisioned; those on the right, students who thought their lives and career were different.

Noncompleters who thought that their lives and careers were similar to what they had anticipated and were satisfied with them (cell 1) had found common threads that linked past dreams with present realities. These continuities were less in their actual lives or careers than in key elements of them.

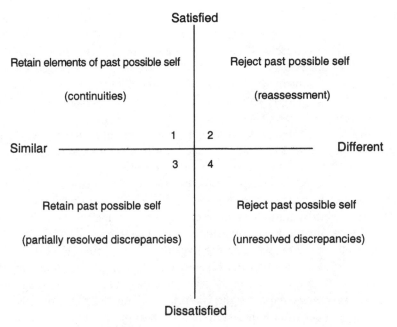

Satisfied

Retain elements of past possible self

(continuities)

Reject past possible self

(reassessment)

1 | 2

Similar ———————————————————— **Different**

3 | 4

Retain past possible self

(partially resolved discrepancies)

Reject past possible self

(unresolved discrepancies)

Dissatisfied

Figure 9.2.   The Relationship between Dreams and Reality and Satisfaction with Life after Graduate School

These students wanted the Ph.D. because they wanted to be challenged intellectually and to be autonomous and self-directed in their careers, because they wanted to participate in high culture and to spend their lives interacting with other bright and intellectually stimulating people. In finding jobs and in living lives that enabled them to enact these core elements of their self-concepts, these students found aspects of the vision that had originally motivated them to pursue the Ph.D.

Noncompleters who thought that their lives and careers were very different from what they had envisioned and, yet, were satisfied with them (cell 2) had resolved the discrepancy by rejecting or downgrading their past possible selves. These students reassessed their dreams in light of their realities and found their dreams wanting. They felt that their current lives and careers were better, fuller, and more rewarding than the lives and careers they would have experienced had their past possible selves become their present selves.

By contrast, noncompleters who thought their lives and careers were similar to what they had desired but were dissatisfied with them (cell 3) retained their past possible selves and had only partially resolved the discrepancy between dreams and reality. Although they were able to find

elements of their jobs or their lives that were consistent with their past possible selves—for instance, teaching their discipline at the school level or
working in a related field—they were not actualizing core elements of their
past possible selves that were still important to them. They had less status,
autonomy, and control than they desired, and they were not interacting
with the kinds of people with whom they had hoped to share their professional and social lives.

Finally, noncompleters who thought their lives and careers were quite
different from what they had imagined and were dissatisfied with them
(cell 4) held tightly to images of self embodied in their past possible
selves; consequently, these past images continued to feature prominently
in their concepts of their future possible selves. Because their past possible selves and their future possible selves were one and the same, they had
not, and were unable to, resolve the discrepancies between the lives they
had planned for themselves and the lives they were living. However, most
hoped someday to resolve this discrepancy by completing their degrees
and getting the jobs and living the lives they desired. The following quote
from Jim succinctly captures the interplay among his past possible self,
discrepant current situation, dissatisfaction, and motivation to action:

> *Jim*: I am still very restless, and I'm not satisfied because I'm not doing music
> full-time. I'm looking nationally to see if I can find a stable prestigious position
> where I can do what I love, what I'm gifted to do, and where I can serve and use
> my gift which is very much a part of my identity. . . . There is still a yearning in
> my soul and spirit to complete the degree. . . . I'm doing well, but I'm certainly
> not satisfied because I don't have a suitable church position where I can more
> fully utilize my talents, gifts, skills, and abilities to serve the church and glorify
> God . . . [I]n order to be satisfied, I need to achieve again, and that to me will be
> . . . when I can find another full-time church position, and then I probably can fin-
> ish my doctorate as well.

Thus, noncompleters' ability to find happiness in their post–graduate
school lives and careers is a function of their ability to resolve discrepancies between the people they had desired to become when they entered
graduate school and the people they subsequently became. Those who resolved the discrepancy by finding continuities between past and present, or
by reevaluating or rejecting the past, had achieved a higher level of happiness and satisfaction in their lives than those for whom the discrepancies
persisted. The larger the discrepancy, the greater the degree of dissatisfaction, and the greater the desire and motivation to resolve the discrepancy
by turning the dream into a reality by going back to graduate school and
getting the Ph.D.

LOOKING BACK WITH REGRET OR
COMING TO TERMS WITH THE PAST

The Ph.D. was a goal to which most of the noncompleters in the survey sample and all of the interviewees aspired. Many attached considerable importance to its attainment, to the status and prestige it bestowed, and to the career paths they believed it opened. In addition, many made considerable personal and financial sacrifices to achieve it. Given the initial significance of the degree to the students, the question arises as to how, six to ten or more years later, noncompleters feel about having left graduate school and how they feel about not having the degree. The survey thus asked the noncompleters about these issues, while interviewees were asked what, if anything, they missed about graduate school and how they felt about not having achieved the Ph.D. The correlates of regret were explored using the same factors as the correlates of emotional distress.

Regrets about Leaving

The survey data show that noncompleters regretted not having a Ph.D. more than they regretted leaving graduate school.[11] As with expressions of distress, the more important the status and prestige of the Ph.D. was to noncompleters when they started graduate school, the more they regretted having left. The more their enrollment in graduate school was motivated by a poor job market, the less regret they had. The former reason reveals a continued commitment to the social meaning of the degree; the latter, a lack of commitment.

With respect to integration, the more academically integrated the students were, the more they regretted their leaving. Lack of motivation to continue increased regret, while realizing that they had been doing the wrong thing with their life decreased it. The former reflects unresolved, unfinished business, whereas the latter indicates an appropriate change in direction. Finally, those noncompleters who pursued additional graduate or professional education after leaving regretted their decision to leave less that those who did not continue in these pursuits.

Over one-third of the interviewees said they missed certain things about graduate school, including the library, computer systems, classroom-based learning, problem solving, doing research, the academic environment, and a measurable sense of growth and accomplishment. However, what the interviewees missed most was intelligent discussions with intelligent people. Charlie captures this nostalgia and longing thus:

Charlie: I do miss being able to joke around and make allusions to things that educated people would get, but noneducated people don't really get. . . . And I miss conversations where people have ideas other than ideas that are presented on TV or in the newspaper.

Scarlett, a biology student who was in a medical residency at the time of the interview, commented that if she had a choice between sitting at a table with a group of graduate students or at a table with a group of medical students, she would not choose the medical students. Thus, although some students do not regret having left graduate school, many miss the intellectually stimulating interpersonal aspects of the experience.

Regrets about the Absence of the Ph.D.

Regret about the absence of the Ph.D. was deeply rooted in students' motivations and commitments to its pursuit (at both the time of entry and the time of exit), their experiences in graduate school, and their reasons for leaving. The interviewees' discussions reveal a complex relationship between the desire to obtain the degree, their current satisfaction with their careers and lives, the meaning and value attached to the degree, and the passage of time (initial feelings and current feelings). Students who had had some graduate education prior to enrolling at Rural or Urban University or who intended to get a Ph.D. when they started regretted not having the Ph.D. more than other noncompleters. High levels of regret are associated with the entering and exiting desire for the status and prestige of the Ph.D., the importance to the student of doing research, having been encouraged to go to graduate school by undergraduate faculty, the desire to teach, and the exiting need for the Ph.D. for one's career.

Degree of integration did not affect subsequent level of regret. However, having had a job off campus and its concomitant pull away from the departmental community and full-time focus on graduate study increased regret. The more satisfied students were with their intellectual development and the less satisfied with their prospects for future employment, the greater their regret. Finally, students who left graduate school because they discovered they were doing the wrong thing with their lives had little regret, whereas those who left because they were advised to leave or because of illness indicated considerable regret.

Meaning and Value of the Ph.D.

As the highest academic degree society can bestow, the Ph.D. is loaded with meaning and value. Indeed, it is often the meaning and value of the degree which inspires its quest and, consequently, affects how students who do not obtain it come to terms with its absence. The Ph.D. appears to have at least three types of meaning or value to those who seek it. At the most personal level, it is an instrument of self-validation. Several students saw it as a way of affirming and confirming to themselves that they were intelligent people who could complete a difficult course of study. At the next, more social, level the Ph.D. is an agent of self-validation through reflected appraisals. Students valued the degree for the status and prestige they believed it would give them in the eyes of others—as a way of announcing to the world that they were bright, learned, and to be taken seriously. In return, they believed the world would honor and respect them. The following exchange with Hugh contains elements of self-validation and self-validation through reflected appraisals.

Hugh: For a long time I felt like I needed the validity of a degree, and I'm changing my feelings about that.

Interviewer: Why did you feel you needed the validity of a degree?

Hugh: I don't know. I was thinking that I would somehow be more worthwhile or something. Or here is a piece of paper that says, "Yes, you know quite a bit about something. This is a person to be taken seriously." It just seemed like it would cap off something and say something and send some kind of notice.

Interviewer: Notice to who?

Hugh: Ah (laughter), I don't know. Those around me. (laughter) I don't know if I was thinking of anybody specifically. It just seemed like a good token of self-validation or affirmation or something.

The third level of value is to see the degree as a certificate of achievement. Ashley viewed the Ph.D. as "a document which certifies to the world that you are a certified scholar." Others saw it as a résumé builder, a way to impress prospective employers.

Students who continued to place one or more of these values on the Ph.D. regretted not having the Ph.D. and still desired it. Several of these students had subsequently enrolled one or more times in doctoral programs. Ashley had just returned to graduate school, Cathleen was exploring the possibility, and Irene had tried once and was hoping to try again when her children were older. Students who had reassessed and downgraded the meaning and value of the Ph.D. did not have any regrets. Some questioned their motivations: "It was simply for show." Others came to view it as "just a piece of paper," which they no longer needed to be who and what they were. This group found other ways to validate themselves as competent and worthy individuals, as shown in the following exchange with Brent:

Interviewer: Why don't you feel so badly about it now? What changed?

Brent: Because I realized it was kind of a strawman. It was just a piece of paper, and, quite frankly, I say that with just a limited amount of modesty. I think I can carry on an intelligent conversation with just about anybody who has a Ph.D., and the ones that I can't, it's because they're talking about their specialty. You see, my whole perception of getting a Ph.D. was that I'd be smart, and it's taken me a long time to realize that I am.

The Passage of Time

A number of interviewees mentioned that they once felt badly about not having the degree but that those feelings were all or mostly gone. Their remarks
prompted probing of initial feelings to understand what causes some students
to change their feeling and others to retain them.

About two-thirds of the interviewees said that they currently had no regrets
or were otherwise not bothered by the lack of a Ph.D. These students were
largely satisfied with their careers and felt the Ph.D. was irrelevant to their
current pursuits. Some had gotten other degrees along the way that were more
meaningful to them than the doctorate. They also believed these degrees
made them more well rounded and more marketable than they would have
been had they completed the Ph.D. Some concluded that pursuing the Ph.D.
was a mistake or just not for them.

One-fourth of the interviewees initially regretted (or had bad feelings about)
not having the Ph.D. but no longer felt this way. These students were distressed
initially because they enjoyed their disciplines and the Ph.D. had been a long-
term goal, part of their life plan. They overcame their negative feelings by reassessing their motivation for pursuing the degree, reconsidering the meaning
and value of the degree, or by leaving a career where the Ph.D. was required.

Students who had bad feelings or regrets about not having the Ph.D. in
the past that had persisted into the present were primarily those who had put
four or more years of effort into achieving the degree,[12] as well as one student who left after one term because of emotional problems. These students
were unhappy and upset about not having the degree, because, like the students who had bad feelings or regrets initially, the Ph.D. had been a long-
term goal and part of their life plan. They felt incomplete, as though they
had left something undone, that they lacked the certification and esteem
(both personally and professionally) that the degree bestowed. Unlike those
who had overcome their initial negative feelings, those who had not done
so were not satisfied with their jobs or careers and still greatly desired to
complete the degree.

Finally, a number of students expressed varying degrees of ambivalence
about not having the Ph.D. They made both positive and negative remarks,
which were sprinkled with a lot of hedges and qualifiers. While most were
content to very happy with their lives and careers, they still valued the degree,
felt as though they had left something undone, and carried with them the desire to complete it. Cathleen's and Tony's responses to the question "How do
you feel about not having the Ph.D.?" are illustrative:

> *Cathleen*: I think it's okay now, but I can see that in a couple years if I still don't have
> it, or if I'm not doing anything toward it, I'd be impatient with myself, unless
> something else wonderful pans out. A Ph.D. is not necessary to a fabulous career

in some way or another, but I guess if a fabulous career is not happening and I don't have a Ph.D., I think I would be kind of bummed.

Tony: Sometimes; like I left some things undone. I don't feel bad about it because I've done so much with what I have. But a little frustrated sometimes. It's like a goal you set. And then there's always someone who [doesn't] believe in you, but I did, and then my wife did. And I got there with bells on my fingers and rings on my toes. . . . I wasn't that lucky, I guess, . . . But then again a lot of things have happened, changes in my life which I believe that they have been a training process for what I do now, which is not economics—it's religious.

In sum, although some noncompleters do regret leaving graduate school, these regrets are not as strong as their regrets about not having the Ph.D., because graduate school is the means to an end and not an end in itself. However, many miss the intellectual stimulation and challenge of their graduate school years, and their colleagues and peers. This longing is related to their initial desire for intellectual and professional development and to not finding the same challenge and stimulation in their post–graduate school lives.

Whether or not they still desire the Ph.D., in time, most noncompleters do manage to come to terms with its absence. This entails changing in one or more of the following ways: losing the desire for the degree, reassessing its meaning, downgrading the value accorded to it, and/or finding satisfaction in one's current career. However, for a small subset of noncompleters the absence of the Ph.D. is a source of dissonance, which most hope to resolve in the future by returning to school and completing the degree. As we have seen, this dissonance motivated some noncompleters to take steps in that direction as many as ten or more years after leaving.

CONCLUSION

How students who leave doctoral programs without the Ph.D. come to terms with their noncompletion, in both the short and long term, is a function of the meaning and value of the Ph.D. to them, their experiences in graduate school, their circumstances after leaving, and the social-psychological processes they do or do not deploy in coming to grips with this turn of events. Figure 9.3 depicts these relationships over time.

At time t_1, the meaning and value students impute to the Ph.D. influences their reasons for pursuing it as well as their commitment to its attainment. These motivators interact with students' graduate school experiences at time t_2. Their experiences in graduate school may alter their feelings about the Ph.D. and their need to have it.

The meaning and value of the Ph.D. to noncompleters at the time of departure, t_3, interacts with the quality of their alternatives (real or imagined)

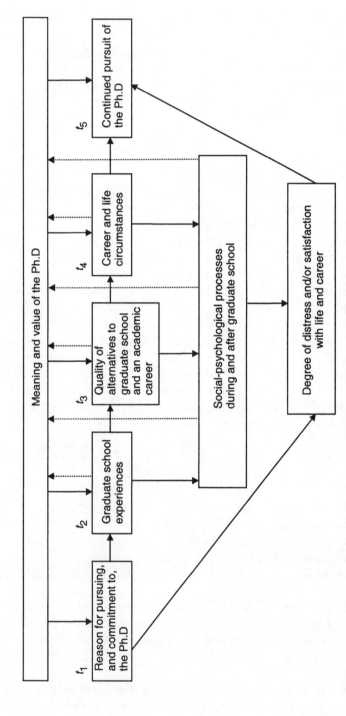

Figure 9.3. Factors Influencing How Noncompleters Come to Terms with Departure from Doctoral Study

and, through a variety of social-psychological processes, affects degree and duration of emotional and psychological distress. As noncompleters' career and life circumstances change, t_4, so may the meaning and value of the Ph.D. as well as the centrality of the Ph.D. to their self-images. Again, these internal changes are mediated by social-psychological processes. The extent to which noncompleters retain or relinquish their Ph.D. identities, and the extent to which they retain or relinquish the meaning and value they initially imputed to the Ph.D., determine their degree of satisfaction with their post–graduate school lives and careers. Finally, noncompleters who in t_4 have not relinquished their Ph.D. identities, and to whom the Ph.D. still has as much meaning as it did when they entered graduate school, hope, plan, or are actually motivated to pursue the Ph.D. at some point in the future, t_5.

NOTES

1. Regardless of status, women's level of self-esteem was lower than that of men's at the time of entry (3.52 vs. 3.77) and the time of exit (3.13 vs. 3.57). However, there was no difference in their level of self-esteem in the present (4.00 vs. 4.08). Male completers exhibit a steadily rising level of self-esteem (3.76 entry, 3.86 exit, 4.15 now), while male noncompleters and females, regardless of status, exhibit a decreasing and then increasing level of self-esteem (male noncompleters: 3.78 entry, 2.87 exit, 3.95 now; female completers: 3.55 entry, 3.45 exit, 3.93 now; female noncompleters: 3.49 entry, 2.77 exit, 4.08 now).

2. These factors are interest in your discipline, desire to teach, desire to do research, career choice required a Ph.D., desire for higher salary, desire for the status and prestige of having a Ph.D., control over your work schedule, spouse or significant other was in or going to go to graduate school (reason for wanting to go to graduate school only), desire for more knowledge, encouraged by faculty (reason for wanting to go to graduate school only), and job prospects were not good (reason for wanting to go to graduate school only).

3. Noncompleters' exiting level of self-esteem by degree intentions are as follows: 2.57 Ph.D., 2.96 not sure whether wanted Ph.D., and 3.22 master's.

4. Completers had a stronger desire for the status and prestige of the Ph.D. than noncompleters at the time of entry and at the time of exit (entry: 2.53 vs. 2.28; exit: 2.45 vs. 2.03). The decrease in strength of desire over time was significant for both groups (completers, $p = .017$; noncompleters, $p < .001$). There were no differences between on-track and at-risk completers in their strength of desire for the status and prestige of the Ph.D. at entry or exit. However, the importance of the status and prestige of the Ph.D. to at-risk completers did decline over time (2.59 entry vs. 2.41 exit, $p < .001$).

5. Degree of academic integration was measured using the academic integration index developed in Lovitts (1997). It contains the following factors: adviser-related variables (had an adviser, method of adviser selection, adviser interest in student), task integration-related variables (type of financial support), and variables that measured participation in academic events/activities (participation in colloquia/brown bags). Degree of social integration was measured using the social integration index developed in Lovitts (1997). It contains the following factors: time spent socializing with faculty other than adviser outside the classroom, participation in department events (sports, socializing on campus,

socializing off campus, other social activities involving graduate students and faculty), and peer support variables (how frequently students discussed their feelings about being a graduate student with other graduate students, students perceptions of how supportive other graduate students were of them).

6. When all the emotions are regressed on duration, the omnibus F is not significant, but the B for sense of failure is ($p = .02$). When happiness and sense of failure are regressed on duration alone, the omnibus F approaches significance ($p = .06$), and the Bs for both emotions achieve significance: the shorter the duration, the happier the student, and the longer the duration, the greater the sense of failure. However, the proportion of variance explained is less than 4 percent.

7. Having a job at the time of exit was defined as having taken zero months to find a job after leaving. Not having a job at the time of exit was defined as having taken one or more months to find a job.

8. Despite many outward measures of success, it was not until I was working on the final chapter of my dissertation, some eleven and a half years after leaving a doctoral program, that I myself finally overcame my feelings of failure, and it was many years before I could talk about my experiences without being on the verge of tears.

9. See Kohn (1977), Kohn and Schooler (1983), and Kohn and Slomczynski (1990) for a discussion of the relationship between values and occupation.

10. Ebaugh (1988, p. 174) call this persistence "role residual." It is an individual's continued identity with aspects of a previous role that can impact on the individual's current role.

11. Noncompleters' degree of regret about not having the Ph.D. was 2.75 compared with 2.35 for leaving graduate school on a 5-point scale (1= *no regrets at all* to 5 = *a great deal of regret*).

12. Number of years includes all years of doctoral study, not just doctoral study at Rural or Urban University.

Chapter 10

Labor Market Consequences of Departure

Students who leave graduate school are frequently demoralized and emotionally distressed. Many have come long distances, leaving family and friends in other cities and others states. Most have barely scrapped by on their stipends (if they had a stipend at all), and many have exhausted their savings and taken out large loans. Consequently, few are financially or emotionally in a position to launch extensive job searches. Those in rural areas may be handicapped by a restricted labor market for people with advanced, highly specialized education. They may have limited access, both physically and informationally, to the national labor market. So, what happens to departers after they leave graduate school? Where do they go and what do they do? Are their decisions affected by the labor market surrounding their university? Do they seek and secure jobs in or related to their graduate training? Does their advanced education, but lack of a credential, help or hurt them? Does their stage of departure affect their fates in the labor market?

Although we know nothing about how departing students actually fare in the labor market,[1] labor market theory suggests that departing students may face structural barriers to job acquisition, occupational and salary attainment, and career advancement. These barriers may be individual, social, or institutional (Bluestone, 1970). To provide a context for understanding students' fates in the labor market, this chapter partially synthesizes three labor market theories: human capital, networking, and credential. It then uses this theoretical framework to shed light on how completers and noncompleters seek and secure jobs and on reasons for differences in their occupational and salary attainment, both in the short and near term.

LABOR MARKET THEORY

Like graduate schools, labor markets are both structures and processes, and, like graduate schools, they interact with students' characteristics, dispositions, and motivations to determine their labor market outcomes. When they enter the market, students confront an array of job opportunities. Positions vary by pay, benefits, career potential, and content (e.g., autonomous and self-directed vs. routine and controlled; abstract thinking vs. concrete thinking). These positions also have a geographic and temporal dimension. Jobs exist in some localities and not others, and the window of opportunity for acquiring a job may be temporally limited and conditional on the state of the economy and the economic sector in which it is located.

Employers and employees find each other through a process known as matching. According to matching theory (Granovetter, 1981), both employers and employees search for appropriate candidates/positions, signal their availability, and screen for optimum fit. Employers search, signal, and screen for such human capital characteristics as age, education, and experience. Prospective employees search, signal, and screen for such job characteristics as tasks, requirements, salary, benefits, career potential, and location.

Labor markets are structurally divided into two sectors—primary and secondary—by occupations (Piore, 1971). The primary labor market is further subdivided into tiers—upper and lower. The upper tier includes professional, technical, managerial, and administrative positions. Jobs in this tier are more creative and less routinized than most other jobs. They are also high paying, high status, and stable and provide workers with autonomy and upward mobility (Kalleberg & Sorenson, 1979; Piore, 1971; Ritzer & Walczak, 1986). The lower tier includes sales, clerical, and skilled craft jobs as well as the female semiprofessions (e.g., teacher, nurse, librarian). The secondary labor market is composed of semiskilled and unskilled nonfarm and service workers. Jobs in this sector are low status, low paying, and routinized; require no training; and offer no stability or upward mobility.

Because many organizations and occupations screen on the basis of the Ph.D. credential, for the purposes of the analyses in this chapter, it is useful to subdivide the primary labor market into two segments by educational requirements. One segment is an advanced-degree (Ph.D.-required) labor market. It includes a narrower slice of the upper tier of the primary labor market such as positions in universities, government, and research and consulting organizations, and such independent occupations as psychologist, which require the Ph.D. for entry and advancement. The other segment is the general labor market. It typically requires at least a bachelor's degree for entry. It includes the lower tier of the primary labor market and that part of the upper tier that does not require the Ph.D. Because of their high level of education, their desire for status and prestige, and their motivation to be autonomous and self-directed in their jobs (see chapter 9), completers and noncompleters should seek jobs in the primary labor market, the upper tier in particular, and completely eschew the secondary labor market. Completers should be concentrated in the Ph.D.-required segment, and noncompleters should be distributed unevenly in the general segment. The more years of graduate education noncompleters have at the time of departure, the higher their representation should be in the part of the upper tier in which the Ph.D. is *not* required.

Human Capital Theory

Human capital theory (Becker, 1964; Mincer, 1958; Thurow, 1970) is the application of standard capital theory to labor market phenomena. It provides insights into the individual factors likely to affect students' occupational and salary attainment. The central idea is that individuals invest in education, training, and experience for the sake of future pecuniary and other nonpecuniary returns such as status and prestige. In return for earnings foregone during the investment period, employers compensate these individuals by providing high starting salaries.

The theory predicts that the more education, training, and experience students have, the higher the rate of return the students should receive on their investment. However, empirical studies find that human capital theory cannot account for the low or even negative rates of return to graduate education (Blaug, 1976). This counterintuitive finding may be a function of the tastes[2] of graduate school–educated people for jobs that may be intrinsically but not financially rewarding and/or the rate at which graduate school–educated people are employed in the academic sector. This sector tends to pay highly educated professionals less than similarly or less educated professionals in the nonacademic sector. Consequently, the salary outcomes for noncompleters as compared with completers are likely to be a function of whether they are employed in the academic sector. A modified version of human capital theory for graduate education based on economic sector would suggest that when departing students obtain high-level jobs in the same economic sector as their completing counterparts, they are likely to be offered lower starting salaries and confront lower ceilings than their credentialed colleagues who have (putatively) invested more in their educations.

Networking Theory

Networking theory provides insights into social factors that affect how students seek and secure jobs. It deals with the role that social ties and social relationships play in the labor market.

Social networks provide job seekers with information and influence. They link individuals to broader social structures such as occupations, markets, and economic sectors than they can connect with on their own. People who use social contacts to obtain jobs often fair better in terms of occupational status, income, job satisfaction, and tenure (Campbell, 1988).

The strength of social ties does not affect all subgroups in a job search similarly (Wegener, 1991). Weak ties (formal professional relationships) benefit individuals with high status. They offer these job seekers a chance to contact someone of rank outside the status range of their own network (Granovetter, 1973). Strong ties (informal, intimate social relationships) benefit individuals with low status. They provide an opportunity for these individuals to contact persons of higher prestige within their own network. By virtue of obtaining the Ph.D., completers achieve a higher degree of status than noncompleters and should use weak ties more than noncompleters. Indeed, completers' job search process should be enhanced and facilitated by exploiting weak ties, whereas noncompleters' job search process should be enhanced and facilitated by exploiting strong ties.

Credential Theory

Educational credentials have become the currency for employment (Collins, 1979). Employers generally look for and screen on the basis of the completion of a degree in a particular discipline. Credential theory provides insights into the institutional barriers departers are likely to face.

While credential theory argues that individuals who lack a degree are structurally disadvantaged in the labor market, it does not distinguish among types of labor markets or labor market segments. Yet, it is reasonable to believe that the lack of a Ph.D. will play out differently in the Ph.D.-required labor market than in the general labor market. Work on occupational and firm labor markets (Althauser & Kalleberg, 1981) indicates that credentials are required for entering and advancing in the occupational labor market (i.e., labor markets defined by educational and professional attainment—chemist, psychologist, doctor, lawyer), while prior training, experience, or education in general are required for entering and advancing in the firm labor market (i.e., labor markets internal to organizations that train workers and promote from within—supervisor, manager, director). It is also reasonable to believe that the lack of the Ph.D. credential will play out differently in expanding, as compared with contracting, or stable labor market sectors (e.g., science and technology sectors as compared with cultural sectors) and that the effect will be a function of labor supply and labor demand.

Strict credentialing theory suggests that students who fail to complete the Ph.D. will automatically be screened out of the advanced-degree labor market during the application process by organizations or occupations seeking Ph.D.-level personnel and that they will find many job opportunities closed to them despite their advanced knowledge and skill. However, work on the mutability of educational credentials (Bills, 1991), indicates that employers are willing to hire one level above and one level below a job candidate's actual schooling, especially if the candidate has relevant prior work experience. Thus, the door to jobs in the advanced-degree labor market may not be closed absolutely but rather may depend on how far along departing students were in their graduate programs when they left and the amount of relevant work experience they have. The supply of similarly or better-qualified candidates relative to demand should also influence departers' chances of securing a job in this labor market: An overabundance of unemployed Ph.D.'s in a low-demand sector will decrease noncompleters' chances; a shortage in a high-demand sector will increase their chances.

Lack of the Ph.D. credential is likely to affect departers differently in the general labor market than in the advanced-degree labor market. In the general labor market, their advanced level of education may cause departers to be viewed as overeducated for jobs for which they have the appropriate bachelor's- or master's-level credential (assuming they admit that they were in, but did not complete, a doctoral program), or it may distinguish them positively from competing bachelor's- or master's-level candidates who were not in Ph.D. programs. The effect is likely to be contingent on a number of factors, including the departing student's prior work experience, the relevance of this experience to the job being sought, the nature of the job (autonomous and self-directed versus routine), the potential for advancement, and the idiosyncratic attitudes and opinions that employers hold of graduate students.

FINDING A JOB

The Local Labor Market and Relocation

Because jobs for highly educated people outside of academe are more likely to exist in large, urban labor markets than in small, rural ones, noncompleters who attend universities in rural areas are under greater pressure to relocate to find a job than noncompleters who attend universities in urban areas. Cities also have flourishing cultural sectors and, therefore, have more job opportunities for students in the humanities than do small towns. Thus, students at universities in urban and rural areas experience different pressures to relocate, as do students in the humanities relative to those in the sciences and social sciences. Pressures to relocate were explored in the survey by asking students (completers and noncompleters) whether they had job opportunities in the vicinity of their university. Interviewees' relocation behaviors were assessed by following up the discussion of the decision to leave with the general question "Then what?"

The size and distribution of opportunity in the labor market near the university does affect students' relocation decisions. Urban students were much more likely to say they had job opportunities in the vicinity of their university than Rural students (41 percent vs. 28 percent). Almost half of Urban noncompleters (47 percent) felt there were job opportunities nearby, compared with less than a third of Rural noncompleters (32 percent). Completers from Urban and Rural Universities were equally likely to say they had job opportunities nearby (33 percent vs. 26 percent). These percentages, which are lower than those of the noncompleters, can be accounted for by a large number of completers entering the national advanced-degree labor market and being offered academic and other Ph.D.-level jobs that required them to move.

Among students who felt that there were job opportunities in the vicinity of their university, Rural students were more likely than Urban students to eventually leave the area (80 percent vs. 62 percent), indicating that Ruraltown has a less favorable labor market for highly educated people than Urban City. The effect holds for completers (82 percent Rural vs. 61 percent Urban) and noncompleters (76 percent Rural vs. 63 percent Urban).

The interview data provide further insight into how the local labor market and noncompleters' economic circumstances affected their relocation decisions. Immediately upon leaving their programs, thirteen of fifteen[3] Rural students left Ruraltown, whereas only seven of fifteen Urban students left Urban City. Two Rural students moved back in with their parents, because they "didn't have any place else to go," and took low-paying, elementary jobs. The two interviewees who stayed in the Ruraltown area had been living there prior to entering graduate school. In addition, three Urban and one Rural student who stayed in their areas had a job prior to leaving. Those who were working part-time converted to full-time.

The domain of knowledge the students were in also interacted with the local labor market and affected their relocation decisions. Overall, Urban humanities students were more likely to feel that they had job opportunities in their area than Rural humanities students (47 percent vs. 33 percent).[4] Urban science students were somewhat more likely than Rural science students to feel that there were job opportunities nearby (38 percent vs. 26 percent). Social science students at Urban and Rural were equally likely to feel they could get a job in their local area (32 percent vs. 26 percent).

Students who did not feel that they had job opportunities in their area were equally likely to relocate regardless of domain of knowledge or university (sciences: 92 percent Rural vs. 93 percent Urban; social sciences: 86 percent Rural vs. 87 percent Urban; humanities: 91 percent Rural vs. 89 percent Urban). By contrast, among students who felt that there were job opportunities nearby. Rural science and humanities students were more likely to relocate than Urban science and humanities students (sciences: 88 percent Rural vs. 72 percent Urban; humanities: 76 percent Rural vs. 57 percent Urban).

Thus, the structure of opportunity in the labor market surrounding the universities influences students' relocation decisions; and the interview data support this contention. However, the pressures on completers and noncompleters are different. Completers, regardless of university, are pulled into good jobs out of the area. By contrast, noncompleters, especially those living in Ruraltown, are pushed out of the area because of the lack of jobs for people with their knowledge and skills. Furthermore, their social and economic dislocation and emotional distress at the time of departure increases the probability that noncompleters will return to their parents' homes or relocate near family and friends for social support and economic security while they regroup and figure out their next moves in life.

Reconstructing a Career

Most of the students had planned an academic or Ph.D.-required career when they enrolled in graduate school. Without the Ph.D. credential, these careers were now closed to most of the departers. Consequently, to understand how noncompleters go about reconstructing their professional lives, the interviewees were asked how they decided what to do after they left and how confident they were in their ability to find a job. Their responses to these questions, and others, indicate that many did not have good cognitive maps of the labor market, of methods for conducting a job search, and even of how to present themselves in job interviews. In addition, their experiences show that employers are flexible about educational requirements in both directions, especially if the job seeker has compensating work experience.

Most of the interviewees were confident that they would find some type of employment, but many were not sure what kind. Those whose self-esteem or self-confidence was diminished when they left had more doubts and concerns about what that something might be than those who viewed their leaving as a good thing. Even though these latter students were quite positive about their ability to find a job, many initially were unaware of the labor market opportunities for people with their educational backgrounds.

> *Boyd*: I never doubted that I could find a job, but I had no idea how easy it was going to be to find that kind of a job. I really didn't even know about that kind of work particularly. But a student in my program, who worked at a private school as an English teacher before, and it sounded like nice environment. . . . He told me how to, you know, there's a couple of centralized ways of going about doing it.

Students with longer durations expressed a bit more uncertainty than those with shorter durations. This may be because the longer students remain in graduate school, the more they have invested in their education, the more committed they become to the academic profession and/or employment in the upper tier of the primary labor market, and the narrower they perceive their field of opportunity to be.

> *Tom*: I think when you initially start looking you have a preference for academic jobs 'cause you just don't have a clue to what nonacademic[s do]. Certainly in my case, I had no clue to what nonacademics — well, other than government jobs doing economic research for the government — I had no clue to what economists did in nonacademic jobs.

By contrast, students of shorter duration have less invested in their education and the academic profession. (In fact, quite a few were turned off by it.) Consequently, they are more willing to explore a wider range of alternative careers and are more willing to take jobs in the lower tier of the primary labor market and even in the secondary labor market as stopgap measures. Many students who sought and secured jobs in the lower-primary and secondary labor markets had durations of one year or less. They simply returned to doing the type of part-time or summer work they had done while in high school and/or college with the intention of working and going to school to prepare themselves for something else. Often that "something else" was not clearly defined.

Interviewees with durations of two or more years, or one year with prior graduate experience, looked for jobs in their own field or in a related field in which they would have control over their work and be able to use their knowledge and skills. A few of the students who left at various points during stage 2 sought and secured full- or part-time college teaching jobs. This indicates that employers in the academic labor market in the early to mid-1980s were willing to hire students without Ph.D.'s, especially if the student had extensive teaching experience. However, students who were at stage 3 and were not already employed in academe self-selected out of college teaching, believing that without the credential, they could not get a teaching position.

> *Interviewer*: So when you went back home and started looking for a job, how confident were you in your ability to find one?
>
> *Beatrice*: Not much at all.
>
> *Interviewer*: Why not?
>
> *Beatrice*: Because I didn't have the education to do what I wanted to do. I didn't have the Ph.D. I don't have teaching credentials, so I couldn't do any of that. . . . I was just so depressed that I just didn't even try very hard from that point of view. I just found a job [as a retail sales clerk] and worked at it.

Similarly, Rhett, who was unable to make progress with his dissertation and who had withdrawn from graduate school a few months before the interview, rejected the idea of seeking a college-level teaching position, despite having taught at a Central American university for several years between spells of graduate education.

Thus, based on the interviews, it appears that duration has some effect on noncompleters' confidence in their ability to find a job, the types of jobs they will consider, and the labor markets in which they search. Advanced education does not appear to deter students from seeking and securing jobs for which they are overqualified. Students who left during stage 2 tried to secure higher-level jobs that were more in line with their education than students who left earlier. In fact, lack of the Ph.D. did not deter students in stage 2 from seeking full- or part-time college teaching jobs. However, it appears to have deterred students at stage 3 who were not already teaching at the college level when they left.

Searching for and Securing a Job

To determine how students were matched with their first job, the survey asked students whether or not they used a variety of specified job search methods (recruited, professor found job for you, contacted employers directly, responded to newspaper ads, used social networks, went through career counseling, started own business, or other). They were also asked which method was most successful for securing a job.

Twenty-five percent of completers and 15 percent of noncompleters already had a job when they left graduate school.[5] Students in the humanities, regardless of status, were less likely to have jobs at the time of exit (15 percent) than students in the sciences (24 percent) or social sciences (25 percent). More men had jobs than women when they left (25 percent vs. 16 percent), and this effect holds for completers (27 percent vs. 18 percent) but not for noncompleters (17 percent vs. 13 percent), suggesting some hiring biases in the advanced-degree labor market.

Completers and noncompleters who were in the labor market[6] used multiple methods to find a job. They were equally likely to have contacted employers directly, to have gone through career counseling, started their own business, and to have used "other" methods (see table 10.1). However, there were differences in the "other" methods. Completers were more likely to have responded to advertisements in professional journals or to have interviewed at professional meetings, whereas noncompleters were more likely to state that they had a job already or had gone on for additional education.

After contacting employers directly, the most frequently used methods by both groups were being recruited, responding to newspaper advertisements,

Table 10.1.   Methods Used for Searching for and Securing a Job by Status (in percent)

Methods	Job Search Methods			Most Successful Method for Securing a Job		
	Completers	Noncompleters	p	Completers	Noncompleters	p
Being recruited	41	19	*	20	9	
Professor finding you a job	15	4	*	5	2	
Contacting potential employers directly	80	83		42	48	
Responding to newspaper ads	37	53	*	13	17	
Using social networks	29	47	*	5	10	
Going through career counseling	15	20		1	2	
Starting own business	3	6		1	3	
Other	22	16		15	9	

$*p < .001.$

and using social networks. However, large differences prevailed between groups in their use of these methods. Completers were more likely to have been recruited than noncompleters, suggesting that the Ph.D. credential played a role. By contrast, noncompleters were more likely to have responded to newspaper advertisements and to have used social networks (strong tie). Although used less frequently by both groups, completers were more likely to have had help from a professor (weak tie) in finding a job than noncompleters. Students' differential use of social ties is consistent with networking theory.[7]

Large and significant differences also exist between completers and noncompleters for the methods they found most successful in securing a job (see table 10.1) and whether those methods resulted in a career track or noncareer track job (data not shown). The best method of finding a job for both groups was by contacting employers directly; 41 percent of the completers and 50 percent of the noncompleters secured a career track job this way within six months of leaving. Responding to newspaper advertisements worked about equally well for both groups, but it is positioned differently in the rankings. Students who responded to advertisements were more likely to find a noncareer track job than a career track job (21 percent vs. 13 percent). However, many of the completers who checked off newspaper advertisements on the survey were probably referring to the *Chronicle of Higher Education* or other professional publications because many of these completers were hired into positions not widely advertised in newspapers (i.e., assistant professorships and postdoctoral research positions). Career counseling worked equally poorly for both groups in securing a job.

Strong ties (social networks) were twice as effective for noncompleters as completers. Noncompleters who secured a job using social networks were more likely to have gotten a noncareer track job than a career track job (60 percent vs. 35 percent). By contrast, completers who secured a job using social networks were eight times more likely to have gotten a career track job than a noncareer track job (81 percent vs. 10 percent). However, completers and noncompleters have different social networks. Completers' social networks include a much larger percentage of Ph.D.'s than noncompleters' (i.e., graduate school friends). Consequently, members of completers' social networks are more likely to be situated in the advanced-degree labor market than members of noncompleters' social networks and can thus help them find better jobs.

Weak ties (professor found job for you) were least effective for noncompleters. Only three noncompleters secured a job this way, and none secured career track jobs. In fact, all got temporary instructor positions. Although, strong and weak ties worked equally well for completers, they do not rank highly among their best means for securing a job. Still, completers whose professor found them a job took career track postdoctoral positions or jobs as assistant professors and industrial researchers.

Finally, the fact that recruitment worked much better for completers than noncompleters suggests that the Ph.D. credential helped completers obtain jobs. Completers who were recruited were more likely to get career track jobs than were noncompleters and to get them in the advanced-degree labor market. By contrast, noncompleters who were recruited entered into the lower tier of the primary labor market and took such jobs as teacher, secretary, library assistant, sales clerk, and mental health worker.

FIRST JOB

Occupational Attainment

Finding a job is not the same thing as finding a career track job. Noncompleters, who do not have the Ph.D. credential and have less years of education, should, and did, have a harder time finding a career track job than completers. The survey asked students whether, within six months after leaving, they had found a career track job, a noncareer track job, looked for but did not find a job, or did not look for a job.

Overall, within six months, 91 percent of the completers but only 71 percent of the noncompleters were employed. The vast majority of the completers (79 percent) had secured a career track job compared with less than half of the noncompleters (42 percent). By contrast, noncompleters were more than twice as likely as completers to have found a noncareer track job

(29 percent vs. 11 percent). Furthermore, noncompleters were five times more likely not to have looked for work than completers (25 percent vs. 5 percent). Among students who did not look for work, noncompleters were four times more likely than completers to have had a subsequent spell of graduate or professional education (62 percent vs. 16 percent), indicating that they transferred to other graduate schools or entered professional schools shortly after leaving. Additionally, while male and female noncompleters were equally likely to have secured a career track job (43 percent vs. 40 percent), male completers were somewhat more likely than female completers to have secured one (81 percent vs. 75 percent). This suggests that women with Ph.D.'s may have been discriminated against in the advanced-degree labor market but that women without the Ph.D. were not discriminated against in the general labor market.

Using information provided by the interviewees about their first jobs, it is possible to analyze how they were initially situated in the labor market on three dimensions by discipline and duration. The dimensions are relatedness to field (in field, related field, or out of field), labor market sector (academic, business/industry, government, or other), and occupational labor market (upper primary, lower primary, secondary, or other).

Before discussing these labor market effects, it should be noted that defining "first job" is not always straightforward. The analysis includes the first job experience subsequent to leaving of the five interviewees who transferred to other universities—only one of whom completed. It also includes the intereducational job of one student who left Urban University for a number of years, worked, returned briefly, and left again. This job was included because when he left the first time, he had not planned to return. By contrast, the work experience of another student who transferred and later stopped out for a year is not counted as his first job because during the stop-out period, he fully intended to return to his program and complete. The analysis is further complicated by the fact that at least three of students held more than one job, two of them taught college-level classes on the side. Thus, the job that the student selected as his or her primary job is the one that was subjected to analysis.

Relatedness to Field

Relatedness to field is a measure of how closely related a job is to the students' academic training. Degree of relatedness was defined as follows. Interviewees' jobs were classified as "in field" if the students were utilizing the knowledge and skills of their discipline in a direct way such as teaching on any level or working in some occupation where training in their field was essential—for instance, a chemistry student in the chemical industry, an economics students at an economics consulting firm, or a music student working for a symphony. Students' jobs were classified as "related field" if their

Table 10.2.   Relatedness of First Job to Field by Domain of Knowledge and Duration for the Interview Sample (number of interviewees)

	Relatedness to Field			
	In-Field	*Related-Field*	*Out-of-Field*	*Other*
Domain of Knowledge				
Science	7	0	2	1
Social science	1	3	3	0
Humanities	4	3	4	0
Duration				
Stage 1	7	4	5	1
Stage 2	2	2	3	0
Stage 3	3	0	1	0

academic training prepared them for the job but the job could be assumed by someone with training in another discipline, and they were not using their academic training in a direct way. Examples of related field include a history student in journalism, an economics student in local government, and an English student employed in publishing or editing. Finally, students' jobs were classified as "out of field" if the job did not require, and the students did not use, academic training in their discipline. Examples include secretarial work, retail sales, waitressing, and farm hand. Motherhood falls into the "other" category.

As shown in table 10.2, the science students were more likely than others to secure jobs in their fields, whereas the social science students were least likely to. Duration in program as well as university departed from (not shown) have little effect on the relationship of first job to academic training, although those who left during stage 3—students with the most human capital—were more likely to be in field than not.

Labor Market Sector

Labor market sector assesses in what broad area of the economy the interviewees were employed. For the purpose of this analysis, the academic sector includes employment at a college or K–12 school. Business/industry is defined as the corporate world or some large, recognized type of for-profit industry such as publishing. The government sector includes working directly for the government (local, state, or national) or being otherwise employed by the government, such as working in a prison. "Other" includes self-employment, retail sales, catering, farm work, church ministry, and motherhood.

Table 10.3 shows that the interviewees were more likely to end up in the business/industry sector than any other sector regardless of field and that students who had left during the stage 1 were more likely to end up there than

Table 10.3.   Labor Market Sector of First Job by Domain of Knowledge and Duration for the Interview Sample (number of interviewees)

	Labor Market Sector			
	Academic	Business/Industry	Government	Other
Domain of Knowledge				
Science	4	5	0	1
Social science	0	2	2	3
Humanities	1	6	0	4
Duration				
Stage 1	2	7	2	5
Stage 2	1	4	0	2
Stage 3	2	2	0	1

students who had left at other stages. Being in the academic sector in some capacity is not a function of duration. However, no student who had left during stage 1 was employed in college teaching—one worked as a high school teacher, the other as a laboratory technician at a university. Finally, of the eight students employed in the "other" sector, seven were from Rural University, suggesting that, despite relocating, they either selected out of, or had greater difficulty accessing, mainstream jobs than did Urban students.

Occupational Labor Market

Although it was predicted that noncompleters would seek jobs in the upper tier of the primary labor market, overall only 57 percent of those interviewed actually secured their first job there. If the three students in the "other" category are removed (two who were self-employed and one who opted for motherhood), the figure rises to 64 percent. As shown in table 10.4, students in the social sciences were the only group to take jobs in the secondary labor market (waitress, farmhand), and students in the humanities were more likely than any other group to be working in the lower tier of the primary labor market. Students who left during stage 1—students with the least amount of human capital—were more likely to take jobs in the lower tier of the primary labor market and the secondary labor market than students who left at any other time, indicating that educational capital does have an effect on initial labor market outcomes.

Excluding the "other" category, two-thirds of the students who did not seek or secure jobs in the upper tier of the primary labor market were female. None of the students in the lower tier of the primary labor market or the secondary labor market viewed their jobs as "career track"; rather, they saw them as stopgap measures on the way to something else. Indeed, three of these students enrolled in classes shortly after acquiring their jobs, and another, a humanities student, quit after a few months to study for actuarial exams.

Table 10.4. Occupational Labor Market of First Job by Domain of Knowledge and Duration for the Interview Sample (number of interviewees)

| | Occupational Labor Market | | | |
	Upper Primary	Lower Primary	Secondary	Other
Domain of Knowledge				
Science	7	2	0	1
Social science	4	1	2	1
Humanities	5	4	0	1
Duration				
Stage 1	7	6	1	2
Stage 2	5	0	1	1
Stage 3	4	1	0	0

Salary Attainment

Assessing differences in completers' and noncompleters' starting salaries sheds light on the role of the Ph.D. credential in salary attainment as well as the relative return they received on their investment in graduate education. Because 45 percent of noncompleters and 9 percent of completers pursued additional education, and because it was often difficult to determine whether the first salary students reported was received before or after that spell of education, the analyses in this section are limited to students who were employed in career and noncareer track jobs within six months of leaving (539 students).[8] Table 10.5 shows the first salary for this group of students by status, domain of knowledge, and discipline rounded to the nearest hundred. Regardless of status, economics students had the highest starting salaries, music students the lowest.

The salary data to be discussed here were analyzed by taking the natural log of salary. Such a conversion allows the contribution of a variety of factors to salary to be discussed in terms of percent. These factors include status, gender, university, domain of knowledge, nature of first job (career track, noncareer track), utilization of graduate training, self-esteem at time of exit, and noncompleters' duration in graduate school.[9]

Controlling for all the factors listed above, noncompleters' starting salaries were 27 percent lower than completers', indicating a high rate of return on the Ph.D. credential. However, for each year they were in graduate school, noncompleters' starting salaries were augmented by 3 percent. This benefit is consonant with predictions about return on investment in education from human capital theory.[10]

The degree to which students use the knowledge and skills they obtained in graduate school in their jobs gets at the pecuniary and nonpecuniary return on investment in graduate education. The survey thus asked students how

Table 10.5.   First Salary for Students Who Were Employed within Six Months of Leaving by Domain of Knowledge, Discipline, and Status (in dollars rounded to the nearest hundred)

Salary	Whole Sample	Completers	Noncompleters
Average	25,900	28,700	19,100
Sciences	27,100	28,600	21,600
Mathematics	26,800	30,300	21,400
Biology	23,600	24,600	21,600
Chemistry	29,000	30,000	21,900
Social Sciences	32,000	33,000	26,400
Sociology	27,700	29,000	16,200[1]
Economics	35,700	36,900	30,000
Psychology	29,700	30,400	22,400[2]
Humanities	19,600	23,400	16,200
English	18,800	22,700	16,800
History	26,600	30,200	17,000
Music	16,800	18,900	14,100

[1] $n = 2$.
[2] $n = 5$.

much they used their graduate training in their first job. Completers used their training a lot, whereas noncompleters used their training only some of the time.[11] The salary attainment data show that the more students used their graduate education and training in their first job, the higher their starting salaries. Each degree of knowledge and skill utilization added a suggestive 5 percent to the students' starting salaries as a whole. In other words, students who made very strong use of their graduate training earned 5 percent more than students who used their training some of the time. Further analysis shows that the effect is limited to noncompleters. They received a 9 percent bonus for each degree of training utilization. Thus, those noncompleters who used their training a lot earned 18 percent more than those who did not use their training at all.

The lack of an effect for completers is probably a function of labor market sector. Most completers entered the advanced-degree labor market, which requires and screens job candidates for the knowledge and skill received during graduate education. By contrast, most noncompleters entered the general labor market, where this knowledge and skill is not required, although often desired. Employers in the general labor market thus appear to be willing to pay noncompleters for their investment in graduate education.

Among the interviewees, only those students who had jobs in their fields said that they used knowledge and skills from their graduate programs. Five out of eight of these students had jobs in the academic sector. Some students, especially those who were teaching at the college level, found their graduate training indispensable. Others indicated that they merely used managerial skills that they had developed from being teaching assistants, or statistical and analytic skills from their statistics classes, but did not use the disciplinary-based knowledge they acquired while in graduate school.

Regardless of status, students who secured career track jobs within six months of leaving said that they used their graduate training more than students who secured noncareer track jobs. Being in a career track job controlling for use of graduate training yields a significant salary premium. Students who secured career track jobs earned 34 percent more than students who secured noncareer track jobs. The effect holds for over status (completers: 35 percent higher; noncompleters: 32 percent higher).

There was also a domain of knowledge effect for use of graduate training. Students in the social sciences used their training more than students in the sciences and the humanities (completers: 2.81 social sciences, 2.70 sciences, 2.71 humanities; noncompleters: 2.45 social sciences, 2.07 sciences, 1.88 humanities). These differences tend to parallel the impact of domain of knowledge on first salary. Overall, students in the social sciences and the sciences received much higher starting salaries than students in the humanities (46 percent and 32 percent higher, respectively), and the effect holds over status (completers: social sciences, 36 percent higher; sciences, 28 percent higher; noncompleters: social sciences, 54 percent higher; sciences, 40 percent higher).

University attended has a significant impact on first salary in general and for noncompleters in particular. The first salaries of students who attended Rural University were 14 percent lower than that of students who attended Urban University. Rural completers' starting salaries were depressed 8 percent relative to Urban completers', but the effect was not statistically significant. However, there were very large differences in starting salaries between noncompleters who attended Urban University and those who attended Rural University. Urban noncompleters' starting salaries were 38 percent higher than Rural noncompleters'. The effect of university persists when the time at which students exited the university's local labor market is controlled for, indicating that the difference in salary between universities has more to do with Urban's prestige than the nature of the labor market surrounding the university.

In chapter 9, we saw that at the time they left graduate school, noncompleters' and at-risk completers' self-esteem had dropped considerably more than that of their counterparts. In addition, we saw that interviewees who spontaneously mentioned decreases in their self-esteem and self-confidence took jobs in the low-paying secondary labor market. Given the potential impact of low self-esteem on the types of jobs students may feel worthy of applying for as well as the potential impact of low self-esteem on self-presentation during a job interview and on one's ability to negotiate for a higher salary, self-esteem at time of exit was included among the factors analyzed as having an influence on first salary. It did, indeed, influence salary by a factor of 4 percent. Thus, students who exited with the lowest level of self-esteem received starting salaries 16 percent lower than students who exited with the highest level of self-esteem.

Also interesting are differences in level of exiting self-esteem by type of job secured. Regardless of status, students with the highest levels self-esteem secured higher-paying, career track jobs within six months of leaving graduate school, while students with the lowest levels of self-esteem secured lower-paying, noncareer track jobs or looked for but did not find a job. The self-esteem of those who did not look for a job (most of whom appear to have gone directly into another graduate or professional program) fell somewhere in between. Self-esteem thus seems to affect both the type of jobs students seek and secure as well as their starting salaries.

Noncompleters' Experiences in and Feelings about Their First Jobs

The interviewees were asked a number of questions about their experiences in their first job. These questions included whether they perceived their first job as a career track job, how qualified they felt they were for their jobs, whether they had any difficulty adjusting to the nonacademic world (if they were employed in the nonacademic world), whether and how much they used knowledge and skills from their graduate programs in their jobs (discussed earlier), whether they were adversely affected by not having the Ph.D., and how satisfied they were with their first jobs.

None of the interviewees who were employed in the lower primary or secondary labor markets viewed their jobs as "career track"; rather, they viewed them as a way to make money and pay the bills while they figured out what they wanted to do and trained for something else. In fact, only six of the interviewees saw their first job as career track, and it was a qualified yes for two of these. Duration in graduate school had no effect on perceptions of first job as career track, although the degree to which the job was related to their field did. Four of the six interviewees who viewed their jobs as career track were working in their fields or in a related field.

Despite the fact that a number of the interviewees were, from an objective standpoint, overqualified for their first jobs, none expressed this sentiment. Rather, they felt they were well qualified for what they were doing or found other ways to rationalize the mismatch between education and employment. Ellen, who worked as a secretary, and Pauline,who worked as a waitress, are illustrative:

> *Ellen*: By that time, I was starting to figure out that things are temporary, and if you take control of your life and you have a goal, and if you have some sort of incremental plan . . . you tolerate at given points in your life things that maybe aren't

quite right in order to achieve the things that you really want. So I think that's how I looked at it.

Pauline: At the time, my new identity came that I am going . . . to medical school. So, that was my identity. "Oh, incidentally, I'm working here while I work to get into medical school." That was the whole thing. It became my new identity.

Only India, an English student who left after one term and went into publishing, felt underqualified for her first job. Her feelings of unease derived from never having done that type of work before.

Given that they had spent most of their adult lives in academe around highly educated people with similar interests, that they had planned to pursue academic careers, and that most had little, if any, exposure to the working world, the question naturally arises as to whether students who left the familiar confines of the university had difficulty adjusting to life and work outside the academy. Very few of the interviewees said that they had difficulty making the transition. Of the four who did, two were at stage 3 when they left. Their difficulties involved not finding their work challenging and not having people to interact with at the same intellectual level as in graduate school.

Not having the Ph.D. could potentially be a double-edged sword in the labor market for noncompleters. Lack of the credential could hurt those in high-level positions where the Ph.D. is common currency and used in making salary or promotion decisions, or lack of the Ph.D. could help students in jobs where holding a Ph.D. might cause them to be perceived as overqualified. Among students who said that not having a Ph.D. had an impact on their jobs, all but one said that the impact was negative, and even in the positive case, the student's feelings about the impact were mixed.

Tom: I would say there is a slight effect. It may affect your ability to testify. I don't think it prevents you from testifying, but it's an additional credential that would have been helpful.

Interviewer: What do you mean by testifying?

Tom: Being an expert witness. So for testimony types of stuff, I think it does make a difference. For any of the rest of the business it does not make a difference. To a certain extent it's a negative amongst some people just because they simply assume you know less rather than more if you have a Ph.D.

Interviewer: Why is that?

Tom: Because they assume you are going to bring a theoretical solution to a problem as opposed to having any practical sense of how businesses really operate.

The majority of those who felt that they were hurt by not having a Ph.D. had jobs that were in their fields. They said that they were hurt in two ways: One was not getting the same amount of respect as colleagues who had Ph.D.'s;

the other was in terms of lower salaries and reduced chances for promotion (see Jacks et al., 1983). James, who taught at a four-year college for several years, is a good example:

> *James*: It was constantly emphasized to me that even though I consistently ranked as one of the best math instructors on campus, . . . even though I got basically excellent job reviews, it was constantly emphasized to me that I would not get tenure without a Ph.D. . . . I would see other people [who] came in . . . at the same time I did or after me . . . who did not do their job as well . . . . When you're placed in a situation [where] you see other people who are not as good at their job as you are, . . . get promoted, or do better simply because they have a degree and it means nothing where they are . . .—they aren't doing meaningful research or whatever— it's just disconcerting. In fact, . . . I didn't get promoted, and the reason I was told that I didn't get promoted was because if they had promoted me—the person on the committee told me that the feeling was I deserved promotion for my work— they felt that in terms of the paper record, if they promoted me, . . . then I could have grounds to sue them if I came up for tenure and they didn't give me tenure because, "Gee, how could you not give this guy tenure when you promote him?" And I just thought that was the most absurd thing I'd ever heard.

Two students whose first jobs were out of field also felt they were hurt by not having the Ph.D. They believed they would have gotten better first jobs with the degree.

Job satisfaction was predicted to be a function of an interaction between how closely related the student's job was to the student's discipline and how close to the discipline the student desired to stay. Across the board, students who were working out of field were dissatisfied with their jobs, and many of these students still desire to get a Ph.D. Stuart, whose first job was as a paralegal doing collection work for a law firm, found the work "distasteful." Ashley, whose first job was in futures trading, "hated" what he was doing because "you deal with a bunch of stupid people whose only interest in life is making money." By contrast, those whose first jobs were in their field or in a related field tended to be satisfied with their jobs and to enjoy their work.

EDUCATIONAL INTERLUDE

As previously indicated, at some point between leaving graduate school and the time they filled out the survey, 45 percent of the noncompleters and 9 percent of the completers had an additional spell of education. These students thus increased their educational capital, and many acquired a credential in the process. However, in doing so, many also removed themselves from the labor force, thereby decreasing their capital of accumulated work experience. Consequently, to fully understand the long-term labor market outcomes for the students in the sample, noncompleters in particular, it is necessary to explore their educational trajectories. Before doing so, it should be noted that the educational data discussed here are far from perfect. Many students did not fill out all or part of the last page of the questionnaire from which these data were obtained, and even when data were available, it was often difficult to follow and accurately code students' educational career paths. These data are meant to be suggestive of the educational strivings of students in the sample, but they should not be interpreted as definitive. In fact, they likely underrepresent noncompleters' actual educational attainments.

Of the students who pursed additional education, 37 percent of the completers and 58 percent of the noncompleters received a professional degree. These degrees include MBAs (9 percent, completers; 7 percent, noncompleters), medical degrees such as an M.D., D.D.S., or D.V.M. (23 percent, completers; 12 percent, noncompleters), law degrees (4 percent, completers; 8 percent, noncompleters) and doctoral degrees (Ph.D., Ed.D.) (30 percent, noncompleters). The rest of the students who had an additional spell of education either received nonprofessional degrees (bachelor's, master's), professional certifications, left their programs without a degree, or were working on but had not yet completed a degree. These students are grouped together has having pursued nonprofessional education.

Among students who pursued additional education, completers in the sciences were twice as likely to pursue additional education as noncompleters in the sciences (80 percent vs. 41 percent), whereas noncompleters in the humanities were eleven times as likely as completers in the humanities to do so (45 percent vs. 4 percent). Equal proportions of social sciences students had an additional spell of education (15 percent, completers vs. 14 percent, noncompleters).

As mentioned earlier, 30 percent of the noncompleters with additional education (14 percent of all noncompleters) had completed the doctorate at the time of the survey, and some indeterminate percentage were in the process. These new doctorates were more likely to have departed from Urban than from Rural (60 percent vs. 40 percent). English students were more likely than students from other disciplines to get the Ph.D. In fact, 85 percent of the English students had been enrolled in Urban's English Department, which weeds at the master's.

CURRENT JOB

Occupational Attainment

Relatedness to Field

Table 10.6 shows that after being in the labor market for, in most instances, six to thirteen years, the noncompleters in the interview sample became

Table 10.6. Relatedness of Current Job to Field by Domain of Knowledge and Duration for the Interview Sample (number of interviewees)

	Relatedness to Field			
	In-Field	Related-Field	Out-of-Field	Other
Domain of Knowledge				
Science	3	1	1	5
Social science	2	2	3	0
Humanities	2	5	4	0
Duration				
Stage 1	5	4	5	2
Stage 2	0	3	2	2
Stage 3	2	1	1	1

equally distributed across jobs in their field, in a related field, or out of field. Science students are the only ones in the "other" category. This category includes one student who, at the time of the interview, was unemployed but looking for work in a related field, a student who had returned to graduate school in his discipline, a student who was receiving disability insurance, and two women who were full-time mothers. Duration in graduate school appears to have little effect on the relationship of current job to discipline of origin.

Labor Market Sector

The survey asked student to identify the sector of the labor market in which they were currently employed (academic, business/industry, government, not employed).[12] While completers and noncompleters were equally likely to be in the government sector or unemployed, completers were much more likely to be in the academic sector (61 percent vs. 38 percent), and noncompleters were much more likely to be in the business/industry sector (47 percent vs. 28 percent). Male noncompleters were more likely to be in the business/industry and government sectors than female noncompleters. Female noncompleters were more likely to be in the academic sector (probably as school-teachers) and to be unemployed (probably working as full-time mothers).

Additional education has little effect on the distribution of noncompleters across sectors, although those who obtained the Ph.D. are more likely to be in the academic sector (60 percent) than in the business/industry sector (40 percent). By contrast, completers who pursued additional education were more likely to be in the business/industry or government sectors (61 percent) than in the academic sector (39 percent). These sector-by-status differences suggest that a high percentage of noncompleters obtained the Ph.D. to move into the academic sector, whereas a high percentage of completers obtained more education to move out of it.

Table 10.7. Labor Market Sector of Current Job by Domain of Knowledge and Duration for the Interview Sample (number of interviewees)

	Labor Market Sector			
	Academic	*Business/Industry*	*Government*	*Other*
Domain of Knowledge				
Science	1	4	0	5
Social science	0	2	3	1
Humanities	3	5	0	4
Duration				
Stage 1	1	8	1	6
Stage 2	0	2	2	3
Stage 3	3	1	0	1

Among the interviewees, the majority of the students' current jobs were either in the business/industry sector or in "other" (see table 10.7). "Other" includes the five students who were in "other" in relatedness to field (discussed earlier), plus four students who were self-employed and one who was in medicine. Students who had left during stage 1 were more likely to be in business/industry or in "other" than students who had left at later stages. Of the four students in the academic sector, three teach at the school level, while the fourth works as an administrative assistant at a small college and teaches a few courses. Only students from the social sciences held government jobs.

Occupational Labor Market

By the time of interview, all of the students had moved out of the secondary labor market, but their numbers in the lower tier of the primary labor market remained relatively stable (see table 10.8). Although they dominate in the upper tier of the primary labor market, less than half of those interviewed were situated there, with a loss of about 10 percent over time. In addition, many moved out of the traditional labor market sectors into "other." Science students, as discussed earlier, are the most likely to be in "other"; humanities students predominate in the lower primary; two of these students are teachers.

Interviewees who had left during stage 1 increased their representation in the upper primary and "other" categories. Three of the stage 1 students in "other" were self-employed, two (both from the humanities) for reasons related to motherhood. By contrast, students who had left during stage 3 reduced their presence in the upper tier and increased their presence in the lower tier of the primary labor market. One went from college teaching to school-level teaching, and the other went from working in management at a symphony orchestra to being an administrative assistant at a college.

Table 10.8.   Occupational Labor Market of Current Job by Domain of Knowledge and Duration for the Interview Sample (number of interviewees)

	Occupational Labor Market			
	Upper Primary	Lower Primary	Secondary	Other
Domain of Knowledge				
Science	4	1	0	5
Social science	5	1	0	1
Humanities	4	4	0	3
Duration				
Stage 1	9	2	0	5
Stage 2	3	1	0	3
Stage 3	1	3	0	1

Salary Attainment

Assessing differences between completers' and noncompleters' current salaries sheds light on the effects of completion and noncompletion of the Ph.D. credential on salary attainment in the near term. As indicated earlier, analysis of the students' current salaries is complicated by the effects from those who pursued additional education as well as by length of time in the labor market. This latter effect was controlled for by including both the year students had left their universities and the total years they were unemployed after starting their first job. The analysis to follow includes only those who were employed at the time of the survey and who supplied all the necessary information about their careers on the last page of the survey (514 students).[13]

Overall, for each year since leaving graduate school or completing the Ph.D., students earned an additional 3 percent. Each year students were unemployed depressed their salaries by 4 percent. However, 88 percent of the students were continuously employed, and only 2 percent experienced four or more years of unemployment. Noncompleters experienced longer periods of unemployment than completers.

Table 10.9 shows current salary for completers and noncompleters, with and without additional education, by domain of knowledge and discipline along with the percentage employed in the nonacademic sector. Overall, there is no statistical difference between completers' and noncompleters' current salaries or between the current salaries of noncompleters who did and did not pursue additional education. However, there are significant differences in salary based on discipline.

Differences between completers' and noncompleters' salaries depend on the amount of further education earned by noncompleters. Noncompleters who had not obtained additional education earned salaries 24 percent below completers who had not pursued additional education. However,

Table 10.9. Current Salary of Completers and Noncompleters Compared with Noncompleters with and without Additional Education and Percentage Employed in the Nonacademic Sector in 1995 by Domain of Knowledge and Status (in dollars rounded to the nearest hundred)

	Completers	Noncompleters	Noncompleters with Additional Education	Noncompleters without Additional Education
Current Salary				
Average	$50,800	$48,300	$50,600	$46,200
Sciences	53,600	55,700	56,200	55,000
Mathematics	42,700	60,400	54,600	66,200
Biology	44,800	58,100	60,500	54,400
Chemistry	60,400	46,800	49,600	42,300
Social sciences	53,300	60,400	60,600	60,200
Sociology	41,200	38,700	37,600[1]	43,000[2]
Economics	61,000	64,900	54,900	76,000
Psychology	51,100	62,700	110,000[3]	42,400
Humanities	41,300	39,800	41,500	38,700
English	37,600	41,400	47,200	37,400
History	50,300	34,700	34,400	34,900
Music	36,700	38,200	30,800	43,300
Percentage Employed in the Nonacademic Sector				
Average	25	75	49	51
Sciences	55	63	65	80
Mathematics	31	65	55	87
Biology	41	57	65	72
Chemistry	67	71	71	83
Social sciences	31	78	84	81
Sociology	28	50	50	83
Economics	29	95	92	100
Psychology	34	64	100	50
Humanities	21	50	60	64
English	12	48	55	62
History	35	50	57	58
Music	19	57	72	70

[1] n = 4.
[2] n = 1.
[3] n = 3.

noncompleters who had been required to get nondegree-producing education or training to get their first job earned salaries comparable to completers. Noncompleters who had pursued nonprofessional education but had not obtained (or had not yet obtained) a degree were no better off than noncompleters who had not pursued further education. Finally, noncompleters who had obtained professional degrees earned salaries comparable to completers' salaries except for noncompleters who had earned a medical degree (M.D., D.D.S., D.V.M.). These students earned a 68 percent premium over the salaries of completers who did not have an additional spell of education.

Completers used their graduate training in their current jobs more than noncompleters.[14] Regardless of whether they had pursued additional education, noncompleters used their graduate training in their jobs to the same moderate degree, an amount that did not change over time from their first job. By contrast, completers who had more education used their graduate training less than those who had stopped with the Ph.D.[15] Despite differences in knowledge and skill use, the use of graduate training did not have an effect on current salary for any group, suggesting that over time, salaries are less a function of the knowledge and skill initially brought to the job than they are of years of work experience and on-the-job training. Data from the interviews suggest that this is the correct interpretation.

Noncompleters in the interview sample felt they used knowledge and skills from their graduate training less in their current positions than in their first jobs. Tom, a dissertator who was working in his field and who was still with the same company after eight years, captures the essence of the durability of graduate training over time:

> *Tom*: I would say when I first started it was 90 percent of the time. I couldn't have done my job without those skills. Now, they're still important, but people are paying me more to think now about problems as opposed to being able to apply the tools to come up with the exact solution. People are paying me now to figure out how to set up the problem. . . . But the reality is it's the thinking skills. It's the skills you develop to know how to approach a problem. That's what I use now.

Even those interviewees who were teaching their subjects at the K–12 school level did not feel that they used knowledge or skills obtained from their graduate programs. Interviewees' whose current jobs were in a related field or were out of field were emphatic about not using their graduate training. They stated, "absolutely not," "it's not necessary," or "it doesn't matter." The only students who felt that they used their graduate training at all were psychology students, one of whom is in a nonpsychiatric branch of medicine and the other who works as a librarian in a correctional institution.

Students in the sciences and the social sciences continued to earn more than students in the humanities (15 percent and 32 percent more, respectively).

However, completion status mediates the effect. Completers in the sciences earned a nonsignificant 6 percent more than completers in the humanities, but completers in the social sciences earned 28 percent more than those in the humanities. By contrast, noncompleters in the sciences and social sciences earned 27 percent and 40 percent more, respectively, than their counterparts in the humanities.

Urban University's prestige and its impact on salary persists long after students have departed. Controlling for all the different educational paths, the salaries of students who had attended Rural were still depressed by 10 percent compared with students who had attended Urban.

Although students' level of self-esteem at the time they left graduate school had a strong impact on their first salary, its effect did not persist into the current period. However, current level of self-esteem influenced current salaries by 8 percent. Thus, students with the highest level of self-esteem were earning 32 percent more than students with the lowest level. Current self-esteem influenced noncompleters' salaries by 15 percent and men's salaries by 9 percent, but it did not influence that of completers or women.

Noncompleters' Experiences in and Feelings about Their Current Jobs

The interviewees' experiences in and feelings about their current jobs were probed in a manner similar to that of their first jobs. The students were asked why they changed jobs, how much they utilize knowledge and skills from their graduate programs (discussed earlier), about the effect of not having a Ph.D., and about their satisfaction with their jobs.

Relocation was the most frequently stated reason for changing jobs, often because of their spouses' job or educational needs (both men and women), or because they had children and wanted to spend more time with them (women only). They also changed jobs because their interests changed, or they realized that their job was no longer satisfying or had become a professional dead end, as well as simple availability. As would be expected, those whose first jobs were in the lower tier of the primary labor market or the secondary labor market and who had gone back to school were currently employed doing whatever they returned to school to do—practice medicine, teach high school, business management.

Few students felt that they were hurt in their current jobs by not having the Ph.D. No comments were made about lack of respect, lower salaries, or reduced chances for promotion, perhaps because the interviewees had self-selected out of the labor market for jobs that required the Ph.D. and were no longer seeking Ph.D.-level jobs. The major exceptions were Jim and Cathleen. Both are ABD in music, both were working out of field, and both would rather have been working in field.

Jim: I am still very restless, and I'm not satisfied because I'm not doing music full-time. I'm looking nationally to see if I can find a stable prestigious position where I can do what I love, what I'm gifted to do, and where I can serve and use my gift which is very much a part of my identity.

Interviewer: Do you feel that not having a Ph.D. has affected your ability to get these kinds of jobs?

Jim: I do think that it has been influential for this dynamic.

Interviewer: Why is that?

Jim: This dynamic, the full-time college teaching positions and church music that once existed are drastically being discontinued. . . . [T]here are a lot of people that have had college teaching positions and have concertized all over the world that are in the job market taking these full-time church positions . . . [I]t's pretty hard to compete against somebody who's been a European, world-class recitalist and has had a doctorate for years and has been teaching with all that experience for years . . . So whereas it used to be for full-time church positions, a doctorate was not required . . . Most of the advertisements I read, if they say something about degrees, they say master's degree preferred. But even so, I have a master's degree . . . and I'm not being very competitive . . . There really isn't a college teaching position that's within any kind of reality for me at this point not having finished my doctorate.

*   *   *

Interviewer: How do you feel about [working as an administrative assistant]?

Cathleen: I'm enjoying it . . . It's a very flexible arrangement. In fact, I've been teaching a music class and advising students. So I've been getting in a little freelancing on teaching and the academic leading end. I enjoy that. But I think in many ways that's another factor for wanting to finish the degree, which is that without a Ph.D. it seems I'm at a dead end. And that if I want to try to take any teaching or any kind of academic administration or whatever a little further, it certainly wouldn't hurt me to have a finished degree. . . .

Interviewer: How do you feel in that environment without the Ph.D.?

Cathleen: As an administrative assistant per se, it doesn't really matter. In terms of a faculty wannabe, so to speak, I feel I do want the degree. Also I'm encountering many people that were ABD. In fact, someone that I do work a lot with is ABD from Urban University and is much older than I am, and he finds himself at this point in his career, in his fifties, saying, "Well, gee, I really wish I had finished the degree 'cause I had been so close and now I can't say I have the Ph.D. and it does close a lot of doors for me." So when I hear those kinds of stories I find myself thinking I don't want to be in that situation in fifteen years. But right now it's okay. But in twenty years I don't want to find myself looking back with regrets.

Interviewer: Do you feel that not having degree hurt you professionally?

Cathleen: Not thus far, no. But I can see that in the next ten years it could. It would prevent me from applying for jobs I might be interested in in terms of teaching or any kind of upper academic administrative job.

Despite the fact that the interviewees appear to have self-selected out of the advanced-degree labor market, those who still desired to teach at the college level were less satisfied with their jobs than those who were no longer interested in college-level teaching. Among those who no longer desired to teach, the more interesting and challenging they found their current jobs, the more likely they were to be satisfied with their jobs. The few who were not satisfied with their jobs liked the kind of work they were doing but not their jobs per se. They were restless and put a premium on their spare time, which they used to pursue other interests. Some hoped to turn these interests into a career.

The survey data on satisfaction with career indicate that completers are more satisfied with their careers than the noncompleters. Rural students were more satisfied with their careers than Urban students. Students who had pursued additional education were no more satisfied than those who did not. Finally, the more students used their graduate training in their current job, the happier they were. Use of graduate training may be capturing how closely related students' jobs are to their discipline of origin. If this is the case, then students who were working in their fields are much more satisfied with their careers than other students.

CAREER ADVANCEMENT

By looking at the changes in occupational and salary attainment that took place between students' first and current jobs, we can gain insight into how they advanced in their careers and into some of the things that contributed to it. These changes are explored by analyzing interviewees' mobility across the three dimensions of the labor market and by examining the factors that influence salary growth.

Occupational Attainment

Relatedness to Field

Table 10.10 shows mobility across job fields over time for the interview sample. The main diagonal indicates no change in field. The lightly shaded cells above the diagonal show movement away from field, while the darkly shaded cells below the diagonal show movement toward the field.

Overall, the data indicate that over time, as they acquire new knowledge and skills or develop new interests, noncompleters tend to drift away from rather than toward jobs in or related to their field of origin. The majority of the interviewees (seventeen), regardless of whether they actually changed jobs, maintained the same degree of distance from their discipline over time.

Table 10.10. Mobility by Relatedness to Field for the Interview Sample (number of interviewees)

First Job	Current Job			
	In-Field	Related-Field	Out-of-Field	Other
In-field	5	3	2	2
Related-field	1	5	0	0
Out-of-field	1	1	6	1
Other	0	0	0	1

Note: Light gray cells indicate movement away from field; dark gray cells indicate movement toward field; central diagonal indicates no change.

Eight students moved away from their discipline of origin, while three students moved toward their disciplines. Students who moved toward their discipline moved as follows: from secretarial work to high school teaching in field (English), from doing political work for the government to doing economic consulting and teaching at the college level on the side (economics), and from retail sales into teaching English as a second language (history)—all three would still like to get the Ph.D.

Labor Market Sector

Less than half of the students interviewed remained in their employment sector of origin. Students in the business/industry sector exhibited the greatest stability (see table 10.11). Shifts off the diagonal show movement across sectors.

Three students shifted into the academic sector, while four moved out. Those who shifted in switched into K–12 school-level teaching or clerical work at a college. Those who moved out include two science students who had been teaching at the college level and one humanities student who taught at a private high school. The one student who remained in the academic sector went from teaching at a four-year college to teaching at a private junior high school.

Table 10.11. Mobility by Labor Market Sector for the Interview Sample (number of interviewees)

First Job	Current Job			
	Academic	Business/Industry	Government	Other
Academic	1	1	0	3
Business/industry	2	7	1	3
Government	0	1	1	0
Other	1	2	1	4

Note: Light gray cells indicate movement across sectors; central diagonal indicates no change in sector.

Four students shifted into business/industry, but five moved out; two for reasons related to motherhood. Similarly two students shifted into government and one out, and six shifted into "other" and four moved out. Those who moved out of "other" left jobs in retail sales and jobs in the secondary labor market. Thus, the various sectors of the labor market appear to be permeable over time, and the students in the interview sample appear to have taken great advantage of the permeability.

Occupational Labor Market

Less than half the interviewees maintained their status in the occupational labor market, as shown in table 10.12. Excluding "other," five students improved their positions (darkly shaded cells), and three worsened their positions (lightly shaded cells). An additional seven students moved out of the occupational labor market entirely (three, self-employed; one, unemployed; one, into graduate school; one, motherhood; one, receiving disability insurance). Most of these students moved from the upper primary into "other." Thus, it appears that while many noncompleters tend to improve their position in the occupational labor market, they are highly mobile and not all move into jobs that, by the tenets of labor market theory, would be viewed as improvements.

Salary Growth

Perhaps the most interesting thing about the students' salary growth is how few factors actually influence it.[16] Students from Rural experienced the same degree of salary growth as students from Urban, and women experienced the same degree of salary growth as men. Similarly, students in the sciences and social sciences saw their salaries grow at the same rate as students in the humanities. The rate of salary growth was also the same for students who started in career track jobs compared with those who started in noncareer track jobs.

Table 10.12. Mobility by Occupational Labor Market for the Interview Sample (number of interviewees)

First Job	Current Job			
	Upper Primary	*Lower Primary*	*Secondary*	*Other*
Upper primary	9	3	0	5
Lower primary	3	2	0	2
Secondary	1	1	0	0
Other	0	0	0	2

Note: Light gray cells indicate worsening of position in the occupational labor market; dark gray cells indicate improvement of position in the occupational labor market; central diagonal indicates no change in position in the occupational labor market.

These lack of effects help explain why the university, gender, domain of knowledge, career-type differences in first salary persisted in current salary.

Very few of the educational factors affected salary growth. Obtaining a medical degree was the only form of additional education that had an influence for noncompleters' (42 percent growth), and it was one of two types of education that had an influence for completers' (51 percent growth). The other type of education to influence completers' salary growth was nonprofessional education (40 percent growth). However, the effect is accounted for largely by chemistry students who held postdoctoral positions before entering the business world as industrial scientists.

Compared with the academic sector, students in the business sector experienced the greatest gains in salary (22 percent gain). However, this effect can be largely accounted for by completers moving out of low-paying postdoctoral positions in the academic sector, as noncompleters who presumably started and ended in the business sector did not experience significant gains.

With respect to changes in use of graduate training over time, 78 percent of the students reported no change in use, 10 percent reported an increase, and 12 percent reported a decrease. Overall, these changes affected salary growth by 11 percent in a positive or negative direction. In other words, students who increased their skill use the most (two-point gain) experienced 22 percent more salary growth than students who did not change their degree of skill use. Similarly, students who decreased their skill use the most (two-point drop) experienced 22 percent less salary growth than students who did not change their degree of skill use. But again, the effect is due to completers. The rate of change in their salaries was 16 percent for each degree of increase or decrease in skill utilization. By contrast, changes in use of graduate training had no effect on noncompleters' salary growth.

There is, however, a relationship between change in use of graduate training over time, domain of knowledge, and labor market sector. Between first and current job, students in the sciences experienced the greatest decrease in the use of their graduate training. Over time, students who were currently employed in the business/industry and government sectors also significantly decreased their use of their graduate training.

Finally, changes in self-esteem over time had a considerable impact on salary growth. Overall, 44 percent of the students experienced an increase in self-esteem, 12 percent experienced a decrease, and 44 percent stayed the same. Each degree of change in self-esteem resulted in an 11 percent change in salary in a positive or negative direction. Thus, those students who had the greatest increase in self-esteem (four-point gain) experienced 44 percent more salary growth than students whose self-esteem did not change. Similarly, those students who had the greatest decrease in self-esteem (three-point drop) experienced 33 percent less salary growth than students whose self-esteem did not change.

CONCLUSION

Students who enter the labor market without the Ph.D. are disadvantaged. However, most of the negative repercussions dissipate over time as they increase their human capital, either by pursuing additional education or by accumulating work experience and dispersing into high-paying segments and sectors of the labor market. In addition to not having the Ph.D. when they enter the labor force, noncompleters must overcome a number of other obstacles. Few know what they want to do with their lives at the time of departure, and most seem unaware of alternative careers for people with advanced education in their disciplines. Consequently, many take jobs that are unrelated to their graduate training and that fall well below their level of education—largely to pay their bills while they regroup and figure out their next moves in life. Attending a university situated in a rural labor market further compounds noncompleters' woes at the time of departure because there are fewer job opportunities for highly educated people in small towns than there are for similarly educated people in big cities—and humanities students are at a greater disadvantage than science and social science students. Not only did Rural University students have to rethink their careers, they had to relocate to get the often poorer-quality jobs they did.

The fact that so many noncompleters pursued additional education and that so many ultimately obtained the Ph.D. or another professional degree is testimony to noncompleters' resilience and their powers of perseverance in the face of apparent failure. Their postattrition educational achievements thus contradict widely held views that noncompleters are not as capable and not as dedicated as those students who complete.

With the exception of those who pursued nonprofessional education, noncompleters who extended their education fared as well as completers in their current jobs. Yet, the effect of further education appears to matter only in the academic sector—the Ph.D.-required segment of the academic sector in particular. Many of those in the academic sector who had not extended their education or who had received nonprofessional education fared less well because they were teaching at the K–12 school level (though it remains to be seen whether they fared better than their colleagues who had not pursued doctorates). Alternatively, they held low-paying instructor, adjunct, or assistant professor positions, either because they are permanently ABD or were completing their doctorates. By contrast, with the exception of noncompleters who earned medical degrees, noncompleters with and without additional education fared as well as completers in the business/industry and government sectors.

Regardless of status, students' salary attainment appears to be a function of their gender, the university they attended, the discipline they studied, and their level of self-esteem. Although women were not disadvantaged relative to men when they first entered the labor market, they became so over time. The gender effects were strongest for female completers in the labor market as a whole and for all women in the business/industry sector. These findings indicate that biases still exist against women in general and against women with advanced degrees in particular.

Urban University's prestige creates a halo effect for all students who went there regardless of whether they completed the Ph.D. As they advance through their careers, the halo continues to cast a glow and bless them.

Irrespective of time period, status, or labor market sector, social sciences students received the greatest return on their educational investments; humanities students received the poorest. Science students fared far better than humanities students in general, though noncompleters, women, and students in the business/industry sector from the sciences received a greater premium for their choice of disciplinary specialization than their counterparts.

Level of self-esteem, a factor not commonly included in labor market studies, had a marked effect on salary attainment and salary growth. Students feelings about themselves at the time of exit appear to influence the types of jobs they feel worthy of applying for, they may also influence their self-presentation during job interviews and their ability to negotiate for higher salaries and better benefits. Although the direction of causality cannot be determined for the relationship between current salary and current level of self-esteem, its effect on salary is as real and as profound as in the earlier time period. In addition, salary growth is, in part, a function of the degree and direction of change in self-esteem over time. Again, the effects are large.

Thus, while noncompleters are genuinely disadvantaged relative to completers at the time of departure, these disadvantages can be overcome over time in two primary ways. One is by increasing their stock of educational capital, often by obtaining the missing credential. The other is by leaving the segments and sectors of the labor market that are causing the disadvantage — the secondary labor market and the advanced-degree segment of the academic sector, in particular. However, while this chapter has focused on the disadvantages of noncompletion relative to completion, what is not known, and would be valuable to know, are the relative advantages noncompleters receive compared with similarly bachelor's- and master's-degreed students who did not pursue doctoral education.

NOTES

1. The one exception is Jacks, Chubin, Porter, and Connolly (1983), "The ABCs of ABDs: A Study of Incomplete Doctorates." However, this work is limited to science and engineering ABDs.

2. In human capital theory, tastes are exogenous to the economic system.

3. Scarlett, whose interview did not record, is included in this and several of the other labor market analyses because my postinterview notes include facts about major events in her life.

4. The effect was strongest among music students (100 percent Urban vs. 34 percent Rural) and persisted across status (completers: 100 percent Urban vs. 30 percent Rural; noncompleters: 100 percent Urban vs. 40 percent Rural).

5. Having a job at the time of exit was defined at having taken zero months to find a job.

6. This analysis excludes students who indicated that within six months of leaving they had not looked for a job. The majority of these noncompleters (62 percent) had a subsequent spell of graduate education, suggesting most of the noncompleters who did not look for work went directly on to another graduate or professional program.

7. There were a few differences in method of job search by completer type and gender. At-risk completers were more likely to have responded to newspaper advertisements and to have used social networks (strong ties) than on-track completers (newspapers: 43 percent vs. 33 percent; social networks: 35 percent vs. 25 percent), whereas on-track completers were somewhat more likely than at-risk completers to have had assistance from a professor (weak tie) in finding a job (17 percent vs. 11 percent). Consistent with networking theory (Campbell, 1988), women were more likely to have used social networks (strong ties) than men (41 percent vs. 32 percent), and men were somewhat more likely than women to have been recruited (36 percent vs. 29 percent).

8. In the process of working with the educational data, four completers were reclassified as noncompleters because they had not been continuously enrolled at Rural or Urban. Rather, they had enrolled between 1982 and 1984, left and attended another university, and then returned to their university of origin and completed the Ph.D. They thus had three spells of graduate education and are technically noncompleters with respect to the first spell. Consequently, from this point forward, all the analyses are based on this reclassification. However, the analyses up to this point have not been redone because these four students represent less than 0.5 percent of the survey sample, and the preceding analyses are unlikely to change significantly as a result.

9. Because the natural logarithm of salary is the dependent variable, the coefficients are approximately equal to the percentage change in the salary associated with a one unit change in the variable. This interpretation of the coefficients is only valid if the coefficient is less than 0.1 and greater than –0.1. For the coefficients B, outside this range, the coefficients were transformed into percentage changes in salary using the formula $e^B - 1$.

10. Duration in graduate school was not tested for completers because it was assumed that achieving the credential is the critical factor in their salary attainment. However, it is possible that inordinately long times to degree could reduce completers' starting salaries, as employers may question motivational and other personality factors that contributed to the delay and view them negatively relative to completers who finished their degrees more quickly.

11. On a scale of 1 = *not at all,* 2 = *some,* 3 = *very much,* completers' level of skill use was 2.73; noncompleters', 2.01.

12. Providing an answer to this question were 751 students; there were sixty-five missing cases.

13. Forty-three students were unemployed at the time of the survey (4 percent of the completers, 9 percent of the noncompleters). Many students did not fill out all or part of

the Life History Data section on the last page of the survey. Consequently, relevant data were missing for an additional 259 students (29 percent of the completers, 37 percent of the noncompleters).

14. On a scale of 1 = *not at all*, 2 = some, 3 = *very much*, completers used their graduate training 2.66; noncompleters, 2.01.

15. Specifically, 2.30 completers with additional education vs. 2.69 without additional education.

16. This analysis is based on a sample of 509 students. It excludes all of the students who were unemployed at the time of the survey. Relevant data were missing for an additional 264 students (30 percent of the completers, 37 percent of the noncompleters).

Chapter 11

Conclusions and Recommendations

This study was motivated by concerns about the causes of departure from doctoral study and why such a high rate of attrition has persisted for so many decades in graduate schools in the United States. To understand and explain these issues, the study focused on social structural causes. The high and persistent rate of attrition was addressed by bringing together attribution theory from social psychology; exit, voice, loyalty, and neglect theory from political economy; and the theory of greedy institutions from sociology. The emergent synthesis located the cause of attrition in the social structure and organizational culture of graduate education. This complex social structure leads observers (graduate deans, graduate faculty, and recent Ph.D. recipients) and actors (the departers themselves) to commit the fundamental attribution error and place the onus of responsibility for attrition on the departing student. Because they hold themselves responsible for their attrition, noncompleters exit without giving voice to their discontent, thereby denying the members of the university community the feedback necessary to invalidate their attributions and redress the underlying causes.

The cause(s) of attrition was addressed by elaborating and extending the theory of integration and uniting it with the concept of the cognitive map. More specifically, the concepts of academic and social integration were invoked and an explanation was provided for why academic integration has a greater impact on persistence than social integration: Academic integration is the primary purpose of graduate education; social integration is the unintended consequence of interactions that take place in the process of achieving the primary purpose. Mechanisms that bring about these two forms of integration were proposed: task integration, working together on a common project; and socioemotional integration, supportive interactions in the academic and social realm.

The concept of the cognitive map was introduced and developed to gain deeper insight into the factors that create conflict between the assumptions and expectations that students have about the process of graduate education and those that the graduate program and its faculty have of students. Two types of cognitive maps were proposed: a global cognitive map of the formal system of graduate education and a series of local maps of the informal interactions that take place in social and academic systems. These maps stand in a reciprocal relationship with integration: The better the student's cognitive maps, the more integrated the student will become; the more integrated the student, the better developed his or her cognitive maps will be: Knowledge and understanding facilitate interaction, interaction fosters knowledge and understanding.

The study was also concerned with the personal and professional consequences of attrition. Insight into these outcomes was developed through analysis of social-psychological and labor market processes. The theories of emotional distress, self-concept, and possible selves were advanced to provide insight into students' immediate and long-term reactions to and feelings about their attrition, while such labor market theories as human capital, networking, and credential were used to help understand and explain students' (completers and noncompleters) occupational and salary attainment.

The section to follow provides a model for how the distribution of structures and opportunities for integration and cognitive map development at five social-structural levels—institutional, disciplinary, interdepartmental, intradepartmental, and individual—interact with students' entering characteristics, loci within the levels, constructions of reality, and with forces external to the system to influence persistence outcomes. A model for how noncompleters come to terms with their attrition was presented in chapter 9, and much more research needs to be done on labor market consequences before a model can be developed.

MODEL OF THE STRUCTURES AND
FORCES INFLUENCING PERSISTENCE

As shown in figure 11.1, universities attempt to cull the best and the brightest students based on demonstrated aptitudes such as students' GPAs, Graduate Record Examination (GRE) scores, and, often, students' integration into the academic profession as undergraduates as evidenced by achievements such as single or coauthored publications and presentation of conference papers. However, as the data on GPA in this and other studies (see Belt, 1976; Benkin, 1984; Berelson, 1960; Tinto, 1987, 1993; Tucker, 1964)

			Social-Structural Level			
Student Entering Characteristics	Institutional Level	Disciplinary Level	Interdepartmental Level	Intradepartmental Level	Individual Level
Aptitude (GPA and GRE)	Degree of selectivity	Intellectual structure	Opportunities for academic integration, social integration, and cognitive map development	Type of financial support	Degree of academic and social integration
Prior professional socialization	Selection criteria	Values, norms, and beliefs about methods of training graduate students	Department culture	Method of adviser selection	Quality of cognitive map(s)
Prior socialization to the graduate school experience	Demands for commitment, time, loyalty, and energy	Job opportunities		Having an office	Type of adviser (high vs. low producer) and quality of relationship with adviser
Degree intentions	Degree intentions				Degree intentions
					Social construction of reality
					External forces (e.g., family, health, finances)

Figure 11.1.   Forces Influencing Persistence Prior to Entry and at Five Social-Structural Levels after Entry

show, aptitude is an inappropriate selection criterion for several reasons. First, the range of variability in aptitude among admitted students is very small, thereby guaranteeing that most admitted students have the requisite aptitudes to succeed. Second, aptitude does not predict creative scholarship and intellectual innovation—which is what graduate education is about. Finally, aptitude provides no information about how well students understand the structure and process of graduate education. However, aptitude may contribute to academic integration because the higher the student's GPA and GRE scores, the more likely the student will be to receive a TA or an RA. Yet, aptitude may also detract from academic integration. Students with the highest GPAs and GRE scores are typically the ones awarded full-university or outside-private fellowships, and possession of these financial free rides deny them access to important structures and opportunities for integration that are entailed in the obligations, benefits, and privileges that come with TAs and RAs. In addition, aptitude provides no information about the type of adviser the student will have or the quality of the relationship the student will have with his or her adviser (assuming that the student even has an adviser). Thus, aptitude provides no information about critical interactional processes that take place after the student has enrolled in the university.

Prior professionalization to the academic profession should be a better predictor of success. However, it paradoxically fails to be so, probably because it implies that a student had a high level of academic integration with faculty and the discipline as an undergraduate, expected the same or higher degree of integration in graduate school, and did not encounter it, leading to disappointment, disillusionment, and disenchantment.

Students' prior socialization to the graduate school experience does, however, affect their persistence. Students who enter graduate schools with good cognitive maps of the formal and informal structures and processes they will encounter integrate quickly and comfortably into the role of graduate student and into the departmental community. Students whose cognitive maps are less well developed often feel ill at ease in their environments and in their interactions with professors and peers unless they receive a high-quality orientation and are provided with opportunities to interact with people (faculty and advanced graduate students) who can help them develop the requisite understandings.

With students' entering characteristics and individual differences held constant, once they have entered graduate school, students' persistence is a function of the social structures and the social and cultural forces operating in the institutional, disciplinary, and inter- and intradepartmental contexts in which they find themselves. The intradepartmental context is embedded in the interdepartmental context, the interdepartmental context in the disciplinary context, and together the interdepartmental and disciplinary contexts are embedded in the institutional context. The social structures and social forces in all four contexts operate on students simultaneously, exerting joint and independent pressures on their degree of integration, the quality of their cognitive maps, their constructions of reality, and, ultimately, their persistence decisions.

The institutional structure and cultural ideal of graduate education structures the experiences of all students. The Ph.D. is a high-status degree that results in highly desirable professional and social rewards for those who obtain it. Consequently, graduate schools present themselves as highly desirable places to be and maintain this elitism by offering selective admission and membership to "The Best." This selectivity allows the system of graduate education to make great demands on students who enter it in terms of commitment, loyalty, time, and energy.

Students who are admitted to this system are led to believe that they are among "The Select." Upon entry, they are placed in competition with one another for the rewards of graduate education (fellowships, assistantships, faculty sponsorship, and job placement). This competition can engender pluralistic ignorance and prevent students from sharing their concerns, as the case of India (discussed in chapter 2) demonstrates so well. Students having problems come to believe that their problems lie with themselves and not with the structure of the situation. Consequently, they commit the fundamental attribution error. They blame themselves rather than the system for their "failings." The situation and the concomitant self-blame it engenders inhibit students from giving voice to their discontent. Hence, they exit silently and alone, thereby denying people in position to effect change the feedback they need to recognize that there is a problem and the information necessary to correct it. This lack of feedback allows key players in the institution (administrators and faculty) also to commit the fundamental attribution error. It allows them to place the onus of responsibility for attrition on the departing student rather than on the university. The social structure of graduate education and its underlying social forces are thus maintained intact.

Disciplines and departments have, by and large, been conflated in this study, in part, because the structure of, and processes that take place in, a department are greatly determined by the parent discipline. However, within disciplines differences exist between departments. These differences affect persistence outcomes independently of the discipline in which the department is embedded.

Disciplines vary not only in their structural organization but also in their organizational cultures. A discipline's culture includes norms, values, and beliefs about how to train graduate students and about the nature of the interactions that take place between and among faculty and graduate students. These norms, values, and beliefs form a social current that impinges on all members of the disciplinary community. In the sciences and laboratory-based social sciences, research is done in teams. Students enter research groups early in their graduate careers. The subject matter is vertically integrated. Students can develop a clear picture of their graduate programs and the type of work they need to do to complete their degrees. By contrast, research in the humanities and most of the social sciences is done individually and in isolation in libraries, archives, and in the field. Because dissertation-related research often does not begin until students have passed their qualifying examinations, students in these disciplines can delay entering into an adviser–advisee relationship until late in their graduate careers. In addition, the subject matter in these disciplines is horizontally integrated. Students are required to make sense of a large body of disparate information, which often has only a tangential relationship to their research interests. Thus, by virtue of the structural and cultural organization of the discipline, students in the sciences and laboratory-based social sciences are provided with more opportunities for academic and social integration with members of their departmental community than students in the humanities and nonlaboratory-based social sciences. Consequently, the probability of attrition for students in the sciences and laboratory-based social sciences is lower than for students in the humanities and nonlaboratory-based social sciences.

Departments are not just social structural units in which graduate education takes place; they are cultures that are independent of the parent discipline and that shape the structures, processes, and interactions that take place within them. Cultural differences among departments are objectified in the opportunities departments provide for cognitive map development and for integration into their academic and social systems. Differences in department cultures are evident the moment one physically enters the building(s) in which a department is housed. Departments send messages about themselves through their displays of photographs, arrangement of bulletin boards, and other hallway and seminar room postings (or lack thereof). Some departments are friendly and welcoming; they say, "We are a family; please join us." Others are cold and austere; they say, "Do your work and leave."

Differences in opportunities for cognitive map development are embedded in the design and content of the materials departments send to students as early as the time of inquiry, at the time of admission, and at the time of enrollment. The culture is personally revealed to students by the manner in which the department characterizes itself to students during orientation (militaristic, powerfully important, social and friendly, no orientation) and provides information to students on all components of their programs (friendly and helpful, deferential to the department handbook and graduate student subculture).

A department's culture is also embedded in and revealed by the opportunities it provides for academic and social integration. Some departments have structures in place to help students plan their programs and choose advisers; others leave students to their own devices. Some departments provide weekly, sometimes daily, colloquia and social hours; others provide them rarely, if at all. Some departments encourage student participation on department committees and in important department decision making; other departments exclude them. Some have holiday and other bonding traditions; others are all business.

These cultural differences have implications for how well students understand the department's formal requirements and informal expectations as well as for their degree of academic and social integration. The more opportunities for cognitive map development a department has, the better the quality of students' cognitive maps; and the more opportunities for integration the department has, the more integrated the students (and faculty) become. Indeed, the existence of an orientation correlated positively with students' understanding of the department's formal requirements and negatively with the department's attrition rate. Opportunities for integration, in general, and academic integration, in particular, also correlated negatively with the department's attrition rate: The less integrated the department, the more likely its students are to leave. The departments' faculty retention rate also correlated positively but not significantly with the department's environment for integration, and strongly and significantly with the department's student attrition rate, suggesting that something in the department's environment influences both graduate students' and faculty's persistence decisions.

While the department's cultural ideal structures the experiences of all its members, departments provide different members of their communities with different structures and opportunity for action and interaction, thereby creating groups of haves and have-nots. The distribution of these structures and opportunities have a differential effect on the haves' and have-nots' abilities to develop cognitive maps of the department's formal requirements and informal expectations, on their ability to become integrated into its academic and social systems. Students who receive teaching and research assistantships are provided with more opportunities to interact with faculty, with more advanced graduate students, and even with undergraduates than students who are not. They are more likely to attend an orientation for new graduate students. They have more opportunity to engage in the activities of the discipline, which enhances their intellectual and professional development. They are also more likely than other graduate students to receive a desk in a gang office, which contributes both to their social integration with other students and to their ability to access the tacit knowledge contained within the graduate student subculture. Consequently, students who receive these opportunities are more likely not only to complete the Ph.D. but never to have considered leaving graduate school without it.

Access to advising is also not distributed equally. Some students do not have advisers; others are assigned to advisers with whom they have not established a relationship and with whom they may have little, if anything, in common; while others select or are selected by an adviser with whom they have some type of interpersonal relationship. In addition, evidence from the interview data and from students' write-in responses on the survey about why they were satisfied or dissatisfied with their advisers suggests that noncompleters and at-risk completers are more likely to work with low-Ph.D.-productive faculty than completers and on-track completers; and low-Ph.D.-productive faculty are less engaged with their students, less engaged in department activities, and less engaged in cutting-edge research than high-Ph.D.-productive faculty. Thus, the nature and quality of noncompleters' and at-risk completers' interactions with their advisers may be different than those of completers and on-track completers because they are interacting with different types of advisers.

The four contexts of graduate education combined—institutional, disciplinary, interdepartmental, and intradepartmental—interact with external factors—health, family, finances—and impinge on individual's mental processes and constructions of reality. Students who are well integrated are provided with resources for persistence that are more extensive than their own. Their interactions in the departmental community are well scripted and taken for granted. Consequently, they are satisfied with their programs and their personal, professional, and intellectual development. They have no reason to question the community and their tenure in it. By contrast, students who are poorly integrated are propelled toward exit because they lack the bonds that glue people to communities and that help people function better. Thrown back on their individuality and their own resources, they come to see themselves as figures against a ground of which they are not a part. Their actions and interactions become effortful. As a result, their performance suffers, and they start to question whether they are achieving their goals, examine their reasons for being a member of that community, and assess whether the benefits of persistence are worth the costs.

Examination of students' reasons for leaving or thoughts about leaving reveal that for a majority of the noncompleters and at-risk completers, lack of integration was often either a direct or underlying cause of attrition. Students who were directly affected by lack of integration cited their dissatisfaction with their program, the faculty, their adviser, and their fellow graduate students, as well as feelings of isolation and social deprivation, a lack of cohesion in the department, and lack of bonds tying them to their programs as reasons for their leaving. Other students cited reasons that, had they been more integrated, probably would not have led to attrition. Reasons for attrition such as loss of interest in the program or change in career plans often resulted from students' disappointment or disillusionment with their graduate programs and the academic lifestyle as lived in their departments. Academic failure often resulted from lack of information about how to meet the program's standards, lack of support or advice from faculty, and a decline in performance because of dissatisfaction with the program. Attrition for financial reasons was also frequently motivated by lack of integration. Unlike well-integrated students, poorly integrated students appear to be less willing to put up with the financial hardship—the benefits just do not seem worth the costs. Thus, noncompleters' individual reasons and constructions of reality more often mask than reveal underlying causes of attrition. Hence, the reasons students provide on forced-choice questionnaires cannot be accepted at face value; the social factors motivating those reasons must be explored.

Finally, many of the at-risk completers indicated that they were most responsible for their decision to continue; that is, they relied on their own internal resources. However, at-risk completers are more integrated than noncompleters. They had more social and academic resources to fall back on—resources that helped them function better in their programs and persist. Again, students' individual reasons for persistence (or nonpersistence) need to be assessed against the social context from which they are proffered.

In sum, with individual differences and factors external to the institution of graduate education held constant, a high percentage of graduate student attrition can be explained by assessing the distribution of structures and opportunities for integration and cognitive map development in the various contexts in which graduate students are located. A student who is in a discipline whose organizational culture and structural organization fosters integration is more likely to complete than student who is in a discipline whose organizational culture and structural organization does not foster integration. Similarly, a student who enters a department whose organizational culture and structural organization facilitates integration is more likely to complete than a student whose department's organizational culture and structural organization is laissez-faire. Finally, a student who is given opportunities to integrate into the department's academic and social communities is more likely to complete than a student who must rely on his or her own resources and ingenuity to become integrated.

The degree to which different universities and departments exert forces on students that are characteristic of greedy institutions and the effect of these forces on persistence remains an open question. However, one can predict that these forces will vary across universities and between departments within universities, and that the force is likely to be exerted more strongly in the more selective and elite universities and departments.

Last but not least, the way in which students construct an understanding of the social circumstances in which they find themselves also affects their persistence decisions. Some students seem to be keenly aware of their degree of integration, while others may sense it but be unable to articulate it to themselves and others, thereby attributing their persistence (attrition or retention) to some other cause. Still other students, by virtue of their single-minded commitment to their goals or other personality factors, may be completely oblivious to their degree of integration and persist when all contextual factors predict they should not. Regardless, integration helps all students function better—socially, emotionally, and academically.

POLICY IMPLICATIONS

Numerous policy recommendations for graduate schools, departments, faculty, and even colleges and professional associations emerge from this study's findings. The ones presented here flow naturally from issues discussed throughout the book. They are meant to serve as guides for those seeking to initiate reform. Colleges, universities, professional associations, departments, faculty, and even graduate students are encouraged to explore and debate the issues and recommendations and determine reforms best suited to their local environments.

Changing the Organizational Culture and Social Structure of Graduate Education

The organizational culture and social structure of graduate education has remained relatively static during the latter half of the twentieth century and into the twenty-first because universities and their faculties resist change. They tend to operate on the assumption that institutional norms, values, and beliefs have been in place forever (Tierney & Bensimon, 1996); thus, they unquestioningly embrace the status quo (Seymour, 1995). When problems arise, they tend to focus on the immediate, the obvious, and not the root cause. This too often results in a "bad apple" approach to problems like graduate student attrition— that is, improve by elimination (Seymour, 1995). This approach further perpetuates the myth that those who survive are "The Best" and that only "The Best" survive. The "survival of the fittest" mentality, in turn, serves to reinforce existing cultural norms, because it ensures that only those graduate students who conform to the norms will survive. Recent work on organizational performance and learning indicates that this approach has only limited ability to enhance the quality of a graduate program and the students in it because their quality is determined by the quality of the system of graduate education (its structures and processes), not its putative outliers (individuals) (Demming, 1992, cited in Seymour, 1995). Universities and graduate programs also resist change because they do not have a customer-driven approach to quality (Seymour, 1995). Consequently, they do not pay attention to things of importance to their customers—students—or worse, they have created a situation in which their customers signal their dissatisfaction by exiting the institution in silence, thereby denying the institution the feedback it needs to change.

To address the problem of attrition, universities and departments—especially ones with high student and faculty attrition rates—need to assess their cultures and their climates. Faculty need to question the system. They need to ask, as this study has done, What are the underlying causes? Common negative experiences are a good indicator that something is wrong with the system and that the system needs to change. Faculty can start the change process by examining what they take for granted about their organizational culture and the structure and process of graduate education.

One of those taken-for-granted assumptions is that new students must conform to the prevailing departmental culture (Tierney & Bensimon, 1996). Instead, faculty need to consider how the organizational culture needs to change to ensure success for all students who they thought were worthy of being admitted to their program. If necessary, they should bring in outside consultants who are familiar with organizational learning to help them identify problems in their climates and cultures and institute appropriate changes.

Universities can best learn about the underlying causes of attrition by opening up channels of communication with current and exiting graduate students. In particular, universities can better learn about students' concerns and discontents by sponsoring focus group discussions with currently enrolled graduate students on an ongoing basis. Ideally, focus groups would involve students from various departments around the campus and at different stages in their programs. For instance, the university might sponsor focus groups that concentrate individually on the experiences and concerns of first-year students, students in stage 2, and students at the dissertation stage. In addition, universities might sponsor focus groups by discipline or domain of knowledge that include students across stages or even groups of students by type of undergraduate institution. They might also sponsor focus groups comprised solely of women and students from different racial and ethnic groups. These kinds of focus groups should help the university learn about experiences and concerns that are specific to stage, discipline or domain of knowledge, gender and race/ethnicity, and even organizational socialization. To encourage openness, focus groups should be facilitated by someone not affiliated with the participating students' departments.

In addition, university administrators should arrange to conduct honest and open exit interviews with departing students. If face-to-face interviews cannot be conducted with them before they leave, then they should be contacted by telephone. These interviews should be carefully crafted to get at underlying causes and be conducted by a neutral third party to increase the likelihood that departing students will be completely honest about their experiences and reasons for leaving.

Using information provided by both focus-group students and exit-interview students, the university should be able to discern problems in its culture and in the structure and process of graduate education, in general, and in individual departments, in particular. Once problems have been identified, universities can work with administrators and faculty to change their value systems and reward structures.

Developing Well-Structured Cognitive Maps of Graduate Education

A large percentage of attrition results from deficiencies in students' cognitive maps of graduate education. These deficiencies can, and need to be, remedied at both the undergraduate and graduate level, and even by professional associations.

Recommendations for Undergraduate Institutions

Data in this study show that prior socialization to the graduate student experience (cognitive map of informal expectations) is a better predictor of success than undergraduate GPA or prior socialization to the academic profession. Consequently, in much the way they have prelaw and premed advising, undergraduate institutions need to establish formal pregraduate advising. Such advising needs to focus on the structure and process of graduate education and provide undergraduates with the best possible preview of the graduate student experience. At undergraduate institutions with Ph.D.-granting programs, this preview might involve having undergraduates spend a day to a week shadowing currently enrolled graduate student mentors. Undergraduate institutions without Ph.D.-granting programs might arrange for their undergraduates to spend a day to a week shadowing currently enrolled graduate student mentors at the nearest Ph.D.-granting institution. The preview might also include having students read a dissertation in their area of interest to demystify the dissertation and to provide them with a feel for the type of final product they will be expected to produce. Pre–graduate school advising should also involve exposing undergraduates to nonacademic career options for people with Ph.D.'s in their areas of interest, perhaps by holding a career day at which prospective graduate students can interact with Ph.D.'s in both the academic and nonacademic world.

Undergraduate institutions and undergraduate faculty should do their best to make sure that undergraduates sincerely want to pursue graduate study and then steer them toward programs that are most congruent with their interests and career goals. They should stop advising them to go the most prestigious schools and programs they can get into if these programs are not best suited to their interests. In a similar vein, undergraduate institutions and undergraduate faculty should encourage students to read publications by potential faculty mentors in their areas of interest and help facilitate some sort of interpersonal interaction (phone, e-mail, letter, meeting) between the prospective student and prospective mentor prior to enrollment, if not application. Graduate schools can facilitate this process by creating homepages for their graduate faculty on the World Wide Web. The homepages should include a brief biography of the faculty, the faculty's current research interests, a list of recent publications, a list of the Ph.D.'s they produced, along with the titles of their dissertations and their current positions as well as the names and research interests of graduate students currently working with them. Undergraduates should be encouraged to contact those graduate students to get their views on what it is like to work with particular faculty members. One benefit of these interactions is that they have the potential to commence prospective students' integration with both potential advisers and with graduate students in prospective departments.

Recommendations for Graduate Schools

Graduate schools need to do more to ensure that there is a good fit between the interests of the students they admit and the intellectual orientation of the department and its faculty. The director of graduate study or a committee of faculty should, at minimum, make telephone contact with all prospective students and explore the match between students' interests and the resources the department has to offer. Departments should stop admitting the "best" students and instead admit students with the best fit, as the data in this study show that paper measures of academic ability and prior socialization to the academic profession are not an effective means of determining who will succeed and who will not.

To the extent that students who had selected graduate programs on the basis of knowledge about individual faculty members were more likely to succeed than those who did not have such knowledge, graduate schools should "force" this type of cognitive map development prior to entry. They can do so by requiring students to discuss the work of a faculty member or research group in the department in which they want to enroll in their applications for admission and discuss why they want to work with those faculty. Such an action on the part of the university increases the likelihood of fit and also helps departments match entering students with preliminary advisers.

Cognitive maps also are enhanced when students visit the campus prior to entry. If the student is displeased with the university or the department during the visit, the student can either choose not to enroll or use the time between the visit and enrollment to come to terms with his or her decision. Regardless, campus visits reduce culture shock. Graduate schools, therefore, should facilitate campus visits for as many prospective graduate students as possible and ensure that prospective students interact with the faculty, especially potential advisers, and currently enrolled graduate students. To this end, organizations that provide graduate fellowships should include money in their awards to cover the cost of a campus visit, thereby increasing the likely return on their investment.

Orientations should be mandatory in all departments for all entering graduate students. During the orientation, details on individual requirements and the standards for meeting them in terms of quality of performance should be discussed and supplemented with individual brochures that students can access when they need them. New students should be introduced to each other, to faculty, and to advanced graduate students as well. Faculty should share their research interests with entering students and provide students with an overview of the first-year courses they teach.

Departments should create and maintain files of high-quality student papers, master's theses, preliminary and qualifying examinations, and dissertations so that students who are approaching these requirements can be exposed to examples of the department's performance standards. Departments should create committees of faculty and advanced graduate students to meet with students who are approaching these requirements and discuss the expectations and standards for achieving them.

Recommendations for Professional Associations

To the extent that new graduate students are often unprepared for, surprised, and turned off by differences between undergraduate and graduate education in their discipline, professional and disciplinary associations can help ease this transition by developing brochures for prospective graduate students which discuss these differences. They can start the development process by bringing together one or more groups of currently enrolled graduate students at different stages of their education from different universities who attended different types of undergraduate institutions (especially small, liberal arts colleges) and have them discuss things that surprised them about graduate school and things they would have liked to have known about graduate education in the discipline before they enrolled. Graduate faculty can contribute to the process by discussing how and why they approach graduate education differently than undergraduate education. Because of the realities of the academic labor market and because some students change their minds about academic careers while pursuing the Ph.D., these brochures should also include a discussion of the different types of nonacademic jobs available for Ph.D.'s in that discipline along with profiles of people in those careers.

Enhancing Students' Academic and Social Integration

The data in this study revealed a relationship between department's environments for integration and student attrition rates. The results suggest that to reduce attrition, departments need to provide more structures and opportunities for integration and distribute them more equitably. Departments should create more occasions for graduate students and faculty to interact formally and informally. Such occasions include regularly scheduled colloquia, brown bag lunches, social hours, departmental research conferences, and so on. A graduate student government could be created to take responsibility for these activities and, in the process, allow students who participate in the government and help organize the activities to become more integrated with each other and with faculty who participate.

Rather than deferring the communication of such important processes such as subscribing to journals and joining professional associations to the student subculture, departments should overtly encourage students to take these actions. Where possible, underwriting or offsetting the cost of subscription/membership for first-year students may prove beneficial in integrating students into the discipline and in helping students develop cognitive maps of the extra-academic roles and responsibilities of disciplinary leaders.

Working together on a common project appears to be among the best means of achieving academic integration. Thus, to the extent possible, departments should do as much as possible to engage all students, especially new students, in the professional tasks of the discipline—paid or unpaid. New students need to work closely with faculty and advanced graduate students on common projects as early as possible in their graduate careers. Special efforts could be made to put students who do not have TAs or RAs on department and graduate student committees, thereby increasing their integration with those with whom they interact. Committee participation should also enhance their professional development and increase their leadership skills.

Although space is limited in most departments, graduate schools should seek ways to provide a desk in a multistudent office to as many graduate students as possible—especially first-year students—for as many years as possible, even if it means students have to share a desk. Overcrowding is better than isolation. Besides, all members of an office community are rarely in the office at the same time. Similarly, departments that do not have graduate student lounges should try to create them. Those with lounges should make sure their lounges are as conducive to social interaction as possible, which might include vending fresh food. These two structures, in addition to increasing students' integration, will help increase student access to the graduate student subculture and the tacit information contained within it.

When students feel that their goals for their intellectual development are not being met, the likelihood of their leaving increases. Interviewees' dissatisfaction with their intellectual development is reflected in their criticisms of the quality of the product they went to the university to consume. To this end, universities need to develop more effective faculty, course, and program evaluation tools and reward or sanction faculty and departments for acting or not acting on apparent weaknesses. Given that most attrition takes place in the first two years of graduate study, the director of graduate study (DGS) or a group of advanced graduate students should meet with first- and second-year students every term to determine whether the program is meeting their expectations and explore ways in which their expectations and needs could be better satisfied.

Improving the Advising Process

A student's relationship with his or her adviser is probably the single most critical factor in determining who stays and who leaves. Therefore, departments need to assess all aspects of their advising process to determine whether it is working in their graduate students' best interests. Among the things departments could do to improve advising is create a staff of faculty members who are explicitly charged with helping predissertation students through their programs until such time as students have secured an adviser. Departments that assign students to advisers should do more to inform students that the assignment is temporary and that there are no penalties for changing advisers. Departments should also establish processes to help students select an appropriate adviser. Ideally the process should enhance students' cognitive maps of the discipline and faculty interests and also begin the process of integration. For instance, departments could hold special seminars for first-year students at which faculty discuss their research. In a manner similar to Rural's Chemistry Department, students could then sign up individually or in small groups and meet with a few faculty to discuss research interests and opportunities in greater detail. Students would then submit a list of their top choices to the DGS, who, in concert with the prospective adviser, could mediate the final selection.

Departments also need to do more to raise faculty's consciousness about the importance of being more supportive of, and interested in, graduate students, their ideas, research, and professional development. As Melanie stated in chapter 8, departments need to regard new students as an investment that needs to be mentored along. To this end, departments could create ongoing forums that discuss issues—and research—related to effective advising and mentoring. In fairness to graduate students and as a means of rewarding and sanctioning faculty, department's should keep records on, and make available, faculty's Ph.D.-productivity rates; that is, they should provide the percent of students who complete the Ph.D. with a particular faculty member as function of the number of students who signed on with that person.

Universities and departments know all too well who on their faculty abuse graduate students. Yet they swaddle these faculty in an unwritten code of silence and sacrifice their students in the process.[1] Working with and training graduate students should be a privilege, not an entitlement. Thus the right to work with graduate students should be taken away from any and all faculty who abuse that trust. To this end, at the time of exit all graduate students—completers and noncompleters—should be required to submit an evaluation of their adviser (and any and all previous ones) to the graduate school. The evaluation should ask students about the ways in which their adviser(s) facilitated or obstructed their progress to the degree. On some regularly scheduled basis, the dean of the graduate school should review these evaluations and reward and sanction faculty accordingly—advising students is, after all, part of their job description. Sanctions could range from peer mentoring by a high-Ph.D.-productive colleague to losing the privilege of working with graduate students.

Finally, universities and departments need to take collective responsibility for their graduate students. Some graduate students leave because either they do not get along with their adviser or the adviser leaves the university, becomes terminally ill, or dies. When this happens, too many graduate students are unable to complete because there is no one else in the department in the student's area of interest or no one else is willing to take the student on as an advisee. The student is thus confronted with tough options: change his or her interest area or research topic, change institutions, or leave graduate school entirely. The first two options cost the student time; the third costs the student the degree. In addition, choosing the first option prevents the student from getting the education he or she went to that particular institution to get.

None of these situations are the student's, the department's, or the university's fault. However, because the university and the department admitted the student into the doctoral program and that admission carried with it an implicit agreement to bestow a degree on the student if the student made satisfactory progress, the university and the department have an obligation to do whatever is necessary to see the student through to completion. In other words, the burden should be on the university and the department, not on the student.

Dealing with the Reality of Attrition

The large differences in attrition rates between Rural and Urban Universities as well as the large differences in attrition rates between departments in the same discipline indicate that attrition rates can be other than what they are. Achieving attrition rates comparable to law and medical schools (5 to 10 percent), although desirable, is probably unrealistic because of differences in the nature of the educational processes, especially the dissertation requirement. However, the current national average of 50 percent is far too high and, at minimum, should be cut in half. Indeed, three departments in this study had attrition rates under 25 percent, demonstrating that this goal can be met.

Disciplinary associations and accrediting agencies need to hold universities and departments accountable for their attrition rates. They can do so by requiring departments to publish this data in graduate handbooks and other materials sent to prospective graduate students and by developing documents that rank departments by attrition rate. University and departmental attrition rates should be included in surveys like those published by the *Chronicle of Higher Education* and *U.S. News and World Report.* Prospective graduate students have a right to know what their chances of completing the Ph.D. are *before* they enroll in a graduate program.

Although some attrition decisions are right for the student and the department, other "decisions" are pleas for help. To this end, faculty need to rethink the way in which they interact with students who indicate they are thinking about leaving the program, especially female and minority students. Many of these students are simply experiencing self-doubt and could be persuaded to continue if they were given appropriate support and encouragement. In addition, faculty need to broaden their view of the purposes of graduate education and be more willing to discuss Ph.D.-level nonacademic career opportunities with students who have decided that the academic lifestyle is not for them but would still like to complete the degree. Graduate students are far better off completing the Ph.D. and not finding an academic or Ph.D.-level job than they are not to finish the degree at all. In the former case, they leave with a sense of accomplishment and can blame the labor market for things not working out. In the latter case, they often leave with a sense of failure and blame themselves for their "failings."

Finally, departments and faculty need to be more open and honest about the reality of attrition. Not all newly admitted graduate students should receive a Ph.D., and some newly admitted students will discover that graduate education is simply not for them. These issues should be discussed with new graduate students during orientation. Students should be informed that deciding or being asked to leave a graduate program does not mean that they are failures. There are other ways to define success and there are other stimulating, challenging, and satisfying careers. Students should be helped to understand this and be helped to leave with their pride and dignity intact.

Celebrating Success

Obtaining the Ph.D. is a monumental achievement, yet there was not a single visible sign of recognition in any department in this study. While many departments had portrait boards filled with pictures of currently enrolled or first-year students, no department had an exhibit of their graduates or even a simple listing of their names. Displays of this nature are easy to create. Departments could easily develop bulletin boards or scrapbooks that contain photos of graduates in their caps and gowns with their advisers. They could post an honor roll of Ph.D. recipients along with the titles of their dissertations and the name of their adviser in the department office or hallway, much the way community organizations honor benefactors. They might also indicate where the student took his or her first job. These types of displays help bond a community by giving members a sense of history with those who came before and a sense of their own future legacy in the department.

UNFINISHED BUSINESS

Most components of this study were highly exploratory; consequently, they are subject to improvement. Indeed, with the advantage of 20/20 hindsight, many things would have been done differently. These aspects of this study suggest directions for further research.

Among the many unanswered questions is a need to determine with whom in university administration graduate students speak when they discuss their discontents, what they talk about, and if and how their concerns are resolved. Knowing this would go a long way toward helping universities establish effective lines of communication with troubled and dissatisfied students.

Better, more subtle measures of students' attributions for their attrition need to be carefully crafted. Forced-choice questions on this topic were not included in the questionnaire for fear that seeing system-blame options in the same context as self-blame options would influence students' responses. The open-ended questions in the noncompleter interviews tried to control for this problem. However, these questions may still have been leading.

Students' durations and stages in their programs need to be captured by direct questions and deeper analysis of cognitive map– and integration-related factors as well as reasons for leaving need to explored relative to them. In addition, spells of prior graduate education need to be controlled for, as does the relationship between duration and stage. For instance, a student with a duration of one year could be in stage 2 because the student entered with a masters' degree from another university. Similarly, a student with a duration of three years could be in stage 3, while one with seven years could still be in stage 2. Reasons for such differences need to be explored.

More standardized, quantitative measures of departments' environments for integration need to be created, and more appropriate weights need to be applied. For instance, it is not clear how much weight "occasionally" should receive relative to "sometimes," nor how often "frequently" is, when these responses are from a nonanchored verbal protocol. It is also not clear that encouraging students to subscribe to journals should receive the same weight as having a graduate student lounge or providing students with office space. Regardless, the fact that the crude measures and weights applied to these factors led to significant correlations is a testament to the strength of these forces on the departmental community. Quantitative studies of departments' environments need to be supplemented with qualitative studies that focus on the nature of interactions that take place during departmental activities and events and in different departmental contexts, and how these interactions influence integration and cognitive map development. They should also assess who (faulty and students) attends which events and why or why not.

The relationship between faculty turnover and student attrition also requires deeper exploration. First, better measures of just who is a member of a department's faculty need to be created, because most departments tend to list all faculty who have some type of relationship with them (joint appointments and other nominal ties) as being members of their faculty, when, in fact, they are physically located in another department and have infrequent contact with departments listing them as members of their faculty. This study did not attempt to control for this problem. Second, reasons for faculty attrition and their relationship to the department's environment for integration need to be explored further. Although retirement or acceptance of a "better" position elsewhere may appear benign, a faculty member's decision to retire or relocate could result more from dissatisfaction with the departmental environment than from the surface reason proffered. Conversely, faculty attrition because of negative tenure decisions may affect the department's environment. Divided and bitter tenure rulings cannot but have a negative effect on the departmental community, and departments in which it is hard to get tenure cannot but affect the relationship among faculty and the department. Regardless, a high faculty turnover rate combined with a high student attrition rate is a signal that something is definitely awry.

Much more research needs to be done on the differences between high- and low-Ph.D.-productive faculty and the relationship between Ph.D. productivity and student satisfaction and persistence outcomes. In particular, studies need to be done in which students are matched with their advisers. Issues such as the relationship between the race/ethnicity, sex, and age of an adviser need to be assessed against the race/ethnicity, sex, and age of the advisee. Qualitative studies that explore the initiation and development of adviser–advisee relationships would provide much needed information about the advising process and its outcomes. High producers could be asked to reflect on their growth and development as advisers. What mistakes did they make along the way? What lessons have they learned?

Although not discussed in the body of the book, different types of faculty emerged within Ph.D.-productivity groups. In particular, the high-productive group included types classified as "father-friend," "friend-friend," "wise counselor," and "halo effect." The friend types were just that—they were faculty who viewed their students as friends. The "father-friends" were faculty who, by virtue of age, had a more paternal relationship with their students than the "friend-friends," who had a more peer relationship with their students. "Wise counselors" were less actively engaged with students and their departments than the "friend" types, but they were readily accessible to their students and enjoyed interacting with them and contributing to their professional development. They also dispensed sage wisdom. Halo effects had many characteristics in common with low producers. However, because they were very eminent in their fields, they attracted the best and most independent students. Therefore, little advising was necessary. Types within the low-Ph.D.-productivity group were harder to establish, in part, because there are a variety of reasons for why faculty may be low-productive, including working in an unpopular area and choosing not to take on students.

A few words of caution on research on adviser types are in order. Survey research on this topic will not be easy to conduct. High and low producers will likely have different response rates, and the reasons for nonresponse between groups will be different. In addition, measures of productivity are not as straightforward as they seem. Not all departments keep records on their faculty's Ph.D. productivity, and not all faculty have spent their entire careers in one department. Most of the high producers interviewed did not know the exact number of Ph.D.'s they produced, although low producers did because their numbers were so low. Pulling productivity rates out of *Dissertation Abstracts International* was a good but nonoptimal first approximation. Some faculty indicated that while they were officially the chair of a student's dissertation committee, they were not necessarily the student's primary adviser—politics sometimes played a role. Furthermore, reasons for low productivity, such as working in an unpopular area as opposed to simply being a poor adviser, need to be controlled. Different disciplines appear to have different productivity rates. A high producer in mathematics with twenty-five years of tenure may have produced six Ph.D.'s, while a high producer with the same tenure in chemistry may have produced sixty. Productivity also varies as a function of department size. Faculty in departments with few graduate students have less opportunity to produce Ph.D.'s than faculty in departments with many. All these factors need to be controlled.

Although this study provided a good first start on the personal and professional consequences of attrition, it has barely nicked the surface. Much more work needs to be done on the immediate and long-term emotional sequelae of attrition. Indeed, the extent to which suicide attempts and completions among graduate students appear to far exceed national averages indicates that a mental health crises exists inside the hallowed halls of academe. It is a clarion call to action.

Much more needs to be known about the educational trajectories of noncompleters and the factors that motivate them to pursue different types of postattrition education. More also needs to be known about the movement and differential fates of completers and noncompleters in the labor market. Although this study tried to address these issues, much of the data was obtained using a life-history inventory. Many students did not fill out this portion of the questionnaire. Consequently, the results are imperfect and incomplete. In addition, at the time they responded to the survey, most of the students were in their mid- to late thirties, so the long-term effects of degree noncompletion are still unknown.

There is a need to conduct objective longitudinal studies of persistence, as opposed to subjective retrospective ones such as this. It is only through conducting objective longitudinal studies—and triangulating the data with other objective sources—that accurate measures of frequency of interaction and changes in frequency of interaction over time with faculty, advisers, and graduate students can be assessed against a baseline. It is only through objective longitudinal studies that changes in the quality of students' cognitive maps over time can be captured and assessed relative to their changing levels of integration. Longitudinal studies can better, more objectively, capture time-relevant information such as when a student received a TA, RA, or an office and how long the student had the experience. They can also accurately determine when the student entered into an adviser–advisee relationship. In addition, longitudinal studies can provide better information on when and how students overcame their emotional distress, how distress influenced their job-seeking behaviors, and students' occupational and salary attainment. Because this study's survey instrument tried to capture the full range of graduate school and post–graduate school experiences, its length caused many of these important time-relevant questions to end up on the cutting room floor. By contrast, longitudinal studies are better positioned to ask both generic questions that measure changes over time and specific stage-relevant questions that focus on time-limited experiences.

Finally, the method of sampling employed by this study—two highly selective universities and nine liberal arts disciplines—restricted its ability to explore ways in which the graduate school experience of minority students (completers and noncompleters) was the same or different from that of majority students, because there were simply not enough minority students in the sample to conduct meaningful analyses. Consequently, the conclusions reached in the study are incomplete. Yet, if the findings are true for mainstream students, one can only wonder how much more true they may be for minority students. What we do know from other research[2] is that for variety of social and cultural reasons, minority students are more likely to be marginalized than majority students, in part, because they often have greater difficulty conforming to the prevailing white male–oriented organizational culture of graduate education. This suggests that they are less likely than majority students to be academically and socially integrated and less likely than majority students to have access to the information necessary to develop accurate cognitive maps of the graduate school experience. Their higher attrition rates support this conjecture. There is thus a great need for careful and deliberate studies of representative samples of minority students, studies that will allow the experiences of subgroups (e.g., Puerto Rican, Mexican American, Cuban American) within broader covering categories (e.g., Hispanic, Asian, Native American) to be explored.

NOTES

1. In one of the graduate programs I was in, the department chair advised me against (read "forbid") me to pursue a particular field because the professor was a well-known abuser of female students (i.e., he was a lech). Rather than sanction the abuser and create an environment conducive to learning, the university protected the faculty member and

expended its students. This experience did factor into my attrition decision, because I (and no doubt many other women) was prevented from getting the education I went to that university to receive.

2. The little that we do know about minority students and their experiences with graduate education comes primarily from quantitative studies. Most of these studies have used nonrepresentative samples of minority students and, consequently, are of limited generalizability (Ibarra, 2000). Also, as demonstrated earlier, quantitative results run the risk of misinterpretation unless a significant sample of respondents participate in in-depth interviews or unless other ethnographic observations can be made to validate the findings.

Appendix

Most and Least Successful Adviser–Advisee Relationships from the Point of View of the Faculty

The faculty interviewed for this study were asked to talk about their most and least successful adviser–advisee relationships to discern elements of the relationship and characteristics of students that make a relationship work or not work from the point of view of the faculty. These questions were designed to parallel a set of questions posed to the student interviewees in which they were asked to talk about a faculty member with whom they had a particularly good relationship and a faculty member with whom they had a particularly bad relationship (see chapter 6).

MOST SUCCESSFUL RELATIONSHIP

Although asked about their most successful relationship, most faculty talked about a particular student, the student's work, and, often, subsequent career. Consequently, after they talked about the student, they were asked, "Why do you view this relationship as successful?" Six high producers (HPs) but no low producer (LP) focused on the type(s) of students with whom they had successful relationships.

The faculty, regardless of productivity type, cited three times as many male students as female students (twenty-one vs. seven). This difference may, in part, be a function of the opportunity the faculty had to work with female students rather than gender bias on the part of faculty, given the smaller numbers and higher attrition rates of women during these professors' careers (most were in their mid- to late fifties and early sixties). However, gender bias should not be ruled out, as the case of Professor Bonnell will show. Although their numbers are too low to generalize from, the female faculty in the sample (two) were no more likely to cite a female student than they were to cite a male student.

Professor McDonough (LP) articulated the nature of the two types of success stories the faculty related. The first type is about students who are "miracles in themselves"—a phrase uttered by Professor Picard (HP). The second type is about students who blossomed.

Professor McDonough described the relationship with students who are "miracles in themselves" as one in which "You never see the students. . . . They're just so self-directed and they have such a command of, mastery of, the techniques and materials, they simply bring [you their work] and you're slightly more than an editor." He opined, "I expect many faculty like those [types of students]." His assessment may be correct given the high frequency with which this type of student was cited. Indeed, more than half the faculty who related success stories related stories about these types of students.

Almost twice as many HPs (nine) as LPs (five) identified students in this category. Analysis of the faculty's narratives confirm and extend Professor McDonough's characterization. Students who fell into this category were described as very smart or intelligent, very talented and creative, and independent and self-motivated. Most of these students identified their own research problems, designed and carried out their research projects independently with particular creativity and insight. They completed their projects in a relatively short period of time and required little input from faculty.

"Students who blossomed" are, according to Professor McDonough, instances in which "the student is a marginal case and you help them meet the standards." He noted, "In some sense there's some satisfaction that you've given some help where they probably would have quit." Less than a third of faculty interviewed (nine) related stories about students who blossomed. High producers were as likely as low producers to identify students in this category (5 HPs, 4 LPs).

Analysis of the faculty's narratives confirm and extend Professor McDonough's characterization. Although the student who blossomed may not have been the most brilliant student with whom the professor ever worked, in almost no case was this student marginal for lack of intelligence. Rather, these students were described as smart or bright, but ones who entered the program underprepared, a little lost, or unfocused. In most but not all cases the student blossomed because the faculty member worked closely with the student.

Deeper analysis of the faculty's narratives provides insight into characteristics of both kinds of students and into different aspects of the relationship itself. One characteristic that emerged from the analysis was specific traits and behaviors. Faculty had successful relationships with students who were very bright, independent, self-motivated, hardworking, dependable, talented, resourceful, mature, articulate, and had good social skills. They liked students who they could challenge and who understood that they were being challenged for the sake of being challenged. A few faculty mentioned things they liked and did not like in students. Professor Stuart's and Professor Clayton's comments about traits and behaviors they do and do not like reflect the qualities students need to be successful in their disciplines, humanities and laboratory sciences, respectively:

> *Stuart (HP)*: I like it best when the student is independent minded, knows what the student wants to do. . . . I like working with a student who's willing to speak his or her mind. And I like to challenge what students write. I like to throw out questions and I like them to come back and tell me why I'm dumb with the questions that I'm asking them. What I don't like is a student who you ask a question of and then the student then becomes enormously defensive about it or decides that the only way to deal with the question is to go out and do an enormous amount of work that, in fact, wasn't the point of the question in the first place. . . . I've had students who understood this instinctively and, therefore, I've always felt really good about working with those students. . . . I like working with people who give me back every bit as good as I give them.

> *Clayton (HP)*: It depends a great deal on the maturity . . . of the student. In my group the students very much have to accept responsibility for themselves professionally. And the students who have done that, we've had a very good relationship and it's worked out very well. Students who expect me to be an authority figure or a father figure or provide detailed guidance as to exactly what they should do, what steps they should march through to get the degree, have a more difficult time in my group. In talking to students about joining my group, I point out to them . . . this expectation of independence and motivation.

For some faculty (five HPs, five LPs), the defining quality of the success of the relationship was the quality of the student's dissertation, even though some readily admitted they played very little role in the students' progress through the program. For other faculty (ten HPs, five LPs), the success of the relationship was defined, at least in part, in terms of whether the student had gone on and had a successful academic career. These faculty seem to be basking in the glow of reflected glory because they highlight not the relationship that led to the success but the success itself.

Regardless of whether students were miracles in themselves or blossomed, one aspect of the relationship the faculty valued the most was the intellectual give and take they had with the student (six HPs, four LPs). They talked about having similar interests but not always having the same point of view; about having interesting, intellectually mature discussions about issues and data; about having wonderful negotiations with students about the students' project; and about the mutual intellectual challenge. A few also mentioned that they saw each other in very human terms, that the relationship was easy-going, and that there was humor in the relationship. Four of the ten faculty (two HPs, two LPs) who talked about these types of interactions also mentioned that they developed a close, social/personal relationship with the student. Professor Johnston is a good example. His narrative also illustrates how social integration develops out of academic integration.

> *Johnston (LP)*: There was a man who came in at a master's level who worked in my area. . . . He knew of my work and he wrote to me, and I told him, "Look, you already know something about this area. If I were you and I were going to graduate school, I would go into another area." . . . Then he persisted. And so I said, "Okay." We worked together and we worked very closely together. We talked about the data all the time. Then he became a close friend. . . . He helped me immensely and I helped him immensely, and even now it's likely that he'll come to my summer home sometime this summer just as he's done many times.

Four HPs but only one LP mentioned learning from the student as an important part of what makes a relationship successful. Their comments also highlight the joy they derive from that type of relationship.

> *Sherman (LP)*: [I view it as a particularly successful relationship] because I've learned at least as much, in my view, from him as he says that he's learned from me. He wouldn't characterized it that way, but I would certainly characterize it that way. And that's what I think should be the defining characteristic of what is a successful relationship with a graduate student: if someone can begin teaching you about things. I've got another one going right now who is probably the brightest student that I ever had. . . . I just learn things from him every week. It's a very wonderful and exhilarating feeling. Maybe it's the case that it took me a while to get mature enough so that I could say I don't have to be the teacher all the time. I can be the pupil here, and at least I can be an equal with you here.

Seven faculty (four HP, three LPs) mentioned that the student(s) with whom they had successful relationships became true peers or colleagues before they completed their degree; two (one HP, one LP) published a few journal articles with the student while the student was in graduate school. This aspect of the relationship appears to be more common in the sciences (three) and social sciences (three) than in the humanities (one).

Another significant component of a successful relationship for many faculty was remaining in touch with the student—personally and/or professionally. Although an almost equal number of high and low producers (seven HPs, five LPs) mentioned that they were still in contact with their students(s), the nature of these relationships were qualitatively different. First, contrast the views of Professor Wheeler (LP), who is not included in this count above, with Professor Stuart (HP):

Wheeler: I'm not sure that one keeps in touch with one's students. . . . In the case of one at a nearby university, we've exchanged other coworkers after that.

Stuart: Almost all of the students, in fact, with whom I have worked on dissertations have remained in contact with me way past the time of the dissertation. . . . I continue to write letters for them. I continue to have a professional relationship with them. On a number of occasions they have, in fact, . . . taken on work for these major editions that I am responsible for . . . so that I have said, in just sort of jesting with students, that the adviser–advisee relationship is really a life-long relationship. It isn't something that ends when the person gets a degree, and I think that's true. I think it's very important, and that's part of this whole thing, considering ourselves professionals and working together.

The other difference between high and low producers is that when low producers remain in contact with their students, their relationships are less likely than those of high producers to be truly collegial. Low producers often continue to advise the student at the students' initiative, whereas high producers interact as professional peers with the adviser contributing as much to the relationship as the student. Compare Professor Hood (LP) with Professor Dalton (HP):

Hood: It seemed like the two of us were not getting anywhere [with her dissertation]. Me giving her constant negative reinforcement. And then suddenly, a powerful thing from my point of view happened [that led to her completion], and so, I think it's why she still calls me from time to time, she says to bounce ideas off of me.

Dalton: I stay in contact with almost all of my students. I regularly visit them. Many of them are in foreign countries, and many of them have prominent positions in universities or government, so I stay in very close touch with them. Or students who are in international organizations in Washington [or] who are now in the business sector and very successful in New York, so . . . I stay in touch with them. And then, when I organize conferences, usually I have a number of my ex-students come to those conferences. So, I have a very active relationship with them beyond graduate school.

No professor said that he had developed a true collegial relationship with a female student prior to or after completion. Only two faculty, both LPs, were still in touch with female students, but in both cases their relationships were advisory rather than collegial. This negative finding may reflect the fact that male faculty often develop relationships with male students through modes of interaction that are frequently closed to female students. Although there is only one clear case of it in this study, engaging in sports and other typically masculine activities (e.g., drinking beer, attending baseball games or Super Bowl Sundays) with male graduate students afford male students greater opportunity than female students to develop academic, social, and even personal bonds with their advisers, which, in turn, help them advance in their careers.

> *Bonnell (HP)*: [inaudible] sort of social bonding with students in a sense that I went hiking with John and I played racquetball with Richard, and we continue to maintain our relationships. . . . . There's an interesting thing that that particular activity allows for regular interacting, so you can have a lot of unplanned commentary on what you're playing around with intellectually and so forth in the course of that that play an important role in building relationships.

When asked whether he played racquetball with his female students, Professor Bonnell was quite adamant that he would not: "No, but they've been usually people who have had courses with me and sort of [inaudible] . . . basically hook on to me." Thus, Professor Bonnell's female students were not afforded the same academic, social, and professional interactional and developmental opportunities as his male students because of his discomfort in being with them in the closed setting of a racquetball court. In addition, female students "hook on" to him, whereas he appears to hook on to male students. Thus, female students may have to make an even greater effort than male students to develop collegial and friend relationships with their advisers.

LEAST SUCCESSFUL RELATIONSHIP

While HPs had a greater tendency to discuss the type(s) of students with whom they had successful relationships, LPs had a greater tendency to discuss the type(s) of student with whom they had unsuccessful relationships. Regardless of productivity type, the faculty cited three times as many male students as female students (twenty vs. six).

Within the context of their discussions of unsuccessful relationships, a few faculty revealed their views of their roles and responsibilities as an adviser as well as their views of graduate students. Professors Picard (HP) and Cromwell (LP) provide contrasting views. Professor Picard takes responsibility for getting his students through their programs, Professor Cromwell abdicates it.

> *Picard*: I don't know if that would mean a student who never finished. That would be, for me, the least successful. And I have had a number of them. These are students who, for one reason or another, I was unable to motivate effectively enough to keep working at it, or students who took much longer to finish than I would have liked to have seen, or students who produced undistinguished dissertations. All of those could be seen as unsuccessful or less successful.

> *Cromwell*: I wouldn't characterize any of them as unsuccessful. And it's hard to even characterize them as less successful. To me, my role as an adviser is to help the student understand what it takes to do graduate-level work, to help the student develop a project that will be suitable as a Ph.D. project—not too much, not too

little. That's a skill that takes some time to develop and . . . most graduate students don't have it. . . . I don't actually feel its any reflection on me if the student decides to drop out of a program or a student decides to go into a different graduate program. I mean, people are different, and I don't at all feel that it's my job to keep cranking out more students in my discipline because the discipline is already overflowing with students. I think that would be irresponsible. So success is measured in whether the student feels they have a successful relationship. They're the ones who are at risk. I have a job. I'm tenured. I'm not going to get fired if a student fails.

Unlike their narratives about successful relationships, which highlighted two archetypal relationships, the faculty's narratives about unsuccessful relationships resolved into three categories with less clear patterns: involuntary termination, voluntary termination, completed the degree.

Six faculty (two HPs, four LPs) discussed instances in which they had to terminate a student. These terminations took two forms: One form involved terminating the student from the program. These students' academic performance did not meet the faculty's expectations. The other form was terminating the adviser–advisee relationship with the student because the professor did not feel he could advise the student properly or because of interpersonal conflict. Although it is not completely clear from their narratives, LPs seem to terminate their students somewhat earlier in their academic careers than HPs, LPs while students are still doing coursework, HPs while students are working on a dissertation.

Burr (LP): I suppose it's least successful; I thought I did the right thing. There was a student who came to work in my field; and I thought she was never going to learn the tricks of the trade. And I persuaded her that she should leave, and she's never forgiven me for it. And she went and got a Ph.D. in another field and kept in touch with one of my colleagues, regularly, to report on her successes in life, which I don't begrudge to her at all. I just, I didn't think it was working out in the context of this program at all. And I foresaw despair down the line for her. The common denominator in the three people that I've tried to guide to completion and who haven't in one way or another really worked out was that they were still very dependent on me. And I saw that they would be indefinitely, and they really never emancipated themselves from that relationship.

Hilton (HP): One of them from many, many years ago, probably twenty-one years ago, something like that. A young woman who kept changing her dissertation topic radically about four or five times and kept taking people off the committee. Kept me as a director, but kept changing the other members of the committee continually without talking to me about it first. Just would sort of do it. And I think on the fourth or fifth dissertation topic change, I said, "Look! I don't think—I just don't think this is working out. I can't really get a handle on this anymore. I think you should find someone else." And she did find someone else, but then ended up dropping out of the program and not completing the degree, and I don't even know what finally happened to her.

Twice as many HPs (eight) as LPs (four) discussed students who left the program voluntarily. With the exception of students who simply quit or disappeared, few clear patterns emerge for these types of unsuccessful relationships. The reasons mentioned for students' self-termination included the student having mental health or emotional problems, the student not being sufficiently motivated or taking too long to complete the degree (ten or more years), the student deciding he or she wanted a career in a completely unrelated field, the student not listening to advice, or not being "up to the mark."

More than four times as many HPs (nine) as LPs (two) cited unsuccessful relationships in which the student finished the degree. Three patterns emerged within this category. The first is the student whose work either did not live up to expectations or one who produced an undistinguished dissertation. The second is the student who, after a promising graduate career, left academe for the business world or high school teaching or had some other "undistinguished" professional career. The third is the student with whom the faculty member had a difficult or conflictual relationship.

Almost half the faculty (fourteen) made comments about the traits and behaviors of students with whom they had an unsuccessful relationship (seven HPs, seven LPs). In a nutshell, these students can be characterized as people who lacked emotional intelligence (Goleman, 1995). While most were characterized as bright, they were also described as people who did not know the fundamentals of collegiality; that is, they were variously described as stubborn, brash, arrogant, antisocial, and people with biting styles, who did not listen to or take advice. They were also often described as needy, dependent, and wanting both structure and freedom, and occasionally as lacking in motivation or intensity.

Included in the narratives of six HPs and one LP were comments about efforts they made to see students with whom they had unsuccessful relationships with through to completion. The difference in the number of HP and LP faculty who engaged in these actions reflects a difference in the way high and low producers view of the role of graduate adviser and the responsibility they take for graduating their students, as well as a the degree of engagement they have with their students. For some faculty, the effort involved giving the student more time, attention, or urging than they normally did.

Stuart (HP): This is a student with whom I met more than I normally meet with students, who really was, seemed to me, a particularly needy student. So we set up a weekly meeting, and she would come almost for an hour at a time, and we would gab and then she'd come back the next, and we'd gab some more and try . . . in a much more [interventive] way . . . to define a topic and . . . to understand how to do it. It seemed to me ultimately that she still felt that I just wasn't enough there for her, but I didn't understand what she meant by being there for her.

For others, especially those who had a student disappear, the effort involved following up with the student over a period of time and encouraging the student to complete.

Clayton (HP): I had a student a number of years ago who got discouraged and just stopped showing up in the lab. And despite conferences and efforts and letters to him and so on, he just couldn't get himself motivated.

Watling (HP): It must be a tenth-year student or something. He never comes to see me, and I'd love to see him if he wants to come. . . . Now I'm not going to call him up every month for ten years—you'd think I was crazy. . . . I made an attempt in the beginning. Yes, I made several attempts.

More than twice as many HPs as LPs (seven vs. three) attached affect to their discussion about a student with whom they had an unsuccessful relationship. Faculty who had to terminate a student were frustrated by students who did not recognize their lack of aptitude and leave without having to be terminated. Unsuccessful relationships also caused distress: "I don't feel good about it. It's always painful." Even though faculty who cited promising students who finished but then went on to nonacademic or undistinguished careers denied responsibility for the students' "failure," they expressed sadness and confusion about the turn of events.

Lee (LP): There is Peter, my most brilliant student, who is now teaching—well, I'm not sure he is still teaching high school; I think he's editing a newsletter. This is a guy—I mean, he is as smart as my smartest colleagues. He is brilliant and he totally loved [literary] criticism, and I still don't quite understand. I don't think it was my failure especially. . . . Sadly, that's a case of I don't know what it is.

Finally, the faculty were most disturbed by students who left the program voluntarily. Their narratives reveal the hurt of a severed relationship and often frustration from being unable to control the situation and retain the student.

Dalton (HP): My least successful . . . was an American student who was fascinated by [a foreign country]. And when he was ready for the thesis stage, I helped him get some money and even contributed some money of my own to make it possible for him to stay a semester in [that country] and gather data. And he came back with quite a bit of data and was here for a year and wrote one chapter, which I liked. And at the end of the year, suddenly he left the place and accepted a teaching job, . . . and I never heard from him again. And I was disappointed, because at least he could have talked to me and told me why he was giving up. But he just disappeared and never—especially considering how I put in some of my own money in sending him down and so on. These things happen. Thank God they don't happen too frequently. I've had about three or four people who suddenly, in the middle, left. . . . I must say, most of them were disagreeable experiences. Disagreeable because there are four students in my twenty-one years who left that way without saying good-bye. And if at least they come to see me and say, "Look, I am not in the position emotionally or for a number of reasons to do it," okay, I understand it. I'll try to talk them out of it, but at least they talk to me. But in all four cases, they just disappeared.

Forrest (HP): I can think of a person who I was never able to make contact [with]. He kept slipping away from me. The way he was writing about things was not compatible with the way I was seeing things. I thought he was smart. We had trouble with him . . .—trouble not in the sense he was a problem, but just that we didn't know how to reach him exactly. . . . I was the secondary person [on his committee] and I never was able to connect, and he actually left. This was one of the three or four [who left] without even telling me. . . . I think that this person really had talent, [perverse talent], . . . and I felt I could never get him to make that perversity turn into something useful to him, and I think he is unhappy.

CONCLUSION

The analysis of the faculty's narratives about their most and least successful adviser–advisee relationships not only reveal characteristics and qualities of students and faculty–student relationships that contribute to more and less successful relationships but also indicate differences between high and low producers in their approach to graduate students and graduate education. Successful relationships are those in which a bright student, one with good social skills, who is self-motivated and independent, completed an often distinguished dissertation with, but more often without, help from the adviser in a short period of time and then went on to have a successful academic career. These relationships are also mutually intellectually challenging, and a true peer or collegial relationship often emerges before the degree is completed— a relationship that continues well beyond graduation day. By contrast, unsuccessful relationships are generally those in which the student left without the Ph.D.—voluntarily or involuntarily—or a promising student failed to live up to the adviser's expectations either in terms of the quality of the dissertation or in terms of his or her career, usually because the student did not pursue an academic career. Unsuccessful relationships are also ones in which the student is difficult to work with, often because the student lacked good interpersonal skills and was not open to advice or criticism.

Some common threads can be found between this analysis and the analysis of the student interviewees' descriptions of faculty with whom they had particularly good or particularly bad experiences (see chapter 6). Good student–faculty and adviser–advisee relationships can both be characterized not only by the contribution the relationship makes to the intellectual and professional development of the parties involved but also by the quality of the interpersonal relationship in which it is embedded; that relationship is pleasant, mutually supportive, and has a human element. Bad student–faculty and adviser–advisee relationships, by contrast, can be characterized by the failure of the relationship to meet or advance one or both parties' intellectual and professional needs and goals. In addition, the interpersonal relationship that surrounds it is often difficult and full of conflict, with one member often failing to take the interests and needs of the other into consideration.

Finally, the analysis highlights further differences between high and low producers in their attitudes, beliefs, and behaviors toward graduate students and graduate education. High producers take particular delight in learning from their students. They appear to be more deeply committed to seeing their students through to completion and work harder to get them there than low producers. Indeed, they view each student as a potential Ph.D. and academic professional, and each student who does not succeed is a personal loss. By contrast, some low producers seem to have a more "survival of the fittest" view of graduate students and make judgments about their ability to complete early in the relationship. Consequently, they do not take responsibility for their losses and these losses do not affect them personally. High producers also take a longer-range view of their students and their relationships with them than low producers. Many expect their students to become life-long colleagues and friends, and they take an active role in maintaining the relationship. By contrast, when low producers remain in contact with their students, it is often in an advisory capacity with the student taking the initiative. In short, high producers are more concerned about and involved in their students' intellectual and professional development, and even their personal lives; consequently, their students become more academically and socially integrated with them than students of low producers. These differences in faculty's attitudes and behaviors combined with students'—completers' and noncompleters'—reasons for their degree of satisfaction or dissatisfaction with their adviser (see chapter 7) further support the conjecture that completers and noncompleters are affiliated with different types of advisers.

Bibliography

Adler, N. E. (1976). Women students. In J. Katz & R. T. Hartnett (Eds.), *Scholars in the making: The development of graduate and professional students* (pp. 197–225). Cambridge, MA: Ballinger.

Althauser, R. P., & Kalleberg, A. L. (1981). Firms, occupations, and the structure of labor markets: A conceptual analysis. In I. Berg (Ed.) *Sociological perspectives on labor markets* (pp. 49–74). New York: Academic Press.

Austin, A. E. (1990). Faculty cultures, faculty values. In W. G. Tierney (Eds.), *Assessing academic climates and cultures* (pp. 61–74). San Francisco: Jossey-Bass.

Baird, L. L. (1969). A study of the role relationships of graduate students. *Journal of Educational Psychology, 60,* 15–21.

———. (1972). The relation of graduate students' role relations to their stage of academic career, employment, and academic success. *Organizational Behavior and Human Performance, 7,* 428–441.

———. (1976). Who goes to graduate school and how they get there. In J. Katz & R. T. Hartnett (Eds.), *Scholars in the making: The development of graduate and professional students* (pp. 19–48). Cambridge, MA: Ballinger.

———. (1992, April). The stages of the doctoral career: Socialization and its consequences. Paper presented at the meeting of the American Educational Research Association, San Francisco.

Barry, B. (1974). Review article: "Exit, Voice, and Loyalty." *British Journal of Political Science, 4,* 79–107.

Basinger, J. (1997, 15 August). Graduate Record Exam is poor predictor of success in psychology scientists say. *Chronicle of Higher Education,* p. A33.

Bean, J. P. (1980). Dropouts and turnover: The synthesis and test of a causal model of student attrition. *Research in Higher Education, 12,* 155–187.

———. (1982a). Conceptual models of student attrition: How they can help the institutional researcher. In E. T. Pascarella (Ed.), *Studying student attrition* (pp. 17–33). San Francisco: Jossey-Bass.

———. (1982b). Student attrition, intentions, and confidence: Interaction effects in a path model. *Research in Higher Education, 17,* 291–319.

———. (1985). Interaction effects based on class level in an exploratory model of college student dropout syndrome. *American Educational Research Journal*, *22*, 35–64.

———. (1990). Why students leave: Insights from research. In D. Hossler & J. P. Bean (Eds.), *The strategic management of college enrollments* (pp. 147–169). San Francisco: Jossey-Bass.

Becker, G. (1964). *Human capital*. New York: Columbia University Press.

Belt, W. T. (1976). Counseling graduate students. *The Graduate Journal*, *9*, 193–202.

Benkin, E. M. (1984). Where have all the doctoral students gone? A study of doctoral student attrition at UCLA. (Doctoral dissertation, University of California at Los Angeles, 1984.) *Dissertation Abstracts International*, *45A*, 2770.

Berelson, B. (1960). *Graduate education in the United States*. New York: McGraw-Hill.

Berscheid, E. (1983). Emotion. In H. H. Kelley, E. Berscheid, A. Christensen, J. H. Harvey, T. L. Huston, G. Levinger, E. McClintock, L. A. Peplau, & D. R. Peterson (Eds.), *Close relationships* (pp. 110–168). San Francisco: Freeman.

———. (1986). Emotional experience in close relationships: Some implications for child development. In W. Hartrup & Z. Rubin (Eds.), *Relationships and development* (pp. 135–166). Hillsdale, NJ: Erlbaum.

Bess, J. L. (1978). Anticipatory socialization of graduate students. *Research in Higher Education*, *8*, 289–317.

Bills, D. B. (1992). The mutability of educational credentials as hiring criteria: How employers evaluate atypically credentialed job candidates. *Work and Occupations*, *19*, 79–95.

Birch, A. H. (1975). Economic models in political science: The case of "Exit, Voice, and Loyalty." *British Journal of Political Science*, *5*, 69–82.

Blaug, M. (1976). The empirical status of human capital theory: A slightly jaundiced approach. *Journal of Economic Literature*, *14*, 829–855.

Bluestone, B. (1970). The tri-partite economy: Labor markets and the working poor. *Poverty and Human Resources Abstract*, *5*, 15–35.

Blumenstyk, G. (1993, 1 September). Measuring productivity and efficiency. *Chronicle of Higher Education*, p. A41.

Bowen, W. G., & Rudenstine, N. L. (1992). *In pursuit of the Ph.D.* Princeton, NJ: Princeton University Press.

Bucher, R., Stelling, J., & Dommermuth, P. (1969). Differential prior socialization: A comparison of four professional training programs. *Social Forces*, *48*, 213–223.

Burgess, R. D. (1989). Major issues and implications of tracing survey respondents. In D. Kasprizyk, G. Duncan, G. Kalton, & M. P. Singh (Eds.), *Panel surveys* (pp. 52–79). New York: Wiley.

Cage, M. C. (1989, 8 November). Alabama panel limits doctoral programs at public universities. *Chronicle of Higher Education*, p. A26.

———. (1995, 28 April). Report says Ph.D. students should prepare for off-campus jobs. *Chronicle of Higher Education*, p. A47.

———. (1996, 15 March). Graduate programs offer training for careers outside of academe. *Chronicle of Higher Education*, p. A20.

Campbell, K. E. (1988). Gender differences in job-related networks. *Work and Occupations*, *15*, 179–200.

Carnegie Commission on Higher Education. (1973). *A classification of institutions of higher education*. Berkeley, CA: Author.

Carnegie Foundation for the Advancement of Teaching. (1994). *A classification of institutions of higher education*. Princeton, NJ: Author.

Chronicle of Higher Education. (1989, 1 November). Iowa debates duplicative programs. P. A20.

——. (1992, 22 January). Yale considers trimming arts and sciences. P. A5.

——. (1993, 10 November). MIT to cut 400 jobs over four years. P. A4.

——. (1995, 24 November). U. of Rochester to cut its faculty by 10%. P. A6.

——. (1996, 9 February). Mathematicians at U. of Rochester reject deal to save program. P. A19.

Clance, P. R., & Imes, S. A. (1978). The impostor phenomenon in high achieving women: Dynamics and therapeutic intervention. *Psychotherapy: Theory, Research, and Practice, 15*, 241–247.

Clarridge, B. R., Sheehy, L. L., & Hauser, T. S. (1977). Tracing members of a panel: A 17–year follow-up. In *Sociological methodology 1978* (pp. 185–203). San Francisco: Jossey-Bass.

Collins, R. (1979). *The credential society: An historical sociology of education and stratification*. New York: Academic Press.

Converse, J. M., & Presser, S. (1986). Survey questions: Handcrafting the standardized questionnaire. Sage University paper series on quantitative applications in the social sciences, No. 63. Beverly Hills: Sage.

Coser, L. A. (1974). *Greedy institutions: Patterns of undivided commitment*. New York: Free Press.

Council of Graduate Schools. (n.d.). *Graduate enrollment and degrees: 1986 to 1996*. Washington, D.C.: Author.

Davies, C. (1989). Goffman's concept of the total institution: Criticisms and revisions. *Human Studies, 12*, 77–95.

Dillman, D. A. (1978). *Mail and telephone surveys: The total design method*. New York: Wiley.

Dolph, R. F. (1983). Factors relating to success or failure in obtaining the doctorate. (Doctoral dissertation, Georgia State University, 1983.) *Dissertation Abstracts International, 44A* (University Microfilms International, 8403341).

Durkheim, E. (1951). *Suicide*. (J. A. Spaulding & G. Simpson, Trans.). Glencoe, IL: Free Press. (Original work published in 1897.)

Dziech, B. W., & Weiner, L. (1984). *The lecherous professor: sexual harassment on campus*. Boston: Beacon.

Ebaugh, H. R. F. (1988). *Becoming an ex: The process of role exit*. Chicago: University of Chicago Press.

Egan, J. M. (1989). Graduate school and the self: A theoretical view of some negative effects of professional socialization. *Teaching Sociology, 17*, 200–208.

Family Educational Rights and Privacy; Final Regulations. 34 C.F.R. Part 99 (1988).

Farrell, D. (1983). Exit, voice, loyalty and neglect as responses to job dissatisfaction: A multidimensional scaling study. *Academy of Management Journal, 26*, 596–607.

Fitzpatrick, S. M. (1996, 9 August). Ph.D. scientists and the job market. *Chronicle of Higher Education*, p. B5.

Frost, R. (1916). The road not taken. *Mountain interval*. New York: Holt.

Gerholm, T. (1990). On tacit knowledge in academia. *European Journal of Education, 25*, 263–271.

Girves, J. E., & Wemmerus, V. (1988). Developing models of graduate student degree progress. *Journal of Higher Education*, *59*, 163–189.

Glaser, B. G., & Strauss, A. L. (1967). *The discovery of grounded theory: Strategies for qualitative research*. New York: Aldine de Gruyter.

Goffman, E. (1961). *Asylums: Essays on the social situation of mental patients and other inmates*. Garden City, NY: Doubleday/Anchor.

Golde, C. M. (1994, November). Student descriptions of the doctoral student attrition process. Paper presented at the meeting of the Association for the Study of Higher Education, Tucson, AZ.

———. (1996). How departmental contextual factors shape doctoral student attrition. (Doctoral dissertation, Stanford University, 1996.) *Dissertation Abstracts International*, *57A* (University Microfilms International Number, 9702896).

Goleman, D. (1995). *Emotional intelligence: Why it can matter more than IQ*. New York: Bantam.

Goodman, N. (1989). Graduate school and the self: Negative resocialization or positive developmental socialization—and for whom? *Teaching Sociology*, *17*, 211–214.

Graduate Record Examination & the Council of Graduate Schools in the United States. (1986). *Directory of graduate programs: 1984 & 1985*. Princeton, NJ: Educational Testing Service.

Granovetter, M. (1973). The strength of weak ties. *American Journal of Sociology*, *78*, 1360–1380.

———. (1981). Toward a sociological theory of income differences. In I. Berg (Ed.). *Sociological perspectives on labor markets* (pp. 11–47). New York: Academic Press.

Green, S. G. (1991). Professional entry and the advisor relationship: Socialization, commitment, and productivity. *Group and Organizational Studies*, *16*, 387–407.

Hall, R. M. (1985). Classroom climate for women: The tip of the iceberg. *Association for Communication Administration Bulletin*, *5*, 64–67.

Hall, R. M., & Sandler, B. R. (1982). *The classroom climate: A chilly one for women?* Washington, D.C.: Association of American Colleges, Project on the Status of Women.

———. (1984). *Out of the classroom: A chilly campus climate for women*. Washington, D.C.: Association of American Colleges, Project on the Status of Women.

Harvey, J. C., Kidder, L. H., & Sutherland, L. (1981, August). The impostor phenomenon and achievement: Issues of sex, race, and self-perceived atypicality. Paper presented at the meeting of the American Psychological Association, Los Angeles.

Hawley, P. (1993). *Being bright is not enough: The unwritten rules of doctoral study*. Springfield, IL: Thomas.

Heiss, A. M. (1967). Berkeley doctoral students appraise their academic programs. *Educational Record*, *48*, 30–44.

———. (1970). *Challenges to graduate schools*. San Francisco: Jossey-Bass.

Heller, S. (1990a, 14 March). The demise of a department sparks a new controversy. *Chronicle of Higher Education*, p. A24.

———. (1990b, 30 May). Former academics move confidently into other fields. *Chronicle of Higher Education*, p. A11.

Hewitt, N. M., & Seymour, E. (1991). *Factors contributing to high attrition rates among science, mathematics, and engineering undergraduate majors*. Unpublished manuscript, Ethnography and Assessment Research, Bureau of Sociological Research, University of Colorado at Boulder.

Hirschman, A. O. (1970). *Exit, voice, and loyalty: Responses to decline in firms, organizations, and states*. Cambridge, MA: Harvard University Press.

——. (1974). "Exit, Voice, and Loyalty": Further reflections and a survey of recent contributions. *Social Science Information, 13*, 7–26.

——. (1976). Some uses of the exit-voice approach-discussion. *American Economic Review, 66*, 386–391.

Howard, J. A. (1995). Social cognition. In K. Cook, G. A. Fine, & J. House (Eds.), *Sociological perspectives on social psychology* (pp. 90–117). Boston: Allyn & Bacon.

Ibarra, R. A. (2000). *Beyond affirmative action: Reframing the context of higher education*. Madison: University of Wisconsin Press.

Jacks, P., Chubin, D. E., Porter, A. L., & Connolly, T. (1983). The ABCs of ABDs: A study of incomplete doctorates. *Improving College and University Teaching, 31*, 74–81.

Jaffe, A., Lipman, J., & Lowengrub, M. (1996, 1 March). U. of Rochester plan to cut mathematics is recipe for disaster. *Chronicle of Higher Education*, p. B1.

James, W. (1911). The Ph.D. octopus. In H. James (Ed.), *Memories and studies by William James* (pp. 329–347). New York: Longmans, Green.

Jones, A. (1990, 1 August). Colleges must help some of their humanities Ph.D.'s to pursue careers outside of academe. *Chronicle of Higher Education*, p. B2.

Jones, E. E., & Nisbett, R. E. (1971). *The actor and the observer: Divergent perceptions of the causes of behavior*. Morristown, NJ: General Learning Press.

Jones, L. V., Lindzey, G., & Coggeshall, P. E. (Eds.). (1982). *An assessment of research-doctorate programs in the United States* (5 vols.). Washington, D.C.: National Academy Press.

Kalleberg, A. L., & Sorensen, A. B. (1979). The sociology of labor markets. *Annual Review of Sociology, 5*, 351–368.

Katz, J. (1976). Development of the mind. In J. Katz & R. T. Hartnett (Eds.), *Scholars in the making: The development of graduate and professional students* (pp. 107–126). Cambridge, MA: Ballinger.

Katz, J., & Hartnett, R. T. (Eds.). (1976). *Scholars in the making: The development of graduate and professional students*. Cambridge, MA: Ballinger.

Kerlin, S. P. (1995, 8 November). Surviving the doctoral years: Critical perspectives [2500 lines]. *Education Policy Analysis Archives* [On-line serial], *3*(17). Available: http://SEA-MONKEY.ED.ASU.EDU/EPAA.

Kleinman, S. (1983). Collective matters as individual concerns: Peer culture among graduate students. *Urban Life, 12*, 203–225.

Kolarska, L., & Aldrich, H. (1980). Exit, voice, and silence: Consumers' and managers' responses to organizational decline. *Organization Studies, 1*, 4–58.

Kohn, M. (1977). *Class and conformity: A study of values* (rev. ed.). Chicago: University of Chicago Press.

Kohn, M., & Schooler, C. (1983). *Work and personality: An inquiry into the impact of social stratification*. Norwood, NJ: Ablex.

Kohn, M., & Slomczynski, K. M. (1990). *Social structure and self-direction: A comparative analysis of the United States and Poland*. Cambridge, MA: Basil Blackwell.

LaPidus, J. B. (1997, 24 January). Doctoral education and the realities of the marketplace. *Chronicle of Higher Education*, p. B3.

Lofland, J. (1971). *Analyzing social settings: A guide to qualitative observation and analysis*. Belmont, CA: Wadsworth.

Louis, M. R. (1983). Surprise and sense making: What newcomers experience in entering unfamiliar organizational settings. *Administrative Science Quarterly, 25,* 226–251.

Lovitts, B. E. (1997). Leaving the ivory tower: A sociological analysis of the causes of departure from doctoral study. (Doctoral dissertation, University of Maryland at College Park, 1996.) *Dissertation Abstracts International, 57A* (University Microfilms International, 9718277).

Magner, D. K. (1989, 15 November). Minority graduate students say the path to the professorate can be rocky. *Chronicle of Higher Education,* pp. 19, 22.

——. (1994, 27 April). Job-market blues. *Chronicle of Higher Education,* p. A17.

——. (1996, 28 June). Science Ph.D. students told to prepare for non-academic careers. *Chronicle of Higher Education,* p. A18.

Malaney, G. (1987, November). A decade of research on graduate students: A review of the literature in academic journals. Paper presented at the meeting of the Association for the Study of Higher Education, Baltimore, MD (ERIC No. ED 292 383).

Markus, H., & Nurius, P. (1986). Possible selves. *American psychologist, 41,* 954–969.

Martin, J. (1992). *Cultures in organizations: Three perspectives.* New York: Oxford University Press.

McMillen, L. (1989, 6 December). Cornell faculty panel urges cuts in jobs so pay can rise. *Chronicle of Higher Education,* p. A25.

Merton, R. K., Fiske, M., & Kendall, P. L. (1990). *The focused interview: A manual of problems and procedures* (2nd ed.). New York: Free Press.

Mincer, J. (1958). The investment in human capital and personal income distribution. *Journal of Political Economy, 77,* 281–302.

Mitchell, M. (1936). *Gone with the wind.* New York: Macmillan.

Mooney, C. J. (1991, 27 February). Financial stresses hit professors but most colleges protect tenured ranks. *Chronicle of Higher Education,* p. A1.

Moore, R. W. (1985). *Winning the Ph.D. game.* New York: Dodd, Mead.

Morgan, D. L., & Schwalbe, M. L. (1990). Mind and self in society: Linking social structure and social cognition. *Social Psychology Quarterly, 53,* 148–164.

Morgan, S. P., & Teachman, J. D. (1988). Logistic regression: Description, examples, and comparisons. *Journal of Marriage and the Family, 50,* 929–936.

National Academy of Sciences, National Academy of Engineering, & Institute of Medicine. (1995). *Reshaping the graduate education of scientists and engineers.* Washington, D.C.: National Academy Press.

National Institutes of Mental Health. (1996, June). *Suicide facts.* Rockville, MD: Author.

National Research Council. (1987). *Summary report 1986: Doctorate recipients from United States universities.* Washington, D.C.: National Academy Press.

——. (1989). *Summary report 1988: Doctorate recipients from United States universities.* Washington, D.C.: National Academy Press.

——. (1990). *Summary report 1988: Doctorate recipients from United States universities.* Washington, D.C.: National Academy Press.

——. (1996). *The path to the Ph.D.: Measuring graduate attrition in the sciences and humanities.* Washington, D.C.: National Academy Press.

National Science Foundation. (1990). *Women and minorities in science and engineering.* Washington, D.C.: Author.

Nelson, C. (1995, November/December). Lessons from the job wars: What is to be done? *Academe: Bulletin of the American Association of University Professors,* 18–25.

Nelson, C., & Berube, M. (1994, 23 March). Graduate education is losing its moral base. *Chronicle of Higher Education,* p. B1.

Nerad, M., & Cerny, J. (1991, May). From facts of action: Expanding the educational role of the graduate division. *Communicator.* Washington, D.C.: Council of Graduate Schools.

Neter, J., Wasserman, W., & Kutner, M. H. (1989). *Applied linear regression models* (2nd ed.). Homewood, IL: Irwin.

Office of Scientific and Engineering Personnel. (1987a). *Minorities: Their under-representation and career differentials in science and engineering.* Washington, D.C.: National Academy Press.

———. (1987b). *Women: Their under-representation and career differentials in science and engineering.* Washington, D.C.: National Academy Press.

Office of Technology Assessment. (1988). *Educating scientists and engineers: Grade school to grad school.* Washington, D.C.: Author.

Parry, O. (1990). Fitting in with the setting: A problem of adjustment for both students and the researcher. *Sociology, 24,* 417–430.

Pascarella, E., & Terenzini, P. (1991). *How college affects students.* San Francisco: Jossey-Bass.

Peterson, M. W., & Spencer, M. G. (1990). Understanding academic culture and climate. In W. G. Tierney (Ed.). *Assessing academic climates and cultures* (pp. 3–18). San Francisco: Jossey-Bass.

Piliavin, J. A. (1989). When in doubt, ask the subject: A response to Egan. *Teaching Sociology, 17,* 208–211.

Piore, M. J. (1971). The dual labor market: Theory and implications. In D. M. Gordon (Ed.). *Problems in political economy: An urban perspective* (pp. 90–94). Lexington, MA: Heath.

Pope, K. S., Levenson, H., & Schover, L. R. (1979). Sexual intimacy in psychology training: Results and implications of a national survey. *American Psychologist, 34,* 682–689.

Qualitative Solutions and Research. (1994). NUD*IST (Power version, revision 3.0.4) [Computer software]. Melbourne, Australia: Author.

Ritzer, G., & Walczak, D. (1986). *Working: Conflict and change* (3rd ed.). Englewood Cliffs, NJ: Prentice Hall.

Roose, K. D., & Anderson, C. J. (1970). *A rating of graduate programs.* Washington, D.C.: American Council of Education.

Rosen, B. C., & Bates, A. P. (1967). The structure of socialization in graduate school. *Sociological Inquiry, 37,* 71–84.

Rosenberg, M. (1979). *Conceiving the self.* Malabar, FL: Krieger.

———. (1990). The self-concept: Social product and social force. In M. Rosenberg & R. H. Turner (Eds.), *Social psychology: Sociological perspectives* (pp. 593–624). New Brunswick, NJ: Transaction.

Rosenthal, R., & Jacobson, L. (1968). *Pygmalion in the classroom: Teacher expectation and pupils' intellectual development.* New York: Holt, Rinehart & Winston.

Ross, L. (1977). The intuitive psychologist and his shortcomings: Distortions in the attribution process. In L. Berkowitz (Ed.), *Advances in experimental social psychology* (Vol. 10, 174–224). New York: Academic Press.

Rusbult, C. E. (1980). Commitment and satisfaction in romantic associations: A test of the investment model. *Journal of Experimental Social Psychology, 16,* 172–186.

——. (1983). A longitudinal test of the investment model: The development (and deterioration) of satisfaction and commitment in heterosexual involvements. *Journal of Personality and Social Psychology, 45,* 101–117.

Sandler, B. R. (1986). *The campus climate revisited: Chilly for women faculty, administrators, and graduate students.* Washington, D.C: Association of American Colleges, Project on the Status of Women.

——. (1991). Women faculty at work in the classroom, or, why it still hurts to be a woman in labor. *Communication Education, 40,* 6–15.

Schmidt, P. (1996, 29 March). Ohio Board of Regents deletes funds for 6 doctoral programs. *Chronicle of Higher Education,* p. A48.

——. (1997, 14 February). Sweeping reviews lead states to consider cutting many academic programs. *Chronicle of Higher Education,* p. A33.

Segal, M. W. (1986). The military and the family as greedy institutions. *Armed Forces and Society, 13,* 9–36.

Serge, G., Begin, G., & Palmer, D. L. (1989). Education and causal attributions: The development of "person-blame" and "system-blame" ideology. *Social Psychology Quarterly, 52,* 126–140.

Seymour, D. (1995). *Once upon a campus: Lessons for improving quality and productivity in higher education.* Phoenix, AZ: American Council on Education and Oryx.

Seymour, E., & Hewitt, N. M. (1997). *Talking about leaving: Why undergraduates leave the sciences.* Boulder, CO: Westview.

Sherlock, B. J., & Morris, R. T. (1967). The evolution of the professional, a paradigm. *Sociological Inquiry, 37,* 27–46.

Silberman, D. (1993). *Interpreting qualitative data: Methods for analyzing talk, text and interaction.* Thousand Oaks, CA: Sage.

Simpson, J. A. (1987). The dissolution of romantic relationships: Factors involved in relationship stability and emotional distress. *Journal of Personality and Social Psychology, 53,* 683–692.

Spady, W. (1970). Dropouts from higher education: An interdisciplinary review and synthesis. *Interchange, 1,* 64–85.

——. (1971). Dropouts from higher education: Toward an empirical model. *Interchange, 2,* 38–62.

Spencer, D. G. (1986). Employee voice and employee retention. *Academy of Management Journal, 29,* 488–502.

SPSS, Inc. (1994). SPSS for Windows (Release 6.1) [Computer software]. Chicago: Author.

Talmon, Y. (1972). *Family and community in the Kibbutz.* Cambridge, MA: Harvard University Press.

Taylor, A. R. (1975). Graduate school experience: Excerpts from essays by graduate students. *Personnel and Guidance Journal, 54,* 34–39.

Thomas, W. I., & Thomas, D. S. (1928). *The child in America: Behavior problems and programs.* New York: Knopf.

Thurow, L. (1970). *Investment in human capital.* Los Angeles: Wadsworth.

Tierney, W. G., & Bensimon, E. M. (1996). *Promotion and tenure: Community and socialization in academe.* Albany: State University of New York Press.

Tinto, V. (1975). Dropout from higher education: A theoretical synthesis of recent research. *Review of Educational Research, 45,* 89–125.

———. (1987). *Leaving college: Rethinking the causes and cures of student attrition.* Chicago: University of Chicago Press.

———. (1988). Stages of student departure: Reflections on the longitudinal character of student leaving. *Journal of Higher Education, 59,* 438–455.

———. (1991, April). Towards a theory of doctoral persistence. Paper presented at the meeting of the American Educational Research Association, Chicago.

———. (1993). *Leaving college: Rethinking the causes and cures of student attrition* (2nd ed.). Chicago: University of Chicago Press.

Tobias, S. (1990). *They're not dumb, they're different: Stalking the second tier.* Tucson, AZ: Research Corporation.

Tobias, S., & Chubin, D. E. (1996). New degrees for today's scientists. *Chronicle of Higher Education,* p. B1.

Tobias, S., Chubin, D. E., & Aylesworth, K. (1995). *Rethinking science as a career. Perceptions and realities in the physical sciences.* Tucson, AZ: Research Corporation.

Tucker, A. (1964). *Factors related to attrition among doctoral students* (Cooperative Research Project No. 1146). Washington, D.C.: U.S. Office of Education.

University Microfilms International. (January 1987a–June 1994a). *Dissertation abstracts international: Humanities and social sciences* (Vols. 47–54). Ann Arbor, MI: Author.

———. (January 1987b–June 1994b). *Dissertation abstracts international: Sciences and engineering* (Vols. 47–54). Ann Arbor, MI: Author.

———. (1995). *Dissertation abstracts on-line* [CD-ROM]. Ann Arbor, MI: Author.

Vetter, B. M., & Babco, E. L. (1989). *Professional women and minorities: A manpower data resource service* (8th ed.). Washington, D.C.: Commission of Professionals in Science and Technology.

Watkins, B. T. (1990, 3 January). 1987–88 Ph.D. graduates: Half have no education debt. *Chronicle of Higher Education,* p. A13.

Webb, E. J., Campbell, D. T., Schwartz, R. D., & Sechrist, L. (1966). *Unobtrusive measures: Nonreactive research in the social sciences.* Chicago: Rand McNally.

Webster's II New Riverside University Dictionary. (1984). Boston: Riverside.

Wegener, B. (1991). Job mobility and social ties: Social resources, prior job, and status attainment. *American Sociological Review, 56,* 60–71.

Weiss, C. S. (1981). The development of professional role commitment among graduate students. *Human Relations, 34,* 13–31.

Widnall, S. (1988, 30 September). AAAS presidential lecture: Voices from the pipeline. *Science, 241,* 1740–1745.

Wilson, K. M. (1965). *Of time and the doctorate: Report of an inquiry into the duration of doctoral study.* Atlanta: Southern Regional Education Board.

Wilson, R. (1996, 18 October). Graduate students face tough choices when programs are cut. *Chronicle of Higher Education,* p. A10.

Withey, M. J., & Cooper, W. J. (1989). Predicting exit, voice, loyalty, and neglect. *Administrative Science Quarterly, 34,* 521–539.

Wright, C. R. (1967). Changes in the occupational commitment of graduate sociology students: A research note. *Sociological Inquiry, 37,* 55–62.

Index

About the Author

Barbara E. Lovitts is a senior research analyst at the Pelavin Research Center of the American Institutes for Research in Washington, D.C. She has worked as a program director at the National Science Foundation and as a program associate at the American Association for the Advancement of Science. She left doctoral programs in psychology and history of science without a degree but subsequently completed a Ph.D. in sociology at the University of Maryland. This study was motivated and informed by her experiences in graduate school, the process of deciding to leave (and return), and her experiences in the labor market.